THE KING RANCH

VOLUME ONE

THE KING RANCH

BY

TOM LEA

MAPS AND DRAWINGS BY THE AUTHOR

RESEARCH
HOLLAND McCOMBS

ANNOTATION
FRANCIS L. FUGATE

BOSTON · LITTLE, BROWN AND COMPANY · TORONTO

Published simultaneously in Canada
by Little, Brown & Company (Canada) Limited

PRINTED IN THE UNITED STATES OF AMERICA

Á TODOS AQUELLOS HOMBRES

KINEÑOS DE VERDÁD

SE DEDICA ESTA OBRA

EN RECONOCIMIENTO DE LO QUE

LES DEBE ESTE RANCHO

CHAPTERS

ILLUSTRATIONS
DRAWINGS

MAPS

FACSIMILES

1824 - 1885

1 *A River Man Finds A Far River*

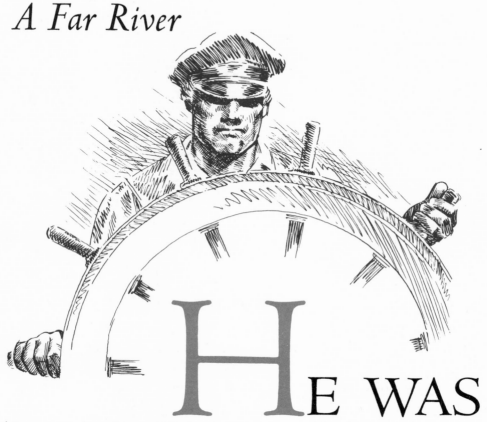

He WAS

his own sole witness. We know no more of his beginnings than he himself chose to tell: no record but his own testimony now exists. If he ever spoke in full and particular detail concerning his parents, or the circumstances of his birth, or his home before he left it, or his young boyhood, no one preserved what he had to say. It is probable that he said very little. In manhood it was his habit to look ahead, not back. Yet he did choose to tell, and to make it a matter of record,[1] how and why and when he began a rough life single handed.

The sailing ship *Desdemona* stood four days out of New York, bound for Mobile.[2] In the choppy waters off Hatteras, a sea detail went below to secure shaken cargo. Deck hands working along the hold heard footfalls and a scrambling in the dark. Throwing a beam of lantern light, searching between the high dark piles of crowded freight, the hands found him. They dragged him up the hatch — he fought all the way. There was something sturdy about him, held in the sunlit glare of the heaving deck with his captors tall around him. They hustled him aft. The captain, standing near the helmsman, peered hard at the boy brought before him. He bent down at the pale face under the mop of black hair, at the tangled ringlets around the dirt-smudged ears, at the tough square cut of the little jaw — the chin trembled — and at the eyes. They were dark blue. The captain frowned into them. Then he rapped out questions; the stowaway, full of dread, answered with the truth.

His name was Richard King. He was eleven years old. He was born in the City of New York. The tenth of July, 1824.[3] His parents came from Ireland.[4] They were immigrants. They were poor. They were poor as any could be. When he was nine they signed a paper. They apprenticed him.[5] To a jeweler. To learn the trade, for board and keep. The jeweler had a shop, there in the city.[6]

He didn't like that jeweler. And it wasn't so much of a trade, what he learned. It was mostly the sweeping, cleaning, scrubbing, fetching and carrying. And rocking a cradle. They made him. They made him mind the baby, like he was naught but a girl. He stood it so long as he could. And then he left. He ran away.

Yes, he did know the penalty. He knew about the paper his people had signed, bonding him out. But — would the captain — not send him back? Please not send him back? He could work — he was used to hard work — he wanted to work — he wanted to show — —

How had he got aboard the *Desdemona?*

Sometimes there was the chance to walk down the street to the docks. He liked the fine ships with the tall masts moving up the river to the wharves and loading and going away so far. There was something about the smell of the ocean and how the ships went out. He thought about it, at the jeweler's. It came to him, and then he thought about it all the time. He went to the docks whenever he could. And watched. It got so he mixed with the roustabouts and they were friendly, some were. They told him about stowaways. It was the roustabouts showed him how stowaways did. And finally he got up the nerve of it and he come with a sack of bread he saved for it and sure one of the roustabouts did help him to hide on the ship and showed him a scuttlebutt where the water was——

The master of the *Desdemona* looked down at the eleven-year-old runaway apprentice. Something about the story, something about the square jaw, something about the size of the figure in the light of the open deck after four days and nights alone in a dark hold, something touched at the hard-eyed, hard-handed skipper. Richard King never went back. The captain gave him a lecture on probity and set him to work.

He served *Desdemona* as a cabin boy. He listened well; he jumped when ordered. He learned the ship and the harsh routine of men who sail a ship at sea. The ship, the routine, the sea quickly forged a new form for his growing mind. He fitted himself to it. He remembered later, when he spoke of it, that his first ship treated him well.

As the days followed each other in their long procession and the ship's bell marked the hours of their passing and the watches changed and the vessel made its steady southing, a softness came to the air, a blueness to the sea. The *Desdemona* sailed through the straits, coasted Florida along the sun-struck waters of the Gulf to Mobile Bay.

The breeze carried a faint smell of flowers, a stronger smell of pine pitch, from the strange shore. Towering sails, white above the sea glare, moved past Dauphin Island through the mouth of the bay. Steamboats huffed choking black smoke, churning their big wheels, nosing in to tie up with their cotton, molasses, lumber, hemp, turpentine, with all their stacked barrels and boxes and crates headed for the plantations inland, beyond the blued hot haze where the trees made a line against the sky.

It was far enough from gray Manhattan. It was where Richard King wanted to stay.

Before the *Desdemona* sailed again, north for New York, her cabin boy had a new berth. The skipper arranged it. He went to a steamboat captain named Hugh Monroe, a friend whose shallow-draft boats plied the coastal waters, and he asked Monroe to give a likely and likeable waif a chance. Monroe did.[7] Richard King went to work in steamboats on the southern rivers.

If necessity made him an earnest worker for his keep, it did not make him solemn. A high spirit, a flavor of Irish that pumped through the toughness of his growing body, made him ready to laugh, eager to venture, anxious to learn—and he was quick at it. Some quality of his young presence, springing either from his earnestness or his high spirit or perhaps from an unusual blend of both, commanded attention from his elders and evoked promise. When he had spent two years on the rivers and was thirteen years old, the generous Hugh Monroe got him a better job. Upon Monroe's recommendation, Captain Joe Holland, whose boat made the big run from Mobile to Montgomery on the Alabama River, took Richard King as his steamboat "cub."[8]

The cub grew. He learned from clanging bells, hissing pipes, fireboxes that roared, gauge needles that trembled, on a shadowy boiler deck where iron shafts whirred naked in greasy great collars, by the high loom of a paddlewheel foaming muddy water.

He came to know the deck of a pilothouse under the rough cobbled soles of his boots, with the feel of the wheel, of the current, of the rudder in his hands; with the threat of snags, slicks, riffles and breaks, tumbling boils, roiling chutes in his eyes; with the stink of the mildew, the musty shallows, the muddy wood yards, the soot of resin smoke in his nose; with the calling far sound of a whistle blowing around a bend, the crowded shuffle and shout of the roustabouts hustling their loads, the cry of the leadsman, "D-e-e-p four! M-a-r-k three! Quarter-less-three—" in his ears; with the named shapes of points, bluffs, islands, bends, bars, reefs, drifts, towheads, cutoffs, lantern-buoys, plantations and landings stretched from Mobile to Montgomery by sunlight, moonlight, starlight— or no light at all— in his head.

And that was not enough. Captain Holland, a man of education, taught his unlettered cub to read and to work numbers; he explained the reason for riverboats, the arithmetic of freight and traffic and how it was accounted. The boy showed a quick understanding of figures, a natural bent for accounts; the captain determined that his promising charge should have some real schooling. He sent this exceptional cub all the way to Connecticut to live with members of the Holland family, to go to school.[9]

There is no record of the exact date, the exact circumstances or the exact locale of this schooling: only the bare statement of Richard King in later years that he went north— reluctant to be so close to a jeweler of New York—to Connecticut where he stayed with Captain Holland's family and went to school for eight months. He mentioned his attachment to the captain's two elderly sisters who cared for him.[10] It was the first home life he had known since he was nine years old and the only formal education he ever received. He is said to have done well in class and to have attracted the favorable attention of his teachers.[11] Yet at term's end, his schooldays were over.

Richard King never told why. Books and decorum probably tasted thin to a tough-fisted boy who had nourished himself on stronger meat: the free life, the excitement, the movement, the roughness of the rivers were in him. For whatever reasons, he left school and he left the Holland family. He never went back to his captain on the Alabama River. He was grateful all his life, but he never went back. He signed on with the crew of a steamboat for service in Florida during the Seminole War.

He served under a Captain Henry Penny. Though Richard King's name is not listed on the muster rolls, he was there.[12] The brawny eighteen-year-old riverman was present on the steamboat *Ocochobee* off Fort Brooke in Tampa Bay in 1841 when the wily Chief Hospetarke and eighteen warriors were enticed aboard to council—again hoping to inveigle whiskey and supplies from the gullible whites before evaporating into the dismal Cypress Swamps to set up ambushes. Colonel William J. Worth had been an apt pupil in the school of the Seminole War; abruptly he announced that all were prisoners. The cabin doors were closed and the trap was sprung.[13] The capture of Hospetarke proved a deciding factor in ending the long-festering conflict.

After the cessation of hostilities in 1842, with a stint at wartime steamboating in shallow waters under his belt, Richard King surveyed his prospects and went to work in the steamboats that carried a growing commerce on the Apalachicola and Chattahoochee rivers.

Well-grown and already wise with more than half a dozen years at steamboating, thoroughly at home with the profane and rowdy ragtag of the rivers, immersed in a rough trade and a hard life for which he was by nature fitted, Richard King, aged nineteen, began his rise.

R. King

His evident ability, in spite of his youth, earned him a pilot's license. There is no record of the date he made this rating, and the first boat whose wheel he officially held is now nameless; yet he was already Pilot King when he met, in 1843, the man who was to loom largest in the making of his fate: Mifflin Kenedy, master of the steamboat *Champion,* recently arrived in Florida waters.[14]

Kenedy was neither profane nor rowdy. He was a Quaker from a devout and well-established family of Friends in Downington, Chester County, Pennsylvania. He had been educated in the private boarding school of the Quaker scholar Jonathan Gause, and he had taught school himself. And though he had shipped as a sailor before the mast on a voyage to India and had worked in a Pittsburgh brickyard and clerked on a Mississippi steamboat,[15] and though he was physically powerful[16] and a competent boatman, there remained about him an air of Quaker rectitude, oddly prim for the boss of a riverboat on the Chattahoochee.

He was seven years older than Richard King and very unlike him. Yet Mifflin Kenedy, solemn in his standards for character and conduct, was drawn to Richard King, a young man ready for a rough-house any time and tough as a knot in the hard pine stacked on his forecastle.

An unpredictable alchemy distilled a friendship, strong and lasting, between Kenedy and King. It may be the two young rivermen complemented each other: they could find different qualities to respect, each in the other. They did find the bond of a trade they both engaged in; beneath the surface of their unlike personalities, they were both ambitious, enterprising, hardy. They may have sensed that they might make a future team. They knew they could learn from each other, and they did.

In the spring of the year 1846, Mifflin Kenedy left Florida to take the *Champion* up the Mississippi and the Ohio to a boatworks at

Pittsburgh for a general overhaul.[17] King expected his friend and the *Champion* back, but they did not come. No news of them came.

As the months went by in that year of 1846, there was other news. General Zachary Taylor and his troops — the biggest United States Army assembled since the War of 1812 — were on the edge of a place called Texas, on a river called the Rio Grande, fighting Mexicans, winning victories. The stir of the news, the war fever, its traffic and its rumor, reached the deck of Richard King's steamboat, churning the murmur of the Chattahoochee more than a thousand miles from any popping of muskets or cracking of horse artillery.

And a letter, at length, reached Richard King: his friend Kenedy was no longer master of the *Champion*. In Pittsburgh he had met Captain John Sanders, United States Army Engineers, who was in charge of procuring vessels to carry Taylor's men and supplies on the Rio Grande. Taylor's orders put him in a desperate hurry for adequate transports — and the Army lacked expert advice on the building and handling of shallow-draft riverboats. Sanders had fastened upon Kenedy, a young man "of the right stamp."[18] On July 2, with a master's certificate, Kenedy sailed on the steamer *Corvette*, for New Orleans, where she was officially purchased for government service. On August 6 Captain Kenedy, with Pilot Prescot Devot aboard, had joined the growing flotilla of steamers heading for the mouth of the Rio Grande.[19]

He had arrived late in August, almost three months after the battles of Palo Alto and Resaca de la Palma, and the occupation of the Mexican towns Matamoros, Camargo and Mier. He had found the Mexican border a sweating place to take a steamboat — the Rio Grande was a vicious stream, crooked, snaggy and variable. Yet the boats were a vital element in Taylor's campaign. There was a crying need for real rivermen. Kenedy wrote that he needed Richard King. He asked him to come.

The date of Kenedy's appeal is not known; Richard King may have started for Texas soon after the receipt of Kenedy's letter, or he may have been delayed in Florida for some time. It was, at any rate, the spring of 1847 before he got to New Orleans to sign on as a steamboat pilot in government service for the duration of the war and to wait for his passage southwestward.

On a day in May, 1847,[20] a quartermaster's sloop from New Orleans came about and lay to before the treacherous bar at the sandy mouth of the Rio Grande. Helm down, with her sails fluttering along the luff, the sloop put her dinghy over the side into the sun-glinting water. One passenger got into the dinghy with the oarsmen, and they rowed ashore. When the dinghy touched the beach, the passenger jumped out with his sea bag, and the boat shoved off again.

The passenger stood alone. Over the tops of the dunes on the other side of the river, he saw the ragged clump of smugglers' hovels, the Mexican place with the joking name of Bagdad;[21] upriver on the Texas side, his eyes found another weather-grayed straggle of shanties, the boatmen's camp lettered on the charts: *Boca del Rio,* Mouth of the River. Beyond it, the metallic shine of the stream wound westward in the haze of the brush.

A faint wind from the sea cooled at the sting of sweat from under his cap as he walked heavy-footed in the loose sand, still feeling his sea legs. The wind caught the rise and fall of the surf, the cry of sea birds, sounding in the silence. The wind moved the summer clouds, casting shapes of shadow on the emptiness north to a prairie horizon where league beyond lonely league of grass rustled, waiting.

Richard King moved inland, carrying all he owned on his shoulders and in his skull. His bootprints marked the wind-carved ripples on the sand of the rise toward the gray shanties up the river where Mifflin Kenedy would come to meet him.

II *The Big Contentious Place*

AT BOCA DEL RIO

there was no familiar face: Mifflin Kenedy was aboard his boat *Corvette* on a passage upriver. Impatient, anxious for orders, Richard King stowed his sea bag and settled himself to wait.

The burly 22-year-old newcomer was hardly a man to be idle while waiting or a man averse to mixing with strangers wherever he found them, and there was a good deal to learn about the big contentious place he had come to. He began to learn it from the turbulent, wild-whiskered assortment of border rogues and boat-men, soldiers and commission merchants, smugglers, deserters and gamblers, that drunk and sober, idle and busy, with orders and without, sought transient shade at a way station like Boca del Rio in the backwash of a war.

It was now almost two years since Zach Taylor, who looked as mild as a tobacco-chewing old farmer on a trip to a mill and who won bloody battles wearing a flop-brimmed palmetto hat and a scruffy old linen suit without brass, had landed an army at the mouth of the Nueces River.

The country south from the Nueces to the Rio Grande had been the primary cause of the Mexican War — or, at least, the formal ex-cuse. It was a disputed strip of territory shaped between the contours of the two rivers like a rough-edged tadpole more than 200 miles long with its head, its big end, butted against the Gulf for 130 miles.

As an excuse for a war, it was a strangely empty place. Across its blankness on the official map prepared in 1839 by the General Land Office of Texas, there was lettered: *Of this section of country little is known—* Other maps labeled its emptiness: *Immense Herds of Wild Horses* or *Wild Horse Desert.* The few men known to frequent its lonely prairies and thickets were mustangers who rode roping and taming wild horses, outlaws who rode from crime and the remnants of a tribe of Indians the Texans called Cronks: Karankawa Indians who did not ride but ran and paddled in dugout canoes along their Gulf haunts, the stinkingest, biggest-built, meanest Indians ever made, the cinnamon-colored seven-foot cannibals, rubbed in alli-gator oil, who had for three centuries murderously disputed the passage of all men since Spanish explorers first set foot upon the land.

Texas claimed this wilderness between the two rivers, Cronks and all, as a part of the land she won when she whipped the dictator

Santa Anna at San Jacinto in 1836. Mexico allowed no such claim.

In the first place, Mexico maintained that the disputed area was never a part of the State of Coahuila-Texas which was split when Texas broke away from Mexico: the strip between the Nueces and the Rio Grande was a part of the State of Tamaulipas and, as such, had nothing to do with any division of Coahuila and Texas. It was a technical point of considerable cogency.

In the second place, Mexico declared that the *tejanos malditos* had never settled, nor administered government, south of the Nueces. Except for the dubious tenure of a *tejano* named Kinney who was running a smuggler's post on Corpus Christi Bay, the country in question was Mexican country, *puro mexicano,* owned by Mexicans who had received existing titles to the land by grants of the Spanish Crown and the government of Mexico. Only the "disturbed" times —and the Karankawas and the lightning raids of Lipans and Comanches—kept the rightful owners from residence upon these lands.

In the third place, and to stop all argument, Mexico wished to point out that she had not recognized the independence of Texas. The defeated Santa Anna had no right to grant, or say he would grant, independence to any part of the soil of Mexico.

Texans snorted, with blood in the eye, with sweat in the gun hand. By the grace of God and the glorious arms of patriots, Texas was obviously independent. She stood so, before the world. And regardless of any damnable Mexican casuistries, the Rio Grande— *not* the Nueces—was obviously the boundary of independent Texas.

For the nine years following Santa Anna's capitulation at San Jacinto, the independent, contentious Republic of Texas had a rocky time. After a long set of internal political quarrels, and a complicated series of manipulations by men of power in Texas and in the United States'—with the governments of Mexico, England and France often throwing pepper that stung—and after many heated exchanges between advocates and opponents of slavery extension in the Union, and between prophets of Manifest Destiny and less prophetic or less greedy Americans, and between anxious investors whose Republic of Texas bonds and script were sinking fast and those feeling no investors' anxiety at all—after nine years of contentiousness, Texas had itself annexed to the United States of America in the spring of 1845.

The contention did not end. Mexico had given warning: she took the annexation as a hostile act and withdrew her envoy from Washington. President James K. Polk, just inaugurated, with ideas about Texas, California, perhaps something more, ordered Brigadier General Zachary Taylor to the Nueces to defend what was obviously now a State of the Union.

Polk also made a motion toward what he thought might be a pacific solution: he sent an emissary to Mexico City to settle United States claims, agree on a Texas boundary and offer up to forty million dollars for the purchase of California and New Mexico.

The aggrieved Mexican government agreed to nothing, refused to receive minister plenipotentiary John Slidell, and prepared an army.

News of the rejection, and the military threat, arrived at Washington in January of 1846. By this time the President of the United States seems to have been constrained to accept the Texan view that the Rio Grande was obviously the boundary line of Texas: he ordered Taylor to move his army to that line.

Taylor's advance across the disputed, empty place on the map was a signal for war.[2] Blood soon stained the sand of the Wild Horse Desert. In two hot battles a greatly outnumbered American force of 2288 men, at Palo Alto on the eighth of May and at Resaca de la Palma on the following afternoon, defeated a Mexican army and sent it reeling. Fleeing in panic south across the Rio Grande, scores of Mexican troops were drowned.[3]

Taylor's instructions from the Secretary of War read: "In case of war . . . your main object will be the protection of Texas; but the pursuit of this object will not necessarily confine your action within the territory of Texas."[4]

It didn't. Nine days after the battles north of the river, Taylor's troops, meeting no resistance, crossed the Rio Grande and occupied the town of Matamoros. As soon as available transport had been gathered — transport was a hampering problem throughout the campaign — Taylor moved advance units upriver to Camargo and Mier.

Using Camargo as his forward base, he spent most of the summer readying an invasion force and organizing a mule train — wheeled vehicles were impossibly few — that could carry supplies on an assault thrust ninety miles overland to Monterrey, the largest and most important city of northern Mexico. Lack of transport compelled Taylor to leave behind, at stations along the river, several thousand of the short-term Volunteers which were arriving from the States.

On the twentieth of September Zach Taylor stood ready for action at the outskirts of Monterrey with a force of 6600 facing a Mexican army of 10,000. In a three-day battle that cost the American army nearly 500 killed and wounded, Taylor's hellbent fighting men breached the strong defensive positions within the city and battled through the streets until early on the morning of September 24 when the Mexican commander dispatched a note proposing surrender, and terms of surrender, which Taylor allowed him. By these terms the Mexican army retreated, carrying their arms, more than three hundred miles south to San Luis Potosí, leaving Taylor in undisputed control of northern Mexico.[5]

The victory demonstrated the fighting talent of the roistering "unmilitary" Volunteers who composed a half of the United States battle force. It also made Zach Taylor a hero.

An enthusiastic press called him "Old Rough and Ready," a sobriquet earned during his Seminole campaign; the name delighted the nation. Old Rough and Ready not only rode a famed horse called Old Whitey, he rode such a rising ground swell of adulation that he heard politicians from afar proposing his name for President.

He was a Whig. The alarmed Democrat Polk and his administration in Washington moved to abort the threat of a Whig hero in the coming election: the sticky boot of politics shuffled out upon the field of Mars.

Turning up no Democrat qualified for high command, Polk did the next best thing for his party. He sent another Whig, the sixty-year-old, six-foot-four Commanding General of the United States Army, Major General Winfield Scott—called Old Fuss and Feathers for his magnificence in uniform—upon a new and bigger campaign into Mexico, a campaign designed not only to defeat the enemy in his capital, but to split in two any politically threatening laurel wreath that might be garnered in war. Old Fuss and Feathers was sent out to steal Old Rough and Ready's thunder.

Scott was ordered to gather necessary forces at the Rio Grande, embark them for Vera Cruz, win that port as his base and strike inland for the capture of Mexico City. His call for troops deprived Taylor of the greater part of his army, some five thousand Regulars and nearly the same number of Volunteers, including most of his artillery. Taylor was ordered to maintain defensive operations only, in territory already held.

With the seat of field command and activity thus shifted, General Scott landed at the mouth of the Rio Grande in December of 1846; for the next several weeks the lonely coast by the river was alive with a gathering and preparation of troops, a great stir. Then in February most of it sailed away, an armada of thirteen thousand men armed for the field, moving south.

Zach Taylor wrote that he wished he had been relieved of his by-passed command.[6] Still, one battle remained to him, a battle that covered him with new glory, and it came about in an unexpected way.

General Antonio López de Santa Anna, that somehow impressive and ubiquitous rascal loathed by Texans, had handsomely fooled the President of the United States. Polk had allowed the exiled Mexican dictator to pass through the naval blockade and return to his homeland, with the understanding that he would seize the Mexican Government and make peace with the United States. He had indeed seized the government. And forthwith raised a cry to repel the felonious gringo invaders. He had also raised a new army, more effective than any Mexican force yet seen, and by the fortunate capture of a courier's pouch[7] come into possession of a dispatch of the highest military value, from Scott to Taylor, detailing all the plans for the expedition against Vera Cruz, including the reduction of Taylor's forces.

Hungry for a victory which both his personal prestige and his country's morale badly needed and sniffing the fragrant opportunity for a victory over Taylor's depleted troops, Santa Anna, instead of moving his assembled army correctly and quickly against a main threat at Vera Cruz, headed north from San Luis Potosí, marching 19,525 men across three hundred punishing miles of desert country to fight Taylor. The 19,525 had shrunk to 15,000 effectives when, at dawn in a narrow place along the Saltillo road near the Hacienda Buena Vista, Santa Anna found Taylor and attacked him.

Old Rough and Ready stood to fight, with his gathered force of 4759 men and about 20 artillery pieces. In the long and desperate day of battle, the twenty-third of February, 1847, Santa Anna lost under fire between 1500 and 2000 of his most aggressive troops, and at the end of it he withdrew, whipped. Six hundred and seventy-three Americans were killed and wounded that day.[8] "In all the annals of American warfare[9] no other such victory as that of Buena Vista can be pointed out. Upon ground unprepared for defense, . . . this little body of well-trained volunteers successfully resisted from daylight till dark the assaults of an enemy of three times its own strength; and at last repulsed him and kept the field." Taylor's men were in no condition to follow victory with pursuit—and their commander had his orders.

In May of the year 1847, when the riverman Richard King arrived on the Rio Grande, the tide of war had rolled past that river. Far in the south, Scott had taken Vera Cruz and fought and marched his way to Puebla on the highroad to the Halls of Montezuma, while Taylor could only settle to a billet in quiet Monterrey.

Taylor's army sat, recounting to itself more exciting times. It sat, wanting to go home. It hunted shade from the heat of the day. It hunted drinks and girls. It gambled and it complained. It grabbed such supply as boats brought up the river. It regularly thumbed through its newspaper the *American Flag*, published biweekly in the occupied town of Matamoros.

Passing the time and hearing the talk at Boca del Rio, Richard King probably sampled the columns of the *American Flag*. They carried news of interest to a riverman; he could read in the issue of April 28, 1847, warm from the press:

> The schooners *Mary Emma* and *Virginia* were stranded Sunday last at mouth river. Everything total loss.

Or the advertisement:

> Received per steamers *Aid* and *Gazelle,* 100 bbls. superfine flour; 20 bbls. dried apples and peaches; 25 firkins superior butter; 40 kegs lard; 12 bbls. molasses; 8 boxes best Virginia Tobaccos; 40 boxes claret; 15 boxes lemon syrup; 100 bales tobaccos on consignment. For sale low by
>
> P. C. SHANNON
> Opposite Postoffice

P.S. Texas claims, located or unlocated, bought and sold.

He may have heard the first whisper of boom times blended with the murmur of the moribund war on the Rio Grande.

Yet if the war of battles had ceased in northern Mexico, the war of supply went on. Whether fighting or waiting, an army ate and wore shoes and carried guns. The quartermaster was busy as ever; so were his boats on the river.

Richard King's first orders arrived from the quartermaster's office. On the thirteenth of June he reported for duty aboard the steamer *Colonel Cross,* as one of three Second Pilots with a salary of $60 a month.[10] At the same time, the master of the *Corvette* was working upon other arrangements. Mifflin Kenedy's friend King served on the *Colonel Cross* just seventeen days and was transferred as a First Pilot to the *Corvette.* On the quartermaster's scale, a First Pilot made $120 a month, only $30 less than the skipper himself. It was good pay, aboard the Army's best Rio Grande steamer. Captain Kenedy and Pilot King were a good team.

A new pilot necessarily assumed his duties first as an observer in the wheelhouse, learning the new run and the new boat, how she handled and what she could do. Before standing a watch at the wheel itself, Pilot King had to build a riverman's practical navigation chart inside his head.

As the *Corvette* moved out the muddy tidal wash where the Rio Grande met the Gulf, there was less than a risky fathom of water, barely enough, above the soft mud bar in the river's mouth. Captain Kenedy snaked his boat over with full engine, stern wheel splashing close by the bobbling channel buoy. Then he turned wide, setting his course north along the low line of the coast. A southeast wind spanked at *Corvette's* pudgy quarter as she steamed a mile offshore, heaving high and falling away in the blue-water swell of the Gulf.

Three miles north from the river's mouth, the new pilot learned the shape of the low break in the line of the coast, Boca Chica, the shallow small inlet separating the mainland from the first of those long and pencil-thin islands that formed a line hugging the Texas coast, like a sandy breakwater. Behind this line stood the musty shallows of the Laguna Madre, an unnavigable bay built by the islands along the mainland's face.

The old Spaniards gave the name of *Santiago,* Saint James — saint of warriors and a battle cry — to the first island north of Boca Chica. Santiago was a low and thin five-mile length of sand; around its north end, between it and the south side of Padre Island, lay a cramped but navigable channel into the Laguna Madre.

This channel and its protected anchorage, the only one for 125 miles north along the coast to Corpus Christi Bay, was important. It bore the resounding title of *El Paso de los Brazos de Santiago,* The Pass of the Arms of Saint James. There was prophecy in that name. Warriors indeed used it: Brazos Santiago was the sea terminal and main staging depot for Old Rough and Ready's army during all its Mexican campaign. Brazos Santiago was where the *Corvette* and the score of shallow-draft boats in her flotilla picked up the cargoes brought by the deeper draft seagoing vessels for the long haul up the Rio Grande.

The new pilot took careful professional measure of the handling of the *Corvette's* wheel as she eased through the S-shaped Brazos Santiago channel in less than two fathoms over a hard sand bottom to quieting water; he studied the bearing dead ahead across three miles of murky green lagoon where a few shacks on a low bluff stood up from the mainland, Point Isabel, with its Mexican customhouse wrecked by war. When the *Corvette* came clear, swinging around the end of Santiago into the anchorage against the island's landward and leeward side, there were masts of sailing ships, high stacks of steamers, in from the sea.

With his boat tied up, Captain Kenedy took the new pilot ashore, beyond the rocking lighters, over the sea-rotted flimsy wharfing, along the glaring sand spit with the sea wind on his face and the gulls wheeling, to the leaning collection of jerry-built shanties and sway-backed warehouses that made the military depot of Brazos Santiago. Arranging the *Corvette's* lading, the new pilot was initiated into the quartermaster's tortuous system of supply.

Most of the cargoes came in holds from New Orleans, and they could be moved from the depot to the army by two ways. Some of the freight could be lightered across the shallows to Point Isabel, then carried by muleback or oxcart over a quaggy roadbed twenty-six miles to the Rio Grande. There, it might be loaded on boats for passage upriver, or it might move on by land transport to its destination. But the necessity of ferrying across to Mexico, the lack of passable roads, the scarcity of workstock and drivers and wheeled vehicles, the bottomless sloughs during rain, the famishing marches during drought, the marauding bands of Indians and outlaws made all land transport maddeningly toilsome and uncertain. By far the greater part of the army's supply moved in shallow-draft boats like the *Corvette* by open sea the eight miles from Brazos Santiago to the mouth of the Rio Grande and thence to various stations upriver as far as Camargo and Mier. Beyond there, supplies for the advance Monterrey outposts were carried overland by mule train. The army's line of supply was rightly called in military parlance "extended."

When Mexican roustabouts and soldiers on detail and the *Corvette's* own deck hands had loaded her for the long haul, she moved out the channel of Brazos Santiago and nosed south, bucking and rolling hard against the steady southeast wind and the chop of its sea. It was plain to anyone, and especially to the seasick passengers aboard, that a tub-shaped mudwalloper was hardly the craft for such wind and water even on a pleasant summer day—and clearly danger-ous in any kind of a blow. Wind blew often, and wind blew hard.

In 1844 one of the hurricanes had blown Brazos Island flat, smashed Boca del Rio, knocked down Bagdad, with the loss of many lives. Old Fuss and Feathers Scott, blowing in an official communication, in 1847, called the vicinity "this terrible coast."[11]

The *Corvette* thrashed again across the bar at the river's mouth and entered to her own element in a chuffing climb against the current's swirl. Past the familiar shacks of Boca del Rio, Pilot King began to plot upon the ever-growing chart inside his head the cranky, crooked river, 250 miles of it.

Three clusters of settlements stringing out along the Mexican side roughly divided the steamboating part of the Rio Grande into three divisions: the 50 miles from the sea to Matamoros, the 128 miles from Matamoros to Reynosa, and the 75 miles from Reynosa to the practical head of navigation at Mier.[12] On primitive roads and trails skirting the river's loops, these distances were shorter. By the road it was little more than 175 miles from Mier to the sea; the difference in mileage was testimony to the twists the river made.[13]

The three river divisions held three kinds of country: sandy coastal flats of dune and marshland from the Gulf to within a few miles of Matamoros; alluvial blackland studded in the low places with semitropical jungles of thorned brush and palmetto, hackberry and light-leafed willow from Matamoros toward Reynosa; and drier, narrowing valleyland hemmed in heavy chaparral of mesquite and cactus, with the first stone ledges and hill slopes outspreading to horizons of rolling prairie, open lands of lonely grass, the Wild Horse Desert, from Reynosa upriver.

The towns, though they resembled nothing Pilot King had seen before, resembled each other. They all possessed a certain settled and easy grace that no poverty or maculation ever hid, fashioned by another people of another tongue, strange, melodious. They were all towns built where timbers were scarce, where walls were raised of sunbaked mud bricks or of rough-layed rock, roofed by grass thatch or wattling packed hard and thick with earth, towns with a few massive dressed stone buildings, always with a church and a cross facing a public square, a plaza where trade and traffic gave the heart of the town its beat. And if they were all something alike, they were all different too, each with a line and air and flavor of its own.

Matamoros was the prettiest. It sat on a level plain, back from the river in the midst of trees and flowers, rich fields, orchards, gardens. It was the largest of the towns; seven thousand people lived within its walls. It was also the richest, fat with trade goods, a great part of them contraband shipped from forwarding houses of New Orleans to be filtered into markets of northern Mexico, to the mines and towns and haciendas, by busy merchants. And Matamoros was the youngest of the towns: it had been an organized municipality less than thirty years when the Mexican War came. The quick growth and increasing prosperity of Matamoros came from its strategic location for trade rather than from any richness of its corn fields, its bean crops, its cotton and cane, or the livestock on its outlying ranchos.

Reynosa was smaller, sleepier, poorer than Matamoros. Less than a third as large, Reynosa was three times as old. In the year 1749 that efficient colonizer for the king of Spain, Colonel Don José de Escandón, Knight of the Order of Santiago, had chosen the site of Reynosa and planted eighty-one families there, as one of the settlements to establish a line of occupation along the Spanish frontier.* Reynosa took root but grew slowly, a town of farmers and rancheros, drawing its unspectacular nourishment from irrigated fields by the river and from herds of livestock it tended on grasslands beyond.

Forty-two miles upriver, the town of Camargo with nearly three thousands inhabitants seemed a different kind of place. The air was

* See Appendix I for a discussion of early Spanish colonial policy and the activities of Escandón.

drier, dustier; there were not so many trees. *La Villa de Santa Ana de Camargo*, established nine days earlier than Reynosa by the grandee Escandón, was not situated on the Rio Grande itself, but upon a high bank over the clear waters of the Rio San Juan four miles above its confluence with the Rio Grande. In the spring of 1846 the San Juan had overflowed the thirty-foot banks, reducing some two hundred adobe houses to crumbling ruins. About half of the almost three thousand inhabitants deserted the inundated town. Though fields were cultivated to use the river's never-failing water, Camargo was predominately a town of rancheros who owned, by grants of the Spanish Crown, immense outlying pastures. Herds of cattle, horses, mules, goats and sheep were the real sustenance of Camargo, and its ranchos formed the center of the livestock trade on the lower Rio Grande.

Camargo was also the nearest point on the river to the important city of Monterrey, and hence a way station on the best route overland to Mexico's interior. The few flat-roofed rock buildings remaining around the plaza were used by the quartermaster as storehouses and commissaries for outfitting troops en route to the interior. Steamboats tied up at the makeshift wharf, close by a steep and narrow roadway slanting up to the level of the overlooking town. The creak of oxcarts and the rattle of mule hooves blended often with the ringing of bells from the neat little church on the main plaza.

Upriver another thirty miles, Mier was neither as large nor as flourishing as Camargo. Founded in 1753 by the same busy Escandón, Mier was also built upon a tributary stream, the little Rio Alamo, about three miles above where it flowed into the Rio Grande. Mier lacked arable land, cultivated few fields and depended upon its herds for a livelihood. The town was well-known for the fine blankets it wove from the wool of its flocks. To Texans it was known for something else. There was a hateful memory and malevolence about the rock walls, the cobbled streets and bare stone plaza of Mier: it was the scene of an inglorious whipping. At Christmas time of 1842, a foolhardy band of Texans had inaugurated an "invasion" of Mexico at Mier—and had been defeated, captured and made to suffer in chains, held in the prison fortress of Perote near Jalapa. On the long way south, the captives of Mier had been decimated by being forced to draw beans; the unlucky drawers of black beans were stood against a wall and shot. The "Mier Expedition" was an uncomfortable memory on both sides of the Rio Grande, one of many memories contributing to the hatred between Mexicans and Texans, the long-standing bitterness that showed itself, whenever opportunity arose, in vituperation or violence.

There were only two hints of future towns on the Texas side of the river. Opposite the mouth of the San Juan, convenient to Camargo, on a high and pleasant bank of the Rio Grande, was a group of well-built houses, storerooms and corrals, called Rancho Davis or, as gringos said, Davis Landing. Its founder, a Colonel Henry Clay Davis, had come into the country in 1839 as a filibustering recruit for the army of the "Republic of the Rio Grande." He had stayed, married a daughter of the prominent de la Garza family of Camargo and become well-established. During the hostilities of 1846 and 1847 he lent his services and his knowledge of the country to the American forces. The Davis Landing was often mentioned by visiting troops as "a beautiful situation" or "the best point on the river." Close to the head of navigation on the Texas side of the river, it had splendid possibilities—which were utilized—as a smuggling base. It was to grow and become known as Rio Grande City.[14]

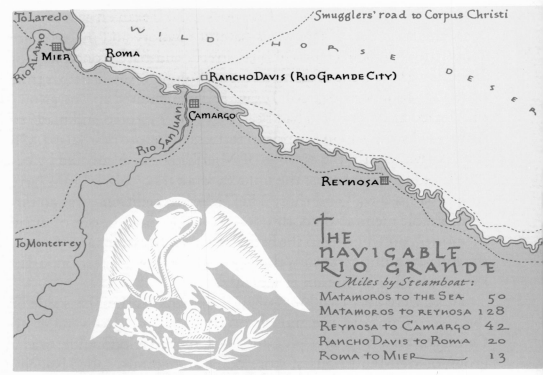

To Laredo

Smugglers' road to Corpus Christi

WILD HORSE DESERT

Rio Alamo

MIER

ROMA

RANCHO DAVIS (RIO GRANDE CITY)

CAMARGO

Rio San Juan

REYNOSA

To Monterrey

THE NAVIGABLE RIO GRANDE

Miles by Steamboat:

MATAMOROS TO THE SEA	50
MATAMOROS TO REYNOSA	128
REYNOSA TO CAMARGO	42
RANCHO DAVIS TO ROMA	20
ROMA TO MIER	13

Aside from a few lonely wood yards, piles of mesquite and ebony chopped and replenished often for the hungry fireboxes of the steamboats, the only other focus of activity on the north bank of the Rio Grande was opposite Matamoros. The development of an American counterpoise to that strategically located and trade-richened Mexican town was inevitable.

Zachary Taylor had first touched the Rio Grande at a point opposite Matamoros. The American flag had first stood on the river there, tied to a willow staff, floating in the southeast wind from the sea, while troopers and horses came plunging down the river bank to drink the muddy water.[15] Taylor had established his first military position there, dubbing his camp Fort Texas,[16] and he had held that fort during all the risky first days of his operations by the Rio

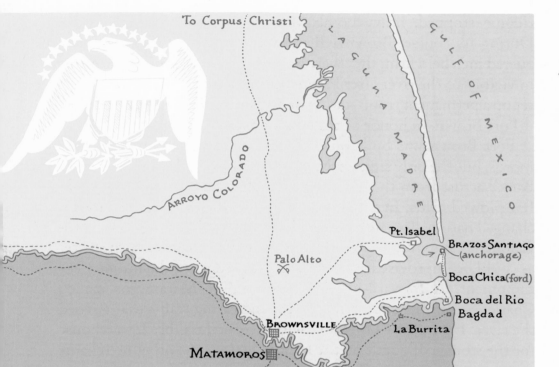

Grande. On the first of May, 1846, when he moved back to probe for the Mexican army which had crossed the river to threaten his rear and his supply base at Point Isabel, Taylor left five hundred men, the Seventh Infantry and two batteries under the command of Major Jacob Brown, in position facing Matamoros. And during the time Taylor's main force was dealing with the enemy at Palo Alto and Resaca de la Palma not many miles north, Brown and his men were besieged. The Mexican Commander Arista had left seven cannon and a heavy contingent of troops as a safeguard to Matamoros, with orders to pin Brown in his isolated position and destroy him if possible. When the church bells of Matamoros clanged, pealing to announce the opening of the Mexican bombardment, Brown's batteries gruffly replied: the church tower toppled. Though the bell ringing stopped, heavy bombardment continued for 160 hours. During its course, Brown fell mortally wounded. But his beleaguered men held firm; they were in place to greet the units returning in victory to the river after Palo Alto and Resaca. Taylor forthwith set up a permanent troop station on the site of the siege and renamed it Fort Brown, in honor of the commander who died there.[17]

Fort Brown was built on the *ejidos,* town commons, of Matamoros, but the only signs of Mexican occupancy there on the "Left Bank" across from the town were less than a dozen poor huts and a few plowed fields. In the summer of 1846 the *ejidos* of Matamoros changed nationality, and changed looks. A motley gathering of provisioners, camp followers and frontier drifters crowded such shelter as could be improvised around the muddy edges of the military encampment. A forward-looking merchant of Matamoros named Charles Stillman built a ferry for the increasing traffic that crossed the river. He followed the ferry with a substantial brick warehouse for the storage of goods on the United States side; other merchants set up competitive establishments and the ramshackle civilian settlement around Fort Brown began to burgeon. When Pilot King first saw it as he steamed around a bend of the river in June of 1847, it was already being called Brownsville and it was feeling the first pulse beats of a boom.

American soldiers were in the foreground along every view of the river, soldiers in crowds on the decks of the *Corvette.* There were few professionals among them: the Regular Army was six months and eight hundred miles from the Rio Grande. One of those Regulars would have interested Pilot King. The Colonel Worth who had tricked the Seminoles aboard the *Ocochobee* six years back in Richard King's life was now the General Worth who had led valorously a brigade, then a division under Taylor, and sailed south as one of

Scott's ranking commanders in the field. Pilot King arrived too late to see him.

He saw the Volunteers. During the year there had been as many as twenty thousand[18] of them in the valley—most of them there under such short-term militia enlistments that they had time only to arrive in Texas and be sent home again, without ever having been of use, without ever having seen action of any kind. Sickness had taken its toll of these untrained soldiers, most of them farm boys whose lives had never exposed them to crowded living and disease. In the unclean camps and sultry air of the Rio Grande came strange and mortal epidemics of mumps, measles, smallpox. The climate, polluted drinking water, carelessness with latrines had racked thousands of men with dysentery, catarrhal fever, bilious fever and chills. A lieutenant from Tennessee wrote, "The Dead March was played so often on the Rio Grande that the very birds knew it."[19]

The Volunteers were willing to leave the Rio Grande to the birds, and the sooner the better. In a great variety of uniforms and illusions, calling themselves warlike names—"Rifles," "Grays," "Guards," "Killers"—they had arrived pellmell from their various states. The "Volunteers of Kentucky," for instance, came wearing three-cornered hats, full beards, and hip boots faced with red morocco. All of them came to win a war in ninety days, despising Regulars as "drillyard slaves" without "pride of free men"—"I'll be blowed if they make a Regular out of me!"

The Volunteers had been loathed in turn by the Regulars, for their rowdy bumpkin sloppiness and rank insubordination, for their conduct in camp and in the towns where there were thievery, riot and sometimes rape.

The pay of privates was seven dollars a month; Volunteers were fond of referring to themselves as "seven-dollar targets." They were thoroughly certain they should be drawing more money than the mere Dutch, Irish, English "foreigners" in the ranks of the Regulars.[20]

Yet the shakedown of war, of service in the field, had winnowed out most of the short-term patriots, the rioting rascals, the malingerers. Pilot King saw Volunteers whose uniforms had long since taken on the common blue of Army issue, whose conduct had settled to the workmanship of veterans who no longer needed to prove anything to themselves or to others.

The steersman of the *Corvette* heard enough opinion about the brown-faced people on the south bank of the river. Soldiers judged soldiers: the American was generally sorry for the Mexican in the ranks wearing his corded and belted coat of blue, his white pants, his leathern shako — and his sandals. He was a pretty good fighting man. There was nothing wrong with his hardihood — Mexican infantry habitually marched thirty miles a day and could do fifty, compared to the American average of fifteen. And there was nothing wrong with his courage. When it came to hitting a target with a musket, he was not so good, and he put too many frills to the business of a fight, listening to too many bugles and too many commands. It was his officers that betrayed him, who brought him defeat. Battle veterans said that Mexican officers with their gold braid and red pipings and waving swords — especially officers of the junior grades — were no good. They did not lead their men, they tried to drive them.

There were Americans whose judgments were as haughty as the Volunteer General John A. Quitman's. He said Mexicans were "a bastard and robber race, incapable of self-government, and only fit for servitude and military rule."[21] Others, looking for causes in the Mexican character, made the kind of observation expressed by a West Point second lieutenant named Ulysses S. Grant at Matamoros: "The better class are very proud, and tyrannize over the lower ... as much as a hard master does over his negroes; and they submit as humbly."[22]

The Protestant and provincial Americans had their observations about the Roman Catholic Church they encountered over the river. Most of them thought that the poor people of Mexico "suffered from the influence of the Church."[23] A lieutenant of the Second Artillery wrote home, referring to Catholic chaplains present in some of Taylor's units: "The priests that come from the States say they could not recognize the Catholic religion in the mummeries practiced here . . . . Religion is a mixture of Indian idolatry and superstition with the Catholic."[24]

Americans judged Mexicans, aware that Mexican attitudes toward the gringo invader were not those of loving kindness. General Mejía, commander at Matamoros when Taylor first arrived on the Rio Grande, had in an official proclamation denounced the invasion as "that most degrading depredation ... of the degenerate sons of Washington."[25] Clerical propaganda issued from San Luis Potosí called the Americans "Vandals vomited from Hell" who "worship no God but gold." The Mexican populace was eloquently asked: "Will you consent . . . to have the holy rights of your church abolished and the sign of your redemption exterminated? . . . Your daughters and your wives will be seized in your sight, and made victims to lascivious passions, even in the streets."[26]

Among the many Volunteers from the many states, there were three regiments Pilot King heard about but did not see: some of their companies had sailed south with Scott, and many of those remaining with Taylor had simply gone home after Buena Vista because they saw no chance of a further fight. These three regiments were the Texans, very troublesome people.

They were the first Volunteers to join Taylor. They came drifting into Matamoros shortly after Palo Alto and Resaca, company by company, horseback men on tough ponies, wearing slouch hats and raunchy clothes, carrying well-oiled rifles and revolver pistols and honed bowie knives. They came looking for a chance to kill Mexicans. A colonel of Tennessee Volunteers, exposed to the "Texians" and their behavior in camp, called them "the wildest and most dissipated men I ever saw; they remind me of . . . Russian Cossacks."[27]

They were hard to handle; their wild ways fretted and peeved Taylor. But he used them. He was glad he had them, for they became the eyes and ears of his army, his cavalry screen, his mounted scouts and spies and advance guards.

The yells of *los diablos tejanos* curdled the blood of Mexican soldiery. At the start of hostilities in front of Monterrey, when whistling Mexican cannon balls began to hit and roll, the Texans rode out before the lines in sheer dare-deviltry and performed horseback tricks, skimming wide circles around the enemy's fortifications. Taylor had to put a stop to it. Next day, the Texans stormed Bishop's Castle, a strong point in the city's defense.[28]

Insubordinate to the formalities of military command, the Texans fought as teams under the control of their own respected leaders. There were stories about all those leaders: wiry Jack Hays who led the Rangers during the hard days of the Republic; poker-faced Ben McCullough; red-haired Sam Walker who helped another Sam named Colt design a revolver; level-headed Rip Ford; Indian fighting Addison Gillespie; stalwart John T. Price; and that veteran of a thousand scrapes including Mier, the kindly giant of them all, Big Foot Wallace.

Running down the middle of a raw borderland marked with bitterness and blood, the muddy current of the Rio Grande went twisting between the two unlike faces of two nations, to the sea. Summer heat baked the low coast and winding valley, and the sweating quartermaster kept his transport hustling, hauling stores from Brazos Santiago to the lethargic units of an occupation army south and west to Monterrey.

Volunteers with travel orders slouched on splintery steamboat decks, recounting in the manner of soldiers and with embellishments certain charms of smiling dusky-busted *chulitas* "in low-cut chemises," recalling bouts with *pulque* poured from pigskins, remembering the flavor of the south, the bite of the sun, the sound of hooves and cries along adobe-walled streets, the rattle of gunfire. But Volunteers remembered most at night, singing on the steamboats, far from the sound of trumpet or the weight of arms and far from home, laments of "The Rose of Alabama" and "Alice Gray."

The steersman at the wheel of the quartermaster's riverboat *Corvette* felt the flavor of all the land, without the burden of nostalgia, in the strength of his youth.

Afloat on wilderness waters, steamboats were arks of pleasant living, furnished with tolerable food, good drink, clean quarters and even soft beds. And the *Corvette*, built originally for passenger service on the Ohio, was among her sisters a de luxe steamboat; the government had bought her in Pittsburgh for $16,000, the highest price paid for any craft plying the Rio Grande.[29] Because of her superior accommodations, General Winfield Scott had chosen her to take him and his staff on the one trip he made up the river to Camargo early in January of 1847.[30] *Corvette's* furniture and equipment were a good deal better than her rough military service required, "but she had been immediately available, and the Quartermaster Department consoled itself that because of her appointments, she would probably be easier to dispose of after the war than less expensive boats. Above all else, she satisfied the requirements of light draught, drawing under twenty inches when not loaded and only thirty inches when carrying good freight."[31]

By their very nature, and by the nature of their duties in treacherous water, steamboats on the Rio Grande were constantly liable to damage or destruction through mishandling, carelessness or simple lack of luck. Hulls were gashed by snags or sprung by hanging on reefs and bars, superstructures were ripped by scraping river banks and overhanging timber on sharp bends when boats swung powerless, caught broadside against a current engines could not stem. Paddle wheels were banged and smashed. Engines had a habit of breaking down—more than a thousand miles from any source of replacement parts. And boilers exploded, scalding and killing.[32]

The professional skill, the vigilance, the luck of two young rivermen named Mifflin Kenedy and Richard King are manifest in the record of their steamer *Corvette:* she suffered no damaging accident in all her service on the Rio Grande. Her skipper and her pilot kept her running, in continuous service for the duration of the war. Captain Kenedy and Pilot King appear to have learned early how to deal with vagaries in steam engines, quirks in rivers and crotchets in crews.

King and Kenedy must often have discussed the requirements of a steamboat designed to operate efficiently from Brazos Santiago to Camargo. The previous summer, when boats were new to the Rio Grande, the editor of the *American Flag* in his issue of August 29, 1846, had made certain observations:

In ordering the construction of boats to navigate this river, there has been an evident want of foresight in not stating the peculiarities of the stream. A boat which may have a speed of six miles an hour against the current of the Mississippi will fall short of two miles on the Rio Grande. A flat bottomed boat will not answer, as in turning the short bends the current has such power on the side of the vessel as to prevent her heading up, and she is invariably swept over to the opposite bank. The most expert steersman cannot handle one of these boats, and several with whom we have conversed say that unless more power is given them, they are in a measure useless. They lack boiler, and their firebeds are too small. The *mosquital* which is the only wood to be had, burns slow and has very little blaze, causing great difficulty in keeping up steam. Should any more boats be built for this river attention should be paid to giving them a sufficiency of boiler. There is little danger of making more steam than can be worked off.

Yet there was more to the problem than that. The year 1846 had been a season of heavy rains, high water, swift current. The following year, when Richard King arrived, rains did not come. The channels carved by the previous year's flooding became shallows invested with newly shaped shoals. Swift current died. By late summer the river was so low that navigation to Camargo was barely possible. The successful boat for the Rio Grande not only needed plenty of boiler, it needed sometimes to stay afloat in soundings about the depth of dew. And for the run to Brazos Santiago it needed a build staunch enough to weather the pounding of an open sea.

In spite of difficulties, boats ran. The average trip from the mouth of the river to Camargo took from four to six days. Actual running time was less. Boats ordinarily tied up at night, attempting no navigation in the unmarked dark, and there were "wooding" stops for fuel and frequent landings to handle cargo and passengers.

During the year 1846-1847 the best recorded time from Boca del Rio to Camargo was made by the boat *Colonel Cross:* 61 hours and 55 minutes, of which 10 hours and 58 minutes were devoted to stops.[33] Shorter runs needed fewer stops and so were relatively faster. The *Brownsville* once churned up the fifty miles from Boca del Rio to Matamoros in only nine hours.[34] During the high water of 1846, before the arrival of Richard King, Kenedy and his Pilot Prescot Devot had pushed the *Corvette* to her fastest time from the river's mouth to Camargo. She had made it in exactly three days, and for this speed she had received a special commendation from military personnel aboard.[35]

Not all the quartermaster's boats on the Rio Grande were government property. Some of them had come to the Mexican border chartered by the government on a *per diem* basis.[36] Depending on the quartermaster's need, these boats went frequently in and out of charter; by August, 1847, the government had discharged them all. Growing trade and traffic had already brought to the Rio Grande a half dozen commercial packets in no way employed by the military, and most of the steamers released from government charter forthwith joined the packets in commercial operations hauling cargo and passengers for private profit.[37] From aboard the *Corvette,* Captain Kenedy and Pilot King watched and carefully noted the increasing number of "independents" plying the river. Notices in the columns of the *American Flag*[38] bespoke new enterprise on the border:

RECEIVING, FORWARDING and COMMISSION BUSINESS

The proprietors of the steamer *Tom Kirkman* would inform their friends and the public that they have erected warehouses at Rio Grande City (Davis Landing) and at Camargo, to which points goods will be dispatched and stored on account of the owners. Shippers may depend that all business confided to their care will be punctually attended to. This boat being of light draught of water will always be able to perform her regular trips to Camargo.

Agents:

CHAS. STILLMAN & BRO., MATAMOROS

P. DOWD, CAMARGO

Matamoros, September 29, 1847.

MATAMOROS AND MOUTH OF RIO GRANDE,
SEMI-WEEKLY PACKET

The owners of the steamer *Laurel* have determined to run her as a semi-weekly packet between the above ports, leaving Matamoros every Monday and Thursday at 8 o'clock A.M. and the Mouth every Tuesday and Saturday at 5 o'clock P.M. This arrangement is expected to accommodate the citizens of Matamoros as well as shippers and travellers generally. Whether profitable or not to the proprietors, no delay whatever, unless by unavoidable accident, will be permitted to break up the regular trips, and the public may rely upon her punctuality.

Passage same as on Government boats. Freight at the lowest rates of other private boats on the river. For freight or passage apply to

BODMAN & CLARKE
Hotel, Steamer *Frankland*
Mouth of Rio Grande

This arrangement will facilitate travel and business, and be of interest to citizens of Matamoros, and to shippers and traders generally.

Matamoros, September 18, 1847.

Late that September, couriers came with long-awaited news from the south. Winfield Scott's campaigners had stormed through battle at Contreras, Churubusco, Molino del Rey and up the heights of Chapultepec itself to plant the Stars and Stripes over the valley of Mexico. On the thirteenth of September, Scott's army had marched into the capital. Mexican resistance had collapsed, Santa Anna had fled to the hills. Peace negotiations were opening.

The army at Monterrey and on the Rio Grande roused itself to cheer and prepared to go home, done with war. But departure was slow. Occupation forces were ordered to remain in Mexico until a treaty of peace was concluded. Meanwhile there were limited withdrawals and preliminary motions toward the dismantling and abandonment of most of the military stations.

On the eighth of November Zachary Taylor said goodbye to his men in Monterrey, and traveled to Mier. His arrival at Camargo on the thirteenth was saluted by artillery salvoes; the next day the Tenth Infantry gave him a grand parade. On the fifteenth he embarked for Matamoros where he at last received his anticipated orders for relief from duty. Leaving General John Wool in command of the troops, Taylor went to Brazos Santiago and on the twenty-sixth of November boarded a vessel for New Orleans.[39]

The boat that carried Old Rough and Ready on his last journey downriver from Camargo to Matamoros was the steamer *Colonel Cross:* and some time during that month of November, 1847, Pilot Richard King became Captain Richard King, master of the *Colonel Cross.* There is no record of the precise date Richard King received this promotion or exactly when he transferred from the *Corvette* to the deck of his own command; there is some possibility that the new captain did carry the old general down the river—which happened to be in the direction that led Zachary Taylor to the White House.

Hundreds of miles to the south of where the new captain named King moved quartermaster's freight along the twists of the river, treaty makers were busy, officially settling some of the contention and bloodshed that river had caused. On February 2, 1848, a *Treaty of Peace, Friendship, Limits, and Settlement between the United States of America and the United Mexican States* was concluded at Guadalupe Hidalgo. Under the treaty's terms, the Rio Grande—not the Nueces—was to be the boundary line; Mexico was to cede Texas, California, and all the territory between. In return, Mexico would receive fifteen million dollars and the cancellation of outstanding American claims. With an American army still stationed as a threat at the heart of Mexico, a majority of the Mexican Congress had no choice but to approve the treaty, and it was sent to Washington. Had it not been already approved by the Mexican authority, there might have been an attempt on the part of the United States to annex all Mexico. Demands for such annexation were growing. Yet, since the treaty had been written under United States domination and had been approved by Mexico, President Polk believed it ought to be accepted. It was ratified in the United States Senate on March 10 and signed by the President. Ratifications were officially exchanged at Querétaro late in May.

By the end of July, the last United States troops had been withdrawn from the shores and borders of a Mexico bereft by war and treaty of one half its total area.

The Volunteers went home finally; their departure left no reason for the quartermaster's system of supply. Warehouses emptied, he tied his steamboats up to await some future disposition by a government remote in Washington. Except for a post of Regulars at Fort Brown and details scattered at such places of vantage as Brazos Santiago and Rio Grande City, soldiers faded from the Rio Grande. The effect of their marches along the far river remained.

Their war marked a new border, made a new frontier, brought new men to it, created new opportunity for new enterprise in an expanding economy, bound by the very surge of its energy to encompass the unsurveyed and unused new breadth of a continent.

Captain Richard King, 24-year-old former master of the Army steamer *Colonel Cross,* released from government service for the second time in his life, surveyed the prospects of the new border frontier, the flavor of the life and of the opportunity it offered. He found the prospects and the flavor good. So did his friend Kenedy. The two young captains were the kind of men a big contentious place could use. They stayed with it.

III *Steamboating for Profit*

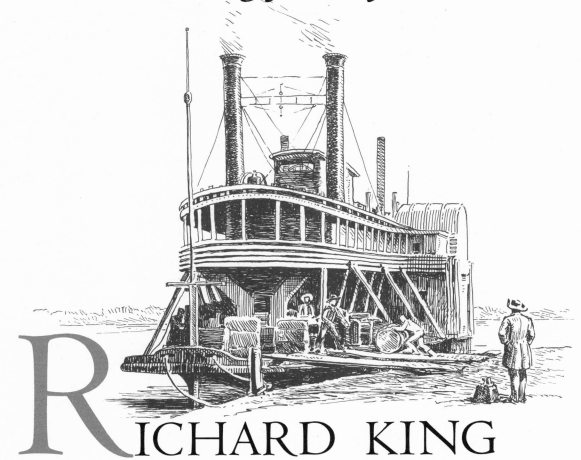

RICHARD KING

went to the steamboaters' shantytown at the mouth of the river to keep a sharp eye for an opening in his trade. It may be that he knew of official plans for a war surplus sale of the immobilized steamboats tied up at Brazos Santiago and that he intended to bid for one of those vessels. If he had any such information or intention, he knew he must wait until the Quartermaster Department stated terms and was ready to sell.

He went in business at Boca del Rio while he waited. Using some of his savings, he rigged up a kind of flophouse and grogshop to catch the rough custom of the boomers who came needing a place to sleep and a little something for thirst. He made himself not only proprietor but bedmaker, bartender and bouncer of the establishment. Later in his life he would grin, saying that years as a cabin boy had eminently fitted him for the wholesale making of beds;[1] he did not mention his qualifications for bouncer or barkeep, but he had a self-evident pair of fists, and a temperament that knew no dismay at the bung of any barrel. During the last months of 1848, he enjoyed himself ashore. He ran a convivial place. It provided a livelihood lively enough, and he heard all the news.

His friend Kenedy was busy up at the other end of the river. He was promoting a new town, named Roma. A paid advertisement in the November 29, 1848, issue of the *American Flag* (newly moved from the old stand in Matamoros to new business in Brownsville) informed the public that Roma was:

... situated on the east bank of the Rio Grande, about midway between Camargo and Mier, on a high stone bluff. The adjacent land is the richest soil, well adapted to the cultivation of the main staples of the south, such as cane, cotton, corn, tobacco, &c., and also furnishing an inexhaustible range for stockraising. On this tract, also, are fine stone quarries for all building purposes, and last, though not the least, steamboat navigation, *certain and sure,* for four-fifths of the year. Besides the town is almost in front of the main road leading to Monterey, Saltillo and Zacatecas. The position is an elevated one, presenting the most interesting views of mountains and valleys to be found on the river — all that is asked is for every person wishing to purchase to come up and examine for themselves.

WM. WILKINSON — J. H. BEAN
Commissioners for Stockholders
M. KENEDY — P. H. PROUT
Agents for Justo García, José María García, and others

The site of Roma, formerly called the García Rancho after the owners of the tract, was a handy landing place on the American side of the river sixteen miles upstream from Rio Grande City. The "Commissioners for Stockholders" and the "Agents for Justo García" *et al* were, in reality, promoting the establishment of a landing to compete with the practical monopoly then held by Henry Clay Davis, who at his Rio Grande City controlled the only existing facilities on the American side of the river for the handling of goods moving up the Rio Grande into the Mexican trade. Mifflin Kenedy had seen opportunity in aligning himself with the interests of Matamoros merchants who intended to by-pass the Davis monopoly by building up Roma; Kenedy was investing in the development of a trade rival to Rio Grande City.

With the year 1848 almost gone, Richard King got the word he waited for. The December 6 issue of the *American Flag* printed it:

NOTICE OF QUARTERMASTER'S SALE

Brazos Santiago, Texas
November 20, 1848

Propositions for the purchase of the following named steamboats will be received in writing until the 20th day of December, 1848. The price offered for each boat must be distinctly stated, and those making offers will be noticed whether they are accepted on the 10th day of January, 1849.

Colonel Hunt	Whiteville	Brownsville
General Jesup	Wm. R. McKee	Hatchee Eagle
Troy	Colonel Cross	Colonel J. Stephens (propeller)
Dragon	J. E. Roberts	

W. W. Chapman
Brevet Major & A. Q. M.

Yet the waiting went on: a public sale was postponed until the fifteenth of March,[2] and again, until the second of April. The next day, the wartime master of *Colonel Cross,* became her peacetime owner:

An official report, to Quartermaster General T. S. Jesup, following this certification[3] by the auctioneer, describes the circumstances leading to the delay and the greatly depreciated prices obtained for the boats:

Asst. Quartermaster's Office
Brazos Santiago, Texas,
April 7, 1849

General:

I have the honor to report, that in consequence of the prevalence of the cholera in this vicinity, and by the advice of Colonel Thompkins, Quarter Master, who was here on the 10th of March, I again postponed the public sale of the Steamboats, at the Mouth of the Rio Grande, until April 2d.

The boats at the public sale were sold at very low prices, — lower than they would have realized when they were laid up last fall — The reasons, however are obvious: — since that time great numbers have left this region for California, and business on the Rio Grande has greatly diminished. Added to this, the universal prevalence of the Cholera in its worst epidemic form, throughout the whole Valley of the Rio Grande, for the last six weeks, has created a perfect stagnation of business.

> I have the honor to be, General
> very respectfully
> Yr. Obdt. Servt.
> W. W. Chapman
> Brevet Major & A.Q.M.[4]

Only six of the eleven boats advertised are accounted for at the public sale. The *Dragon* had been wrecked near the mouth of the river on November 26;[5] the *Colonel Hunt* disposed of by private sale. The other unaccounted vessels may also have been sold privately on written bids, as advertised. Though his name is not found in the record as a purchaser, the powerful Matamoros merchant Charles Stillman was acquiring war surplus vessels; he saw in a fleet of steamboats the key to control trade on the Rio Grande. His merchant partner Samuel A. Belden bought both the *Hatchee Eagle* and the *Troy* at the public sale, probably acting for Stillman.

Richard King acted for no one but himself. He was on his own. In coming to ownership of the *Colonel Cross,* he paid $750 for a steamer which had cost the government $14,000 at Pittsburgh only three years before. She was battered but she was a bargain. As her most recent skipper, he knew with accuracy her condition for further service — and he could swing her price from his savings on the river. Escaping the cholera, disregarding "a perfect stagnation of business," he left his bedmaking and bartending at Boca del Rio, hired a crew, put his boat in repair, fired up his boilers and went in business hauling cargoes for merchants of Matamoros, engaging in a trade which had a history tinged with romance and flavored with profit.

In early times one of the great grievances held by the Rio Grande settlements and all northeastern Mexico against the rule of Spain was the Crown's monopoly of trade. All imports were by law compelled to pass through the port of Vera Cruz.[6] Without a nearer port of entry, goods had to be hauled hundreds of miles north through a dangerous frontier and on execrable trails, a procedure that made most goods either entirely unavailable or prohibitively costly. Contraband crept in by difficult short cuts, but the quantity was negligible in the face of the demand. The people of northern Mexico wanted and needed a closer and more convenient legal port of entry; when Mexico severed itself from Spain, such a port was one of the prime demands of the settlers along the Rio Grande and in the towns of the interior farther west.

With the restraint of the Crown's monopoly removed, geography itself contributed to the difficulty of establishing a convenient port. There seemed to be no safe and practical harbor in all the 450 miles of coast from Indianola to Tampico.

Since the expedition of Alonzo Alvarez de Pineda in 1519, seafarers along that coast knew of the existence of the passage between Brazos and Padre islands, *El Paso de los Brazos de Santiago.* Its tricky channel and scant anchorage for three centuries brought it small consideration as a port, though the quiet water in the lee of sandy Brazos had surely served as an occasional haven and hide-out for shady gentry as famed as Jean LaFitte, and for less legendary smugglers, who operated along the great south-swinging curve of the Gulf shore. However it had served infrequent and undercover mariners, suddenly Brazos Santiago became the port the people of northeastern Mexico looked for. Credit for its "discovery" belongs to an able and aggressive ranchero from Tamaulipas who became the successful impresario of a Texas colony during Mexican rule, Martín de León.[7]

From his rancho at the mouth of the Aransas River, Don Martín in the year 1823 drove a large herd of horses and mules to market in New Orleans. He sold them at a fat profit. During what was obviously celebration in the celebrated atmosphere of New Orleans, the ranchero, fresh from his ride in the sticks, encountered two affable and well-spoken gentlemen, a Spaniard by the name of Carlos Lazo and a Frenchman named Ramón Lafon. When conversation came upon the topic of the long coast, Lafon remarked that he knew a good harbor near the mouth of the Rio Grande. The ranchero showed an unmistakable interest. It developed that Lafon and Lazo were in fact, and most conveniently, the owners of a schooner which was out of charter at the moment. They could—They were indeed ready—They could take the Señor de León to the secret port—And take some merchandise along. There was one small difficulty: for some unjust reason, Lafon and Lazo felt that they might be wanted on a charge of piracy along the Mexican coast. The ranchero Don Martín searched his own feelings and decided that one small difficulty should not be allowed to stand in the way. It could surely be resolved happily. He chartered the schooner, loaded it with the kind of New Orleans luxury goods he knew would find demand amongst his neighbors south and west, paid for it all with his horse and mule money, and got aboard with Messrs. Lafon and Lazo. The story has all the earmarks of a badly worn and badly written piece of fiction, with villainy to come. The outcome was neither fictional nor villainous.

Don Martín and his new friends sailed safely down the coast. Just eight miles north of the Rio Grande's mouth, they brought their vessel neatly through the channel between the two islands to quiet, convenient anchorage at Brazos Santiago. Transporting his cargo on by muleback to the nearby settlements, Don Martín not only made a huge return on the sale of his goods, he went into his native Tamaulipas and, from the proper authority, got pardons for Lazo and Lafon.[8]

To judge by their historical results, the pardons were well-deserved. Mercantile houses and traders of New Orleans had for years been trying to pry open a practical and profitable trade route into northern Mexico. A ranchero and his bluff trust in two pirates showed the way.

When the news got back to New Orleans, it called forth a stream of venturers in best-sailing-time, following the trade wake of Martín de León. From that year 1823 onward, goods moving toward the populated areas of northern Mexico went to the port of Brazos Santiago.[9] Until 1846, when war brought Point Isabel into use as a depot for overland freight and when steamboats plying the Rio Grande handled cargoes with immensely greater efficiency, everything unloaded from the ships was carried by muleback or oxcart along the desolate five-mile length of Brazos Island to a primitive ferry at Boca Chica, where the road crossed to the mainland. From there, mules and carts carried their heavy loads across dunes and sloughs to the Rio Grande. There was a crossing at Burrita and another, more frequently used, thirteen miles farther on, at Matamoros itself, the *entrepôt* of all the trade.

In 1765 Matamoros had not even its name: it was a rancho with a chapel, known as *San Juan de los Esteros*.[10] Thirty years later the little village grown around the rancho was being called *Congregación del Refugio*. When goods from Brazos Santiago quickened it, the Congregación changed to the *Puerto* (Port) *del Refugio*. It took its final name in 1826, chartered and incorporated as *La Villa de Matamoros* in honor of the soldier-priest Mariano Matamoros, martyred in the struggle for independence from Spain. The church on the Plaza de Armas was finished in 1831; by 1836 Matamoros had seven thousand people and was bigger than any town in Texas. Trade made it so.

The real reason Mexico wanted the territory between the Nueces and the Rio Grande, the real reason for the bitterness and for the war upon that issue, was not twenty-five million empty acres of grassland between the two rivers. *It was the location of the little port of Brazos Santiago, the only practicable funnel through which commerce poured into northern Mexico.*

The merchants who poured that commerce at Matamoros were an assorted lot, coming in many colors, pale and deep-dyed, like goods they sold. There were few Mexicans of any consequence among them, and many French. Arriving originally as agents for New Orleans houses, or with Creole connections, French firms were thickly studded in the roster of merchants at Matamoros: Pretat & Co., Gautier & Fils, Dessommes & Co., Monstiet, Brougnoir E. Chassignet and half a score more. Some of the French names arrived in Matamoros through colorful channels: it is said that when LaFitte sailed away from Campeachy and over the horizon, some of his pirate crew did not sail with him; drifting down the coast, they established Bagdad as a smuggling base and then seeped up to Matamoros. The French were not the only foreigners among the merchants on the Rio Grande. There were Spaniards, *gachupines,* by habit hard with their pesos and dollars. There were some with grand manners, like the very rich Basque Don Francisco Ytúrria.[11] In the *pot-pourri* were Italians, Germans, Irish, Scotch, English. And there were Yankees, with trade in their blood.

Like the frontier that stretched out boundless about them, the merchants of Matamoros were on the make. To stay in business, they stayed sharp; if they managed to stay, they managed to get rich. The Merchants of Matamoros were the Merchants of Venice, Rio Grande style.

They handled profitable quantities of goods. In the boom following the Mexican War, the trade is said to have brought through customs merchandise valued at from ten to fourteen million dollars annually[12]—a surprising trade, practiced under every difficulty of transportation and brigandage on a rough and remote frontier. One of the fortunes made in Matamoros developed the National City Bank of New York. Operators on the Rio Grande were not playing with marbles.

Their merchandise was of a kind to satisfy the wants of the mines and towns and ranches of northern Mexico: machinery, tools, implements, wagons, harness, utensils, hardware, cutlery, firearms, glass, paper, dry goods ranging from coarse *manta* and plain calico to fine linens, woolens and silks from the looms of Europe, notions, furniture, Virginia and Havana tobaccos, wines and liquors, fancy groceries, comestibles in bulk like corn and lard, rough-sawed lumber for towns where timber was scarce, bales of cotton for textile mills at Monterrey and beyond.

Mexico was an early and unremitting proponent of protective tariffs, both for her manufactures and her raw stuffs; import regulations prohibited the passage of many standard articles of trade. Merchants of Matamoros handled these goods, as contraband. They brought huge profit. Tobacco, for instance, was a principal item on the prohibited list, and the same hundredweight of tobacco which could be bought for a dollar or a dollar and a half in New Orleans could be sold, when baled up and smuggled into Mexico, for between fifty and seventy-five dollars.[13] Enjoying that kind of reward, smuggling became a border industry. If it was not legal, neither was it considered disreputable. Smuggled goods were often necessities; purchasers welcomed them and attached no stigma to those who furnished them. The arrangements for running contraband ordinarily were not arduous. Mexican customs officials, and many higher in government, were seldom averse to holding out a hand and closing an eye. There was little difficulty. Properly greased, the channels were smooth and—except to the purchasing consumer—wonderfully profitable for all concerned.

Payment for goods in the trade, legal or illegal, came in Mexican specie, bullion from the mines, or barter exchanges, usually in the form of raw wool or beef hides. Each of these items worked to the advantage of the receiving Matamoros merchants. Bullion, either gold or silver, needs no comment as a desirable article subject to premium in changing hands. As for the coined silver Mexican peso, it was legal tender in the United States until 1857, and it was more than that: most of the state mints of Mexico produced a peso of greater weight and fineness of silver than the American dollar; in the border trade, merchants could take a peso at par of one dollar and get more than a dollar for it by shipping it to American brokers who paid a premium for its silver content. And the wool and hides, principal products suitable for export from the grass-rich huge pastures of northern Mexico, formed convenient cargoes, subject to profitable price speculation, for ships that otherwise would have returned in ballast to New Orleans.

Following the Mexican War, pig lead from Monterrey and Saltillo became a heavy article of export. In addition to beef hides, manifests often listed sheep, goat, deer—even jaguar—skins. A few mules, some salt, some bones and tallow were occasionally shipped to New Orleans. Late in the 1840's "a typical cargo of a New Orleans-bound schooner contained 338 bales and 75 sacks of wool, 1339 beef hides, 24 bales and 50 bundles of skins, 58 bales of goat skins, 537 pigs and 164 slabs of lead, and $408,300 in specie and bullion."[14]

Angry Mexicans had naturally discriminated against American merchants at Matamoros during the Texas troubles and the American invasion of Mexico. Merchants of other nationalities had received preferred treatment and gained advantage in the trade. When the Rio Grande became the boundary of the United States, Americans were at last in position to swing a hatchet on their foreign competitors. To control the distribution of goods arriving on the American side of the river was to control the Matamoros trade. And Brownsville, that new place within the friendly jurisdiction of the dependable United States Government, sat astride the vital flow of goods from Brazos Santiago. "Brownsville replaced Matamoros as the great *entrepôt* of trade with Northern Mexico because the United States was in possession of the best harbor in the Lower Rio Grande, because steam navigation of the river was in the hands of Americans, and above all because a great discrepancy in tariff rates, together with relative ease of smuggling, made it highly desirable to keep goods for the Mexican market on the American side of the river until they could be removed to the interior of Mexico."[15] The advantages of Brownsville came playing about the heads of Yankee traders like little flames with silvery-golden tongues.

One of the richest and shrewdest of those traders had taken heed of the tongues early. He had built a dependable ferry service from Matamoros *to* Brownsville. He had built a large brick warehouse at the head of that ferry, to store his goods *in* Brownsville. He had bought title (which was later to be in litigation for decades) to those *ejidos* of Matamoros surrounding Fort Brown, hired a surveyor to lay out the townsite, and organized a company to sell the lots and develop the boom *of* Brownsville.[16] And he had bought the government's war surplus river craft, putting James O'Donnell, a steamboat captain, in charge of operating them,[17] to control transportation *around* Brownsville. Charles Stillman was a rough competitor in any department. He came of a competitive race.

Among the very first representatives of that race at Brazos Santiago was David Willard Smith, a Connecticut Yankee. He entered the trade sometime before 1824 and received an appointment as the first United States Consul at Matamoros in 1826.[18] Smith was enthusiastic about it. He probably communicated his enthusiasm to his former business partner, Francis Stillman, another Connecticut Yankee trader. In 1828 Stillman loaded the ship *Albion* with a cargo of trade goods and on February 2 registered its arrival at the port of Brazos Santiago.[19]

Stillman's eighteen-year-old son Charles came with him. There was delay in the sale of the goods, and Francis Stillman left his son in Matamoros to dispose of the merchandise. He did, at such profit that he decided to stay in Matamoros to receive and sell goods his father shipped him.

From that first transaction onward, Charles Stillman evinced a pushing eagerness in life: the making of money. In that regard, a contemporary stated, "Stillman had little to learn."[20] He toiled at it. He had been ready with goods and services during all the Texas revolution. Ten years later, when the eight American merchants of Matamoros were interned by the Mexican commander Ampudia and sent south into Tamaulipas at the beginning of Taylor's campaign, "Carlos" Stillman got away.[21] He hid in the brush. Five weeks later he was on hand to pursue his eagerness in the midst of a friendly occupation army on his old stomping ground in Matamoros. Peace or war, he used what he made to make more.

When Richard King fired up the boilers of his *Colonel Cross* early in the year 1849 and solicited the business of hauling merchandise and passengers on the Rio Grande, the steamboats of Charles Stillman, under the management of James O'Donnell, were King's chief competition.

Stillman did not put all his purchased government vessels in commission on the Rio Grande. Some were sold for service elsewhere. Some were found to be unserviceable anywhere and were junked for their parts or tied up and used as houseboat-hotels, as in the case of the *Whiteville*.[22] O'Donnell was probably unable to operate at any one time half a dozen of Stillman's boats, including his first and privately bought vessel, the *Tom Kirkman*.

The steamers of all other competitors, such as the firm of Bodman & Clarke, could not have totaled more than four or five. It is improbable that at any one time during the postwar boom there were more than ten steamboats operating on the Rio Grande.[23] The trade did not justify a greater number — and the boats themselves presented difficulties.

In private ownership, operating for profit and without a wasteful amplitude of public funds for maintenance, it soon became apparent that the boats on the Rio Grande were not satisfactory. They broke down too often and they stuck aground, losing revenue in delays and costing money in repairs. Their build was not sturdy enough for the rough sea from Brazos Santiago to the river mouth; on the river their patched, cranky engines lacked power when they ran and lost custom when they stalled.

Richard King, owner-master-pilot of a single vessel, had some advantage over his competition. He operated without having to hire captain, pilot or clerk, and with his knowledge of boat engines he could bear a hand to help his engineer. Cutting the payroll to a minimum by hiring only an engineer, a cook, and not more than a dozen Mexican stokers and deck hands, Captain King managed to run the *Colonel Cross*. There was business enough, and to keep it moving there was work enough, twenty-four hours a day. As the banks of the Rio Grande and the months of 1849 slid by and wild tidings came from California, Richard King realized the wheelhouse of the *Colonel Cross* was no bonanza.

On the runs upriver he saw his friend Mifflin Kenedy at Roma. Kenedy was finding that time and money in the promotion of river real estate did not make a bonanza either. Roma was a slow thing, like the progress of the *Colonel Cross* with a boiler clogged.

Kenedy's eyes had often looked west following the lines of pack mules and the dust of wagons fading in distance, into Mexico. Kenedy's ears had listened to the talk of traders come back to Roma on the river, back with big money. They hauled goods to the great fairs in Mexico's interior, Saltillo in September, Aguascalientes in October, Allende in November, San Juan de los Lagos in December. Merchants and peddlers came to the fairs as paying customers for the imported merchandise; they bought it and moved out retailing it to the remotest hinterlands.[24] The thoughts of 31-year-old Captain Mifflin Kenedy, former steamboat man, ranged westward where not the lightest-draft mudwalloper would float.

He entered into a joint venture with Samuel A. Belden and Captain James Walworth.[25] Belden had come into the Matamoros trade backed by the prominent New Orleans merchant, William Alling, and had prospered to become a member of the firm of Stillman & Belden.[26] He had connections. Walworth was an ex-skipper from New England who had come to the Rio Grande during the war and, like Kenedy, accumulated modest funds.[27] The three venturers put up their money and bought mules, wagons and merchandise—probably to the profit of the firm of Stillman & Belden. Their objective was the famed fair of San Juan de los Lagos, six hundred harsh miles across Mexico. A good day's travel for a wagon train over Mexican roads was ten miles. To arrive upon the date of the fair, which began at San Juan on December 5 and continued for eight days, the joint-venturers Belden, Walworth and Kenedy loaded up and left the Rio Grande no later than the first of October, 1849, probably much earlier. They never reached San Juan de los Lagos. The demand for their goods was so great in the war-shorn back country through which they traveled that in Zacatecas they sold out everything they had, including the wagons and mules, and dissolved the joint venture.[28]

Sometime before the end of 1849, Mifflin Kenedy came back to the Rio Grande with new Zacatecas money in his sweaty saddlebags. He used it in a new venture, on his own. Buying another stock of goods in Matamoros, he loaded it all on muleback and headed west again. He sold out in Monterrey.[29]

In late January or in February of 1850,[30] when he returned to Matamoros with the proceeds of his mule train, Mifflin Kenedy got word that Charles Stillman wanted to see him.

Their interview carried portents.

Stillman knew from the wartime performance of the big boat *Corvette* what kind of a riverman Kenedy was; moreover, Sam Belden had reported Kenedy's business sense in the joint venture to Zacatecas. Sitting at his desk, close by his ledgers, Stillman opened his mind and his hand to the sober Quaker. He made Mifflin Kenedy a proposition.

He told Kenedy there was something wrong with the management of the Stillman boats on the river. Far from expectation, the steamers were bringing in less than their cost of operation, and Charles Stillman wished to state that he was not in any business for the purpose of losing money. A remedy must be found. He did not know exactly what that remedy might be. It was out of his line: he was a merchant, not a steamboater. Would Captain Kenedy, whose line it was, care to come in as a partner to put the Stillman boat venture into profitable operation?—Could he?

Careful Mifflin Kenedy did not know. He did know the difficulties of operating the kind of boats Stillman had. Yet the offer carried blandishments to a steamboater with saddle galls, just arrived from dry Mexican hills. It was an offer to summon up an old music in his mind, a rattling winch, a dinging bell, an engine thumping steady under the planks of a wheelhouse deck. It was no matter of music, however. It was arithmetic. It was his good friend King's kind of horse sense river arithmetic.

Kenedy's mind worked with the possibilities. When he had considered them, he spoke.

He told Stillman that if anybody could make steamboats operate on the Rio Grande at a profit, it was a man named King. They would need him. If Stillman would bring King into the partnership—if King would come so would Kenedy. It would be a team.[31]

Stillman could find no objection to the prospect of transforming a competitor into a partner.

Kenedy went to find his friend on the river.

When the partnership offer was outlined to him, Richard King's reply was not without the emphasis of a long lean year on the *Colonel Cross*. The young captain said no. *Hell no!* Not with those goddamned government smoke scows. He was trying to run one. One was enough. They were no goddamn good!

Quaker Kenedy spoke quietly: it was opportunity. They would be working together. Just what was the matter with trying?

Didn't Kenedy remember the *Corvette?* Not built right to begin with! There were only seven steamers left on the river.[32] And they were falling apart. The boats were no good for their job.

Did Captain King have any ideas? One thing was clear. Mr. Stillman had the money—and the desire—to operate boats—

Hell yes, Richard King had ideas. If Stillman actually wanted to operate, he'd sink the damned clinkers and start over. He'd get the right kind of boats built and then run them the right way—

What way?

Fourteen years of river lessons came moving Richard King's tongue: the Rio Grande was a peculiar deal. What it needed was a different way to handle cargo. The old boats were too light for the outside sea run and too heavy for the inside river run. There ought to be two kinds of boats. One kind ought to be a big and stout brute side-wheeler built to carry real payloads from Brazos harbor to the river mouth and on as far upstream as practical, maybe a dozen miles of easy water, to a place like White Ranch. A decent terminal ought to be built there for handling and storing what the big boat carried. And from there cargo ought to be taken by the other kind of boat. A stout little upriver rascal built with hell's own kicking boilers and a bottom that could float in a light sweat! What the Rio Grande wanted was system: a big boat for big loads direct from ships at Brazos to a transfer point on the river *and* a team of high-powered stern-wheeled mudskimmers to go on from there. There would be one clear aim and object in it: sure profit, through the lowest possible cargo handling cost. The system would cut out most lightering and all but one transshipping when the big outside boat unloaded at the downriver terminal. During high water, the big devil could pull as far as the wharf in Brownsville with *no* transshipping. If Mr. Stillman actually cared to get in real business on the river, Richard King could design boats— both kinds. He could run that big brute over the bar at the mouth himself, he could see it now! He could keep those loadings *rousted* by God —with the right kind of boats.

The horse sense river arithmetic, both mechanical and negotiable, not only persuaded Mifflin Kenedy, it convinced Charles Stillman.[33]

A new firm, M. KENEDY & CO., of Brownsville, Texas, organized for business on March 1, 1850.[34] The firm was composed of four partners holding equal shares, Charles Stillman, Mifflin Kenedy, Richard King, and Stillman's steamboater James O'Donnell. It was organized for the purpose of putting into operation Richard King's plan; its efficiency was soon to transform and to monopolize completely all commercial transportation on the Rio Grande.

Stillman furnished the money. O'Donnell was brought into the firm for reasons of loyalty and to act as Stillman's agent in steamboating matters. Kenedy and King were to furnish the drive to establish and maintain the enterprise.

The new vessels were the first order of firm business. King straightway set to work on his diagrams and specifications. If he was not entirely easy with a pen, he was downright familiar with a steamboat; he knew what he was after, and he put it down.

When everything—including the cautious use of funds—had been discussed and agreed among the partners, Kenedy put a sheaf of papers in a portmanteau and got aboard a ship at Brazos, bound for New Orleans and then Pittsburgh, to place an order for the building of two steamers.

They were to be named *Grampus* and *Comanche.*

The *Grampus* was to be a blocky, bluff-bowed, heavy-stanchioned 500-ton side-wheeler, about 150 feet long, of exceptionally wide beam, equipped with power and ruggedness to butt hard seas and rock over the bar at the river mouth, drawing just three feet of water. Because of her short run, her fuel spaces were to be limited in favor of more deck for payload. She was expected to make the run from Brazos to a river landing in from three to four hours in most weathers.[35] The *Comanche* was to be an easy-handling stern-wheeler of 200 tons, a powerful light "mudder" with a draft of less than twenty-four inches loaded.[36]

Kenedy placed contracts for them at a Pittsburgh yard and supervised the early part of their construction before he returned to the Rio Grande early in July. There is no record of what the *Grampus* and the *Comanche* cost, but they were made to special order, strongly built and expensive. The *Grampus II,* built in 1857, cost $31,559.95; and the *Ranchero,* much like the *Comanche,* in 1855 cost $27,538.18 "for delivery in Brownsville.''[37] These prices suggest the extent of M. Kenedy & Co.'s initial investment in steamers.

When the company organized it evidently assumed ownership of the *Colonel Cross*.[38] Until the new craft arrived from Pittsburgh and the old boats could be disposed of, the firm operated with what it had. Captain Richard King spent the spring and part of the summer of 1850 on the worn and familiar decks of the *Colonel Cross,* impatiently.

His impatience for the arrival of two steamboats was blended with a disquietude of a very different kind. Captain King had met a young lady.

On a day of that same fateful February[39] when Mifflin Kenedy had returned from Monterrey and Charles Stillman had studied disagreeable figures in a ledger, Richard King brought the *Colonel Cross* on a run upriver toward Brownsville.

The going was hard. High water had carved silt to new shapes of deeps and shallows along the crooking channel. The *Colonel Cross* was sluggish with her load. Her engine pounded and slipped, losing headway often in a tedious upstream fight against the suck and swirl of mud-thick brown water. It was not a trip to put a riverman in the best frame of mind.

Near the end of his run, Captain King stood nursing his turns on the sweat-slicked grips of the wheel. When finally he gave hard left rudder and swung straining against the drift of the last bend leading to the welcome sight of the Brownsville riverfront—a boat stood moored, blocking the slip where the *Colonel Cross* customarily unloaded. It was the old *Whiteville,* and it was in the way.

Captain King swore. He had to back engine to snake around, sweating his boat into where her hawsers could secure at the bollards and a plank could go down. When it did, he came from the wheelhouse letting rip, like a blare from the steam whistle over his head.

Who in the bychrist name of bejeesus had the green gall to tie that goddam tub *Whiteville* in the way? *Who?*

One of the loungers on the quay looked up and grinned. He made a gesture cautioning quiet. The *Whiteville*, he said, was a houseboat now. Rented by the new preacher. Just come to town—the Reverend Some—

Reverend? Well bygod Richard King would just as soon dock alongside hell with the hide off as that bygod trap for rats named *Whiteville!* Just *who*—

A listener he had not seen moved into the sunlight, to the tidy gunwale of the *Whiteville.* The listener was a young lady.

She wished to inform him—he saw her dainty prettiness—that the *Whiteville* was a great sight, *a very great sight* cleaner—he saw the outraged flash in her eyes—than *that* unsightly thing with the horrible molasses running down its perfectly filthy sides—he heard the well-bred accent of her angry voice—and *certainly* cleaner than a shameless beastly profane tongue! *Indecent* tongue unfit for the ears of decency! *The very idea!* As for rats in the vicinity, he could be assured they would not be on the *Whiteville.* It was perfectly apparent where they *were*—he saw her toss her head.[40]

The captain of the *Colonel Cross* stood, red-eared and squelched, as the young lady stalked out of sight. Wordless rivermen watched her go as if an hallucination moved fading, voice and figure of another world, a world unknown. The big-fisted *indecent* skipper of the *Colonel Cross* stood smitten.

The crew unloaded his boat quietly that afternoon, hiding brownfaced grins. The mind of their *Señor Capitán* wandered somewhat from a strict consideration of river business. And the deck was scrubbed clean of molasses.

Before the *Colonel Cross* moved on, Mifflin Kenedy found her and came aboard to see his friend. At a certain stage in conversation

Kenedy was asked, casually enough, about the new preacher, over there on the *Whiteville*. It happened that the serious-minded Quaker had indeed the recent privilege of the clergyman's acquaintance. He was the Reverend Hiram Chamberlain, just arrived from Tennessee, come to establish what would be the very first Protestant church on all the length of the Rio Grande.[41] He was a Presbyterian, a very sober and godly man. Kenedy approved, and said so.

About the — uh — Reverend Chamberlain's family? Kenedy had met them?

Kenedy saw the light. He was not a light-minded man, but when he found a situation to relish, he did. He told Richard King he had met the minister's family. A splendid wife, two little sons, an infant.

Uh, there wasn't a daughter?

Ah, Kenedy said, of course! He had forgotten. A daughter. Her name was Miss Henrietta Maria Morse Chamberlain. She was seventeen. Kenedy's eyes were enjoying themselves.

Well. Did Kenedy suppose he could introduce a friend?

Kenedy's eyes enjoyed themselves even more. He would consider introducing Captain King to the young lady. That is, if Captain King would on Wednesday evening attend the prayer meeting and church social aboard the *Whiteville*.[42]

In his whole life Captain King had not been to a prayer meeting. Or a — church social. Wasn't his friend making it pretty hard?

His friend was enjoying himself. The prayer meeting and church social were the only way, Kenedy said.

Richard King nerved himself up to it — but he met her beforehand, on the Wednesday afternoon. As Kenedy and King walked together on a Brownsville street, she came toward them; Kenedy performed the introduction.[43] Miss Chamberlain had bright brown eyes, and they recognized Richard King. It may be they perceived a soul to save.

Richard King may have borne himself with a self-consciousness toward amenities and refinements he had yet to learn, but he was not shy. He was smitten. He was not deterred from the prayer meeting, or the church social. He went, and he went again. He met the Reverend Chamberlain, who was not much drawn to a burly young riverman, captain or not, seeking the refined company of a Christian daughter.

The 53-year-old Hiram Chamberlain from Middlebury College, from Princeton Theological and Andover Theological seminaries, possessed a soul like a redoubt built with the frosty stone of his native Vermont.[44] As a warrior against Sin, he was aware of the drama of life, especially his own. Aged twenty-six, he had written a letter to his betrothed, setting forth the drama as he felt it:

> . . . I am attached to one of the daughters of Eve, educated among the wild rocks of Vermont. I do not blush to confess this attachment. It is *open* and *announced.* It is neither *unlawful* nor *base.* It is *innocent* and *honorable.* I am indulging the passions of love, I am the affectionate, the constant, the manly friend. I am not the whining, whimpering wretch who sighs and swoons his life away, when his lov'd fair one's gone. Duty is the *pale star* of my conduct.[45]

The pale star had led him as an ordained Presbyterian minister and zealous worker in the Home Missionary Society to bring Gospel light to the frontier of Missouri, and then Tennessee. In the course of his ministries, he had been twice a widower and thrice joined in bonds of holy wedlock.

His daughter Henrietta had come into the world on the twenty-first of July, 1832, at Boonville, Missouri, born of his first wife, Maria Morse of Dorset, Vermont.[46] Maria had died in 1835, and Hiram Chamberlain had remarried. Four years later, without further issue, he, with his daughter Henrietta, had again been bereft.[47] In October of 1842, he had taken unto himself another daughter of

Eve, Anna Adelia Griswold, who had blessed him with three sons, Hiram Jr., Milton, and Peter Bland.[48]

The child Henrietta, healthy and strong, had lived in a home that moved often, following her father's various ministries; and since the age of three, the mother love her heart required had been supplied by stepmothers. These circumstances of her childhood had nourished a self-reliance and a certain loneliness at the same time, though affection within the family circle had always been given her. When she was fourteen, her father had sent her away to school, and she had suffered homesickness. She had missed most of all the affectionate presence of her little half brother Hiram; when her feelings crept into the letters she wrote home, her father had answered by reminding her of her own *pale star:*

Miss Henrietta Chamberlain
Female Institute
Holly Springs, Mississippi

Via Memphis   Sommerville, Tenn.
                                                     January 22, 1847.

My Daughter:
    We send you a few small presents. Your mother sends you a fine handkerchief, which cost a dollar. . . . and I send you a little money. . . .We have received the letter with the little book for Hiram. He pretended to read it, and was much pleased that you sent it to him. He professes to understand what you say about him, and becomes very much animated.
    You say you dream about him. This gives me some uneasiness. I fear you are getting nervous and unhappy in being away from home. That will never do. It will injure your health, and your mind, and prevent you from making suitable improvement in your studies. You must determine to get above it. Think of what I write to you and it will help you to rise superior to all such depressing thoughts. It is your *religious* duty. We were not made to be *perfectly* happy here. We must wait till we get to heaven for that. If we desired noth-

ing but what was right, and had all we desired, Earth is not the place to enjoy perfect bliss. God has reserved that for a better world. We are *here* to glorify Him.

This we cannot do unless we deny ourselves, and like our Savior, bear the Cross. We can never do any good without making some sacrifice for it. Your father had to leave home, and dear friends to get *his education.* Our officers and soldiers have to do the same, to fight the battles of their country. Your grandfather left *sweet home* to enter the Revolutionary Army. He slept on cold frozen ground, and exposed his life where the bullets whistled, and the sword of our fierce enemy gleamed on the field of death. *He,* and others like *him* did all this to secure the blessings which you now every day enjoy. And can't you show some of his spirit, and resolution? Can't you be a soldier for a few months? Have you not some of his blood circling in your veins?

Try now, and put on a noble resolution, and show that you have. Make everything yield to a sense of duty. Who knows what good you may do in the world yet. And you may perhaps benefit your brother hereafter more by staying away from him than you could by being with him.

I expect to come and see you about the time our Presbytery meets in Salem in April. I know you will try to be contented and learn. And I don't blame you for loving your brother & home. It is perfectly natural that you should. I am only advising you to that which is best.

So the Lord be with you and bless you, my dear child,

Your Affectionate Father,

H. Chamberlain

You should put *Rev.* to my name, and not *Mr.* They don't know, who is meant.[49]

Henrietta Chamberlain appears, from her father's further correspondence, to have put on the noble resolution. When she had conquered her loneliness, Hiram Chamberlain had further advice:

It will greatly assist you in all your duties to live a life of prayer, and to sanctify every thing with prayer that you attempt to do, or that you are permitted to enjoy. . . .[50]

Attending the classes at Holly Springs for two years, she had devoted herself not only to the standard curriculum but to a study of music, to the writing of verse properly sentimental and religious, and to the hand-painting of flowers on sashes of white velvet.[51] Her New England father had been assiduous in supervising an education and accomplishment suitable to a lady.

In the year 1848 or 1849, with Zachary Taylor and exploits on the Rio Grande fresh in the mind of the nation, Hiram Chamberlain had heard a call, a missionary challenge, from the far border of Texas. When his infant son Peter Bland was nearly a year old and at a suitable age for travel, the clergyman had put his wife, his daughter and his three sons into a coach and set out for Brownsville. It is said that he himself rode a mule to the border, by the side of the conveyance that carried his family.[52] It was a long journey. The Chamberlains had arrived to find no quarters in the booming crowded town; they had rented the moored *Whiteville* on the river and set up housekeeping there until something better might be found. Hiram Chamberlain had come to the frontier "staff and Bible in hand, to preach the Gospel." Now for his labors he had found a vineyard big and boisterous enough. His daughter had of course become a charter member of the First Presbyterian Church of Brownsville. She was a singer in its choir, an embodiment of culture and an active Presbyterian partisan of the Lord.

In confronting Miss Henrietta Maria Morse Chamberlain, Captain Richard King found himself on unfamiliar ground. It was formidable, fascinating and not very comfortable.

The discomfort was with him during all those days when his mind dealt with the beginnings of the new firm, with the business of M. Kenedy & Co. There were times, as he sat putting images of the *Grampus* and the *Comanche* on paper, when another image stood beyond any paper or any diagram Captain Richard King could make. A new ingredient had come to his thought, and if the Reverend Chamberlain plied it with a certain cold abrasive, certain bright brown eyes soothed it with a warming lotion.

Captain King arranged his business so that he was often tied up at Brownsville, especially upon Wednesday evenings. He found the way difficult. As those sermons invariably pointed out, nothing good was ever easy. Meanwhile, the *Colonel Cross* went slogging again in the heat along the brush-bordered twists of a lonesome river.

The town of Brownsville was a busy noise in the summer quiet. It hammered and sawed, strident above the plash of the brown Rio Grande. The new county seat of newly organized Cameron County, Texas,[53] watched a two-story Market House with open arches and a high cupola arise upon its crowded public square. Shop fronts and warehouses sprang up. Freshly painted galleries shaded sidewalks from the heat of the day. Streets lengthened out, knocking thickets flat, raising up new lanes of houses, farther and farther back from the river. A German sea captain, Henry Miller, took over the inn named Cameron House and transformed it to the hospitable Miller's Hotel, a haven for border travelers.[54] Affluent Charles Stillman[55] and his merchant partner Belden built themselves brick residences, the first of those show places giving rise to the town's epithet for the rich and uppity, "the brick house crowd."

A quality of the Spanish tongue, and the venerable and unhurried life that tongue portrayed, softened the crude corners and seams of Brownsville. Painted walls and iron grilles lent a gentle touch of New Orleans to the bordertown streets. The power of the sun and the sea salt of the air worked mellowing at all rawness. Flowering vines grew quickly, gracing the new walls; palmetto fronds made exotic tropical shapes against the sky; leafy shade gave new gardens deeps of cool. A spice of life from many lands, a certain flair of lively-gathered rascals and *bon vivants* and ways civilized and uncivilized, from many nations, brought a tone to the air. Along the streets of Brownsville in the late afternoon came a fragrance compounded strangely of mesquite smoke and orange blossoms and parching coffee.

One evening in July, when constellations of far southern stars stood misty over the dark emptiness toward the Gulf, a warmth of yellow lamplight shone from the open doors and shutters of Miller's Hotel on Elizabeth Street. Inside there was high jollity: friends of Captain Richard King had come from all along the border to celebrate his birthday. He was twenty-six. And his partner Kenedy was just back from Pittsburgh with tidings. The *Grampus* and the *Comanche,* those two big-boilered brain children of M. Kenedy & Co., would soon be arriving ready on the Rio Grande. It was an evening for double celebration. Henry Miller himself was one of the hosts. Viands were tasty and drinks copious. The rough stag gathering was as hearty as the prospect of prosperous tomorrows and noisier than any seemliness aboard the moored steamer *Whiteville.*

A carousing was in full swing when two horsemen dismounted in front of Miller's Hotel. They were a strange pair, sauntering into the light and racket: One was slender and handsome, dressed with a dash of fashion no stain of travel could hide, the other was heavy-set and ugly, rigged like an armed mustanger direct from the Wild Horse Desert. Richard King noticed the entry of the ill-matched strangers. The oddness of the team caught his eye and his curiosity. Feeling a glow, he asked his host Miller to find out what such a pair might be, and to invite them over for a drink.

Miller went to them and asked their pleasure. They sought lodging. The trim young gallant introduced himself.

He was Dr. Charles Berthoud Combe, of Owensboro, Kentucky, stopping over on his way to Mexico City to begin the practice of medicine. His companion — Miller glanced at him with some uneasiness — was a trusted comrade of the road, the long road, the rough road, across the wilderness of Texas.

Miller had his doubts about the companion, but the peremptory self-assurance of the young doctor overbore them. So Miller grinned, and pointed.

Captain Richard King, the husky gentleman over there, wished to invite the two travelers to have a drink.

Captain King, did Miller say? Indeed yes, Doctor Combe would be delighted.

There was no chance for an introduction. King had leveled his gaze on the young stranger as he approached.

"Wait a minute," King said. A wry pull came to the smile in the corners of his mouth. "People who come to Texas these days are preachers or fugitives from justice or sons of bitches. Which one of those fits you?"

The young man's eyes took the challenge.

"Captain King, I am Doctor Combe. Back in Owensboro, Kentucky, sir, I was the treasurer of the Methodist Church. I raised the money to build a new church house. Well—that church was never built—and here I am in Texas! *Now*, Captain King, which category do *you* come under?"

Richard King's jaw thrust out as he grinned, "You'll do for Texas, Doctor! You and your friend—sit down!"[56]

IV M. Kenedy & Co.

THE STEAMBOATS

Grampus and *Comanche* arrived from Pittsburgh in August of 1850 and were put into operation sometime before the twenty-first of that month.[1] They proved themselves, and the soundness of their design, quickly: their performance as "outside boat" and "inside boat" was a success from the start.

When the new craft had been given trial runs, M. Kenedy & Co. chose two of its old steamers to maintain as upriver auxiliaries for the *Comanche's* work and confidently sold or junked the obsolete remainder.[2] Members of the firm set about the business of putting into effect Richard King's plan of operation for the *Grampus-Comanche* team.

Captain King spent most of his time ashore arranging new facilities for the *Grampus* at Brazos Santiago and watching construction of a terminal at White Ranch. While this work went on, Captain Kenedy superintended boat operation and maintenance, and himself skippered the *Grampus*.[3] Captain O'Donnell worked at the firm's office in the Stillman Building on the riverfront at Brownsville, and possibly filled in as temporary master of the *Comanche* or an older boat upriver. Charles Stillman took on the vital task of providing and disbursing the money to set up the new operation.

In his work ashore Captain King drove hard, showing his knack for cutting costs and saving time. At Brazos Santiago, M. Kenedy & Co. put up a sturdy warehouse at dockside, repaired and converted several cheaply acquired government shacks for use, and equipped a lightering system to function in the harbor with no waste motion. At White Ranch, ten miles upriver from the Rio Grande's mouth, the firm erected riverside storage and service structures and built a landing, bringing business and the shouts of roustabouts to a lonely marshland.

When shore installations were ready, Captains King and Kenedy moved to more permanent positions in their plan. King settled down to command of the *Grampus* and management of the Brazos Santiago-White Ranch sector: he became the "outside" man. Kenedy moved to the *Comanche* as her master, supervised her auxiliaries, and took charge in the upriver sector of company business: he worked the "inside."[4] O'Donnell stayed at the Brownsville office, and Stillman, using his multifarious connections, roped customers.

With the four partners in these positions, M. Kenedy & Co. began to make money.[5]

Fair weather and foul, Captain King kept loads moving and the *Grampus* shuttling. His big-beamed boat was a husky tool and he dug hard with it. When timing did not permit the *Grampus* to meet a schooner in the Brazos harbor for cargo handling from deck to deck, M. Kenedy & Co. roustabouts unloaded freight to the company dock and warehouse, awaiting the *Grampus* schedule. But every effort was made to keep that schedule timed, both to the arrival of schooners at Brazos and to the presence of the *Comanche* at White Ranch, so that transshipping could be kept to the minimum, obviating multiple handlings and the wasteful procedure of moving cargo from deck to dock to another deck. In time of high enough water, the operation was simple: the *Grampus* plowed all the way to the quay at Brownsville or the unloading slip for Matamoros, delivering freight directly to the two principal destinations of cargo on the Rio Grande.

The system allowed a reduction in carriage charges that spelled ruin to competition; the whistles of big *Grampus* and little *Comanche* brought pain to the ears of rivals. Steamers of other packet lines, like the converted side-wheeler *Del Norte* of Bodman & Clarke, when loaded were seldom able to negotiate the bar at the river's mouth; their payloads had to be lightered ashore at Boca del Rio or, worse, hauled overland from Brazos to deep water on the river, making high rates mandatory. The *Grampus* could load cargo shipside at Brazos and deliver to the *Comanche* for any point upriver, on a through bill of lading. Other operators found they could not compete. In less than two years, by early 1852, the *Grampus-Comanche* team drove everything else from the river, and M. Kenedy & Co. controlled the carriage of all water-borne goods into the north Mexican trade.[6] It was a most profitable and long-lasting monopoly.

In 1852 O'Donnell withdrew from active participation in company business, but not from its benefits; the firm continued to pay him, then his heirs, a full one-fourth share of dividends for at least three years following. A notation among the Charles Stillman Papers now at Harvard[7] states that in the year 1855 M. Kenedy & Co. paid an equal dividend to Kenedy, King, Stillman and "the Estate of James O'Donnell." It was not until after the death of O'Donnell and the above notation dated April 4, 1855, that O'Donnell's interest was bought back into the surviving partnership.

Only once was the transportation monopoly held by M. Kenedy & Co. threatened. During the fall of 1855, John Young and José San Roman brought the steamers *Swan* and *Guadalupe* to the Rio Grande, hoping to skim some of the profit of the trade from *Grampus* and *Comanche.* This competition proved worrisome enough to cause M. Kenedy & Co. to buy it out. In May, 1857, Kenedy, King and Stillman paid Young and San Roman a total of $20,000 for the *Swan* and *Guadalupe,* half the sum in promissory notes, the other half consisting of title to one undivided one-eighth interest in all properties and business of M. Kenedy & Co. The ownership participation on the part of Young and San Roman was brief, and their one-eighth interest in the firm returned by purchase to the hands of the original partners. A deposition dealing with a legal claim concerning the year 1858 names only "Mifflin Kenedy, Richard King and Charles Stillman, partners under the firm name of M. Kenedy & Co."[8]

Captains King and Kenedy were to be associated in the Rio Grande steamboat business until 1874. When Charles Stillman withdrew from the firm after the Civil War, the company reorganized and took a new name, KING, KENEDY & Co. During twenty-four years of continuous business the two companies built, bought and operated a total of about twenty-six boats. After the two original steamers, first replacements were *Ranchero* in 1855 and *Grampus II* in 1857. In the hard wear and tear and the inevitable mishaps of steamboating during more than two decades, the partners built and operated "outside" boats named *Grampus, Grampus II, Matamoros, Camargo, Tamaulipas, Tamaulipas II,* and *Matamoros II.* These were supplemented at various times by boats, bought but not specially built for the firm: *Mentoria, Swan, Mexico, Alamo* and *Sellers.* The upriver mudskimmers built to order following in the wake of the *Comanche* were *Ranchero, Mustang, James Hale, José San Roman, John Scott, Alice, Jesse B., Leo* and *San Juan.* Other upriver craft purchased by the company, not built to order, were *Guadalupe, El Primero, Enterprise* and *Jerry Galvan.* And there were others, like a *Cora* and a *Colonel Holcomb.*[9] Confusion awaits any attempt to come to an exact total; during certain Civil War expediencies some of the above-named vessels flew the Mexican flag, and in changing registry, some of the boats also changed names. In any event, the company clearly spent a total of more than a half million dollars building and buying the boats it operated.

There are no records extant by which profits of the firm can be determined, but there are entries preserved in the Charles Stillman Papers upon which estimates can be founded to indicate the kind of returns King, Kenedy and Stillman received from their steamboats over the years. For example, there is record that Stillman received $5,734.30 as his share of the dividends on the earnings of all boats between May 1 and October 14, 1857. Assuming that the other five and a half months of that year brought an equal dividend — a reasonable assumption because the spring months were times of large mercantile shipments into Mexico — it will be seen that Stillman probably received about $10,000 in the M. Kenedy & Co. operation for 1857. If this sum represents a one-fourth interest in the firm's profit, M. Kenedy & Co. made about $40,000 during that year. And if the capital of the company was $80,000—calculated from the $10,000 value of the one-eighth interest as shown in the Young and San Roman transaction—it appears that M. Kenedy & Co. paid something like a dividend of more than 50 per cent in the one year of 1857, a dividend which was, if not wildly spectacular, at least a very substantial return![10]

Another entry in the Stillman Papers shows something about the costs and profits involved, during the 1850's, in the operation of a single steamboat. Between April 16 and December 31 of the year 1855, the newly arrived little *Ranchero* brought receipts amounting to $35,699.49, some $30,000 from freights and the remainder from passenger fares. Operational expenses for this period, including wages, wood, stores, et cetera, but excluding allowance for capital outlay or depreciation, were $16,877.67. The profit shown for the twenty-one trips the *Ranchero* made in the eight and a half months was $18,821.82.[11]

Early in the 1850's M. Kenedy & Co. moved its Brownsville headquarters from the Stillman Building to its own newly built brick warehouse and office on the riverfront. Stillman's role in the firm became increasingly that of a silent partner mainly engaged in receiving the returns due from his investment. Captains Kenedy and King ran the business and determined its policy. In mutual co-operation Stillman left Kenedy and King to steamboating and they left Stillman to his other enterprises, which were many. As the firm's business expanded, partners Kenedy and King found it necessary to devote more of their time to management and less to navigation. They hired skippers to run their boats. Kenedy permanently relinquished command of the *Comanche* to attend the business from ashore, and with growing frequency King was absent from a wheelhouse. The May 8, 1852, issue of the *American Flag* gives the name

Brown as the master of the *Grampus*. By that time she was the only steamer meeting the schooners in from the sea at Brazos Santiago.

Kenedy and King both engaged in joint ventures outside the firm's prime business of hauling goods. When a profit was indicated and the opportunity offered, they bought cargoes of wool, hides, bones, tallow or an occasional herd of livestock from the Camargo area to haul and sell downriver. These ventures were usually pursued separately, often with outside partners, and had nothing to do with the firm except that use of company steamers made such ventures advantageous. The profits from such deals were private profits. In making them, both Kenedy and King were careful not to compete with the mercantile arrangements of their partner Stillman, or his cohorts in the Mexican import trade who furnished the patronage of M. Kenedy & Co.

Richard King's business on the Rio Grande was essentially that of a carrier, not a merchant. His interest in goods was their transportation, not their trade. He never became a trader, and he does not appear to have been called to that avocation of traders, the smuggling of goods. It is improbable that he concerned himself with any moral standard of conduct in smuggling or not smuggling. All other considerations aside, for any happy long-term operation of M. Kenedy & Co. he knew the wisdom of legality. Confronted with the possible profits and the certain involvements of running contraband, he knew he could not have the former without the latter and, believing he could do better without either, he left both of them alone. He was a rarity on the Rio Grande, a man his contemporaries did not accuse of smuggling. And he appears to have been one border man who never brought that accusation against anyone else.[12]

The boats of M. Kenedy & Co. became key factors in the economy of the lower Rio Grande and a wide section of northeastern Mexico. They brought visible changes along the river. The terminal

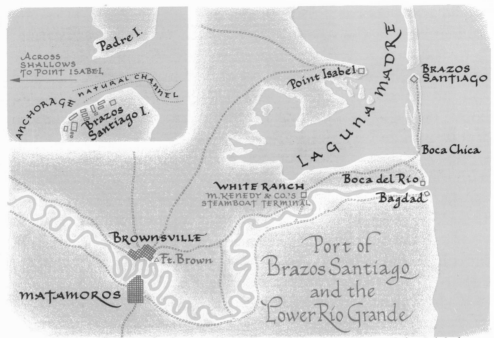

Across
Shallows
To Point Isabel

ANCHORAGE

NATURAL CHANNEL

Padre I.

Brazos
Santiago I.

Point Isabel

BRAZOS
SANTIAGO

LAGUNA MADRE

Boca Chica

WHITE RANCH
M. KENEDY & CO.'S
STEAMBOAT TERMINAL

Boca del Rio

Bagdad

BROWNSVILLE

Ft. Brown

MATAMOROS

Port of
Brazos Santiago
and the
Lower Rio Grande

at White Ranch caused the decay and abandonment of the old shantytown at Boca del Rio. Roma began to grow. Rio Grande City became a lively place, augmented by the founding of a new Army post, Ringgold Barracks, at the edge of town. Assured by the presence of the military to offer some protection against Indian raids and brigandage, and by the regular operation of M. Kenedy & Co. steamers to bring supplies and provide a dependable channel to markets, new settlers took up land to begin farming and stock raising along the Texas bank of the river. An empty frontier began to be a little less empty.

Richard King studied the change. Signing his receipts with a gaunt and roughly formed R. KING, he prospered.

Prosperity neither shut his eyes, nor swelled his head, nor softened his fists. Behind the roughness and the drive there was an equitable mind and a natural courtesy. An ability to inspire confidence, which he had possessed as a homeless boy, grew formidable in the mature man. Command had settled within him. He tempered it to mildness on most occasions; but his eyes, ice-blue around the black sharpness of the pupils, could drill holes into the heart of recalcitrance. The set of his weather-roughened mouth and the spread of his muscled jaw spelled comfort to a friend and trouble for an enemy. There was a power in his presence that overmatched the accounting in his firm's ledger books, however successful. Men along the border began to watch him. They were interested in what Captain King did. They listened to what he said.

It was not his habit to tell them much about what he thought.

His feeling, as well as his thought, during the months and years that saw the rise of M. Kenedy & Co. dwelt often upon another monopoly more difficult to achieve: the hand of Henrietta Chamberlain. In that affair the details of his conduct, his dogged and doubtless circumscribed courtship, do not survive. A hint of them is set forth on a single small sheet of paper, with a crumbled edge singed by fire.[13] Upon it are unsteady letters, written in an aging feminine hand, forming the words: "In time Reverend Hiram Chamberlain grew to admire the young Captain's sterling upright qualities."

If wooing made Richard King mindful of virtues he had not previously considered, and even smoothed his parlor manners, it did not dull his enterprise on the river. The captain held at least one thing in common with the Reverend who did not "sigh and swoon his life away."

From the time of his first arrival on the border, Richard King made friends on both sides of the Rio Grande. The south bank interested him. It may be that some singing attribute of his Irish blood caught the tune of Mexico and Mexicans, to give him understanding. As he became acquainted with the people, from the patient brown-faced peons rousting the heavy loads and feeding the fire-boxes on his boats to the high-blooded gallants riding silver-studded saddles and Barb horses from Randado, he liked them. They evidently liked him. He was impressive even when he amused them — an amusement they politely did not show — by his awkward Spanish. The captain's tongue was one of those that did not shape easily to the demands of another language. He acquired fluency but his accent was barbarous. The effort he made in bringing Spanish from his lips was marked by a sound like a shifting of linguistic gears, for he commenced most of his Spanish salutations with a pidgin preface peculiar to himself: *"Alal, ven pacá—"*[14]

Conducting a business along the living artery of the border, traveling its length, knowing the people who lived in it and meeting most of those who moved through it, Richard King was in a salient position to hear news. He and his partners usually knew what was going on. It was a necessary part of their business operation, commercially profitable. Although a war-surplus cannon stood mounted on the deck of each M. Kenedy & Co. steamboat, a factor of greater importance to preparedness and safe passage along the lonesome and lawless river was the information the firm had constantly at hand. It came from a kind of voluntary intelligence service formed from trusted friends, not only from all kinds of fellow citizens on the north bank of the Rio Grande, but from many Mexicans, town dwellers, rancheros, and deck hands, who knew all the plazas, all the country roads, all the talk, from Bagdad to Mier.

The trade served by M. Kenedy & Co. was highly sensitive to the internal condition of Mexico: the struggling *República* had been exhausted by her war with the United States. Though she mounted no major revolutionary upheaval in the years immediately following the war, she suffered a chronic state of governmental perfidy and a mismanagement that brought her economy to the edge of chaos.

The two large factions of Mexican politics, each composed of various shifting parties and powers, and each guilty of corruption and faithlessness, were the Centralist and the Federalist forces. Centralism roughly represented the reactionary impulses of entrenched military power, privileged landholders, and the Church; it flourished under the dictatorial regimes of Antonio López de Santa Anna. Federalism, colored by a Mexican brand of liberal thought and exemplified in uniquely idealistic form by a governor of Oaxaca named Benito Juárez, roughly represented the impulses of those who stood for the advantages of a local autonomy, something like States Rights as against despotism and spoliation by a central government.

The central government was always in trouble. To make payments on the national debt, and even to meet current budgets, Mexico from about the year 1825 had become increasingly dependent upon foreign loans, especially from England. By 1850 the incurred obligations of Mexico were so great that the president, General Mariano Arista, was forced to mortgage three fourths of his country's total customs duties in order to soothe the wounded feelings of unpaid British bondholders. Even so, the debt was too large to be met by any resource of the leaking Mexican treasury.[15]

Among remedial measures was a stiff increase in Mexican customs duties. This increase was not merely irksome to merchants, it was a threat to the existence of any profitable foreign trade. To counter the threat, importers—including those merchants for whom M. Kenedy & Co. carried cargoes on the Rio Grande—made deals. They plied local authorities with such bribes that collectors in different Mexican customhouses began to compete with each other in the reduction of duties they were supposed to collect, defying the law and the central government.[16]

This was only one manifestation of an insurgency that had become the ordinary state of Mexican affairs. Bandits raided the countrysides and went unpunished. Political generals "pronounced" and led their factions into seamy uprisings against constituted government.

One of these miniature revolutions took place on the lower Rio Grande. Its aims touched at the fortune and future of M. Kenedy & Co., and the partners of that firm, amongst many others, supported the rebellion.

In September of 1851 General José María Jesús Carvajal summoned the Liberal Party he had brought to life in the State of Tamaulipas and, in convention at Hacienda de la Loba, issued a manifesto which came to be widely published as the *Plan de la Loba*. It was a flowery call to arms, for a redress of government wrongs against the citizens of northeastern Mexico.

Not all the *Plan* met the eye. There are grounds for believing that an arrangement existed between General Carvajal and two other generals with large interests in Tamaulipas: the President of Mexico himself, Mariano Arista, and the General-in-Chief of all militia in northern Mexico, Antonio Canales. Whatever the arrangement was, in its main outlines it appears to have been a plot to make northeastern Mexico a separate and independent state called *La República de la Sierra Madre,* to be offered, in the proper course of time, for annexation to the United States.[17] Meanwhile, the three generals were to organize a government friendly to American interests, abolishing all customhouses and establishing within the boundaries of the new state a free trade zone. This mercantile millennium on the border could hardly be unprofitable for Generals Carvajal, Arista and Canales. And it could hardly fail to engage the support of Texans, Yankee expansionists, and all merchants and firms involved in the Rio Grande trade. It was from these interested parties that General Carvajal, as front man for the scheme, expected to receive the necessary aid and abetment for revolution.

Carvajal was peculiarly fitted to inspire confidence in non-Latins. He was himself a Texan, born in San Antonio about 1810. He had not only a bilingual and binational background, he seems to have possessed a personality that appealed to all sorts and conditions of men. He had spent seven years of his youth in Kentucky and Virginia and acquired an education in the English tongue. As a friend and protégé of Stephen F. Austin himself, young Carvajal had surveyed Texas lands; his abilities had brought him the position of official surveyor for the de León Colony, and there he had married the daughter of the colony's founder, Martín de León, that doughty "discoverer" of the port of Brazos Santiago. When Texas fought for independence, the Carvajals and de Leóns were among those Latin families who lined up against Mexico. One of Carvajal's brothers was killed with Fannin at Goliad. Another fought as a lieutenant in Texas cavalry. Carvajal and his brother-in-law Fernando de León saw no combat; captured aboard a coastal schooner at the beginning of hostilities, they did not manage to escape until after the battle of San Jacinto. In their absence, they found that Anglo-Texans had trumped up a charge of disloyalty against the de Leóns, for the purpose of confiscating their extensive holdings. The family, in straitened circumstances, was forced to exile in New Orleans, and Carvajal went with them although his own loyalty was never in question. The despoliation of the de Leóns alienated Carvajal so that he never again considered himself a Texan, though he retained many ties of friendship north of the Rio Grande.[18]

Carvajal had lived as a prominent citizen of Tamaulipas for more than eleven years when he prepared the revolt initiated by his *Plan de la Loba.*

In September, 1851, President Arista withdrew all regular army units from the frontier. At the orders of the co-conspirator Canales, only militia garrisoned the border. Carvajal mobilized his Mexican followers on the Texas side of the river near Rio Grande City, and prepared for an auspicious re-entry into Mexico. By agreement, the opposing militia stationed at Camargo was to surrender after a show of battle, and Carvajal's coup was to move on in triumph after triumph.

To summon up the generosity of his friends north of the Rio Grande, for the purpose of acquiring money, arms and supplies to pursue his campaign, Carvajal privately divulged certain plans and made certain promises. He is said to have been a Mason and to have used the Lodge for the communication of his plans and promises.[19] There was an enthusiastic response. Interested parties in Brownsville and Matamoros, including M. Kenedy & Co., supplied some money and matériel, together with great quantities of good wishes.[20] Then more than a hundred non-Mexican volunteers came into Carvajal's camp, armed, ready, and too loud. To alerted citizens of Tamaulipas, the noble crusade of the *Plan de la Loba* looked exactly like a pro-American filibuster.

In the combat that ensued when the crusade crossed the Rio Grande, the foreign volunteers were Carvajal's right arm—indeed, they proved to be the only arm he had, for his Mexican rebels had a tendency to wither away under fire. The freebooters who fought Carvajal's battles under the command of Texas Ranger Captain John S. "Rip" Ford acquitted themselves splendidly in the field, but their presence ruined the *Plan*. The Mexicans, hating the intruders, resisted too seriously and too much, beginning at Camargo. The bloodshed caused by Carvajal's non-Mexican colleagues angered both President Arista and General Canales. They withdrew their co-operation. Carvajal found himself standing alone with his plans and promises, supported by the merchants of the border trade and a hot handful of fighting Texans.

If perfidy compounded can partake of comedy, Carvajal's position had its comic aspect. Regarded beyond comedy, his revolution shed blood. And it did not spring from any blameless breast of patriotism either for Texas or for Mexico. Carvajal was later to become a General-of-Division and a distinguished public servant of Mexico. During the French Intervention, Benito Juárez would send him to the United States as an emissary entrusted "not only with the honor but with the credit" of his country, a mission he would fulfill with integrity. But in the affair of the *Plan de la Loba,* José María Jesús looks like an operator a little too familiar with two tongues, two countries. He was perhaps the first eminent man who could be called in the border slang of later times a *pocho.*

Fighting lasted from September of 1851 to March of 1852. It consisted of forays, skirmishes, and less than half a dozen battles along the Mexican side of the river from Camargo to Matamoros, with one engagement as far west as Cerralvo, halfway to Monterrey. After each tussle Carvajal crossed his force to the north bank of the Rio, licking wounds, recruiting, receiving aid and encouragement from his friends there.

The high point of Carvajal's revolution was reached in October when Carvajal with Rip Ford's Texans almost took Matamoros. Ford himself was wounded and carried to friendly Brownsville, and his men fought on. The Matamoros commander, General Francisco Ávalos, raised a cry to repel the invaders, and the entire citizenry of the town joined Ávalos' soldiers in arms. The siege lasted eight days. Then General-in-Chief Canales moved in toward the relief of Ávalos, and Carvajal ordered the besiegers to withdraw. In their retreat toward Reynosa twenty-nine mounted Texans under Walker, fighting as rear guards, faced four hundred of the enemy armed with artillery and drove them back. But Matamoros was delivered from its peril. A grateful legislature appended an official adjective to the city's name, which survives to this day and must be written in all legal documents: "The Heroic City of Matamoros."

When Rip Ford was well enough to travel on an M. Kenedy & Co. steamer to rejoin his chief at Reynosa, he asked Carvajal why he had withdrawn from the siege. Carvajal replied that he did not wish to bear arms against his old comrade Canales; General Canales had also sent word of the unseemliness he would feel in having to fight his old friend Carvajal.[21]

There was another factor in Carvajal's lack of success. General Ávalos had already published a sudden decree abolishing *all* tariffs in his Matamoros district. It had caused a stampede of mercantile interests, switching their money and their influence.

While Charles Stillman and most of his merchant cohorts went over to Ávalos to make hay while there was sunshine, a number of men connected with the Rio Grande trade, among them Richard King and Mifflin Kenedy, did not. King and Kenedy not only distrusted Ávalos and the duration of his decree, they demonstrated a conduct which was consistent throughout their lives on the frontier: they were loyal to their friends, right or wrong, up or down. They stayed with José María Jesús. Shortly after the siege of Matamoros, Kenedy went up to Reynosa with an offer to Carvajal recounted by Rip Ford:

General Carvajal stated to the writer the substance of a proposition made to him by Capt. M. Kenedy of the firm of King and Kenedy, [M. Kenedy & Co. at this time] to organize a provisional government, place himself [Carvajal] at the head of it, and become thereby commander-in-chief of the army, but to confer the control of the army in its active operations upon another.[22]

It is obvious that Kenedy was asking Carvajal to make Rip Ford the commander of all troops in the field.

The acceptance of the proposition was to be attended by an advance of supplies of ordnance and other war materials. The General declined.[23]

The steamboating members of the firm of M. Kenedy & Co. continued in their support of Carvajal. They furnished him with free transportation for men and matériel on the river, and they may have been contributors toward some of his supplies. But in gambling on Carvajal, they were backing a loser.[24] Such ultimate reward as partners Kenedy and King got for their part in the Carvajal revolution was a lesson in the equivocal nature of such affairs, and in the lack of dividends earned by a filibuster.

Carvajal's insurrection caused a temporary trade recession along the river. The risks of buying or selling goods and the hazards involved with safe delivery and payment made merchants cautious, and money tightened. Prosperity dwindled on both sides of the river. The business of M. Kenedy & Co. took a drop as the volume of cargoes shrank.

Contracts with the United States Army for the transportation of military stores were cushions for M. Kenedy & Co. in hard times, and during the Carvajal trouble an Army contract helped to keep *Grampus* and *Comanche* operating on schedule without loss. Details of this contract are set forth in a report made by the Assistant Adjutant General of the Army, Brevet Lieutenant Colonel William G. Freeman, who inspected the military installations in Texas under orders dated April 22, 1853:

Fort Brown and Ringgold Barracks are the only posts that receive supplies through the Brazos. The stores are transported by contract—a steamer running from the depot to Fort Brown [*Grampus*] in connection with one from that post to Ringgold Barracks [*Comanche*]. This contract was entered into by Bvt. Maj. Chapman, Assistant Quartermaster, with M. Kenedy & Co., for two years from February 10, 1852. The rates paid . . . seem high to me, but they were doubtless the most advantageous that could be obtained at the time.

. . . The transportation paid, under contract, from Brazos to the post [Fort Brown] is as follows:—corn and oats 15 cents per bushel; hay $2 per bale;

lumber $10 per 1,000 feet; shingles $1.25 per thousand; for all pound freight, 30 cents per 100 lb.; for all measurement freight, 10 cents per cubic foot; soldiers $3 per man; horses and mules $5 per head. For subsistence stores, the rates paid are:— flour, bread, apples, onions and potatoes, 50 cents per barrel; beans, rice, coffee, sugar, salt and bacon, 60 cents per barrel; pork, molasses, kraut, vinegar or any other *wet barrel,* $1 per barrel.[25]

Such a contract was in no way a subsidy, but it was in every way an insurance for a dependable minimum of business. Kenedy and King, both former employees of the Quartermaster Department, culti-vated such insurance as a continual policy during all their years of steamboat operation. King in particular had consistently cordial dealings with officers of the Army, and he handled most of the firm's business with the government.

The disturbance caused by Carvajal brought orders for an alert, and for reinforcements, to the small United States Army force sta-tioned on the Rio Grande. Though its command seems to have been friendly enough to allow Carvajal and his followers unmolested asylum on the Texas side of the river between their sorties into Mex-ico, pressure eventually arrived from a higher level to stop their armed border crossings.[26] On the eighth of March, 1852, the Army politely put Carvajal under arrest for violation of United States neutrality. Arraigned amongst friends, in the United States District Court sitting at Brownsville, he was released on bond. The arrest marked the beginning of the end of his active revolt, but it did not destroy the hopes of his friends for another more successful try. The hopes of Kenedy and King were warmed to a considerable heat when their steamer *Comanche* once in March and again in May was hotly fired upon from the Mexican side of the river.[27]

In the press of these affairs, Mifflin Kenedy found time to win a lady's hand. He had known her perhaps since the days he had lived at Roma, and the background for his wooing had differed vividly from his partner King's efforts at romance in the atmosphere of New England Presbyterianism. The quiet-spoken Quaker had fallen in love to the tinkle of guitars on the far side of the river, and paid court to the dark-eyed daughter of a landholding family at Mier, Petra Vela de Vidal, 26-year-old widow of a colonel in the Mexican army, and the mother of five. "A notably handsome woman, of tall and commanding figure,"[28] she was wed to Mifflin Kenedy on the sixteenth of April in ceremonies performed both by the civil authority and the church,[29] the bridegroom accepting the faith of his Catholic bride. Though no record exists, it is probable that Richard King was his friend's best man at the altar.

As Mifflin Kenedy settled to happy domesticity in a Brownsville house with an attractive bride and a ready-made family of small children, his steamboating partner decided to take a trip.

A ruddy-faced and famous gentleman of fortune named Henry Lawrence Kinney had asked him to come up to Corpus Christi in the month of May, to enjoy an event unprecedented in Texas, a great State Fair. As the intrepid pioneer and swashbuckling founder of Corpus Christi, as the ardent organizer of the Lone Star Fair, as the busiest promoter and most complicated entrepreneur the Gulf Coast had ever seen, Kinney was not only interesting, he was eloquent. Advertisements for his Fair had gone as far as England and Germany. Men of eminence would attend. The exhibitions and entertainments would be stupendous. Corpus Christi and its environs were bursting, Kinney said, with business opportunities for men of vision. And, he added confidentially, a large gathering of able and influential men would take decisive steps to refurbish the revolutionary fortunes of their mutual friend General Carvajal — who would appear as a featured speechmaker at the Fair. It is doubtful if

Richard King knew that Kinney was in Brownsville at the time not only to extend such invitations to his Fair, but to negotiate (unsuccessfully) the sale of a steamboat to the recent Heroic Defender of Matamoros, General Francisco Ávalos.[30] Yet Kinney's gift of many tongues was always engaging. His invitation appealed to Captain King.

One of its appeals was the country he could see in going to the Fair. During five years of running steamboats on the Rio Grande, he had found little opportunity to explore much beyond the margins of the river. He had never been out upon the big prairies; and there is every reason to believe that one of his friends in particular had interested him in seeing for himself the untenanted huge tracts of grassland stretching northward toward the Nueces.

It is possible that Richard King met Gideon K. "Legs" Lewis when that young Texan bravo and war hero was riding dispatches for Taylor's troops during the Mexican War.[31] It is certain that King knew him by 1851, when Lewis as a captain of a company of Texas Rangers was operating in the vicinity of Lake Tampaquas, cleaning out desperadoes that infested the district.[32] The ranger camp was about ten miles from an M. Kenedy & Co. wood yard on the river; when rangers rode in from the brush to meet supplies delivered to them by steamboat, hospitality awaited them aboard, and an exchange of border news. Captains King and Lewis became friends at these riverside meetings. The two men were exactly the same age, and much the same kind. In their conversations there is every likelihood that Lewis mentioned the possibility of setting up a livestock venture to use some of the tall grass going to waste on the deserted prairies north of the river, and there is no question that King had begun to have certain ideas of his own, along that line.

Yet there is no evidence that Richard King had any definite plan beyond his journey to and from the Fair at Corpus Christi, on the morning late in April of 1852 when he put his unaccustomed foot to stirrup and became a steamboater on horseback. He had no way of knowing, when he rode out upon the Wild Horse Desert where the gray mesquite thorns stood newly clothed in vivid green, that the many fates who go weaving at the pattern of a man's life were about to introduce a new design.

V *A Cow Camp on a Creek*

B
Y THE OLD ROAD

north it was 165 miles from Brownsville to Corpus Christi; the trip horseback ordinarily took four or five days. Camps were made near water and, except when recent rains had filled sinks and potholes along the way, watering places were few and far between. Every early traveler through the region mentioned the scarcity of water. When, for instance, Zach Taylor's troopers had toiled south across the dry emptiness in the spring of 1846 and his thirst-gaunted men and horses had plunged at the flowing stream of the Arroyo Colorado, the water they found there rasped their throats with salt.[1] It required a man familiar both with the country and the season to locate the seeps and sweet-water bogs where thirst could be slaked.

In the dry spring of 1852 when Captain King rode north, it is certain that he rode with men who knew the way and the water, and it is certain that he rode in a company large enough to stand against way-laying bands of Indians and brigands in what the Mexicans were calling *El Desierto de los Muertos,* the Desert of the Dead.[2] It seems no less certain that he rode with friends, but there is no record of who they were. One of them making the same journey at about the same time was José María Jesús Carvajal. As an interested partisan, Captain King may have ridden to Corpus Christi in the general's cavalcade.

Winding through palmetto thickets and snaggy chaparral around the edges of boggy *resacas* away from the river, the road led within a mile of the battlefield of Palo Alto, then over lowlands of dry grass and thorned *bosques* for twenty miles to the sandbanks of the brackish Arroyo Colorado. Twelve miles beyond stood a camping place at the crumbled huts of a deserted rancho named *El Sauz.*

The hooves of riders' horses printed tracks north by northwest, mile by mile. A brooding loneliness of the land, like the hazed blue of the flat sky, hung in silence over the world's flat floor. Long gray-green lines of live oak wavered in the shimmer of heat at the prairies' edges where grassless sides of mounded dunes stood pale in the sun, blown bare by winds from the sea. Riders in motion brought life into the unmoving stillness; antelope and deer jumped away bounding through brittle grass; turkey flocks and quail coveys whirred from gray thickets. On the prairie rims the winds lifted pennons of tan dust from herds of mustang horses running wild and free as game, their long manes and tails streaming.

A hundred twenty-four hard miles north of the Rio Grande the road led through grass growing stirrup-high and came to a flowing stream. Thirsty, sunburned horsemen rode into the arching shade of trees there and heard, for the first time in all the miles since the salt-rimed banks of the Arroyo Colorado, murmur of living water.

It was a creek called the Santa Gertrudis, something to remember.

Forty-five miles farther on, across a black loam flatland, lay Corpus Christi and its bay, the domain of the hustler in the wilderness, Henry Lawrence Kinney.

He had come to the uninhabited shore of that bay in 1839 and, in company with an Alabama trader, had set up an odd establishment on land he did not own. When the owner, Captain Enrique Villareal of Mexico, came with three hundred armed men to dispossess him, Kinney not only coolly bluffed Villareal from an attack, he contrived to buy ten square leagues of Villareal's best land, mostly on credit, and to become the only Texan holding legal title to any tract of land south of the Nueces River.[3]

The explanation for his establishment and its success was clear. Under the protection of General Mariano Arista, commander in Tamaulipas and later President of Mexico, Kinney set himself up on the strategically located lonely bay to corner the operation of the Mexican smuggling trade.[4] His partner handled the goods while Kinney handled the warfare, the customers, the politics and the promotion. It was rough business. The blockhouse and stockade built as headquarters by the bluff overlooking Corpus Christi Bay had to be defended from Comanches, Lipans, what was left of Karankawas, Mexican brigands, Texan outlaws and competitors. Trade goods were laboriously lightered in over the bay's unnavigable shallows, loaded on oxcarts or muleback, and hauled out under guard across the Wild Horse Desert on a short cut which by-passed Matamoros and unfriendly customs regulations, directly to Camargo and the interior. Kinney was too astute to try handling all the contraband trade himself. He allowed others to share it—for a price. General Arista's protection was a very desirable advantage: wise smugglers learned that to achieve such advantage they must first make arrangements with the general's enterprising friend.

His friend was selling to all sides. Operating under the auspices of a Mexican commander, he was at the same time upon cooperative terms with authorities of the Republic of Texas. It made what would be called in the Spanish tongue which Kinney spoke so well, a delightful *bola*—and it occasionally made difficulties. A spiteful rascal by the name of Quin, for instance, informed influential Texans that Kinney was not only trafficking with Arista, which he was, but that he was working hand in glove with Mexicans as a traitor to Texas, which he wasn't. The accusation caused Kinney's arrest and detention—until suitable explanations had been made.[5] The still spiteful Quin then proceeded to Arista, to inform the general that Kinney had betrayed the general's confidence, which he hadn't, and was working deceitfully against the interests of Mexico, which he was. Arista withdrew his protection—until suitable explanations had been made.

Kinney was as convincing as he was complicated.

He was also the only Texan who owned and lived upon lands south of the Nueces; as such, he was made a delegate to the Republic of Texas Convention assembled to ratify annexation and to write a state constitution. Kinney's eloquence among lawmakers was as convincing as his rifle among Cronks: the Rio Grande, not the Nueces, was in truth the border of Texas. Henry Lawrence Kinney was living proof of it. The proof penetrated to the ear of President Polk in faraway Washington, and the biggest army since the War of 1812 came smack upon the beach of Corpus Christi Bay, right into the doors of Kinney's trading post! He found himself not merely supplying the quartermaster, he became the quartermaster. In a few months the place called "Kinney's Ranch" was a boom town of two thousand inhabitants, exclusive of troops.[6]

Selling land, selling goods, selling subsistence stores, selling Mexican mules, selling ordnance, acting as a quartermaster, taking the field as a staff officer for the governor of Texas, furnishing trusted spies for Taylor, carrying dispatches through the Mexican lines, fighting gallantly at Monterrey, Colonel Henry Lawrence Kinney served his country without stint, and got rich.

The boom was gone when he came home after the fighting, but he had seen a teeming bright vision there on his beach. He forthwith managed the organization of Nueces County, State of Texas, with its county seat at Corpus Christi, and set about using his money to make the land around his shallow bay—which he planned to dredge—what he called in advertising pamphlets "The Little Naples," "The Italy of America."

When its first census was taken in 1850, Nueces County contained 698 inhabitants, 149 of whom could neither read nor write, and 151 dwelling places—with neither a church nor a school. Kinney kept boosting, writing letters, bringing in visitors. The agents he hired in Europe were empowered to offer each family of prospective emigrants upon their arrival at Corpus Christi "10 cows on shares for 10 years; 100 acres of land for $1.00 an acre; 1 yoke of oxen and 1 horse. All to be paid for at the end of 10 years." By 1852 new settlers, most of them from England, Ireland, Scotland and Germany, had begun to enlarge "The Little Naples." Shallow-draft vessels were entering the bay through a channel Kinney managed to dredge. His town lots were selling for as high as $350 each. There were a Methodist and a Catholic church, and a courthouse under construction. Corpus Christi was incorporated, with a mayor and a city government. Drinking water, in that year of drought, was selling in town for $1.50 a barrel.[7]

Colonel Kinney's hopes were sanguine and his persuasive powers were high, but his money was running low. The Lone Star Fair marked the full tide, and the beginning of the ebb, of fortune for Henry Lawrence Kinney.

There were such rare and merry entertainments on the Fair grounds as circus and theatrical performances, contests in riding and tailing wild bulls and in feats of horsemanship, fireworks, cock-fights, bullfights, and "lectures on philosophy and literature." At a livestock show and an exhibit of the agricultural, mechanical and fine arts, there were prizes distributed in the shape of silver goblets, bowls and pitchers valued at a total of $3,000. It so happened that Kinney himself won three of the prizes. Even his wife was awarded one. An exhibitor by the name of Gail Borden, Jr., also received acclaim, for a specimen of meat biscuit. "The circus tent was nightly filled with 'elegantly dressed American and Mexican ladies, officers of the army, fashionable gentlemen in white kids, frontiermen with their fine shooters in their belts, and the handle of a Bowie knife peeping from their bosoms, friendly Comanche and Lipan Indians, Mexican rancheros, and a fair sprinkling of darkies'."[8]

Visitors presumably found an abundance of liquid refreshment to supplement the expensively barreled drinking water, and there was an abundance of oratory to make throats dry. A large audience heard Dr. Ashbel Smith introduce José María Jesús Carvajal in ringing apostrophe, and then listened to the general's prepared address, a speech of "great force and beauty." When it was done, General Hugh McLeod, "responding to the call" of the audience, arose to make a spirited reply expressing the hope that "the eloquent and forcible address of the distinguished stranger might receive that consideration it so justly merited."[9] Yet the words produced no action. Neither money nor volunteers necessary to warm over the Carvajal crusade were forthcoming. Ranger Rip Ford, present to lend his support to the proceedings, wrote later that his old chieftain Carvajal made a rousing address, but "Fate seemed against him. The revolution was virtually at an end."[10] Ford added that the main reason in Mexico for Carvajal's defeat seemed to be expressed in the words, *"está muy agringado"*—he is very gringo-ized.[11] It was a damning judgment south of the Rio Grande. His friends in the north provided no remedy.

The Lone Star Fair became a disappointment. "Noted personages" did not arrive in anticipated numbers and, what was more serious, neither did cash customers. During the entire Fair not more than two thousand visitors braved the risks of travel to get there. Kinney's land and livestock sales were nothing like his expectation. An ungrateful public criticized the manner in which the silver premiums were awarded to certain exhibitors, and called the bullfights "a humbug." The gala air grew gray. Yet at the final program the unquenched Colonel Kinney read a list of committee members for next year's Fair. It was sheer bravado, not very complicated or convincing either; the colonel was going broke. There was to be no Fair the next year, or any other year in Kinney's life. An annual State Fair of Texas would not arrive for more than three decades, but Henry Lawrence Kinney, along with many dreams, dreamed it first.[12]

One chain of events growing out of the Lone Star Fair became a success beyond the purview of any dream Kinney built in his agile mind.

A steamboater set up a cow camp on a creek.

The exact circumstances that brought "King's Rancho" to birth went unrecorded at the time. A century later, the data available is a set of likelihoods and inferences. Only one thing is certain: Richard King found his friend Legs Lewis at the Fair. In the course of their association before King's return to the Rio Grande, a ranching partnership evolved. Lewis probably proposed the original arrangements.

In the boom atmosphere of a frontier it was almost automatic for a man to consider the rewards of investment in land. The kind of land King chose for an investment was a new departure among the Anglo-Saxon settlers on the Texas border. How he arrived at his choice, how much his friend Lewis had to do with it, is unknown. King turned in an unprecedented direction for his lesson in the kind of land to buy. He looked across the Rio Grande, not the Mississippi. He concerned himself with no standard pioneer vision of future plowed fields or city streets to come. He saw pastures. He put money on land that would raise no crop but the grass that stood right before his eyes. Mexico had developed a way of harvesting that grass. He proposed to import that system, improve it, make it pay. Looking beyond the river, he saw a ranch. "Land and livestock have a way of increasing in value," he would say to Kenedy later. "Cattle and horses, sheep and goats, will reproduce themselves into value. But boats—they have a way of wrecking, decaying, falling apart, decreasing in value and increasing in cost of operation."[13]

He had ridden to Corpus Christi with the seed of such an idea ready to sprout. The waiting prairies provided the seed with a generous soil.

He knew some of the Rio Grande families who by old grants from the Spanish Crown or later grants from the Mexican government owned the immense tracts he rode over.* He knew how little these families thought of their abandoned holdings under a foreign flag, a gringo flag, in a region so scourged by decades of rapine and bloodshed that they called it the Desert of the Dead. No one had tried to buy land in the heart of that desert for seventeen harsh years: he knew how little owners would ask for property they were afraid to

* See Appendix I for a brief history of early Spanish and Mexican land grants and a map of the area.

live upon. And he knew the titles they could offer for sale had been upheld; an act of the Texas Legislature in February had confirmed the ownership of original Spanish and Mexican land grants to rightful heirs and succeeding purchasers.

The titles were unclouded by the law; the vast acreage ought to be about as cheap as land could be, and the grass grew upon it. There was one difficulty. No establishment on that land was feasible without a body of armed fighting men to defend it from Indians, hide peelers, mustangers and assorted roaming cutthroats.

It was Ranger Legs Lewis who provided the answer to the difficulty. He got himself appointed captain of the company of Texas Mounted Volunteers mustered to patrol and protect the region of Corpus Christi, and led the company in a discharge of such duty from September 1, 1852, to March 13, 1853.[14]

During those months, King with Lewis put together a cow camp composed of a primitive shelter and corral, some cattle and horses, and a few herdsmen to tend them at the most promising spot between Brownsville and Corpus Christi. They found that spot on a green and pleasant rise of ground by the strong seep springs that fed into Santa Gertrudis Creek.

The camp began as a side speculation on a very modest scale, a working agreement between a steamboat captain who knew a good deal more about cutwaters than he did about cows, and a ranger captain who had a print shop, along with a real estate and a mercantile deal, at Corpus Christi.[15]

The agreement evidently started with a plan for partnership like this: Lewis as a commander of rangers could reasonably guarantee some protection for a cow camp, and as a man who had handled livestock he could reasonably undertake the building up of a herd; he would be both armed guard and overseer for the work; absentee

King would continue with his business on the Rio Grande and from it furnish funds necessary for the development of the venture.

In operation the plan soon changed. Though Lewis did protect the camp with rangers during the first few months, and though he did prove lively in the enterprise, King proved to be no absentee silent partner. Instead, he was absent more and more from the river, devoting himself to the nascent rancho. Its problems lured him. Its rough life pleased him. He took hold of it shortly after its inception. The cow camp found itself managed by the signature R. KING and the big-shouldered man who wrote it.

"KING'S RANCHO"
THE BEGINNINGS
1854

Nueces River

CORPUS CHRISTI

CORPUS CHRISTI BAY

San from camp to town

Oso Cr.

San Fernando Cr.

45 miles

Petronila Cr.

Tranquitas Cr.

Santa Gertrudis Creek

COWCAMP HQ

Rincón de Santa Gertrudis Grant
3½ square leagues
15500 acres

de la Garza Santa Gertrudis Grant
12 square leagues
53000 acres

Los Olmos Cr.

BAFFIN'S BAY

LAGUNA MADRE

PADRE ISLAND

To Rio Grande City
80 miles

To Brownsville
95 miles

At the time the camp came into being, the partners appear to have been in concurrent negotiations for at least two and probably three separate tracts fronting on the water of the Santa Gertrudis. Legal processes involved in the purchase and transfer of title to Spanish or Mexican land grants required time; the camp was in operation for several months before any purchase was consummated.

The first parcel of land to come under the ownership of Richard King, the tract that became the nucleus around which the future holdings of the King Ranch developed, was an irregularly shaped piece of wilderness measuring three and one half square Spanish leagues and called the *Rincón de Santa Gertrudis* grant. The town of Kingsville now stands within its boundaries.

Situated about forty-five miles southwest from Corpus Christi, in the forks formed by the Santa Gertrudis and the San Fernando Creeks near where they join and flow into an inlet of the Laguna Madre, the Rincón de Santa Gertrudis had been originally granted by the State of Tamaulipas to one Juan Mendiola of Camargo. A glimpse of the sorrowful history of the whole region was contained within the legal jargon of the abstract of title:

. . . that the said tract had been surveyed . . . by Antonio Canales [This was the later Commander-in-Chief of Militia and "old comrade" of Carvajal who was also a surveyor.] the Surveyor General of the State of Tamaulipas, on December 21, 1832; that the said tract was granted to said Juan Mendiola in the year 1834 by the government of the said State of Tamaulipas and that all sums due from the said Mendiola had been duly paid at the time; that the title for said tract . . . was in all respects in good faith and was also perfect, with the exception of the formal placing of said Mendiola in possession of same by the proper authorities, which had been prevented by the disturbances of the time; that the said Mendiola had actually taken possession of said tract at the time of said survey in the year 1832, and had retained possession of same, having thereon a house and pens and cattle and horse stock, until the year 1836, when he died, and the tract was shortly after abandoned because of the incursion of the Texas Revolutionists.

Less than a score of years later nothing but the lonely land itself, with the grass and the water, was left.

Dealing for the property without his partner Lewis, King located the heirs: the widow of Mendiola, his three sons and their wives, and the widow's daughter by a second marriage. None of them remotely considered a return to the forsaken property.

At Rio Grande City, County of Starr, State of Texas, on the twenty-fifth day of July, 1853, "being all the existing heirs to the said tract of Santa Gertrudis, originally granted as aforesaid to Juan Mendiola, deceased," they set their hands and seals to a warranty deed conveying the beginnings of the King Ranch to Richard King for "three hundred dollars, the receipt of which is hereby acknowledged." The sum came as a windfall to the Mendiolas for a holding considered useless. And with that sum Richard King bought title to about 15,500 acres of land at a little less than two cents an acre.

To acquire it was easier than to ranch it, as the Mendiolas had learned.

The deed was not filed at Corpus Christi until November 14, 1853.[16] Meanwhile, King sold Lewis an undivided half-interest in the tract — for $2,000! Such hard dealing with a partner could not have been as hard as it appears. There is every likelihood that Lewis knew exactly how much King paid the Mendiolas; the $2,000 was doubtless involved with side trading in which both the partners were engaged.[17] Nueces County records show that Lewis bought at least two parcels of land nearby, the Manuel Barrera tract of five leagues, the Juan Villareal Rancho of two leagues, and sold King at least one undivided half-interest for $1,000. Both buying from grant owners, they both traded in cash sums to balance their holdings. In two years their undivided partnership interests grew into a complicated set of ramifications. The deed conveying to Lewis an undivided half-interest in the Rincón de Santa Gertrudis was filed at Corpus Christi upon the same day, November 14, as the deed from the Mendiolas.[18]

King's interest in the ownership of land, perhaps even its poignancy for a man who had been a landless runaway apprentice—or perhaps only hurry and efficiency—is demonstrated by the way he used his time a week later in that same November. He was one of the five chain carriers for the surveyor Felix A. Blucher, who came out from the county seat to make an accurate resurvey of the Rincón de Santa Gertrudis.[19]

Early in 1854, King and Lewis negotiated together for the joint purchase of a much larger property. Due west of the Rincón and touching its boundary at one point was a rectangular tract of flat grassland four leagues long and three leagues wide, known as "the Santa Gertrudis grant," "the Big Santa Gertrudis," or "the de la Garza Santa Gertrudis," after the family name of the original grantees. The creek flowed its whole length for more than twelve miles; several other stream beds on it ran water during seasons of rain. It was altogether one of the best pieces of ground for ranching in the region.

The rich and powerful de la Garzas of Camargo had understood its advantages as a site almost half a century before King and Lewis saw it; the Spanish Crown had made a grant of the twelve square leagues to Don José Lorenzo de la Garza, and his two sons José Domingo and José Julián. It had been surveyed to them by the Surveyor General Don Antonio Margil Cano in 1806, and after title had been issued from distant San Luis Potosí, at length on January 25, 1808, the "Spanish government caused the said parties severally to be put in possession of the said tract of land."*

* See Appendix II for a literal translation of the Santa Gertrudis de la Garza land grant.

To put a grantee into formal possession of hitherto ownerless land and forge the first link in a chain of cadastral title, Spanish law, and Mexican law later, required a picturesque ceremony. When a grant had been surveyed and documents of title drawn up, it was necessary for the chief magistrate of the district or his appointed representative to accompany the grantee to the new property. After a formal inspection of it, the magistrate was required to take the grantee by the hand and lead him upon the soil of the new land. The grantee then ceremoniously and ritually, in the presence of witnesses gathered for the purpose, "pulled grass, threw stones, spilled water, and said to the bystanders, 'Gentlemen, be you witnesses that this possession is taken without opposition.' To which they answered, 'How good! How, how good! How good, may it profit you!' "[20]

Juan Mendiola, as mentioned in the abstract of title to the Rincón grant, had been prevented from performing this ceremony of possession, by "the disturbances of the time" — namely, *los diablos tejanos.* But in 1808, when Spanish soldiers were patrolling the area and the Indians were quieted and Texans had not yet arrived, the de la Garzas had been enabled to take possession of their new property with all the formalities, build houses and corrals suitable for an unpretentious frontier hacienda, settle herdsmen for the range work, and stock the pastures.

Yet the development of the Santa Gertrudis did not last long. Troubles began for the de la Garzas, as for every other family trying to maintain isolated ranchos between the Rio Grande and the Nueces, with the advent of Mexico's revolt from Spain in 1811. Spanish soldiery left the frontier to quell uprisings in the south. Local administration of law and order withered. Comanches, Lipans and Karankawas swept in, raiding, laying waste to defenseless outlying settlements.

Don José Lorenzo de la Garza was murdered on the Santa Gertrudis in the year 1814, "whilst shaking hands with barbarous Indians."[21] The butchery intimidated his sons. On June 12, 1814, they relinquished title to the Santa Gertrudis in payment of a debt to Don José Peréz Rey, proprietor of the Laureles grant east of Santa Gertrudis on the shore of the Laguna Madre.

The Peréz Reyes suffered continued violence both at Laureles and Santa Gertrudis. "The disturbances of the time" drove them back to the Rio Grande and caused the complete abandonment of their exposed northern holdings. Looted houses sank to ruin. Horse stock went wild, prey to mustangers and Indian eaters of horseflesh. The increase of untended cattle, feral as deer, were driven from the land by pillaging Texans.

These Texans had begun to strip the country south of the Nueces in 1836 when Texan General Rusk, to feed his troops, detailed mounted men to collect and drive beeves from Mexican ranchos. The meat-bringers were ordered not to raid north of the Nueces: there was plenty of free beef in "the Tamaulipas part of Texas" south of the Nueces line.

In May of 1837 when the Texan government could not find pay for its soldiers and Houston had given them furloughs to go live off the country, those who had been driving cattle from south of the Nueces for the Texan army decided to keep driving cattle from the same place, for themselves.

Roughriding bands of ten to fifteen horsemen would gather 200 to 500 head of the wild cattle and keep them in a punishing run for as long as twenty-four hours, gradually slowing their gait until they could be controlled. Goliad, where Mexicans were hated with passion, is said to have contained the first pens built to hold the stolen cattle and to offer them for sale. Central and western Texas was largely stocked in this way, by Mexican cattle stolen from south of the Nueces. The wholesale theft from deserted ranchos like the Santa Gertrudis went on until about 1840—when there were no more cattle left to steal.

The thieves, "largely young men of the country who served in the army and whose fathers had lost all their personal property in the war," went in gangs referred to as *"Cow Boys."* The generic name for future practitioners of the most celebrated legend on the continent thus was given birth, in the region of the Santa Gertrudis.

Before they became cowboys, Cow Boys were handier with bowie knives and muzzle-loading rifles than with guitars and pearl-button shirts. Cow Boys cut throats, bovine or human, for a living; graduated as brigands or filibusters; made the Wild Horse Desert untenable.[22]

Don José Peréz Rey, owner of the de la Garza grant on the untenable Santa Gertrudis, left one heir, a daughter Eugénia. She in turn left one heir, a son by the name of Praxides Uribe,[23] who lived in Matamoros. He claimed a "full and complete title to twelve leagues of land situated in the County of Nueces and State of Texas, and known as the Santa Gertrudis grant," but he did not possess the perfected documents to prove it.

King and Lewis went to see him. To facilitate ensuing negotiations, Uribe appointed one Manuel Ramírez Elisondo, who lived among Americans in Brownsville, as an agent with power of attorney in an instrument dated May 13, 1854, at Brownsville. This contract between Uribe and Elisondo conveyed the original de la Garza Santa Gertrudis grant to Elisondo for a consideration of $1,800—which Elisondo was to pay when Uribe delivered to his hand documents of full and complete title to the big tract.

Upon the same day, Elisondo in turn made a contract with King and Lewis. By this second contract Elisondo reconveyed title in an agreement which stated:

In consideration of said title, said King & Lewis are to pay to me when said title is perfected, the sum of $1,800.00 being the amount agreed upon for said twelve leagues of land, or the sum of $150.00 per league. And it is further agreed that until such time as I may be enabled to deliver unto said King & Lewis a full and complete title to said lands, this document shall be considered as a complete deed to them from me for said lands, authorizing them, or any person or persons, under them to take possession of said lands and hold the same, or sell the same, as they may think best for their own benefit, hereby annulling all powers of attorney or documents of any kind that I may have heretofore given. And it is further agreed that King & Lewis deliver to me their notes payable in the City of Brownsville for the sum of $1,800.00 redeemable on the delivery by me of a perfect title to them for the aforesaid lands.

King and Lewis were being careful of any possible title hazards. Nine small blocks of unpossessed land, seemingly issued as scrip in payment for services to soldiers of the Texas Republic, were indicated on the State of Texas plat of the de la Garza Santa Gertrudis area. The partners wanted to be sure their title from Uribe was full and complete, stemming from an original Spanish grantee, in order that it could be upheld by law under the Act of Confirmation passed by the Texas Legislature two years before. The final purchase of the Big Santa Gertrudis was made subject to the delivery of a clear title, and no money changed hands at the time. But the Uribe-Elisondo contracts granted to the two cow camp proprietors the immediate rightful occupancy and use of about 53,000 more acres of grass. They rode with their documents from Brownsville to Corpus Christi, and filed them for public record in Nueces County a week later, on May 20, 1854.[24]

Their holdings grew and their stakes became greater as they enlarged the rough headquarters for their enterprise, bought more livestock, hired more men from the Rio Grande.

Their fortified camp on the Santa Gertrudis was the beginning of the permanent conquest of the violent land between the Nueces and the Rio Grande. Every predecessor in that struggle had lost. The two captains intended to win. Rip Ford wrote later:

In 1852 Capt. Richard King, in company with Capt. G. K. Lewis, better known as "Legs Lewis", established a cattle ranch on the Santa Gertrudis creek. They made their headquarters near where Capt. Ford's old camp stood in 1849. This cattle-camp became a stopping-place of wayfarers, a sort of city of refuge for all classes, the timorous and the hungry. The men who held it were of no ordinary mould. They had gone to stay. It was no easy matter to scare them.[25]

The stopping place of wayfarers was something more. It was in a literal sense the rough cradle of a vast enterprise reaching out into a future neither King nor Lewis could foresee: the livestock ranching industry of the United States. It was born on the Santa Gertrudis.

VI First Shapes for A Ranching Pattern

M

ORE THAN

three hundred years before Richard King and Legs Lewis put a cow camp together, the shipwrecked *conquistador* Álvar Núñez Cabeza de Vaca, of Jérez de la Frontera, Spain, wandered naked and hungry in the region of the Santa Gertrudis. He recorded an opinion of the wilderness he found: *All over the land are vast and handsome pastures, with good grass for cattle; and it strikes me the soil would be very fertile were the country inhabited and improved by reasonable people.*[1]

It was natural for Cabeza de Vaca to think of pastures. His people had a tradition as herdsmen; they carried livestock with them wherever the arms of Castile and León were planted. Before Hernando Cortés had actually secured the City of Mexico, Spaniards sailing to Vera Cruz in 1521 brought to the shores of North America the first cattle.[2] This landing of domestic kine was an act partaking of destiny for the western half of the New World, an event of huge economic portent for the waiting land of unexplored plain and plateau and mountain slope where natural rainfall would never bring crops but always brought grass.

The hardy and tough-sinewed Spanish cattle, tinged with the savage blood of the fighting bulls of the *plazas,* seemed exactly fitted to thrive in the new continent's wilderness. Running wild, they increased enormously. And the transplanted stockmen who had learned their husbandry upon the pastures of Spain were not long in adjusting their methods to the spacious and splendid grasslands of Mexico's sunny upland interior.

Great livestock haciendas sprang into being. Years before the founding of any English colony upon the American coast, a single owner "in the Mexican province of Jalisco was branding 30,000 calves a year, and in Durango and southern Chihuahua were individual herds numbering tens of thousands."[3]

The haciendas to which such herds belonged assumed a common pattern. The headquarters, or *casco,* was ordinarily located at the most pleasant and plentiful source of water on the widespread property. The most imposing building at the *casco* was the *casa grande,* the big house of the owner, built like a fortress around a square, green-gardened patio. Clustered about the big house were the huts of the herdsmen and retainers; corrals, sheds and stables for livestock; storerooms, granaries, workshops, a forge; and always a church or chapel with a high cross and a bell. A thick and tall adobe wall, fitted with an iron-studded main gate and loop-holed towers at vantage points, enclosed the entire *casco*, making it a walled village for defense against the raids of Indians or brigands. A watering pool was usually within the enclosure; outside were irrigated fields. Laborers whose work kept them at a distance from the central *casco* lived upon outlying rancherías built at springs or water wells. Where stone was available, great pastures were fenced by leagues of rough rock walling, laid up without mortar. Under a never-ending threat of pillaging Indians, and of losses caused by wild beasts of prey, the hacienda's herds and flocks—sheep, goats, horses and mules as well as cattle—were penned and guarded by night, and pastured only by day.

The hacienda's work developed a picturesque and unprecedented type of New World herdsman: the vaquero. It was this vaquero of Mexico who invented a technique for the horseback handling of half-wild cattle on an open range. He became adept at tossing a coiled rawhide rope he made with a sliding noose. He sat a saddle with a pommel he designed and built as a sturdy snubbing post for his rope, to hold what he caught. He rode a strong-legged and tender-mouthed pony he trained for the work of herding and roping. He used the branding iron derived from Spain to burn the mark of ownership into an animal's living hide. The tools and techniques created by this horseback vaquero set into operation a practical method, for the "reasonable people" Cabeza de Vaca mentioned, of harvesting the New World's grass.[4]

In the year 1853 when Richard King paid $300 for a first parcel of land, his own race of Anglo-Saxon pioneers had done little, beyond a limited imitation of Mexican ranching, to devise a method of livestock husbandry suited to the nature of the frontier upon which they had recently arrived. To be sure, Texans north of the Nueces had used a branding iron as early as 1832;[5] they had gathered and driven range cattle to markets; but the colonists who had come to Austin's Texas from the east and north were by heritage tillers of arable lands, woodsmen, dwellers amidst trees. They had no experience in, or tradition for, the handling of great herds upon great prairies, and it took them a while to learn what to do with what stood before them.[6] The 1850 census of Nueces County clearly shows that the settlers there were still farmers: they had not yet learned to *ranch.* The total value of all livestock in that county was set at only $63,000; the very list of animals bespeaks the property of plowmen: 616 horses, 61 mules, 2541 milk cows, 462 oxen, 7072 cattle, 5600 sheep, 15 hogs.[7]

No one agent brought the burgeoning of a livestock economy in Texas. No single man caused the growth of an occupation so successful that a branding iron became the very hallmark of Texas. It was the natural and inevitable product of many hands and minds. In the workings of history, the Spanish cattle engendered the Texas Longhorn. The Mexican vaqueros became the prototypes who furnished the ready-made tools, the range techniques, even the lingo, from which sprang the cowboy of song and story. The Mexican haciendas provided the primal outlines for the pattern which produced the later Cattle Kingdom of the American West. Pre-eminent as a medium through which these things came to pass, was Richard King.

For his cattle he turned naturally to the south, to the ranchos where the cattle were; and for his herdsmen he hired vaqueros, not only for a skill, but for a wisdom possessed from long living with the traits of the land and the livestock. Then to this basic Latin material for ranching, he added an Anglo-Saxon dynamic, a new thought. Ranching was not a subsistence, it was a business. It was a financial enterprise, susceptible to an organized efficiency. It could be engaged in not merely for a way of life, but for a systematic yield of profit. Ranching and steamboating were the same: only the materials differed. To improve a method of harvesting grass was as strong a challenge to Richard King as the design of a better steamboat for the risky Rio Grande.

It is more than probable that his first plans for a ranching business actually grew from the fact that he was in the shipping business. He saw a connection. The only widely marketed and steadily profitable products from cattle raising in Mexico were hides and tallow. The meat went largely unused; there were no channels for the profitable movement of beeves from remote pastures to centers of population. Such beef as Mexican stockmen sold was usually limited to the occasional driving of small herds of culls to the nearest towns, for haphazard sales to butchers. In the economy of Mexico, where so much beef grew, the sale of meat was a local and small-scale affair. Richard King, aware of what prairies of grass produced when inhabited and improved by reasonable people, anticipated a day when meat to feed multitudes would not go wasted. As a man who could remember the hunger on crowded streets of New York, and as a man who had spent years in the transportation of desirable goods, it was not difficult for him to understand the reward awaiting a man who could raise herds of cattle where the great grass was, and ship meat in volume to cities where the great market was.

The herds came first. Markets might come later. Meanwhile there was an investment to make and a trail to blaze.

The years during which the rancho first took shape, 1853 and 1854, were years of extreme drought over the whole region. The Rio Grande's flow was so diminished that steamboat passage above Brownsville became difficult, and above Reynosa, impossible. There is no question that the low stage of the river, its troublesome uncertainties as a navigable stream and the temporary immobilization of upriver traffic, had much to do with the turning of Richard King's attention to land and livestock. With boat operation at a minimum he had time to devote to the Santa Gertrudis, and a mind to devote to the desirability of a sound business hedge against the threat of a dry river.

Of course the problem of water was as crucial to a rancher as it was to a riverman. One of the first acts of Rancher King after he had title to a parcel of land was to augment its available water for livestock by raising a rough dirt dam across the bed of Tranquitas Creek. When the stream ran with rain, its flow was impounded; the lake thus formed made the only place between the Nueces and the Arroyo Colorado where a thousand head of horses or cattle could be watered at one time. The building of tanks by dirt dams across dry creek beds was a common practice on Mexican haciendas where peon labor was plentiful and cheap, but King's tank on the Tranquitas was the first such "engineering" improvement between Brownsville and Corpus Christi.[8] It represented an investment of capital and it hinted early at the enterprise a steamboater could demonstrate in creating the pattern for a ranch. He entered into his creation as a long-term venture without prospect of immediate profit-taking of any kind, and it was characteristic of King's systematic mode of thought that he made his place ready for livestock, plenty of livestock, before he did much about stocking.

On the creek banks by the quiet flow of the Santa Gertrudis there were only the faint marks of a few old camps and the scattered ashes of travelers' fires to tell of men who had passed there earlier, only the faint paths of savages whose pictures decorated old Spanish maps of the area. Nothing was left of the ruined de la Garza or Mendiola establishments of the previous decades, though there is a statement that a few shallow wells on the property were still usable when partners King and Lewis came.[9] They started from scratch in a wilderness.

After the Corpus Christi company of Texas Rangers was disbanded in March of 1853, it became necessary for King and Lewis to maintain their own defense: the only protection the rancho could depend upon was the protection it provided for itself. At a time and in a place where marauders would kill for a hatband, the growing works on the Santa Gertrudis made a tempting prize. "The country was infested by companies of Mexicans, who frequently united the business of corraling mustangs and murdering and robbing travelers. The Comanches made descents into this district, ostensibly to capture horses to ride and eat, but really to kill the men and to make prisoners of women and children, to make mistresses and slaves." By no means all the depredations attributed to Indians were committed by Indians. Brigands from south of the Rio Grande and renegades from north of the Nueces rigged themselves in Indian trappings and went looting and murdering, careful to leave moccasin tracks. In 1854 an outlaw band disguised as Indians assaulted Roma and Rio Grande City, looting the churches and even attacking United States troops. Only two of the masqueraders were caught. They were hanged on the Roma road, with their white skins exposed.[10]

To protect the solitary establishment on the Santa Gertrudis, King and Lewis hired their friend Captain James Richardson, an intrepid gunman and veteran of the Mexican War, to guard and command the camp in case of attack and to act as foreman of the works during the absences of Lewis in Corpus Christi and King in Brownsville. When occasion required, Richardson had an associate, another captain who was also a veteran of the war, William Gregory. "Richardson was at his post at all times. He was Capt. King's head man, in whom he placed implicit trust. He was brave and careful . . . a skilful opponent of Indians. . . . Capt. Gregory was equally as brave,

. . . and was always at the call of the owner of the Santa Gertrudis ranch when danger menaced."[11]

Raiders could seldom move without being observed and promptly reported. Informants were constantly on the alert, and warnings traveled with speed. The same sort of intelligence system which aided the safe passage of M. Kenedy & Co. boats on the river, now operating along the frontier by information from friends, made a surprise attack upon the Santa Gertrudis almost impossible to achieve.

A rough stockade and blockhouse were probably the first real construction works on the camp site by the seep spring. War surplus cannon from the steamboats were freighted in and mounted on the compound, more for the value of their noise in Indian fights than for any effectiveness they possessed as weapons.

The organization of the herdsmen and workers under the watchful eye of a man like Richardson, the operation of an alert ranchero intelligence system, and the presence of a fortified blockhouse solved the problem of protection for the growing establishment. There are no specific details now on record of Indian and bandit raids at the King and Lewis rancho. There were snipings, skirmishes, livestock thefts, occasional attempts to probe the strength of the rancho's defense, but it is probable that raids of real force were never made. While there is no indication that Captain King ever hired a man for the sole purpose of carrying a gun, clearly he chose men for ranch work who could, and would, fight. As a result, there was a minimum of fighting to do. With easier pickings available, Indians and brigands had no stomach for the rigors of an assault on the Santa Gertrudis.

Some of the best help on the ranch came up from the river with Captain King. One of the earliest of these was "a Mexican that worked a great deal with him on the steamboat," Vicente Patiño.[12] Another boat hand who became formidable on horseback was Faustino Villa, a man of prodigious strength and great heart who was to live a long life of remembered exploits and warm loyalty in the service of King and his ranch. The captain made men of this strong stamp a foundation stock from which grew the straw bosses for the labor that built the ranch, and the foremen for the vaqueros who handled the herds. King referred to these men as "my friends." They were.

A grandson of men like these, who became one of their kind, a King Ranch vaquero named Victór Rodríguez Alvarado, remembered in his old age what his folks had told him about the dim beginnings on the Santa Gertrudis: "In order to build his first houses, King went to Bobedo Ranch [the Rincón de la Bóveda grant, some dozen miles south of the Rincón de Santa Gertrudis] and got my grandfather, Francisco Alvarado, to build houses or *jacales,* . . . My [other] grandfather, my father, and their families also came to build in 1854. They made the first houses of wood and dirt with thatched roofs. They also made corrals of the plentiful wood. The water they used from the dug water tank, because there wasn't any arroyo. These water holes were bedded with sacahuiste. . . . There were two brothers, Pedro and Anselmo Flores, natives of the city of Guerrero, Tamaulipas, Mexico. From them Mr. King bought his first cows and a *canelo* [cinnamon roan] bull, and he also bought on that ranch a remuda of horses from a man that also lived there, Victoriano Chapa, called *El Comanche.* Some men knowing that Mr. King was making his ranch and buying herds, would come and sell him many mustangs, of which there were many in those days. King bought 25 or 30 mares and a stallion. The first cowboy that took care of these mares, Damón Ortíz, was my grandmother's brother, and in order that these mares wouldn't get away from him, he punished them by putting hobbles and sticks on their front feet. . . . Cowboys earned twenty-five pesos a month and food in abundance.

King employed as head of cowboys, Señor Santiago Richardson."[13]

The steamboat captain who considered ranching a business enterprise was not long in setting up a businesslike accounting of it. His first *Ranch Account Book,* preserved at Santa Gertrudis, carries entries during the two years of 1854 and 1855. The bookkeeping was done in Brownsville, probably at the office of M. Kenedy & Co., where records could be conveniently made and safely kept; he did not forget to write things down.*

Immediate and minute details of daily living still glint from the pages of the account book; the terse entries stand in ledger lines like flickers of light seen through apertures too narrow to reveal and too wide to hide exactly what happened behind the wall of the past:

powder and hard bread	$ 1.25
Capt. G. K. Lewis one pair boots	5.50
one large wagon taken in pawn	60.00
cash paid Bill Houston on the road 8th inst.	10.00
cash paid Fradin repairing guns pistols etc	25.00
advanced to men at Mungillas (they run off)	18.00
making cattle brand	2.00

Beyond such vignettes, the account book provides some solid fact concerning the early operations on the King and Lewis Rancho. It clearly shows that King, not Lewis, paid all the bills.

Payroll entries indicate about two dozen names like Francisco Alvarado, Juan Villareal, Damón Ortíz, Ylario Chapa, Frylan and Lucián Cabazos, Chili Ebano, Juan Cantú; and, in addition to James Richardson and William Gregory, there are a dozen employees with names like William Houston, Tom Craig, Luke Hart, some of whom seem to have been busy catching mustangs and handling horses, while others were journeymen, or simply laborers, working on improvements around headquarters or the dam of the Tran-

* Facsimile pages from the original King Ranch Account Book are reproduced in Appendix III.

quitas. Accounts refer often to items "at lower house" — evidently the first rough bachelor dormitory on the Santa Gertrudis, and one of the first ranch bunkhouses anywhere.

Drought conditions during 1854 and 1855 worked to the advantage of King and Lewis in the prices they paid for their first herds. It was a good time to buy. The earliest entry on the purchase of cattle is dated January 12, 1854, "for 42 cows taken in by Juan Cantú, $208.00, with 20% duties, charges and expense on same, $54.60," indicating that cows were selling at about five dollars a head somewhere near the border in Mexico, and that they cost about six and a quarter dollars a head delivered at Santa Gertrudis. There is an entry on March 29, 1854, "cash paid Flores" — this is doubtless either the Pedro or the Anselmo Flores, or both, remembered by old Victór Alvarado — "for 419 cows at $7.00, $2,933.00." In the fall of that year there are recorded: "Nov. 28, Record of stock bought from Ramírez amounting to $799.00" and "Oct. 31, paid G. K. Lewis draft for $1200.00 — 200 cows 26th inst., $1,200.00," a six-dollar price indicating that the cost of a Mexican range cow did not vary much during 1854.

Horses were bought in smaller bunches than cattle, but made larger cumulative investments. Mustangs were cheap: "March 9, 1854, 18 mares at $6.00, $108.00;" "Captain R. King for 10 mares, 2 horses and colt paid for by him Nov. 9, 1854, $68.00;" something a little better, "Feb. 3, 1855, one blk. pacing pony, $15.00;" and something a little worse, "Jan. 8, 1855, horse, $3.50," "Feb. 18, 1855, for mustang horse, $5.00." From the very beginning, entries in the account book indicate that King was buying not only cheap and plentiful mustang stock, but stud horses of real quality for up-breeding purposes and for use under saddle and harness. He liked good horses, and he himself used that kind. On August 3, 1854, the ranch paid $200.00 "for an American gray stallion," and on the same day $300.00 for "a bay American stallion of William Wright." Late in 1854 "Ranch Santa Gertrudis" bought "5 American horses for $735.00," "one American mare $135.00," "one American horse 'Joe' to R. King $100.00." On November 28, 1854, Richard King paid for a single stallion exactly twice as much as he had paid for the whole Rincón de Santa Gertrudis grant: "one sorrel stud called 'Whirlpool' at Lott's, $600.00."

The account book proves that King and Lewis by no means limited their livestock to cattle and horses. They were trying everything: "paid E. D. Smith on 376 sheep 'Ballí' $282.00;" "cash paid to J. H. Durst for 10 merino bucks $100.00;" "paid Seeligson for one Jack $50.00, mare $10.00, mule $15.00;" "for sheep and goats bought through Lewis Mallett, $145.00, charges and expense on same, $13.00;" "H. A. Caldwell for 130 goats $97.50;" and "for 2 breeding sows at mouth of the river $10.00."

First sales of livestock, comprising two of the very few income entries during 1854 and 1855, are shown as "June 19, 1854, stock sold—mules and horses, $223.00," and a week later, evidently cleaning out some mustangs, "June 26, 1854, $1000.00 worth of mares to White & Gardner."

Building the herd, buying not selling, King and Lewis held their cattle. An entry dated February 27, 1854, shows that beef was scarce on the Santa Gertrudis, and that the herd was not being touched: "ranch account paid for beeves of Blas Falcón $22.00."

The account book reveals that in 1854 Richard King paid out the surprising total of $12,275.79, a sum considerable enough to indicate that the riverman had scraped from the river all the cash he had, and probably some he borrowed, to risk on the future of his rancho. Many entries relating to operation and building expense are not included in the accounts of 1855, but it is clear that the outlay was smaller than in the previous year.

The stocking of the Santa Gertrudis brought a minor cattle boom at a welcome time to the cowtowns of Camargo and Mier.[14] Rancheros drove herds in from thirsty ranges. *Con dinero y sin miedo,* Captain King bought and sent the bony stock across the trickle of the Rio Grande, up the dry trails, to waiting pastures in the north.

In that cattle buying, sometime during the early months of 1854, he became a *Señor Capitán* in the tradition of a former age, and the usage of another race. He led an *entrada*. When a certain hamlet, its name now lost without a trace, in the dusty hills of Tamaulipas had offered its drought-starved herds for sale and King had bought them, it was evident that the village had little left to sustain it. The captain made a proposition: he offered to settle the entire community on the Santa Gertrudis where they could build homes, have jobs and get regular wages paid in cash. Whetted by the promise of that rarity, regular wages paid in cash, and with nothing to lose but the sentiment attached to the famished home place, the village decided to move. The resulting *entrada* was composed of more than a hundred men, women and children with all they could pile upon, and all that could be driven at the side of, their rickety high-wheeled *carretas* and pack-saddled burros.

This straggled procession heading north in the glare of the Mexican sun presented sounds and lineaments long familiar in the founding of all New Spain: the choking dust, the cries of the herdsmen urging their beasts, the strident screech of dry-hubbed cart wheels, the wailing of babies, the squawking of cooped poultry, the stately sway of yoked oxen, the dainty-footed jounce of donkeys cruelly laden, the sore-footed jog of yellow-eyed dogs in the moving shade of the cart beds.

A *Señor Capitán* by the name of King, responsible for an *entrada* across a Wild Horse Desert, felt his distance from a jeweler's apprenticeship on Manhattan—even his distance from the clang of an engine bell in a wheelhouse. The *capitán* was becoming *ranchero*.

His transplanted hamlet from Tamaulipas took root, nourished by the waters of the Santa Gertrudis; it furnished some of the seed for a tough, proud, special breed of vaqueros called *Los Kineños*, the King People.[15]

A strong establishment like the King and Lewis rancho on the unprotected reaches between the Nueces and the Rio Grande was like a signal for the resettlement of the empty land. Only a few scattered and ruined ranchos, kept alive by brush-and-mud camps of herders and squatters risking their lives for a living off the land, were inhabited in 1853. Soon thereafter some of the sturdier families of original grantees began to return for a new try at their deserted holdings. King and Lewis actively encouraged the arrival of neighbors; King once said that he "could not have kept on and held on if Andrés Canales had not been adjoining."[16] It has already been noted that Santa Gertrudis bought beef from Blas Falcón, a descendant of the founder of the Rancho Real de Santa Petronila, who still held some of those lands. Families like the Canales and the Falcón came back. Others sold their inherited grants to an increasing number of Texans who were beginning to see the possibilities of pastures.

As early as December 28, 1852, Major James H. Durst, Collector of Customs for the District of Brazos Santiago and a friend of Richard King, bought four fifths of the La Barreta grant forty miles south of Santa Gertrudis.[17]

In 1852 Mifflin Kenedy had taken a try at ranching at Valerio on the Nueces River. Two years later he bought a tract of ranchland on the San Salvador del Tule grant sixty-some miles northwest of Brownsville. He did not become a rancher there but kept supplies on hand for the men he employed.[18]

The other partner of M. Kenedy & Co., Charles Stillman, who had owned deserted land in the Laureles grant since 1844, made arrangements to stock it, and bought another tract for absentee ranching north of Brownsville.

Two lawyers, F. J. Parker of Brownsville and W. G. Hale of Galveston, joined in a partnership to buy the Santa Rosa grant about twenty miles south of the Santa Gertrudis, and hired a manager to live at the rancho and work it.[19]

Richard King's early friend, Major W. W. Chapman, the Assistant Quartermaster, who had changed station to the new Corpus Christi Army depot in 1852, invested some of his money in a small livestock venture on the Santa Gertrudis operated by a James Bryden who worked for shares. And close by, under the auspices of Richard King, Captains Richardson and Gregory, the guards of Santa Gertrudis, ran another small outfit referred to as Rancho Viejo.[20]

There were others. Though the country was still largely empty during the middle 1850's, the establishment on the Santa Gertrudis was not alone.

The ranges of course were open. There were no fences yet. A brand signified an animal's ownership; a livestock operation was the building of a branded herd, and the holding of it, by horseback vaqueros, on the grass by the water.

The hundred and twenty miles of lonely road from Santa Gertrudis to Brownsville became as familiar to Captain King as a stretch on the river. It was necessary to travel that road often on journeys between the river where the money came from and the ranch where the money went. The business of M. Kenedy & Co., after the slump during the Carvajal disturbance, slowly improved and, in spite of the difficulties of navigation caused by drought, earned profit. A principal source of this profit was the contracting for transportation of Army stores and equipment: the firm had made its services almost indispensable to military supply on the Rio Grande. When boats could not navigate, M. Kenedy & Co. undertook the delivery of contracted freight by wagon trains. This demanded the kind of management Captain King in particular had learned how to furnish; his firm's dependability and his own cordiality made strong friends among the military. Santa Gertrudis would one day soon be supplying mules and beeves on Army contract.

Business was by no means the sole reason for journeys to Brownsville. The prominent—the persistent—thirty-year-old riverman and landowning ranchero was making a splendid progress at the Presbyterian parsonage. Somehow the Reverend Hiram Chamberlain was at last persuaded, as his daughter had been long before, of "this young captain's sterling upright qualities."[21] Henrietta Chamberlain and Richard King were to be married.

It had been four years since the pretty young lady standing on the deck of the *Whiteville* angrily squelched the rough master of the *Colonel Cross.* In the busy enterprise and considerable success those four years had brought to Richard King, his desire to win that young lady's hand appears to have been without deviation. The burly and untutored man from the boat decks labored mightily to make his conduct and his prospects acceptable to Miss Chamberlain and to her father. In so doing, there were surely times when big-fisted Captain King found it impossible to keep from blowing steam—at a reasonable distance from the parsonage. But the sterling qualities proved sterling enough. They repaired all falls from grace.

It is regrettable that no single detail of the long courtship survives, no word of the captain's manner of proposal or of its acceptance, no anecdote of calls at the parsonage, of the holding of a hymn book at divine service, of meetings on the way to or from Henrietta Chamberlain's Presbyterian teaching duties at the newly founded Rio Grande Female Institute,[22] of a stroll upon a balmy evening under the trees of Elizabeth Street shyly to consider a site for a cottage next door to the home the happy Kenedys had built.[23]

On December 9, 1854, the Deputy County Clerk of Cameron County, Budd H. Fry, issued a license "to join in the bond of matrimony Miss Henrietta Chamberlain and Captain Richard King."[24]

At the evening service of the First Presbyterian Church of Brownsville on Sunday the tenth of December, Miss Henrietta M. Chamberlain sat at her accustomed place in the choir. Captain Richard King sat in a less accustomed pew. His suit and boots were probably new, and it is safe to say he was nervous, glancing up at Miss Chamberlain, whose hand could have betrayed a tremor in holding the music as she sang. The gown she wore was most certainly new, especially made and extraordinarily becoming, of a peach-colored ruffled silk, with a front of white silk mull "shirred and trimmed with beading, and white baby ribbons under sleeves of white lace."[25] The hymns, the prayers, the sermon seemed long, eternally long, that Sunday evening.

When the service came to its end at last, the congregation remained seated and another ceremony began. Henrietta Chamberlain arose from her seat and came from the choir. Richard King stepped forward. Standing before the pulpit, Hiram Chamberlain solemnly united his daughter and the captain in bonds of Holy Matrimony. Such festivities as there may have been among wedding guests following the ceremony are unrecorded, but the solemnity surely slackened in the gathering of friends. Next day the Reverend Chamberlain promptly went to the courthouse where he wrote:

This certifies that the parties named in the preceding license were duly married by the undersigned, an ordained Minister of the Gospel, in the 1st Presbyterian Church of this city, on the evening of the 10th of December, 1854.
H. Chamberlain.

For a wedding journey and a honeymoon, Captain King took his bride to the Santa Gertrudis. There is an entry in the *Ranch Account Book* dated November 28, 1854, "one large closed carriage and harness now in Corpus Christi $400," and a December item "fit out, to go the trip to Rancho $25," which would seem to be the nearest the captain ever came to recording in writing any detail of a great event in his life.

The "large closed carriage" was a stagecoach; the trip it made from Brownsville to the bridegroom's rancho took four days. Armed outriders paced their mounts alongside the dust-whitened coach by day and stood guard at the camps by night. A ranch cook handled skillets and pots on coals by a golden fire in the December dark. Blurred shapes of oak mottes and dim thickets of thorn stood upon a night horizon of prairies in starlight, and coyotes sang. Camps moved early: horses snorted in the chill at the first gray light, and harness rings clinked when the travelers took the jolting road again.

Across the matted grass of a drought-dusty prairie 120 wilderness miles from the amenities of Brownsville, the bride saw the rancho for the first time. Under bare December trees on the rise by the seep spring stood a cluster of earth-brown wattled huts, a gray tangle of shaggy mesquite corrals, a thatch-roofed commissary, a gaunt-faced blockhouse and stockade garnished with a brass cannon glinting in the quiet sun.

Captain Gideon K. Lewis, Captain Richardson, Captain Gregory, leading brown-faced grinning vaqueros, doubtless rode out with their dusty hats in hand, welcoming the newlyweds to the Santa Gertrudis.

Delighted rather than dismayed by the wilderness miles around her, 22-year-old Henrietta King felt more than courage "circling," as her father said, in her veins. She was happy with Richard King. Nearly six decades later she wrote the memory of her first days with him: "When I came as a bride in 1854, the little ranch home then —a mere *jacal* as Mexicans would call it—was our abode for many months until our main ranch dwelling was completed. But I doubt if it falls to the lot of any a bride to have had so happy a honeymoon. On horseback we roamed the broad prairies. When I grew tired my husband would spread a Mexican blanket for me and then I would take my siesta under the shade of the mesquite tree. . . . I remember that my pantry was so small my large platters were fastened to the walls outside. In those days large venison roasts were our favorite viands. . . . At first our cattle were long horns from Mexico. We had no fences & branding was hard work."[26]

Richard King called his bride Etta, sometimes Pet. It would seem that she called him Captain. The happiness of her marriage is reflected in a letter from her grandfather who wrote from distant Vermont on November 29, 1855:

You speak of your conjugal union as very blissful. I rejoice that it is so. In this dark world, full of evils consequent upon the introduction of sin, life is often embittered by "unequal yoking," and if you have found a mate of congenial tastes and sympathies with your own, you have abundant reason for gratitude to Him.[27]

The Kings lived on the rancho for several months following their marriage. From the day of her arrival at Santa Gertrudis, Henrietta King seems to have considered it home. She was attached to it immediately, and she immediately brought to it some of her own decorous and civilized substance. She also brought it her Scriptures. Probably the first change she instituted around headquarters caused a very careful hiding and a very furtive use of any lurking whiskey or mescal jugs on the place.

Her energetic grace quickly brought luster to the already well-known hospitality of the rancho: she added a polish to its generosity and made it famous. The doors were always open to welcome any traveler decently disposed, friend and stranger alike. Strangers learned what friends already knew: there was never anything to pay for hearty food and cheerful lodging at the stopping place on the Santa Gertrudis.

Henrietta M. King

Excellence as a helpmate and as a hostess came naturally to Henrietta King. To that excellence she added a proclivity natural to the daughter of a border mission worker: the welfare of her *Kineños*. She dosed and nursed the sick, she supplied the needy and, when occasion demanded, she used her authority for good as she conceived of good, and her conception was strongly defined. *Kineños* called her *La Madama* or *La Patrona* with a respectful sweep of their doffed hats.[28]

There were none of her kind, there were none like her, in all the Wild Horse Desert. When the captain was away, and she was left with a guard of her ranch people, "so resolute a woman was she that it was said the outlaws and renegades who infested the neighborhood preferred to approach the house when Captain King was at home than to try it when his wife was there alone."[29]

There is no record of Henrietta King's response to the personality of her husband's ranching partner, the dashing Captain Lewis. His conduct could have been nothing less than impeccable in the presence of a lady like Mrs. King. But if she heard rumors, certain of his improprieties in less correct company could have evoked from her nothing but censure. Legs Lewis, nicknamed during the punishing fatigues of the Mier Expedition for "his unusually long and strong lower limbs" was notably gifted with the ladies. When Legs Lewis went to town, any town, his gifts did not go unused.

Yet his energies were limited to no such single field. He had other business. After a career—printer's devil, reader of law, newspaper editor, soldier and ranger—which at the age of thirty had brought him little but reputation, he had plans and prospects for gain. In addition to his printing office, his real estate speculation and his mercantile interest with John Willett, in Corpus Christi, he was a working partner at the Santa Gertrudis. He not only entered into land purchases, such as the Juan Villareal and Manuel Barrera tracts, which added to the partnership holdings; entries in the account book show Lewis engaged in the rancho's operation, in livestock deals and in the delivery of herds. A May, 1854, entry in the *Ranch Account Book* recorded "advance G. K. Lewis 14th inst. to pay for land $200.00."

In January, Lewis had obtained a power of attorney from Guadalupe Ballí, niece of Padre Nicolás Ballí, grantee of Padre Island, "for presentation and settlement of all my interests."[30] Apparently Lewis never acted upon this document, but the association might well have prompted Richard King's purchase of some 12,000 acres on Padre Island for $200. The transaction took place on April 12.[31] Precisely why Lewis and King were interested in the isolated Padre Island property is a matter for conjecture. It never became a working part of the rancho. Either it appealed to them simply as a bargain, or it indicates that they dreamed of shipping cattle from coastal watersides, at Corpus Christi or Brazos Santiago, and Padre Island seemed to them a good holding place for a future operation of that kind. Lewis at the time owned wharfing rights in Corpus Christi Bay.[32] There is reason to believe that from the beginning the two ranching partners had their eyes on the development of the port of Corpus Christi as a means of shipping the future products of their rancho to the markets of New Orleans, Havana and the Atlantic seaboard.

In the midst of good auguries and promising affairs, early in 1855 the well-known and warmly popular Captain Lewis decided to run for Congress. His campaign was under way when his career came to a sudden end. At Corpus Christi on April 14, an irate husband shot Legs Lewis dead.

The *San Antonio Herald* of April 26, reprinting an account from the *Galveston Journal,* reported:

It appears that Dr. Yarrington suspected Capt. Lewis of improper and familiar freedom with his (Yarrington's) wife. Convinced of the truth of the supposition, by letters intercepted from both parties, and other circumstances correlative, he "put his wife away from him." They lived separately for a short time, when Lewis, hearing that Dr. Yarrington held in his hands such and such letters, came to the Doctor's office and demanded them. Yarrington refused to deliver them, whereupon a wordy altercation ensued, attended however by no serious result, and the parties separated. Twice afterwards, we are told, Lewis repeated this visit, demanding the letters and failing to receive them. At the third visit Yarrington told him that "if he came again it would be the last time." He called again, and prepared with a double-barrelled shot gun, Yarrington shot him down. The unfortunate man lived but a short time after the discharge.

The letters were clearly injurious to the reputation of a candidate for Congress, and Lewis was clearly determined to have them back. Always fearless, and a gallant to the end, he approached the wronged husband unarmed.

The esteem in which Legs Lewis was held is curiously reflected in the letter Dr. Yarrington himself wrote to the *Gonzales Inquirer* published April 21. It was almost an apology for killing his wife's paramour.

Indianola, 17th April, 1855.

Dear Sir:—I drop you a line hastily, to inform you that I had the misfortune to kill Capt. G. K. Lewis at Corpus Christi on the 14th inst. The reason was, he seduced Mrs. Yarrington from me and my children, then added insult to injury by continually coming to my house, and also trying to steal my children from me, and for trying to force from my possession certain letters, which I intercepted, addressed to my wife.

I have written the truth, so help me God.

Truly your ob't. serv't.,

J. T. Yarrington

P.S. I am in charge of the sheriff, Mr. Graham; we are bound for Galveston. I am free of all bonds.

Y

The *San Antonio Herald* on May 2 said a last word:

We announced in last week's *Times* the tragic death of Capt. Lewis, so well known throughout the State of Texas, as her bold and daring defender in the early days of the Republic. Perhaps no man of his age in this country had participated in more of the stirring events which have marked our history, than the deceased. In his earliest boyhood he was engaged in the bloody scenes of Revolution, and by the force of his own genius, unaided by any of the advantages of education save that which was acquired during a short apprenticeship in a printing office, he arose to a distinguished position in the State, and maintained an enviable rank in the hearts of his countrymen. But few braver men could be found where all were daring, than G. K. Lewis. Deeply imbued with a love of adventure and justifiable pride in Texan chivalry, he was always ready to defend the home of his adoption. While the mantle of charity is thrown over his errors, let us drop a tear to the memory of the boy-prisoner of Mier.

Henrietta and Richard King may have been at the Santa Gertrudis, or in Brownsville attending to details in the building of their new cottage on Elizabeth Street, when word of Lewis' death arrived.

Whether Henrietta King was able to draw the mantle of charity completely over the circumstances of Captain Lewis' death is a matter for conjecture. But there can be no doubt of the personal sorrow Richard King felt for the loss of the engaging companion and the trusted partner who played so large a role in the very creation of the rancho on the Santa Gertrudis.

VII *A Varied and Engaging Life*

LEGS LEWIS

died without leaving a will, and he had no heirs. His estate, tangled with joint holdings of a value difficult to determine and weighted with much unfinished business, was eventually settled by a succession of three administrators appointed by the Probate Court of Nueces County.[1]

The sudden demise of his partner brought problems to Richard King. The two principal properties essential to the ranching operation in which he had already invested so heavily were the Rincón de Santa Gertrudis and the de la Garza Santa Gertrudis grants. The Lewis estate owned an undivided half-interest in both tracts. Determined to maintain complete control, King had no intention of allowing the Lewis holdings to pass by purchase into strange or intractable hands when the Lewis estate came to be settled. Lacking cash to buy these interests outright, King took steps to insure continued possession and control.

When the public sale of the Lewis property was by court order held in Corpus Christi on July 1, 1856, King made arrangements to have his friend Major W. W. Chapman present to bid on the Lewis undivided half-interest in the Rincón tract. Chapman and King were to engage in a partnership for the joint purchase of the Lewis interest, and King evidently cautioned Chapman not to be outbid by any means at the auction. The major was already engaged in a livestock venture operated by James Bryden on the Santa Gertrudis, and doubtless entered into the bidding for the Rincón viewing it as an enlargement of his ranching venture in further association with his good friend King.

At the sale Chapman had to bid higher than anticipated, but he did successfully acquire, in his own name and in King's, the Lewis interest in the Rincón for the sum of $1575.00, payable by notes due one year from date of purchase, with title subject to forfeiture unless the notes were so paid.

Only a few days after making this purchase Major Chapman received sudden and unforeseen Army orders: a change of station from Corpus Christi to California, effective immediately.

He barely had time to ride out to the Santa Gertrudis to make his arrangements with Bryden, and to inform King of what had taken place. King was not on the ranch, and Chapman could not wait. He left word with Bryden to tell Captain King "that I purchased the land belonging to the Lewis estate, that I regret that I had to pay such an extravagant price owing to the opposition of Captain Fullerton. Say to Captain King that I am ordered to California, that I have established Bryden in the stock business, that I have not the means to justify me in retaining a half interest and request the Captain to release me from my obligation therein. Say also that I will write him shortly on this subject." In a deposition made years later, Bryden said, "This matter was not heard from again until 1866 when on a visit to New York, Mrs. H. B. Chapman informed me that she had found among her husband's papers [Chapman died in 1859] a memorandum referring to this transaction. I explained to her in the language used above, the Major's own words and at that time she seemed perfectly satisfied."[2]

The abrupt departure of Chapman deprived King of any help in paying the notes held by the Lewis estate, and King was late in clearing up the obligation. There are letters on file from the final administrator, attorney Hamilton P. Bee of Corpus Christi, dunning King for payment in October, 1857, and later. King's answers are lost, but he clearly delayed full payment for some time.

The eventual control of the big de la Garza Santa Gertrudis grant was a more complicated matter. King and Lewis had never paid any money for it—their notes were not due until they received documents of clear title—and they did not own it, though they were in legal possession of it in accordance with the "Contract in King and Lewis" signed by Manuel Ramírez Elisondo.

Since the signing of that contract on May 13, 1854, Elisondo had not fulfilled his obligation to Praxides Uribe, owner of the property. According to terms of the agreement between Elisondo and Uribe, Elisondo was to deliver his own notes to Uribe "payable in the City of Matamoros for the sum of one thousand eight hundred dollars redeemable on the delivery of a perfect title." Elisondo had not given Uribe any such notes and, until he did, Uribe refused to deliver to Elisondo the documents of title which had been perfected. The disagreement or distrust between these two brought the whole transaction to an impasse.

Late in the year 1856 Richard King made an entirely new approach to the matter. He interested his friend Captain James Walworth, a canny steamboater who saved his money and had a comfortable amount of it at hand for investment, in buying the de la Garza grant. Walworth was employed as master of an M. Kenedy & Co. steamer when King talked to him; he had been Mifflin Kenedy's partner on the wagon train venture to Zacatecas in 1849 and was warmly respected by both King and Kenedy.

When Walworth signified a willingness to invest in the ranch, King and Walworth made arrangements with Uribe, who appointed a new "agent and attorney in fact," Diego Castillo Montero, to handle the transaction. Through Montero, Walworth bought from Uribe on December 26, 1856, the entire de la Garza Santa Gertrudis grant. Uribe's price had gone up considerably in two and a half years. Walworth had to pay $5000.

The old contract of King and Lewis was in mutual agreement formally cancelled on January 6, 1857, by signers Praxides Uribe, Manuel Ramírez Elisondo, and R. King. This cancellation and the warranty deed to Walworth were both filed before the end of that January, and Walworth found himself actual owner of a large part of the pastures comprising the Santa Gertrudis operation.[3]

It would seem that Walworth entered the venture primarily as a friendly accommodation to King, with some unrecorded partnership arrangement not now ascertainable. It is known that Walworth kept title to the land in his own name and paid the taxes on it,[4] while the livestock and equipment on the property were owned and operated by rancher Richard King. Whatever the arrangement was, King had the control he desired. Furthermore, the cancellation of the "Contract in King and Lewis" effectively cleared from the transaction any claim that might arise from the Lewis estate. No claim was ever made.

In all of Richard King's affairs there are two constantly recurring and ever prominent motifs: his friends and his lawyers. His friendships were strong, and his legal guidance was expert.

Largely unread, he admired the attainments of lettered lawyers. From his beginnings in business, he used the best legal counsel he could find. A lawyer-scholar has said of him, "Any deal or transaction of Captain King's holds water. It is good, clear and *legal*."[5] As his operations in steamboating, land buying and stock raising increased, he conducted the ramifications of his business more and more through lawyers. His principal lawyer, Stephen Powers of Brownsville, was also one of his strongest friends.

Powers was a cultivated man, astute of mind, quiet of manner, a native of Maine, and a practicing attorney in Buffalo at the age of twenty-one. Before he was thirty he had been a United States consul in Switzerland and a *chargé d'affaires* for the American government in several German states. The Mexican War found him returned to his practice in Buffalo; commissioned by President Polk as a lieutenant, Powers at the age of thirty-two reported to Zachary Taylor for duty at Matamoros as a member of the "Commission for the Government of Occupied Territory." The border appealed to Powers. In 1849 he opened a law office in Brownsville, and immediately took his place as a leading legal light in south Texas. A staunch Democrat, he became party whip and boss on the Rio Grande, with powerful connections: among his friends were Millard Fillmore, Martin Van Buren, Lewis Cass, James Polk, Zachary Taylor, Franklin Pierce, Sam Houston, Thomas Rusk. Taylor appointed Powers postmaster of Brownsville in 1849. Pierce made him collector of customs in 1853. His identity with the border country was further established early in 1855 when he married Pauline Victoire Impey, widowed daughter of one of the pioneers of the whole region, John R. Butler, leading citizen of Point Isabel. During a long career Powers held a number of offices and many irons in political fires, yet he allowed nothing to interfere with a skilled practice of the law, for which he was fitted by nature, education and a background far broader than the Texas frontier. To other gifts he added a talent for evoking esteem, a thorough knowledge of Spanish, and a tight-lipped rectitude in fulfilling all trusts.[6] Stephen Powers and his law firm, as it changed members in the course of several decades, were a formative influence not only upon the affairs of Richard King, but the continuing affairs of the ranch he founded.[7]

After the long stay on the Santa Gertrudis following their marriage, Henrietta and Richard King moved into their cottage next door to the Kenedys on Elizabeth Street in Brownsville. Depending upon the demands of the captain's business, the Kings divided their time then between two households, one with the convenience of town dwelling, another with the roughness of pioneer ranching. Frequent commuting made the households like two contrasting sets of rooms within a single home. Its owners lived a varied and engaging life.

That life appears to have required little spicing from the social affairs of Brownsville. Probably out of deference to Henrietta's Presbyterian opinions upon frivolity, the Kings took small advantage of the *entree* they commanded among their Elizabeth Street neighbors, those affluent gentlemen and their ladies the townfolk of Brownsville dubbed the Brick House Crowd. The Kings took pleasure in neighborly visits and amenities amongst friends and families like the Chamberlains, Kenedys, Dursts and Powerses, without the tone of much attendance at opera, or functions of the Army set at

Fort Brown, or evening galas in Matamoros. Henrietta enjoyed her homemaking duties and her church; the captain, when not hard at work and when opportunity arose, enjoyed a frolic or a cup in somewhat less formal surroundings than those afforded by "society."

Henrietta's journeys to the ranch were temporarily discontinued early in the spring of 1856; at the Elizabeth Street cottage on April 17, a daughter was born to the Kings. They proudly named her Henrietta Maria. With two Henriettas in the family circle, confusion was avoided by calling the little girl Nettie.

Rains came, bringing grass to pastures and water to the Rio Grande, in 1856. M. Kenedy & Co. had a surge of business. The firm's new *Comanche*-type steamer *Ranchero*, which had arrived in the drought of the previous year, was able to navigate on a regular schedule upriver to Roma, and to show the kind of profit she had been designed to earn. River affairs, especially Army contracts,* demanded the presence of Captain King. During 1856 he seems to have spent less time at the ranch and more time at Brownsville operating riverboats.

Early that year, partner Mifflin Kenedy made a trip East. At Washington he presented a letter of introduction to Quartermaster General Jesup, signed by Texas Senator Thomas Rusk and Congressman P. H. Bell, soliciting consideration of Captain Kenedy as an experienced and dependable contractor for the transportation of Army supplies on the Rio Grande.[8] That this consideration met with favorable response and was deemed "consistent with the public interest" is shown by two due bills for service to the Army filed by M. Kenedy & Co. with the quartermaster at Fort Brown in November, one certified for $4,150.00 and another for $12,973.32.[9] These are only two items, though probably among the largest, in the firm's receipts for 1856. During that year Kenedy and King also appear to

* See Appendix IV for facsimile reproduction of a typical Army contract signed by Richard King.

have begun operation not only as transporters but as suppliers of the Army on contracts—probably not large—for mules, horses, feed and possibly some commissary staples.

On a trip upriver during the fall of 1856, Captain King made the acquaintance of a visiting officer of the Army present at Ringgold Barracks to sit on a court-martial in session there. The introduction may have taken place on the military post in October or aboard the *Ranchero* on November 1, the day that steamer churned away from the mudbank at Rio Grande City carrying the officer toward sessions of another court-martial convening at Fort Brown.[10] A warmth of friendship kindled between Captain King and the arrow-straight military passenger on the deck of the *Ranchero,* Lieutenant Colonel Robert E. Lee, Second Cavalry, USA.

Colonel Lee was no stranger to the Rio Grande, though it had been nine years since he had last seen it. On January 16, 1847, Captain Lee had mounted a mare named Creole and left Wool's force in northern Mexico on orders to report to Scott at the Brazos Santiago staging area, for embarkation to Vera Cruz aboard the *Massachusetts.* Captain Lee had sailed from the mouth of the Rio Grande just three months before Pilot King had arrived there.[11]

Since his last ride along the muddy current of the border river, Robert E. Lee had smelled smoke of battle in the Valley of Mexico, built fortifications at Baltimore, been Superintendent of the United States Military Academy at West Point, and, as a prominent career soldier commanding two squadrons of a line regiment, returned for a second tour of duty in Texas.

A man of Lee's perceptive mind doubtless had questions to ask about the borderland and the people he had encountered nearly a decade before, and he doubtless found no man to provide him with more incisive answers than the Captain King he found on the riverboat *Ranchero.* The distinguished soldier was seventeen years older than the big-shouldered steamboater. King commanded Lee's interest, then his lasting regard and respect; Lee's character and bearing had such impact upon King that the friendship of Robert E. Lee was a proud possession of, and an influence upon, Richard King for the rest of his life.

Lee made a like impression, treasured and lasting, upon Henrietta King.

Soon after his arrival at Fort Brown, Lee accompanied by younger officers made a formal call at the King home. The captain, perhaps on business at the White Ranch landing or at Brazos Santiago, was away at the time, and Mrs. King received the callers.

In a letter recounting it to his wife, Lee wrote, "The King cottage was removed from the street by well kept trees and shrubbery in the yard, among which were several orange trees filled with ripening fruit. Mrs. King's table was loaded with sweet oranges and many other things tempting to the eye." The colonel considered that it was not proper to appear interested in food at a correct call, and reported to Mrs. Lee, "I tasted nothing." This propriety left room for complaint from the junior officers, who, after their departure told Colonel Lee that in other Brownsville homes they had been "entertained elaborately" with "cold meats, coffee, tea, fruits, and sweets." This brought a quiet reprimand from the Virginian, who regretted that it was far too prevalent for young officers to call upon townspeople and delay in hopes of being asked to supper.[12]

Though the colonel "tasted nothing" on that first call, there were subsequent occasions when he enjoyed not only hospitality, but food, at the Kings'. He undoubtedly joined the Kings at church, worshiping with the Reverend Hiram Chamberlain's congregation in the church on the corner of Elizabeth and Ninth streets.[13]

The long-drawn procedures of dull courts-martial were trying, even to tempers as equable as Lee's. Sessions at Fort Brown dragged through November, December, past Christmas, through January, and on until the eighteenth of February, 1857, when the court closed *sine die*. Much of the time was spent in idle adjournment waiting for witnesses to make their slow ways to the remote Rio Grande, and, with much time on his hands and many thoughts of his family at far Arlington, Lee took long walks and longer horseback rides. He felt the need of being away at times from his brother trial officers at Fort Brown, and wrote to his wife, "My daily walks are alone, up and down the banks of the river, and my pleasure is derived from my own thoughts and from the sight of the flowers and animals I there meet with."[14]

On some of the horseback jaunts he made during these months, riding and hunting north of the river, he was not alone and his companion was Richard King. It seems likely that during the longer adjournments of the court, Lee rode with King as far as the Santa Gertrudis. Whether he did or not at that time, he did, during duty in Texas from 1856 to 1861, make several visits to Santa Gertrudis, that "seat of hospitality" which had made itself a way station for travelers in the area.[15]

Half a dozen decades later Henrietta King proudly told a granddaughter, "In those days the houses were few and far between and owing to this I can recall with pleasure the many distinguished guests I entertained. Among them I recall General Lee, then Lieutenant Colonel. I am sure if General Lee were here to recall those days, he would say that a dinner served off our tin plates on this old ranch was more appetizing than many a banquet accorded him in later years." She went on to say, "Captain King previously had hunted on horseback with Lieutenant Colonel Lee and he approved of ranching in South West Texas. So your grandfather thought with advice like Lee's he was safe in embarking on the then untried venture of ranching here."[16]

Henrietta King's admiration for every word and deed of General Lee's magnified in her mind sixty years later Lee's role as an advisor in the founding of the King Ranch. Operations on the Santa Gertrudis were three years old when Lee first met King; moreover, King depended upon assurances from no man, not even Robert E. Lee, concerning the feasibility of ranching in "South West Texas." King was already embarked, safe or unsafe.

At the same time, there can be no doubt that he discussed ranching, anxious for Lee's opinions. Lee's very character made him a mentor. His background of agrarian estate made him also a knowledgeable advisor on land and livestock. Lee was impressed by the illimitable grass, confident that wilderness pastures ought to be developed to sustain huge and profitable herds. He said so to King. Though in private letters the polished Virginian wrote sometimes of the frontier's dreary rawness, he was convinced of the future of the land, and he felt its power.[17]

At a time when King had spread himself thin gambling the profits of one business upon the future of another, and at a time when he was in the midst of such uncertainties caused by the death of a partner that he actually owned little of the land upon which his gamble and his hope stood, Richard King got from Robert E. Lee not advice to start ranching but confidence in what he had already started.

One thing Lee told King the rancher never forgot. It came to be a cornerstone in the structure of King's business. Lee said, *"Buy land; and never sell."*[18]

And in another manner Lee left his mark on the ranch itself. Not only as a warrior but as an engineer, Lee had an eye for terrain. There is every reason to believe that he was asked for advice upon the subject and that he did choose the site on the high ground for the building of the permanent ranch home at the Santa Gertrudis headquarters.[19]

When the court-martial at Fort Brown closed, Lee moved by the *Ranchero* upriver to Ringgold again, thence overland by way of San Antonio to Indianola, for yet another court. There is some evidence that from San Antonio he traveled out of his way to Santa Gertrudis, and that his friend King then rode with him north to Indianola.[20] There is also an authentic story that King organized and operated a wagon train as an accommodation to Lee, and delivered troop supplies at remote points where Lee needed them.[21] It would be in keeping with King's policy of friendly attention to the Army for business reasons, but in this instance it was doubtless more. From the first meeting, Lee summoned from King an especial esteem. And it is certain that whenever in the course of his duties Robert E. Lee stopped at the Santa Gertrudis, Henrietta King heaped high with "viands" the very largest of her "large platters."

Not long after the birth of little Nettie, Henrietta and the baby began journeying with the captain to the ranch. Few details of their mode of travel are recorded. It is likely that they made it a practice to leave secretly and quietly, in darkness before dawn, to avoid notice in setting out upon a road where travelers were often way-laid. It is logical to assume that they went in the most comfortable conveyance at hand, the heavy coach, accompanied by a spring wagon or ambulance carrying servants and supplies and guarded by out-riders like the redoubtable Faustino Villa. There were times when the King family risked the 124 lonely miles without entourage and upon one occasion at least trouble came close.

On an evening, probably late in 1856, when the Kings were making camp by the side of the road, a lone Mexican appeared from the brush and asked permission to join camp for the night. King gave permission and sent him out for wood. As the captain bent over lighting twigs to start a fire, his wife was tending the baby and Nettie sat on a blanket spread by the coach. Henrietta King looked up, suddenly frightened in the dusk, and called out, "Captain *King! Behind you!*" With the practiced twist of a veteran riverfront brawler, King swept back both his powerful hands and grabbed tight—to an arm holding a knife. He jerked swinging the whole weight of his assailant overhead, slamming him to the ground with the knife arm twisted helpless. In that time and in that place most men would have killed the would-be assassin. King only told him—with emphasis not hard to imagine—to get out of camp and stay out. Whether the rogue had lurking confederates in the brush or not, nothing more happened.[22]

In a country "menaced by hostile Indians and roving bandits" Mrs. King once suffered a fright within the very walls of the adobe *jacal* at Santa Gertrudis. Nettie was an infant, in a cradle by the door. Her mother, alone and busy setting out loaves of freshly baked bread at the back of the room, turned to see a half-naked Indian standing silent on the threshold. When Mrs. King faced him, he jumped to the cradle and stood over it, brandishing a club. With his other hand he pointed at the bread, grimacing that he wanted it. Iron-nerved Mrs. King gave him all the bread he could carry; he stalked wordless from the door and disappeared.[23]

No roughness discouraged the captain's wife from residence at the ranch. As the headquarters grew, the roughness gradually diminished. The date of the Kings' removal from the adobe *jacal* to the comfortable quarters called the "original" ranch house is not known, but it was sometime between late in 1857 and early in 1859. The location of the building, chosen by Lee, was the site upon which the present great house at the ranch now stands. The "original" was low and rambling, built of frame, with an attic or half second-story and an inviting, bannistered front gallery. The dining room and kitchen, built of stone to avoid the hazard of fire, formed a separate building at the rear and was connected with the living quarters by an unroofed walkway open to the weather. A little to the north of this main house was the stone-built commissary and store, together with a kitchen, eating space and sleeping quarters for extra hands, teamsters and those who came seeking work at the ranch. By the commissary stood a watchtower, and a men's dormitory for buyers, visitors and chance travelers. Farther to the north were stables, corrals, carriage and wagon sheds, a busy blacksmith's shop and a rough line of small houses where ranch employees lived with their families. Sometime in the 1860's a one-room school was established for children on the ranch, doubtless under supervision by Henrietta King.

Much of the lumber used in construction around headquarters was secondhand material bought from the government when the Army abandoned its post and depot at Corpus Christi, for removal to San Antonio, in 1857. King's friend Chapman was in charge of the dispersal of the government property and undoubtedly kept King informed of the materials available for sale.[24] Other timber for buildings at the ranch came from Louisiana and Florida to Corpus Christi by shallow-draft boats and, like the government lumber, was hauled by oxcart and heavy wagon to the Santa Gertrudis.

Ranch operation remained primitive. Land itself had value only when it had water. At that time, before the incursion of the mesquite which made brush jungle of much of the country a few decades later, this land was in great part rolling prairie, its treeless open vistas only infrequently broken by mottes of live oak, laurel and scattered *bosques* of mesquite. Ranching was simply the ownership of branded herds roughly controlled on unfenced prairie near a possessed supply of scarce and precious water. The only cattle a rancher owned were cattle half-wild, quick and fierce, armed with long horns and hard to handle. The only horses a rancher owned were subject to the wildness of open ranging; to be held under herd and used, they had to be incessantly guarded against the feral influence and example of running bands of untamed mustangs. The only herdsmen a rancher hired to work such herds of half-wild cattle and horses were half-wild men, tough centaurs working for wages to the jing of big-rowelled spurs and the sing of rawhide lariats.

A gathering of such centaurs was no drab spectacle.

For herd work in the earliest versions of what came to be named a roundup, the first regularly used gathering place on the King Ranch was a site in the shade of anaqua trees by the big water at the dam of the Tranquitas.[25]

A cookfire and the earliest version of what came to be named a chuck wagon stood at the heart of the camp. Out beyond, upon the other hand from the margin of the water, rode the centaurs in the knife-edged light and glare-edged dust. A stench of burnt hair under irons from branding fires made incense to blend with a primal music, a counterpoint of bawl and bellow and shout in the rustle and rattle of hooves. When the sun bore straight down upon the dusty crowns of hatted centaurs, by relays they unsaddled. They walked stiff-legged, fang-hungry and grinning, into shade at the wagon, to squat and eat, tearing cooked meat with their teeth, licking grease from rope-burned fingers, wolfing white fluff-lumps of hot bread, gulping black coffee, to ease then with their saddles for pillows, sprawled *contentos* in the noon-glint under the anaqua trees for a while, until it was time again to rope a new mount and ascend to the state of centaurs on four fast-moving steel-sinewed legs until the coming of dusk, and meat and bread by a fire in the dark, and song wild as the cry of wolves beyond the Tranquitas, beyond the moon, and sleep until the coming of the Morning Star when centaurs rose again.

The Tranquitas was not far from headquarters. Henrietta King, the little girl Nettie and other King children as they arrived often rode a spring wagon to the motte of anaqua trees by the water at noon, where a blanket was spread in the shade, and Richard King sat with his family and his *Kineños,* to eat by the gathering of his herds. These were the first picnics and feasts *al fresco* of the King family on the King Ranch. In the long years, in another century, in another world, when the City of Kingsville crowded at the remains of the embankment that once had been the dam of the Tranquitas, a few anaqua trees were spared to cast their shade today not upon the nooning ease of centaurs but upon the earth-encasing pavement of a municipal street.

The earliest of the many marks Richard King's men burned into the hides of his herds was a brand the captain himself designed, called the *Ere Flecha,* and made thus ꝶ.

Shortly after his marriage he brought another brand into use, built from the initials of his bride, an H and K connected, HK. Henrietta King recalled to grandchildren her pleasure at first seeing that brand, on a herd of cattle driven to the Santa Gertrudis from Mexico: "I remember well going out to see them with my baby Henrietta in my arms, and to my surprise my brand was put upon them HK."[26] It was the first of the King Ranch brands officially recorded in the brand registry of Nueces County, filed in the name of "Mistress Henrietta M. King, wife of Richard King" on March 20, 1859.

Though the *Ere Flecha* had been used as early as January, 1854 King did not register it until June 27, 1859, along with another brand described as his own, an L and K connected, Ӄ. This was undoubtedly the Lewis and King partnership brand. On the same day of June, 1859, King also entered into the registry "King and Walworth's Brand," a part of the arrangement with James Walworth who owned the de la Garza Santa Gertrudis tract at the time. For

this new partnership mark, he merely added a V at the top of the old L and K connected so that it became ⅄.

During the first several years, all livestock branded at the Santa Gertrudis wore ℞ or HK or Ƙ or ⅄. Richard King was to use them, and buy and register and discard others, before he would begin to burn the ultimately superseding mark, the Running W, which he brought to lasting fame in range history — and which ornaments nearly every page of this book.*

Herds brought their natural increase as the seasons passed and, as the numbers of livestock grew, it became evident that King's policy of upbreeding horse stock with the blood of good studs, and of choosing only the best available Mexican bulls and range cows for his breed herd, was producing animals of a noticeable quality. The investment their owner had made, and the trail he had blazed, led his ranching enterprise first to the possession of good and plentiful stock, and then to the largely unsolved problems of markets.

It has already been mentioned that the ranch's first receipts were from horse sales. Captain King had a sportsman's interest in fast and fine horseflesh, but beyond that, he had clear business reasons for the emphasis he placed on horse and mule raising in the early days at the Santa Gertrudis. Good horses were prime necessities in operating his own ranch. Horses and mules were needed in the wagon train business with which M. Kenedy & Co. was increasingly involved. Saddle and harness and pack animals were in constant demand by the Army. And in a day when livestock had to be driven, not shipped, to remote markets, horses and mules were more quickly moved and efficiently delivered than cattle. Widespread demand for good stock made the Santa Gertrudis horse and mule business lively and profitable from the beginning.

Increasing and improving his cattle, during the first several seasons

* See Appendix V for facsimile reproductions of the original registrations of early King Ranch brands.

of his ranching, King sold only steers. How long this program continued is not known, but King Ranch cattle were being sold in fair numbers during the later half of the 1850's. The most profitable outlet for cattle at that time was their sale as breed stock to other ranchers. King had already made his cattle noticeable for flesh and strength: buyers were attracted and came from a distance—from as far as Monterrey and Saltillo below the Rio Grande.[27] These sales at the ranch brought from twelve to eighteen dollars a head and made a considerable business. Yet King kept a constant eye upon the possibilities of wider markets. The records are missing but there are good reasons to believe that in the late 1850's he had some of his cattle driven to markets as far as New Orleans, and that he even shipped cattle experimentally by coastwise steamer to New Orleans, then by riverboat to a railhead at Cairo, Illinois, and thence by rail to the market of Chicago.[28] Yet such expensive (it cost six dollars to ship a cow to New Orleans)[29] and punishing shipments for livestock offered no real solution to the problem of volume markets, and King knew it.

There was of course the long-established trade in hides and tallow —which ranchers along the Texas Coast were beginning to engage in—but it would seem unlikely that with the prices King got for stock on the hoof he disposed of many cattle by way of slaughter for mere skinning and rendering at that time. There is evidence that he did establish his first works for trying tallow as early as 1859.[30] However, this was probably to process and turn to profit, however meager, an unsaleable surplus of culls from his herds.

King kept to his vision of adequate transportation supplying good beef to a remote mass market. He wanted to *ship meat,* not by long drives, not by bulky and wasteful transport on the hoof.

That vision led him to an imaginative experiment. Long before the machinery for chilling beef was available, Richard King attempted to preserve beef carcasses for long distance shipment. As his preservative, he thought not of ice but of salt. Familiar with salt meat since his boyhood in the boats, he set up an elaborate experiment to impregnate beef with salt—not by merely salting down chunks, but by forcing a strong brine injection into the veins of a large section of beef. When his engineering and his salt solution both failed, he regretfully but promptly quit tinkering as an inventor and got back to less visionary means of moving beef to existing markets.[31]

Corpus Christi was forty-five miles from ranch headquarters; Brownsville was almost three times as far away. The ranch operation naturally linked itself to the nearest town and supply point—and the county seat of the county in which the Santa Gertrudis stood. The old vaquero Alvarado said that "from the time King formed the ranch of Santa Gertrudis, he put a man to carry the mail two or three times a week from Corpus Christi." King's supply wagons and King himself were regular travelers on the Corpus Christi road. As the ranch prospered, the influence of its owner became a factor in Nueces County affairs.

Corpus Christi was gradually emerging from the ups and downs of its origins as a smuggling post and the busted boom town advertised as "The Little Naples."

In 1855 its complicated founder, advocate and prophet, Colonel Henry Lawrence Kinney, had tired of waiting for merely local dreams to come true and had departed southward to more radiant fields, to far Nicaragua, on a genuinely grandiose filibustering dream. Three years later he returned with his dream bedraggled. Among other troubles, Mrs. Kinney had divorced him during his absence. Regardless, his old Texas friends wined and dined him, and at a banquet listened to him "relate his adventures in Nicaragua."

Yet the Kinney eloquence had somehow lost its mellow ring of imminent glory.

The frontier as it filled seemed to lose its room for the expansive Henry Lawrence Kinney it had created. It somehow passed the colonel by without ever quite catching up with him, strangely enough, and left him to his own diminishing devices, or vices, as some said. He died by violence, in troubles caused by the old Mexican custom of maintaining a *"casa chica,"* a little house outside wedlock—in this case tenanted by a former mistress and a bastard daughter grown nearly to womanhood: he was shot on a dark street of Matamoros in the troubled year of 1862.[32]

Corpus Christi lost color and gained solidity. When government business and payrolls were withdrawn by the abandonment of the Army depot, the town managed to survive the blow and develop its own resources. As one of the resourceful citizens of Nueces County, Captain King became a leader in the development. Businessmen like early-comer William P. Aubrey,[33] and late-comer Perry Doddridge[34] who had been an employee of M. Kenedy & Co. and who established a commission house and the first bank in Corpus Christi, prominent residents and officeholders like Forbes Britton[35] and William Mann,[36] the picturesque civil engineer and surveyor Felix Blucher,[37] the first mayor Benjamin F. Neal,[38] the enterprising Henry Maltby[39]—a long roster of pioneer citizens—sought King's counsel and backing in local affairs. Kinney men, like the Reuben Holbein who had been Kinney's agent in Europe, looked for a new chief and found Richard King. After holding office as County Clerk of Nueces County, decorating a vast number of legal documents with his accomplished calligraphy, Holbein moved to the Santa Gertrudis[40] where he exercised both his probity and his penmanship for decades as the ranch's trusted accountant and amanuensis. With King's steadiness in contrast to Kinney's flamboyance, the ranching captain became a kind of successor to the promoting colonel around Corpus Christi.

At the same time, King acquired an increasing prominence in the commercial and political affairs of Brownsville and Cameron County. Standing with his lawyer Stephen Powers and his partner Mifflin Kenedy, King was a strong Democrat and States Rights man, active in their councils and election strategies. He carefully maintained the Elizabeth Street cottage as his legal homestead;[41] his shipping firm, completely identified with Brownsville and its future, was an essential cog in the business of the town and the economy of the whole valley. Ranger Rip Ford wrote: "Kenedy and King were sort of head men. . . . They became a support to the citizens of their section, and stood by them in prosperity and adversity. The charge was not made against them that, they consulted their own interests in public matters, and left the people to take care of themselves. They were with the people, and in all political matters they oftener took the lead than they aimed to avoid responsibility."[42] In Brownsville at that time, Democrats were called the "Reds" — as opposed to the "Blues." Elections were so heated at times that even the school children of Brownsville wore red or blue shoestrings to display their families' feelings.

There was a strong civic and commercial rivalry between Corpus Christi and Brownsville. Bitterly complaining of the preponderance of shipping at Brownsville's Brazos Santiago, Corpus Christi labored to make itself the center of a competing wagon train trade to handle a flow of goods toward the interior, pecked more or less continually at the deepening of a boat channel through the mud flats of its bay, and railed against the "monopoly" and the "exorbitant rates" of shipping through Brazos Santiago to Brownsville and upriver. The weak point of the Corpus Christi argument was that wagon train rates were much higher than riverboat rates.[43]

Though Richard King stood at the very heart of Brownsville's shipping "monopoly" and "exorbitant rates," he also found himself the operator of a leading enterprise in the vicinity of Corpus Christi. Geography made him a connecting link between the interests of both towns and both counties; holding a view that the interests of one were eventually the interests of both, he served as their catalyst in the eventual development of the whole region.

There was another rivalry. It became more than rivalry and grew to an ugly consequence for all citizens between the Nueces and the Rio Grande. This was the antipathy between Latins, who had first possessed the land, and non-Latin newcomers, who appeared as usurpers in Latin eyes.

The two races facing each other across the narrow water of the Rio Grande had the immemorial failing: each firmly believed that its own manners and opinions were right for the unequaled reason that its manners and opinions were its own. Men everywhere find themselves ready to resent that which they must make any effort to understand. The different dynamics of the two races, founded upon different quotients, predicating different results as modes of life, went willfully misunderstood each by the other, and mutually despised.

In their encounter, Americans were apt to feel superior and Mexicans were apt to feel abused. An ordinary American was more prosperous—because he paid more attention to "prosperity"—than an ordinary Mexican, so that an economic division generally conformed with the racial cleavage to more sharply align the border's array of old resentments and mistrusts.

There came to be an almost ideal atmosphere for bloodshed. In the spring of the year 1858, the government of Mexico published a decree creating a free zone "six miles in width, and extending along the entire northern frontier of the State of Tamaulipas" into which goods could be imported from foreign countries free of duty.[44] The zone attracted every foot-loose smuggler, thief and cutthroat that could get there, and brought a riffraff primed for violence to the banks of the Rio Grande. In these far from tranquil circumstances, the bumbling commander of the Department of Texas, General D. E. Twiggs, foolishly decided to order all United States troops away from the border; on February 5, 1859, the Army began an abandonment of every post between the Rio Grande and the Nueces.[45] Stripped of protection, the frontier stood handsomely ready for trouble.

A vast trouble appeared in the durable shape of a man with the haunting name of Juan Nepomuceno Cortina. His cousin called him "a desperate, contrary fellow," and so the border found him.[46]

He was a wellborn rascal.[47] A blood of Castile gave him fair skin, reddish hair. He had green eyes. His intimates shrank the bell tones of his baptismal name to "Cheno," and from the time he was a little boy he was contrary if not yet desperate. Refusing to learn to read and write as became his estate, he preferred the learning of knives, ropes, firearms and fast horses. From early youth he accompanied his elders on forays against Indians, practiced the arts of the vaquero, attended *fandangos* and frequented the company of knaves. The intractable boy grew to personable manhood, unlettered but high-mannered, "fearless, self-possessed, and cunning."[48]

He tasted his people's defeat and felt race hate first stir his heart when at the age of twenty-two he fought against Taylor's men at Palo Alto and Resaca. His devotion, however, was not solely to his invaded country; he had a marked propensity for personal gain. One of his enemies stated on oath that "during the Mexican War Cortina murdered his employer, stole his mules, and sold them to the United

States Army."[49] When the war was over, Cheno Cortina worked for the United States quartermaster trains at $25 a month; his superior found him "faithful and effective in the discharge of his duties" but he had trouble with American teamsters. They were taking no orders "from a Mexican." After two fights and much bitterness, Cheno Cortina quit, took his pay and went out upon his mother's land. It was on the Texas side of the river.[50]

His mother, the twice-widowed and genteel Doña Estéfana Goseascochea de Cortina, granddaughter of María Gertrudis de la Garza Falcón, was heiress to one sixth of the 59-square-league Potrero del Espíritu Santo grant which in its vast acreage happened to include the town site of Brownsville. Members of the large family to which she belonged had set up a claim in Texas courts that the land composing the town site was still a family property which had passed through the hands of faulty title holders wrongfully to the ownership of Charles Stillman and his partners of the Brownsville Town Company. The claim, answered by counterclaims, initiated a monstrously complicated and protracted litigation.[51] Watching the law's tangle and delay, and the fees of lawyers consuming leagues of land, the son of Doña Estéfana saw only what he wished to see for the nourishment of his bitterness: thievery and chicanery, practiced by hated aliens upon his own ill-treated family and his martyred race.

When he went out upon his mother's property early in the 1850's, he found it not only pleasing but profitable to practice a little thievery himself. In building up a rancho at a place called San José north and west of Brownsville, he became an accomplished horse and cow thief. San José became a roost for rogues. There were times when Cheno Cortina's talents took a turn to bring applause: joining with a company of Mexican-Texan rancheros in 1857, he helped to wipe out an entire band of cattle-stealing Indians which may have been the last of the Karankawas.[52] A matter for less applause was his own activity with other people's livestock. In the course of almost a decade, indictments were brought against him, not only for theft but murder. Yet he was never prosecuted. His own, his brothers' and his near relatives' political sway over a strong bloc of Mexican-Texan voters made it "inadvisable" for the elected authorities to bring the "bold and turbulent man" to court.[53]

The boldness and bitterness of the man himself, the smolder of ill will between two races, the unhindered presence of a large and criminal riffraff, and the absence of the military neatly set the stage for a violence known as the First Cortina War. The green-eyed equestrian named Juan Nepomuceno Cortina became a scoundrel champion of his race and brought to a spilling boil an old brew of trouble on the border.

On the thirteenth day of July, 1859, Cheno Cortina with some of his vaqueros rode in from the rancho to Brownsville for morning coffee. As they sat sipping at their cups in Gabriel Catchel's café, they saw City Marshal Robert Shears arrive to arrest a Mexican drunk. The culprit happened to be a former servant of Cheno Cortina's. In making the arrest, Shears happened to use unnecessary brutality. Cortina saw, stepped up to the marshal and asked him, mildly enough, to treat the man more easily. Marshal Shears thereupon started a war: he cursed Cortina—who jerked a gun, shot Shears in the shoulder, mounted, pulled the drunk up behind him and galloped from town.[54]

Before the dust of his ride to the rancho had settled, news had traveled. Cheno Cortina was the hero of his people. He was their gallant and wellborn *campeón de la raza,* not afraid to shoot a despised representative of the gringo law for the blessed sake of justice to a humble man of his own race, their own race! It had all the trimmings.

And no despised representative of the gringo law went out from Brownsville to bring in Cheno Cortina.

Cortina's open and unanswered defiance of authority gave him a sense of power. It brought him not merely admirers but recruits, ready for such plans as he might devise. During the next sixty days his exact whereabouts were uncertain. Adrift along the river were vague words about a secret "society." The words were explicit, if florid, when later divulged: "First, a society is organized in the State of Texas which devotes itself sleeplessly until the work is crowned with success to the improvement of the unhappy condition of those Mexican citizens resident therein: exterminating their tyrants, to which end those who compose it are ready to shed their blood and suffer the death of martyrs."[55] A certain quiet came to the border as the dog days wore away and the sun stood farther in the south.

On the sleeping streets of Brownsville at three o'clock in the morning, September 28, the quiet broke with sudden shouts, *"Viva Cheno Cortina; Mueran los gringos; Viva Mexico!"*

Leading an armed and organized force of something like a hundred men, Cortina had crossed the river and captured the town in the dark. He took it unopposed, with a cool competence. Establishing his headquarters in the ironically deserted garrison of Fort Brown, he disposed his men at well-chosen points in Brownsville's streets and loosed a manhunt for the gringo enemies he had proscribed. Marshal Shears successfully hid himself and others managed to scramble for cover, but five citizens were shot down, including the city jailer. All Mexican prisoners were set free. Cortina threatened to burn some of the houses in town where certain sworn enemies were thought to be in hiding; as the sun came up he was searching stores at the riverfront for turpentine to aid in setting the fires.[56] A curious thing happened.

Completely stunned, stripped of defense, the helpless town of Brownsville found deliverance. If gringos could not save it, Mexicans would: Matamoros rescued Brownsville on the morning of its shame.

It happened by an act of Providence, and Mexican politics, that the commander of troops in Tamaulipas, present at the Matamoros garrison, was none other than the former revolutionary and former Texan of friendly memory, General José María Jesús Carvajal. When he went down to the levee at daylight, resolved to end the mischief-raising on the river's other bank, he took with him his commander of cavalry, who happened to be Cortina's own cousin, Miguel Tijerina, the same who called his green-eyed kinsman a "desperate, contrary fellow." Carvajal, catching sight of Cortina on the opposite bank, ordered Tijerina to cross with troops and persuade Cortina both to desist from madness and to return to the Mexican side immediately, for conference. And he did. How Carvajal and Tijerina prevailed upon Cortina to withdraw peaceably and promptly is not of record. But Brownsville was saved. It is said that Cousin Miguel took Cousin Cheno's horse by the bits and led Cortina with his bravos from the town.[57]

Two days later at the rancho six miles out of Brownsville, on the American side, inflamed with growing fame, Juan Nepomuceno Cortina issued a proclamation bidding defiance to the law, assuming the protection of his downtrodden people and denouncing lawyers who despoiled them of their lands. About some of the lawyers, there was truth enough to cause discomfort. And there was rhetoric enough: "We have careered over the streets of the city in search of our adversaries. . . . *Our personal enemies shall not possess our lands until they have fattened it with their own gore.*"[58] Volunteers flocked to Cortina from the other side of the river, augmenting his force for a real fight. The riffraff from the free zone swarmed, rubbing its hands at the prospect of pillage. Cortina sat upon "a lofty perch in the eyes of the hero-worshiping Mexicans; and there was a general belief among them that Cortina would drive the hated, oppressive gringos north of the Nueces." [59]

Brownsville was scared.

Mayor Stephen Powers—who had been politically friendly with Cortina and had not yet crossed words or swords with him—set about organizing a defense of the town while calls for help went to General Twiggs in San Antonio, Governor Runnels in Austin, and even President Buchanan in Washington. Local citizens rigged themselves in companies for civilian defense and maintained guard watches. The cooperative General Carvajal sent over a detachment of troops, which were quartered in Fort Brown. Over that erstwhile United States Army post a Mexican flag was raised —to protect Brownsville. As an affair between two races, Cortina's War was queer.

Brownsville forces made two irresolute sorties toward Cortina's rancho. Both ended in loutish retreats back to the safety of the town. For more than two months Cortina had it all his own way, holding Brownsville in what amounted to a cowed state of siege. The first help sent to relieve it was a company of Texas Rangers under the undisciplined and ineffective command of Captain W. G. Tobin of San Antonio. Cortina continued to hold the environs of Brownsville completely under his control, capturing the mails, stealing cattle, looting "unfriendly" ranchos, ambushing travelers, shutting off all commerce on the river and roads. [60]

No units of the United States Army, nor any real aid, arrived on the border until the fifth of December when 117 Regulars under the command of Major Samuel P. Heintzelman marched into Brownsville. Heintzelman was a soldier. Leading his own men and a force of about 120 of Tobin's rangers and Brownsville volunteers, he found Cortina at La Ebronal on the morning of December 14 and attacked. Eight Cortinistas and one ranger were killed, and two Regulars wounded. Cortina fell back, and his forces melted into the chaparral beyond pursuit.

Feeling no defeat, Cortina re-grouped his rabble and for the next ten hard-riding days led them raiding along the lower reaches of the Wild Horse Desert, plundering, burning, murdering. Leading a force estimated at from 450 to 700 men and carrying two pieces of artillery, Cortina swept into Rio Grande City on Christmas to loot, roister and set fires in the defenseless town.

Meanwhile, there had appeared upon the border an old hand and master of its warfare. Rip Ford was back again on the Rio Grande.

There were deeps beyond the soundings of gunfire in John Salmon Ford. He was no mere fighting man, though they did call him Rip for the way he went at it. A good mind and a just sensibility gave an uncommon quality to the mettle in him, and made of Rip Ford the ranger, the captain of scouts, the soldier of fortune, the State senator, the newspaper editor, the writer of *Memoirs,* the loyal friend, the hard foe, a most uncommon fighting man.

Walking down Congress Avenue in the capital of Texas on a fall morning of 1859, Ranger Captain Rip Ford met State Senator Forbes Britton of Corpus Christi. Wild news of Cortina's insurrection had arrived. It was even rumored Corpus Christi had been sacked and burned. As the two men discussed it, the Governor of Texas came walking up Congress Avenue and stopped to hear. The senator from Corpus Christi, in imagining the plight of his ravaged constituency, became so agitated that "his eyes danced wildly in their sockets."

The governor was alarmed.

"Ford!" the governor said, "you must go! You must start tonight —and move swiftly!"[61] He then and there commissioned Ford a

Major of Texas Rangers, to command all state forces in putting Cortina down.

Next day Ford marched his army south. "It numbered eight men on horseback; it carried one or two guns, a few pistols, and perhaps a little grub lashed to the saddles. It did not have one dollar of public money, for the simple reason that the treasury was empty."[62] Rip Ford was accustomed to that; he used leadership, not money, and he recruited as he went. A company of fifty-three well armed and mounted volunteers, equipped with an ambulance and a supply wagon, arrived at Brownsville on the morning of December 14,[63] honing for a fight. It was the day of the engagement at La Ebronal. Ford galloped his men toward the sound of distant firing—and reached the field too late to strike a blow.

He had to wait almost two weeks to find his enemy. Combined forces composed of Heintzelman's Regulars, with a troop of the Second Cavalry under Captain George Stoneman, and the rangers of Tobin and Ford were sixteen miles down the river from Rio Grande City on the day after Christmas when they learned Cortina had taken the town.

Ford immediately moved out with ninety men, hurrying upriver in advance of the main body, and before dawn of December 27 reached contact with enemy pickets near the town. At daylight Cortina opened fire with his two artillery pieces. Ford did not wait for the arrival of the support he knew was coming—outnumbered five to one by forces holding a strong and well-chosen line, he joined battle. After silencing the artillery, repulsing a cavalry charge, seeing thirteen of his rangers fall around him, and advancing into crossfire that was murderous, Rip Ford led an assault hot into the enemy center, toward Cortina himself standing with his bodyguards. As the rangers came at him through the fire, Cheno Cortina had his first dose of the medicine Rip Ford would administer thenceforth. The center folded, the bodyguard melted: United States Army wagon tops were in sight. Stoneman and his troopers came rolling up a flank, and Cortina joined a rout—headed for the river. Heintzelman's official report of the action stated: "Major Ford led the advance, and took both his [Cortina's] guns, ammunition and baggage."[64]

Beyond that dry summary, the battle had its inevitable measure of detail and anecdote. A single incident will indicate its spirit. One of Ford's fire-eating volunteers was a colonel of the Kentucky style and manner, named Loughridge. At one point in the onslaught he found himself out of ammunition, and very considerably bothered by a particular enemy marksman who was taking due advantage of his situation. As another ranger moved up within hearing, the colonel called out, "Good morning, Mr. Morris, will you please kill that Mexican?"

Morris did.

The colonel gave a measured bow. "Very much obliged to you, Mr. Morris."[65]

Cortina was never without sagacity as a commander of troops. The obvious personal fearlessness which he added to his other talents as a leader and fighter did not blind him to plain and often hard facts. He was quick to learn from them. After the too ambitious essay at Rio Grande City, he was careful to employ the large lesson it taught him: a pitched battle using ranchero and riffraff volunteers against resolute ranger sharpshooters or disciplined professional troops was out of his class and over his head. Rio Grande City taught him that he was a leader of mobile guerillas. Unless his superiority of force clearly guaranteed a result, he saw the absurdity of standing to fight. With one exception—at the battle of La Bolsa—Cortina's tactics became those of a raider only, a plunderer of isolated ranchos and a killer of outnumbered men. For the next few months he kept the whole border in a taut state of alarm.

Late in March, 1860, the new commander of the Department of Texas, Lieutenant Colonel Robert E. Lee, arrived with orders from the Secretary of War to force an end to the violence. Pressure by an increased number of United States troops, and by the unremitting, trigger-ready patrols of Ford's rangers on both banks of the Rio Grande, soon made raiding too dangerous and too profitless for Cortina to continue.[66]

By early May, it was clear that the incursions into Texas had ceased, and Lee left the Rio Grande. His route back to San Antonio took him by the Santa Gertrudis where he spent the night. In his Memorandum Book he recorded for May 12: "At 7 miles reached San Gertrudis—Capt. King's ranch—A beautiful place on a knoll in a mesquite plain, new house . . ." The party spent the night, and undoubtedly the Colonel was served from Henrietta's "large platters," before resuming the journey the following morning.[67]

The First Cortina War came to a kind of undeclared truce. It adjourned *sine die*. The uncaught Cheno retired into the hills of Mexico, for a stint at the internecine affairs of Mexican politics, until times might be ripe again for the scourging of *gringos malditos*.

Just once during the five months between his lesson at Rio Grande City and his retirement, did Cortina stand to fight a full-fledged battle. He planned it as a calculated risk believing it was justified by the richness of the stake involved. The risk was greater than his calculation: Rip Ford not only thrashed him again, he nearly killed him. The stake was the steamboat *Ranchero*, property of the firm M. Kenedy & Co.

River traffic had been at a complete standstill since the capture of Brownsville late in September. After Cortina's defeat and flight south from Rio Grande City, it was deemed safe to send a steamer upriver to break the stoppage of trade, which had brought the economy of the whole region to a stifling halt. On January 9 the *Ranchero* was dispatched upriver, and steamed safely to Rio Grande City. There a heavy cargo of urgent merchandise, passengers, and an accumulation of about $300,000 in bullion and specie awaited transport to Brownsville.

The passage upriver was widely noted; so was the cargo awaiting shipment. Rumors arrived that Cortina intended to attack the *Ranchero* on her return trip, at one of the horseshoe river bends called La Bolsa, thirty-five miles north of Matamoros. The *Ranchero* delayed departure, arming herself with the two artillery pieces captured from Cortina and taking aboard a unit of Army Regulars to man the guns and defend the decks. Alerted, Ford's rangers and two troops of cavalry under Stoneman came up from Brownsville to patrol the La Bolsa vicinity, and wait. Over beyond the Mexican bank of the river, Cortina brought together a force, later estimated at from 200 to 400 men, and built a strong earthwork well-placed for the delivery of a raking fire upon the steamer when she tried to negotiate the acute La Bolsa bend.

On the twenty-ninth or thirtieth of January, with trouble thus prepared, and with Tobin's rangers pacing as escort alongside, the laden *Ranchero* shoved off to run the gauntlet.

Nosing into the bend on February 4, she met a furious burst of fire from Cortina's prepared position. The steamer's skipper, Captain Martin, was able to con so that his well-served guns came nicely to bear and to pin the attackers behind their earthwork. In the late afternoon during this completely unexampled amphibious engagement, Rip Ford took a beachhead. Crossing the river with forty-six rangers and using the riverbank as cover, he maneuvered his men upstream until they had fought their way past the end of Cortina's earthwork, flanking him. Then they charged, with six-shooters and the Texian yell. The enemy broke in panic. Their leader was the last to flee; Cortina emptied his gun at close range before he spurred away. Bullets struck his saddle, hit his belt and clipped a lock of his hair. Rip Ford, who wrote with a stiffness he did not employ in combat, recorded: "But for the obscurity, it being almost dark, the frontier pirate would have been killed."[68] Four days later the *Ranchero* came steaming safely to her mooring slip on the Brownsville levee and delivered her cargo at the office of M. Kenedy & Co.[69]

In the whole course of the excitement known as the First Cortina War there is a total lack of documented information as to the whereabouts or activities of Richard King. Neither he nor his family are mentioned as present in Brownsville at any time from September 1859 to May 1860. Henrietta King's half brother, Hiram Chamberlain, Jr., matriculated at Centre College in Danville, Kentucky, that fall; there is some indication that the King family accompanied him to Kentucky, and that during the trip Captain King bought some good Kentucky horses for shipment to Texas.[70] If the Kings were absent at the inception of the Cortina uprising, when they returned they must surely have gone directly to the Santa Gertrudis, where they remained until the troubles nearer the Rio Grande had subsided; it does not seem likely that the captain would have subjected his family to the risks of a return to Brownsville at that time.

As for himself, it would be difficult to believe that King did not make various trips to the river in the interest of M. Kenedy & Co.'s business at Brownsville, White Ranch, Brazos Santiago and up-river, during the violence. Yet his main concern must have been the protection of the isolated Santa Gertrudis. A Cortina raid there was clearly within the realm of possibility, and he doubtless stationed himself at the ranch ready to defend it. He must have been there early in December, though no record proves it, when Rip Ford came by the Santa Gertrudis on his recruiting way from Austin to Brownsville. King and Ford were fast friends: there is little reason to doubt that the ambulance, the supply wagon, some of the horses and some of the arms with which Ford had equipped his company when he arrived to fight came from Richard King on the Santa Gertrudis.[71]

By June of 1860, with Cortina gone south and with the river trade booming after several months of repression, King was back in Brownsville. Among many other things, he was busy filing claims against the United States government for damages suffered during the Cortina uprising.

In association with a lawyer named W. B. Chace, King seems to have taken charge of presenting claims not only for M. Kenedy & Co. but for at least seven other property owners up and down the river, whose ranchos had been wrecked by the raiding. For his own firm he stated that all boats and other equipment had been forced to remain idle during all the period of the Cortina disturbances, with the exception of the one trip of the *Ranchero,* and that as a consequence all trade had been diverted to overland routes between Indianola and Laredo, and between Corpus Christi and Rio Grande City, thus destroying the business of the petitioners, to their damage in the sum of $250,000.[72] The several other claims when added to M. Kenedy & Co.'s obviously inflated figure made a total of $336,826.21 in damages asked.[73]

The United States government did not even consider the claims when they were presented. Although there is a notation on the back of a Santa Gertrudis account book indicating that King and the lawyer Chace expected percentage fees from all claims collected, and although King certainly pressed the affair for a payment of monies to the petitioners, it is hard to believe that King thought the government would actually pay. He appears to have had another reason for presenting claims for damages, whether the government paid or not. These claims—and King made his own firm's fat enough to attract attention—served as pointed protests against the failure of the United States government to protect its own border. General Twiggs' stupid withdrawal of the Army from the Rio Grande had been the enabling cause of Cortina's depredations. The claims were a way of presenting a demand for better protection, of calling the government's attention to its responsibility. King held tenaciously to this idea of demanding protection or else reparation from a government that could give it. More than a decade later he would be heading a movement for the payment of much larger claims growing out of a continuing border violence.

As men looked about them in the year 1860, there were bodings of violence immeasurably vaster than a raider along a border river might ever stir. Rising far to the north and east of the Rio Grande, a black and storm-filled cloud shadowed the land. Studying it, men used the words "Secession" and "Civil War."

The two rivermen, Richard King and Mifflin Kenedy, were not blind to the waters ahead if the black cloud spilled its deluge. Like two good boatmen, they readied their craft for the roiling chutes and snags of floodtime.

Foreseeing the impossibility of replacing M. Kenedy & Co.'s steamers if war came, and aware of the vital rôle they might be able to play at a divided country's border port, members of the firm took careful inventory; Mifflin Kenedy went to Pittsburgh to order for immediate construction and delivery another big boat, to be named *Matamoros*,[74] as a teammate for the *Grampus II* on the outside Brazos Santiago run. At the same time he placed orders for two additional upriver mudskimmers, the *Mustang* and the *James Hale,* for future delivery so that if hostilities opened, the firm would command a flotilla of seven steamboats operating on a strategic border. During the latter half of 1860, the business of hauling trade goods along the Rio Grande was very good.[75] So was the prospect of hauling materials for war. The postmaster of Brownsville wrote in June: "Capt. King is here—He talks of going on the boats again—"[76]

Yet the boats were only one consideration in making ready for a looming storm. The ranching operation on the Santa Gertrudis needed shoring up to meet the rigors of the business weather ahead. Captains King and Kenedy doubtless had discussed it often: in November of 1860 they became partners not only on the river but on the ranch.

The Cortina raids, and the probability of more like them, had made Kenedy's pasture lands in the San Salvador del Tule grant a risky place for ranching. They were too near the Rio Grande. During the destructive sweep just before the battle of Rio Grande City, while Kenedy was standing guard as a captain of civil defense at Brownsville, Cortina had laid waste to the San Salvador del Tule rancho and scattered or stolen its livestock so that only a remnant was ever found. Kenedy had ordered his vaqueros to drive that remnant to safety farther north; all the livestock he owned, 1595 cattle and 87 horses,[77] were already on the Santa Gertrudis in the care of Richard King. Kenedy was still mightily interested in ranching, he could raise money for a further investment in it,[78] and a new partnership with his oldest and best friend, on property more than a hundred miles from the border, appealed to Kenedy in every way.

His entry into the Santa Gertrudis operation also solved problems facing Richard King who had not, since the death of Legs Lewis, consolidated titles to the lands upon which the ranch depended.

Henrietta King had property of her own, which her husband had begun to give her as soon as they were married. This property was mostly composed of livestock branded HK — but on June 28, 1859, Richard King had bought in his wife's name, so that the land was deeded to her, a one-half undivided interest in the twelve leagues of the de la Garza Santa Gertrudis grant owned by James Walworth.[79] At the time of Kenedy's entry into the ranching partnership, Henrietta King and James Walworth each held actual title to as much of the ranch's land as King himself, who owned only the three and a half leagues of the Rincón de Santa Gertrudis and a nearby smaller tract known as the Puerta de Agua Dulce.[80]

A new arrangement brought all titles together as property of a new firm styled R. KING & Co., established on the fifth day of December, 1860.[81] The Kings, pooling their separate interests, put into the firm their livestock, the ranch improvements, and land titles to the Rincón, the Agua Dulce, and one half of the de la Garza Santa Gertrudis. Walworth put in the other half of the big tract, possibly some cash, and probably his share of the King and Walworth livestock branded K. Kenedy came in with money and other consideration the amount of which is not now known, and the remnant of his livestock from the desolated San Salvador del Tule. The shares in R. King & Co. were divided three ways: three eighths to Richard King, three eighths to Mifflin Kenedy, and two eighths to James Walworth.

With this organization among friends thus strongly knit, the three steamboat skippers eyed the increasing portents of rough water ahead and divided their watches. Walworth, busy with the political aspects of the storm, became a Cameron County delegate to the Texas convention for secession. Kenedy stayed in Brownsville, close by the river, manipulating the boats of M. Kenedy & Co. with a sharp weather eye. King had moved his family from the Elizabeth Street cottage to the Santa Gertrudis, where all the Kings could be on deck while the captain made the ranch shipshape under the approaching cloud.

There were five Kings in the family that made its home in the ranch house on the Santa Gertrudis the year the Civil War came. A very blue-eyed small sister to little Nettie had arrived in Brownsville on April 13, 1858, and had been given the name of Ella Morse King. Then, almost at the very time of the move away from Elizabeth Street, a son was born on December 15, 1860, to Henrietta and Richard King. They named him Richard King II; when he had children of his own he would tell them that he was "born in a stagecoach while mother was hurrying to Brownsville."[82] Whether this was in jest or not, Brownsville was formally recorded as his birthplace. The captain's joy in a son and namesake is easy to imagine.

On the third of December the Reverend Hiram Chamberlain had made a note: "This day Captain King commenced packing up for a general move to the Rancho del Santa Gertrudis. I am truly sorry to part with them. But I suppose it is all for the best. This is a world of changes."[83]

The Confederacy's Back Door

ONE APRIL MORNING

in a red dawn more than a thousand miles from the Wild Horse Desert, guns of rebellion trained on Fort Sumter opened fire. The crack of the cannonade, the flash of bursting shell brought an end to the nation's sickness of foreboding and began the bloodshed of the Civil War.

The Rio Grande frontier, still in darkness of night when red dawn came to Sumter, was half a continent away from high councils of war, from drumbeats of great armies, from fields of decisive battle. But war, following an inveterate habit, reached out to find the contentious place along the far river.

More than a month before the gunfire at Sumter, Texas had proclaimed in convention at Austin—in spite of dissenting voices—its secession from the Union.[1] Two weeks before that, awaiting no proclamation, Ranger Ben McCulloch, as military commander representing the rebel convention, had led an armed force into San Antonio. Confronted by it, the antique Major General D. E. Twiggs, of rebel sympathies himself, had surrendered the entire United States Army Department of Texas to poker-faced Ben McCulloch without a shot. McCulloch's motley men, carrying loaded frontier rifles, had invested the government arsenal, taken possession of its stores. By the hurried terms agreed upon in Twiggs' bloodless capitulation to rebellion, loyal United States troops stationed in the state had been allowed "all necessaries for a march out of Texas" and had been promised an unmolested exit which, it was suggested, ought to commence.[2]

Lieutenant Colonel Robert E. Lee, arriving by Army ambulance in San Antonio on the afternoon of McCulloch's coup, looking about the Plaza in surprise, had inquired, "Whose are these men?"

"They are McCulloch's," he was told. "General Twiggs surrendered everything to the State this morning."

Lee's eyes filled with tears. "Has it come so soon as this?" Robert E. Lee asked.[3]

Texas lost no time organizing for war. A Committee of Public Safety moved energetically to mobilize the state, without waiting for the arrival of administrative machinery yet uncreated by the newly born Confederate government. Texans went remembering the days of their own Republic when Texas stood alone.

The convention for secession divided the state into three areas for military defense. It appointed as commander of the "Military Department of the Rio Grande" a man well-acquainted with that station. He arrived at Brazos Santiago in February, while the last units of United States troops were being evacuated north and while his Texas troops, about fifteen hundred of them, were reporting to the Rio Grande. The new commander's name was Rip Ford, Colonel Rip Ford.[4]

Disposing units of his volunteers, many of them his old Ranger hands, in salient positions over terrain he knew by heart, he conceived of his mission on the border—until a tangible enemy force appeared—to be the nourishment and protection of the Rio Grande trade and the cultivation of friendly relations with Mexican authority in preparation for unhindered pursuance of that trade during the war emergency. He issued orders accordingly.[5]

Among the many border men happy to welcome Colonel Ford to his post were his good friends Richard King and Mifflin Kenedy. He found them busy with their boats. Captain King came often from the ranch to confer with his partners and employees at the office on the Brownsville levee and aboard the shuttling steamers *Grampus II*, *Matamoros*, *Mustang* and *James Hale*. His firm was also operating a fifth boat called the *Mexico*,[6] mostly on the outside run from Brazos, where it aided the *Grampus II* and *Matamoros* in handling a first spurt of wartime business.

Early in February the *Mustang* had carried departing United States troops downriver from Ringgold Barracks;[7] the outside boats had aided in the evacuation of Fort Brown. When units of Ford's forces arrived from Houston aboard the steamer *General Rusk*, Captains King and Kenedy, both strong for States' Rights and Secession, had hauled Texans and supplies aboard M. Kenedy & Co. boats, flying the Lone Star flag to posts upriver.[8]

Examining his situation, Colonel Ford estimated the port and depot of Brazos Santiago indefensible in case of bombardment by

Union naval guns. On April 18, the Commander of the Military Department of the Rio Grande addressed a letter to Captain Mifflin Kenedy requesting the use of steamers to move to greater safety up-river all United States military stores which had been seized and held by Texans at the Brazos Santiago Army depot.[9] Colonel Ford recorded later that Kenedy and King, and the steamboats, "performed many useful purposes for the South."[10]

Except for spies and fugitive Southerners of Northern persuasion —the border called them *renegados*—who began to infest neutral Matamoros, enemies in the shape of Unionists did not appear. An enemy in another shape furnished the only action Rip Ford's forces found on the Rio Grande during the first year of war. It was almost like old times: Juan Nepomuceno Cortina came again.

Tempted by news of the *tejano* rebellion and reports of confusion in which raiding might go unpunished, the foxy Cheno came out of the Burgos Mountains in Mexico, gathered a crowd of rascals and headed for mischief. His judgment of an auspicious time for a strike could not have been more mistaken; his choice of a spot to strike, a fortified ranch on the site of what became Zapata, Texas, was entirely inopportune. There on May 19, 1861, he found himself forced into a fight with a newly recruited company of Texas State Cavalry composed mostly of Texas-Mexican rancheros under the redoubtable and later very important command of a Captain Santos Benavides, *un hombre todo valiente.* Benavides hit Cortina, whipped him, chased him across the river and, unlike United States troops or Texas Rangers hampered by orders not to cross the international boundary, Benavides continued pursuit. His rawhide horsemen ran Cortina into the town of Guerrero, Tamaulipas, where the raiders melted away.[11] The most unpleasant exercise furnished by Benavides convinced Cheno that times on the border were awry. He headed south, far into the south, and the Rio Grande with trouble enough went untroubled by the green eyes of Cheno Cortina for more than two whole years.

In July of 1861, the battle month of Bull Run during which the nation had its first plunge into the long blood bath ahead, a Union naval blockade was officially extended to include the Texas coast. The order brought rumors and alarms to the Rio Grande, but no Union ships. Boats of M. Kenedy & Co. steamed as usual, without hindrance.

While a wartime economy gripped at the border but no warring arrived, Captain King spent most of his time on the Santa Gertrudis managing the ranch, traveling to the river only when his presence was required by Captain Kenedy, who spent most of his time at Brownsville managing the boats. The third partner of R. King & Co., Captain Walworth, elected from Brownsville as a delegate to the Secession Convention,[12] stayed at Austin, while the third partner in M. Kenedy & Co., Charles Stillman, at work in his profit-taking web behind intricate business fronts and joint ventures,[13] kept himself in sensitive touch with the pulse of border trade and the prognosis of war, and from his offices in both Matamoros and Brownsville kept his partners informed.

The livestock affairs of the ranch on the Santa Gertrudis were complex enough to demand the constant care of a hard-driving ranch boss, quite aside from the multitude of Captain King's other daily concerns. Captain King was a busy man. In 1861, R. King & Co. owned something like 20,000 head of cattle and 3000 head of horses.[14] Military demands stimulated trade in horses and mules; these were marketable and ready assets of the ranch throughout the war. Though armies and civilians both needed beef too, the cattle market in Texas was a different story. Disruptions of war, but mainly the old difficulties of transporting beef from remote Texas to large centers of demand, brought a catastrophic drop in the market during the first year of the war. "The price of cattle . . . sunk to $2.00 per head without finding buyers."[15] Prices offered in New Orleans were better, but so many cattle were driven there in spite of the distance, the war-endangered roads and the problem of crossing herds over the Mississippi, that the New Orleans market became glutted and unprofitable to drovers from Texas.[16]

Ranch records are absent to show it, but there is every likelihood that R. King & Co. cattle were driven to New Orleans early in the war. It is just as probable that in later phases of the struggle R. King & Co. herds were driven to East Texas and even beyond the Mississippi for delivery as contract beef to Confederate army forces, but this again is not of record.

In general, such market as existed for R. King & Co. cattle during the Civil War was confined to a limited and troubled local demand and to the furnishing of contract beef for Confederate forces in the nearer vicinity of Santa Gertrudis. There is some evidence of a market for Texas cattle in Mexico; by August, 1862, prices had risen so that beeves were selling at Matamoros, "age seven years old, fat, at $11."[17] Such a market had its obvious limits.

Most of the marketable cattle on pastures at the Santa Gertrudis clearly would not make their way to any market during the war. Their unculled increase at war's end would be immense. That increase would create new problems of adequate pasturage, water, herd handling and control.

A wartime development of the hide and tallow trade offered little solution to the market problem. These wasteful ranching products might be produced in plenty, but war restricted their transportation and marketing — even though a leak in the Union blockade did make hides from Texas available to European buyers and M. Kenedy & Co. boats did haul hides to the mouth of the river for carriage charges of one dollar per hundred.[18]

Alert to enlarge ranching income, early in the war Captain King essayed a new venture. A salt shortage in the Confederacy made the extracting of salt from saline lakes on the boggy coastal prairies near the Santa Gertrudis a modestly profitable enterprise. He gathered and sold salt.[19]

There is no indication that he ever quit work on the expansion of the ranch, war or peace. Early in 1862, while he was somehow finding time in the midst of other business to act as supervisor of affairs on Charles Stillman's Laureles rancho east of Santa Gertrudis, Captain King proposed to purchase more than 90,000 acres of the Laureles tract, an acquisition which the ranch eventually made.[20] In the same year of 1862, R. King & Co. bought the William Mann ranching property of some 22,000 acres in the Casa Blanca grant north of the Santa Gertrudis, including the livestock and brands that went with it.[21]

A shooting war, which had not arrived on the north bank of the Rio Grande in spite of alarms and preparations, appeared without much alarm or any such preparation on the other side of the river in July, 1861: a war between factions backing rival candidates for the governorship of Tamaulipas, the *Rojos* and the *Crinolinos,* flared in Matamoros. When the *Rojo* candidate Jesús de la Serna was declared elected, the Tamaulipas legislature ordered a new election, alleging fraud on the part of de la Serna. His *Rojos* refused to accept the order, armed themselves, and bloody fighting began all over the state. In September, the *Crinolinos* managed to take possession of Matamoros, driving the *Rojos* to refuge in Brownsville—where they were allowed to regird and recruit under the leadership of Rip Ford's remembered comrade-in-arms, the hardy perennial General José María Jesús Carvajal. Re-entering Mexico and augmenting his force with *Rojos* from deep in Tamaulipas, on November 21, 1861, Carvajal put Matamoros to prolonged siege. Buildings were wrecked and burned. Gunfire, musketry, hand-to-hand fighting raked the streets. The siege was not raised until February 25, 1862, when Carvajal conceded failure and withdrew.[22]

This clash of *Rojos* and *Crinolinos* was a local manifestation of the disorder enveloping all Mexico. *Rojos* were of the general political complexion which supported the reform president, Benito Juárez; *Crinolinos* were a splinter of the reactionary clerical-military-land-owning coalition fighting Juárez's reforms. And while the siege of Matamoros was in progress, French, Spanish and English troops had added a new note to Mexico's chaos: a punitive expedition had landed at Vera Cruz to force debt payments from the riven, bankrupt nation.[23]

The Rio Grande found itself flowing between tumults on both river banks when another tumult, bearing no aspect of combat and working from vast distance, arrived to make the Rio Grande an actual theater of war.

This tumult appeared in the quiet, dusty shape of a wagon piled with cotton bales.

By late in the year 1861, the seaports of the Confederacy had felt the first choke of the Union blockade. At the same time, thousands of autumn-brown fields, which had been tended through summer-green by hundreds of thousands of strong black hands, stood harvested of thousands of millions of fluffy white bolls. In country sheds, in city warehouses and out in the pale November sunlight at the gin yards, the South's baled cotton crop of the war year 1861 waited, with the world waiting for it, and with no accustomed way to go.

Then across Texas on rough roads leading to Mexico, on long inland ways around the tightening coastal blockade, came wagons, a few at first like pathfinders, then a growing tide of rumbling wagons and creaking oxcarts carrying cotton to merchants standing on neutral ground offering foreign gold for the South's packed bales of white fluff.

The maintenance of a huge textile industry across an ocean at Lancashire, Bremen and Lyons depended upon that fluff. When its delivery was threatened by blockade, the powerful tentacles of trade had reached out, quick to seize at a neutral port where cotton might be delivered to neutral ships and sail, evading the stoppage of the American blockade. Entrepreneurs, brokers, agents and consuls from Europe had not been long in arriving at Matamoros, that town with the ancient aroma of devious and extravagant profit, to grease channels for a commerce which could offer gold or fabricated materials of war in exchange for cotton. To initiate this trade, European cargo ships had begun to anchor off the mouth of the Rio Grande in open waters just south of the river, Mexican waters, facing the beach at Bagdad. That forlorn knot of smugglers' huts had come suddenly and galvanically to life. It had grown riotous with promise. Its wharfage, built behind the river's mouth and inside its protection from sea and wind, stood piled with war goods lightered in from the vessels offshore and with bales of cotton waiting to be lightered to those vessels' holds for a voyage to Europe.

It would be difficult to believe that Captain King and his partners did not foresee the unique strategic situation of the Rio Grande and augur the arrival of the cotton boom the border named *Los Algodones.* Cotton entered like a thick and malleable wire of gold into the tangled skeins of wars on both sides of the river. And the mouth of the Rio Grande became the Confederacy's back door.

Captain King stood planted by fate in the middle of that door. The road the cotton took came across his pastures to the very threshold of his house on the Santa Gertrudis and moved to the decks of his steamboats on the Rio Grande. Captain King did not go to war:

the war came to him. It sought him at home. He fought his part of it on strenuous but familiar ground.

Before the New Year of 1862 arrived, he could stand on the watch-tower at ranch headquarters and see the cotton wagons moving south on the road across his pastures toward Brownsville. He could talk to the train bosses and the teamsters and the brokers' agents who stopped to camp under the trees by the Santa Gertrudis water, who came into the ranch commissary to buy camp supplies, who bought horses and mules and beef for the last leg of the long haul to the border.

Strangers bringing cotton from afar, to trade for the hard money offered at Matamoros, had their difficulties delivering the travel-stained bales into the hands of dependable brokers. Moreover, the passage of cotton into Mexico was soon restricted by taxes and attempted controls; official agents and buyers and collectors sent out by the Confederate government and the Military Board of Texas appeared with confusing orders and inconsistent demands and competitive instructions. From his point of vantage on the cotton road, Captain King quickly found himself an adviser of cotton-owning strangers, a counselor and assistant of government agents, a contractor for the cartage of cotton to the river,[24] and a speculative cotton buyer himself. By March, 1862, the ranch headquarters at the Santa Gertrudis was an official receiving, storage and shipping point[25] for the bales arriving from East Texas, Louisiana, Arkansas and finally as far as Missouri.

The boom went into full swing when the fighting of *Rojos* and *Crinolinos* ceased on the streets of Matamoros late in February of 1862. At its inception the Matamoros cotton market was dominated by English and German mercantile agents; the speculation was principally based upon whether or not the Lincoln government would seriously attempt a blockade of the Mexican port.

The excitement in the first flush of *Los Algodones,* the sudden appearance of the first Union blockader, the rôle of M. Kenedy & Co.'s steamers and even their carriage charges as lighters delivering cotton to vessels offshore are set forth with considerable pith in a communication from a partner to Captain King at Santa Gertrudis, written from Matamoros upon the day the siege lifted, February 25, 1862:

Yesterday we were all in great glee. Kenedy saw a hundred thousand in his vaults, twelve vessel[s] reported having arrived in the offing, with a prospect of shipping 20,000 bales of cotton at $5 per bale $100,000 upwards freight, would repay running expenses. Such was our imaginations, evening set in, a beautiful one too, when up comes another courier announcing the arrival of one of Lincoln['s] sloops of war the *Portsmouth* of 22 guns, a permanent blockader undoubtedly. The *Matamoros* was at the Mouth, with a full cargo for the *English Propeller.* The *Mustang* had left that morning with a full load of cotton. The *Matamoros* retreated back to Cobb's Rancho and is waiting orders. This knocks us, cotton and all. . . . You see, *all is vanity,* except cows and mares. A blockader cannot prevent them from having calfs and colts.

Yours truly
Chas. Stillman[26]

If the steamboats were to operate within range of the twenty-two Union guns, something had to be done. The measures taken by Stillman and Kenedy are outlined in another letter to their partner on the Santa Gertrudis, written from Matamoros two weeks later, March 11, 1862:

Our boats have ceased to run and two boats have obtained Mexican papers and doing what little lightering that is done. Yesterday we had a Junto, Judge Treviño, Ford, Kenedy, San Roman, Maloney, the English Counsul, Oetling and myself, we came to the conclusion to sell the boats to Hale y Co. Uhdy y Co. Oetling y Co. and they to obtain a Mexican licence to navigate their waters. The Military Commander to give Ford assurance that he will protect the property whilst in Mexican waters, and Ford swears that if it is molest he will blow them to that place we read of. So I am in hopes we shall see them with Turkey buzzard at their masthead in a day or two. A commission consisting of the English consul and some Mexican officials, are to wait on the Capt. of the Man of War, to ascertain if their property will be respected, or if he is blockading Mexico.

Affairs look dark ahead, prepare for squal[l]s, and keep your affairs snug as you can, and settle the Laureles affair before we are stampeded.

Yours truly,
Chas. Stillman[27]

Use of the neutral flag of Mexico referred to by the disrespectful Stillman as the turkey buzzard, and then the loaded query to the captain of the man-of-war asking if he were "blockading Mexico" in reality became the solution to the problem of keeping the steamboats running cotton — though they were not sold to the English or German firms of Hale, Uhdy or Oetling.

M. Kenedy & Co. found a neater solution. Sometime in the spring of 1862, the steamers went behind a front of Mexican ownership and registry which placed titles in the names of some of the firm's Mexican friends and business connections at Matamoros.[28] Flying the Mexican flag, without change in crew-personnel or in supervision by Mifflin Kenedy who soon had an office operating in Matamoros, the boats began a boomtime business hauling cotton under the noses of the Union blockaders.

Union naval officers demanded and were shown certificates drawn by properly sworn Mexican authorities documenting the ownership of all cotton leaving Bagdad in foreign bottoms. Though these certificates invariably indicated neutral ownership and the papers were invariably in order, the Union sea dogs at the mouth of the river were acutely aware of the obvious: the cotton was Confederate cotton, of great aid and comfort to that enemy, and ought to be seized.[29] To avoid any possible stoppage of trade on these technical grounds, all Matamoros cotton speculators by the summer of 1862 were taking technical precautions: they bought their cotton and transferred its title to the names of bona fide Mexican citizens and branded the bales accordingly, *in Texas,* before the cotton ever crossed the river. Blockaders were then unable to say, much less prove, that cotton moving through Matamoros and Bagdad was not the property of neutrals. The ancient skills of Matamoros merchants had not been acquired for nothing.

The skills possessed by Charles Stillman enabled him to form a conclusion which he expressed to his partner King as early as March 18, 1862, and which proved to be a most reliable forecast: "let me tell you cotton will be exported from Matamoros. . . ."[30]

In April, English and Spanish forces withdrew from Mexico, leaving France alone to pursue an adventure in empire—which would create new tumults to richen the wartime trade at the Rio Grande. In that same month of April, 1862, Union forces captured and occupied New Orleans, depriving the South of its greatest port and channeling cotton in a swollen flow over inland roads across Texas toward the unblockaded Mexican border. By October, 1862, the boom at Matamoros had entered a heyday. The mouth of the river was a port of world importance, the only Confederate entry for foreign supplies. Millions of dollars worth of munitions and medical supplies came through Matamoros in exchange for the cotton of the South.[31]

Although "King Cotton" was clearly the chief resource of the South, the means by which the South could finance war, the Confederate government fumbled away its opportunity to make cotton the potent economic weapon it could have been. Eighty-four years before the Civil War, an early and wise American on a war mission to Europe had confronted a smaller but similar opportunity and had grasped at it with more gumption. At Paris in 1777, Benjamin Franklin contracted to deliver from his country to France 5000 hogsheads of York and James River tobacco, by this contract adding to his country's war fund 2,000,000 most welcome livres.[32] The sum was no decisive factor in that war, but the contract was a realistic response to a fact: control of an export commodity which is in world demand and for which there is no substitute is a means of procuring money for waging war. Unlike the sensible Franklin, the high councils of the Confederacy chose to consider devious diplomatic potentials rather than the forthright financial advantages inherent to a unique supply of a commodity for which world trade competed. Jefferson Davis and his Confederate cabinet made a ruinous miscalculation at the outset. They entertained a chimerical fancy that the *withholding* of cotton from world trade could be made an effective short cut to winning the war, on the mistaken assumption that European textile mills if totally *deprived* of cotton would bring such pressure upon their governments that these would persuade the shattered Union to let the cotton states go in peace.

Only one member of the Davis cabinet took a realistic view. Shrewd Judah P. Benjamin urged that the Confederate government buy up all available cotton, ship it to Europe and warehouse it there as a basis for the credits necessary to waging war. But Confederate Secretary of Treasury Memminger, deluded by a chimera of his own which he called sound money, opined upon the unsoundness of any such device as foreign credits for cotton and Benjamin was overruled.[33] Benjamin then did what he could, arranging for purchases and exportations of cotton by private enterprise. There is little doubt that he had a hand, possibly a very active hand, in the first big transaction for the exportation of cotton through Texas when in 1861 Colonel M. T. Johnson of Tarrant County and Rhyne Bros., capitalists of North Texas, formed a partnership and bought all the cotton they could find in the North and East Texas market, more than three thousand bales, for which they paid ten cents a pound and for which they operated three hundred heavy wagons in transporting their bonanza to Matamoros.[34] Such ventures were more successful in lining the pockets of operators than in effectively furnishing the Confederacy with "sinews for war."

By the autumn of 1862, the Davis cabinet had come to understand that its war might be financed by cotton. Official agents were circulating through all the South, authorized to buy and sell cotton for profits which were to be used in supplying the army. For additional revenue, a tax of five dollars was imposed upon each bale. In 1863 the tax rate would be increased to a tithe, so that one bale in ten, or one tenth of the selling price of each bale, would be impressed by the government. Operating under no efficient administrative control, with no consistent regulation of channels for volume purchase or transportation or exportation of cotton, and implemented by politically appointed agents many of whom were incompetent or rascally, the Confederate government's handling of its one great economic asset was in a constant muddle and a frequent scandal.

The government's cotton agents competed not only with sharp private speculators but with each other, senselessly wasting public monies. In Texas there were cotton agents sent out by the state's Military Board to further complicate the scramble. Honest confusion joined with dishonest greed to cheat soldiers in the field of arms and supplies they might have had. One cotton buyer stationed at San Antonio was accused of "misappropriating" three million dollars.[35] The latitude allowed an official cotton agent and the opportunity officially granted him for growing rich while his countrymen died in battle can be seen in a form letter issued by a London stock company and addressed to the city's commercial circles on November 24, 1862:

We may state for the guidance of any friends who may be desirous of shipping to America that arrangements have been made for the dispatch of a vessel by us to the Rio Grande about the first week of December; that cost of freight and insurance on goods can be paid at the port of delivery. The services of the highly respectable firm of Messrs. Brown, Fleming & Co., at Matamoros, have been secured; also those of Mr. Redgate, Lloyd's agent, an expert in cotton, and who has been resident nearly forty years in Texas and Mexico. . . . a Mr. Bisbie, of the Confederate States of America, holds a contract from that Government whereby he is to receive 100 per cent. on invoice cost, payable in cotton at specie value, clear of all charges of freight, &c., for any goods he may deliver into the Confederate States. . . . He is willing to share same—say to the extent of 50 per cent,—with any houses who may feel inclined to ship.[36]

190

The cotton grab was by no means confined to the Confederacy. It overreached opposing armies and worked within the Union's lines. Charles A. Dana, writing from Memphis early in 1863, reported to the War Department in Washington that he found "a mania for sudden fortunes made in cotton, raging in a vast population of Jews and Yankees." Under Union permits this "vast population" was buying cotton low from planters in Union-occupied areas and selling high to textile works in New England. Dana himself happened to be partaking of the mania he decried: he had just put "$10,000, with a like amount from Congressman Roscoe Conkling and gone into partnership with a cotton expert." Expecting a fortune, Dana could at the same time piously write to his Secretary of War, "I should be false in my duty did I . . . fail to implore you to put an end to an evil so enormous, so insidious."[37]

Planters in the deep southeastern states were cut away from markets by the blockade. These planters sold their cotton, for there was no other outlet, to Confederate government cotton agents, and were paid, because there was no other money, in a Confederate currency which constantly depreciated. To dispose of the cotton thus acquired, the Confederate government fitfully depended upon the limited and uncertain operations of maritime blockade runners.

On the other hand, cotton producers west of the Mississippi were not constrained to sell to the government's agents for payment in the government's paper money. Western planters learned early in the war that their cotton could be hauled to the Mexican border where private speculators not only offered higher prices but paid in gold. Yet the Confederate government's policy displayed no evidence of understanding or wishing to understand that since the cotton growers of Texas, Arkansas and western Louisiana had a gold market for their cotton at Matamoros, they were not interested in selling to the government for Confederate money, on the government's own terms. Hard money in Mexico attracted cotton bales like a magnet —and gave government agents and their paper money an almost hopeless time.[38] Higher authorities in Richmond angrily fretted over uncontrolled specie finding its way from the faraway border cotton trade into the private pockets of farmers; officials denounced this foreign infusion of coin as a principal cause for the depreciation of Confederate currency.

The ineffective competition of such currency with the hard money of Matamoros evoked an order from the Confederate States Trans-Mississippi Department, dated October 14, 1862, and signed by the commanding general, Theophilus H. Holmes, *prohibiting* the exportation of cotton by anyone other than authorized agents of the Confederate government.[39]

This and subsequent orders concerning cotton, which emanated with various contradictions and cross-purposes from the seat of government at Richmond, from the Trans-Mississippi headquarters at Little Rock and from the Texas Military Board at Austin were never effectually enforced. The scramble went on, though the government did consider the cotton road to the Rio Grande vital enough to exempt from military service all teamsters employed on wagons carrying authorized government cotton. Even this exemption of teamsters was ineffectively administered; the roads to Matamoros and that town itself were thick with conscription dodgers and exempted teamsters illegally hauling private cotton.[40]

No confusion or seaminess could halt *Los Algodones.* At the beginning of the war, the market price of cotton in East Texas was around ten cents a pound.[41] The price at Galveston early in 1863 was as low as six cents a pound[42] and subsequent developments in the war doubtless brought it lower. Prices were even more depressed at the southeastern interior of the Confederacy where the blockade, the gradually gathering military gloom and the sinking of the currency sent prices paid to cotton planters on a downward curve from a few cents to fewer cents per pound. In contrast, the prices paid at Matamoros were in a climb during the whole course of the war. The following prices paid in hard money per pound of cotton delivered at Matamoros explain very clearly why neither government orders nor long roads nor any other difficulty could stem the flow of cotton to the Rio Grande:

August 1862	16 cents
Late in 1862	25 cents
April 2, 1863	36 cents
The year 1863	20 to 74 cents
November 1863	80 and 90 cents
The year 1864	82 cents (only one price cited)
The year 1865	68 cents to as high as $1.25 [43]

To correspond with these mounting prices there were the growing numbers of cargo vessels anchoring at the mouth of the river off the Bagdad beach. Sample counts recorded by eyewitnesses show:

September 1862	20 ships
March 1863	60 to 70 ships
March 1863	92 ships
Late in 1864 and early 1865	200 to 300 ships[44]

In return for the South's cotton, there came to Mexico to pass through the fine-fingered hands of merchants and "neutral" customs officers certain quantities of goods: cases of Enfield guns labeled with some nicety "Hollow Ware," barrels of gunpowder branded "Bean Flour," boxes of percussion caps bearing the legend "Canned Goods," cargoes of lead marked "Bat Metal."[45] Yet the authorities comfortably ensconced at the headquarters of the Confederacy's Trans-Mississippi Department some seven hundred miles from the Rio Grande showed an obtuse nonchalance, even disdain, for the mighty possibilities of the trade moving through the Confederacy's back door. The politico-military Southern Gentlemen at headquarters seemed to consider the Confederacy's back door a rather bothersome tradesman's entrance unfit for military use. Throughout the war the Department suffered a great lack of arms and equipment—and never deigned a well-organized attempt to exploit the ready uses of its ready back door. The high order of military intelligence displayed by the Department's command did not even consider that the back door needed protection. In the summer of 1862, with *Los Algodones* building toward a trade of world importance at the only open port then available to the Confederacy, Rip Ford received orders to abandon the line of the Rio Grande.[46] He was to move his troops northeastward in Texas to counter a threat of invasion from New Orleans. Ford obeyed orders, establishing his station at San Antonio, spreading his troops impossibly thin, leaving only a handful of his command to guard the whole border.

A somewhat less than formidable invasion threat materialized on the seventh of August when a Union force made a farcical attempt to take Corpus Christi from the seaward side and was driven back to its boats by a few home guards.[47] In a more serious move and mood, a large Union landing party closed on Galveston during October and the Confederate defenders gave up that port without a fight.[48] Galveston was nearly 350 miles up the coast from the mouth of the Rio Grande and its capture had no apparent effect upon *Los Algodones* — though mill owners in New England were urging their government in Washington to stop the flow of cotton to Europe.

Late in the year 1862, countermeasures were set in motion against the Union lodgment at Galveston. Major General John Bankhead "Prince John" Magruder, fresh from the Peninsula Campaign before Richmond, arrived to assume command of the Texas District and to enliven somewhat the military scene. In a combined land and sea operation on the last night of the year, Magruder sent out the Confederate "cottonclads," four old steamboats armored by cotton bales and manned by brave men, which steamed into a Union squadron off Galveston and handsomely routed it while Magruder moved by land and next day took the town, along with three hundred Union prisoners.[49]

Confederate forces were on their way back to the line of the Rio Grande: Magruder's estimate of the situation brought a temporarily quickened perception of the Rio Grande's military value. But the shake-up in command following Magruder's arrival in Texas deprived the Rio Grande of the one man best fitted to command there. Rip Ford was relieved.[50] His orders sent him, a fighting man, to ride a desk chair as Chief of the Texas Bureau of Conscription. In shunting John Salmon Ford to paper work the wasteful Confederacy wasted one of the most gifted field commanders and potential general officers that might have served the South.[51] He was replaced at Brownsville by a political brigadier general from Corpus Christi, the lawyer Hamilton P. Bee whom Richard King knew well as the administrator of Legs Lewis' estate. Bee assumed command in January, 1863, under Magruder's orders "to hold the Rio Grande at all hazards."[52]

A Confederate company of Texans on the march south as reinforcements to Ringgold Barracks late in 1862, camped at the Santa Gertrudis. They were hungry for fresh meat. When certain members of the company went to inquire about buying a beef, they were politely stalled by the ranch's brown-faced cowboys. Several requests to see Captain King were met with several unsatisfactory responses. The troopers had returned to their camp when Captain King himself suddenly appeared amongst them, "being satisfied, I suppose, that our company were Rebels and friends," said a Confederate veteran named Keepers, recalling it in later years. "We got the beef and spent the night there. The place impressed me as did the owner, as an oasis in a savage wilderness, where a man must be assured of the intentions of his visitors before he would meet them. Two cannon mounted in the top of the house also impressed me and strengthened my feeling that I had got out from under our Lone Star flag. The next morning we rode away to Ringgold Barracks."[53]

In those days of late 1862 when friendly troops had been almost entirely absent from the border since summer, Richard King labored under the responsibility of maintaining his own guard for the ranch, for the cotton stored there and for his family. "The disturbances of the time" — that phrase ancient to the Wild Horse Desert — had not yet become disturbing enough to keep Henrietta and the children from the captain's side.

As the more disturbing year of 1863 dawned, Nettie King was almost seven years old, Ella was nearly five, young Richard was two — and there was a baby sister at the ranch house built on the rise above the creek. A little girl had been born there on the twenty-ninth day of April, 1862. Part of her name was a memorial to the place where she was born; she was Alice Gertrudis King, with brown eyes like her mother's.

The new year 1863 found the prairies seared by months of drought. The lake behind the weedy earthen dam of the Tranquitas had so shrunk that it was margined with slopes of sun-hardened mud, dried in crackles around stems of yellowed sedge where water had once stood. The road across the prairies was a tan ribbon of dust. Powdery clouds of it rose from under the churning hooves of twenty-mule teams pulling tall wagons toward the empty horizon in the south; there were a dozen bales — six thousand pounds of cotton — piled on each rocking, dust-coated wagon bed.[54] The road from the Santa Gertrudis to the Rio Grande was marked with an emblem of the times: tags of white fluff were snagged on the thorns of the chaparral, where they hung graying, tattered reminders of far fields and blood-shed and purses of gold.

Vaqueros on the Santa Gertrudis moved herds to find grass where it grew thickest on the browned ranges and reported to Captain King the lessening number of watering places. Cotton trains moving south made dry marches and found dry camps. As the months of the year 1863 advanced, men and animals suffered increasingly along the lint-marked road. Drought shallowed the water in the Rio Grande and brought further concern to Captain King. His partner Kenedy reported from Brownsville that the *Mustang* and the *James Hale* were navigating upriver with greatest difficulty; cotton which made its way on the Rio Grande City road to the border had to be ferried laboriously across to Camargo and carted down the Mexican side of the river to where a steamer could lade. It finally became necessary to move most upriver freight by wagon, oxcart or muleback along the droughty river roads. The organization and supervision of these M. Kenedy & Co. overland cargo trains fell mainly to Captain King and made it necessary for him to leave the ranch often.[55]

A British military observer named Fremantle, on his way into the Confederacy from Matamoros, reported a rare rain and a short visit to the Santa Gertrudis during the dry spring of 1863. Colonel Fremantle wrote in his journal:

19th April (Sunday) At 1 A.M. this morning our slumbers on the bullock rug were disturbed by a sudden and most violent thunder storm. . . .

The rain lasted two hours; and at daylight we were able to refresh ourselves by drinking the water from the puddles, and effect a start.

But fate seemed averse to our progress. No sooner had we escaped from the sand than we fell into the mud, which was still worse.

We toiled on till 11.30 A.M., at which hour we reached King's Ranch. For several days I had heard this spoken of as a sort of Elysium, marking as it does the termination of the sands, and the commencement of comparative civilization.

We halted in front of the house, and after cooking and eating, I walked up to the "ranch," which is a comfortable, well-furnished wooden building. Mr. and Mrs. King had gone to Brownsville; but we were received by Mrs. Bee, the wife of the Brownsville general, who had heard I was on the road.

She is a nice lively little woman, a red-hot Southerner, glorying in the facts that she has no Northern relations or friends, and that she is a member of the Church of England.

Mr. King first came to Texas as a steamboat captain, but now owns an immense tract of country, with 16,000 head of cattle, situated, however, in a wild and almost uninhabited district. King's Ranch is distant from Brownsville only 125 miles, and we have been six days in reaching it.

After drying our clothes and our food after the rain of last night, we started again at 2.30 P.M.

We now entered upon a boundless and most fertile prairie, upon which, as far as the eye could reach, cattle were feeding.

Bulls and cows, horses and mares came to stare at us as we passed. They all seemed sleek and in good condition, yet they get nothing but what they can pick up on the prairie.[56]

Captain King was absent from the ranch for good reason. Important business was afoot. At Brownsville the three partners of M. Kenedy & Co. were negotiating a contract which would make them suppliers to the entire Confederate force stationed on the border.

The supply of troops in the Rio Grande sub-district of the Trans-Mississippi Department was in a jam. Contractors for military supplies on the border emphatically refused payment in Confederate currency and demanded specie or its cotton equivalent in the hard money market of Matamoros. The Confederate cotton agent in charge, a Major Simeon Hart, had not found it possible to acquire and deliver enough cotton to pay for the supplies being delivered to the troops by Matamoros contractors. Quarrels had mounted on both sides: suppliers were doubting the Confederate ability to pay for goods and were shutting off credit; Confederates were tiring of the profiteering gouges exacted by contractors. Yet one thing was certain: to maintain the troops on the border, the Confederate government had to get its hands on more cotton. Major General Magruder, not without heat, outlined the situation to the Adjutant and Inspector General at remote Richmond:

I have this moment received a copy of a letter from the Secretary of War, dated January 20, 1863, to Lieutenant-General Holmes, countermanding the orders of the latter in relation to the restrictions on the cotton trade [these were the orders prohibiting exportation of cotton by anyone except authorized Confederate agents], and, of course, repealing my orders on the same subject, . . . These instructions from the War Department may make it necessary for me to fall back from the Rio Grande and give up that frontier to the enemy from the difficulty of supplying troops there except through the means of cotton. I feel assured that this result could not have been contemplated by the honorable Secretary of War and I therefore hasten to Brownsville to examine into the state of affairs personally, before taking steps which may lead to such disastrous results. The loss of the entire trade would be the immediate consequence of the withdrawal of troops from the Rio Grande. . . . Major Hart, quartermaster and Government agent [has made excellent arrangements for the purchase of supplies by means of cotton]. He has pledged the faith of the Government for the payment of these supplies, and if this pledge is not redeemed these supplies will not be forthcoming. . . . I will of course seize cotton of individuals on the Rio Grande and use it, rather than fall back; but its impressment would create great dissatisfactions, . . .

I will . . . resort to impressments should all other means fail, taking care to impress the cotton of the largest speculators. Our money is valueless on the Rio Grande, . . . I have to request earnestly that I may be supplied with $100,000 in foreign exchange every alternate month to enable me [to pay and supply the troops there] the means heretofore resorted to having been disapproved by the War Department.[57]

At Brownsville, where he went about the middle of April to "examine into the state of affairs," Magruder

discovered that it would not be prudent to depend on any foreign house for our supplies, if we could procure them with equal economy and certainty from a house having the same credit and means, whose property was in our country, and, therefore, in our power, and King, Kenedy & Stillman, a house in Brownsville, having agreed to furnish supplies at lower rates than any house in Matamoros, I advised Major Hart to enter into a contract with them, which was done through Major Russell, quartermaster, C.S. Army.[58]

A contract making the three partners of M. Kenedy & Co. responsible for supplying Bee's whole force on the border was signed April 28.* To finance these supplies the agreement called for a delivery by the government to King, Kenedy and Stillman of five hundred bales of cotton per month for six months. The further terms were outlined in an official communication written by Bee's brigade quartermaster, Major Charles Russell:

In regard to the supply of troops on this line . . . by and with the advice of the major-general commanding I have contracted with Messrs. Richard King, Mifflin Kenedy, and Charles Stillman, of this city, for a supply of quartermaster's and subsistence stores for six months, commencing June 1 proximo, at an advance of 15 per cent. on the original cost and charges of the articles delivered, they receiving the cotton in the interior, providing the necessary transportation, and selling it on account of the Government, charging a commission of 2½ per cent. for selling and 2½ per cent. for advancing. These gentlemen are too well known to render it necessary to speak of their ability to comply with this contract.[59]

* The entire contract is shown in facsimile, Appendix VI.

Taking the Matamoros cotton price of thirty-six cents a pound in April and eighty-five cents a pound at the end of the year and arriving at a likely average value of sixty cents a pound, the 3000 bales to be delivered would be worth a total of something like $900,000—in gold, not in Confederate notes which at the time had already depreciated to four for one.[60] If the government managed to deliver all 3000 bales and the proceeds were entirely expended on supplies, the contract on the cost-plus percentages would bring about a fifth of the cotton value: $180,000, or possibly $60,000 for each partner. This rough estimate—no records survive to make any figures more exact—would not include added profits such as those derived from furnishing Santa Gertrudis beef, horses and mules as supply items, or receipts from the transportation charges for moving the cotton, or jobbers' markups Stillman might apply to the items he could furnish from his mercantile web—this last, not likely to be shared by King or Kenedy. Regardless of the exact proceeds in prospect for Captain King that war year of 1863, the contract he signed was for a big operation offering a big reward.

If the sum involved was large, so was the toil to earn it. The contract venture demanded of Richard King the sweat of his brow, for it was he who took charge of finding and delivering enough cotton branded CSA to cover the costs of the supplies the quartermaster called for.[61] His task might well have been impossible had not new cotton regulations come in force during 1863 whereby the Confederate government impressed cotton, taking a tithe of one bale in ten.

King and his partners were called upon to make heavy advances of supplies before the arrival of any cotton to trade: during the previous five months, the cotton agent Hart had been able to deliver a mere forty CSA bales to the Rio Grande.[62] On June 23, Brigadier General Bee was writing to Trans-Mississippi headquarters:

... allow me to say that the pressure of the contractors, King & Kenedy, on Major Hart is easily to be accounted for. Their contract did not go into effect until the 1st of June, yet as Major Hart had left the command on the Rio Grande without supplies, and with a credit perfectly prostrated in the market of Matamoros, it became necessary to call on these contractors for supplies for the month of May, and two months' supplies for the troops ordered to Louisiana, thus calling at once for three months' supplies, even before their contract commenced.

In closing this communication, Bee stated that for such advances made before the contract began, he "felt under obligations to the patriotic contractors."[63]

Through that summer and fall of 1863, Captain King was a hard rouster of government cotton, pulling it from depots farther north in Texas to the cotton station on the Santa Gertrudis and pushing it from there through the dust of a drought-withered wilderness south to the river. His partner Kenedy hustled the bales into Mexico, where he and his partner Stillman sold it and moved it, on the decks of their steamboats flying the Mexican flag, to the waiting holds of the ships anchored off Bagdad. And the supplies Bee's troops needed came steadily to the stores of Quartermaster Russell at Brownsville, on schedule.[64]

Bad times were on the way. Less than six months after writing orders commanding Bee "to hold the Rio Grande at all hazards," the changeable General Magruder wrote orders which set into operation a chain of events by which the Rio Grande was lost. Early in the summer Magruder grew concerned over a renewed activity of Union troops in Louisiana. The resultant orders from headquarters carried an old story: troops were to be stripped from the Rio Grande frontier and moved to counter a threat at the opposite border of Texas, five hundred miles northeastward.

Bee's concern fully matched Magruder's. While his troop strength was suffering drastic reduction, Bee was listening to foggy rumors that twenty thousand Union troops were gathering in New York for an invasion of the Rio Grande; Bee was worried enough to be hiring spies with New York contacts to check for information.[65]

It so happened that textile operators in New England did understand, if Confederate councils did not, the importance of an unplugged leak in a blockade. The governors of the New England states had persuaded President Lincoln that the leak at the mouth of the Rio Grande must be forcibly plugged. A military expedition for that purpose was mounting, though New York was not its staging area. Major General Nathaniel P. Banks, commanding Union operations in Louisiana, was feinting to lure Confederate troops to East Texas and at the same time preparing a force at New Orleans to steam to the mouth of the Rio Grande and stop the cotton trade.

The Confederate command seems to have had information of the enemy's plan, or at least strong intimations of it, and seems to have taken no steps whatever to defend the Confederacy's only open door to the outside world.

When autumn came, the lonesome General Bee was still at the Rio Grande, with just four companies of the Thirty-Third Texas Cavalry commanded by Colonel James Duff, one battery of light artillery, two siege guns at Brownsville, a few thin companies of mounted militia like that of Santos Benavides based upriver, and some bands of civilian home guards of doubtful dependability — all told, a total of not more than 1200 men.[66] Even Duff's cavalry and the battery were scheduled to leave the border. Feeling his isolation, worrying over his inadequate strength, concerned with his responsibility, General Bee got jumpy.

Since assuming command he had been troubled, more in mind than in the field, by the guerrilla plottings and prickings of a band of *renegados* based at Matamoros and led by one E. J. Davis, the future Scalawag Governor of Texas. Early in Bee's command some of Duff's troopers while "off duty" one evening had crossed the river at Bagdad, kidnapped Davis and his henchman, Captain W. W. Montgomery, hauled them to Texas, and promptly hanged Montgomery to a mesquite tree for his brutal murder of a respected *tejano* named Isidro Vela.[67] Bee had managed to bring Davis into custody before he too was hanged, and had returned him to the Mexican side of the river, with apologies to the Governor of Tamaulipas for the violation of neutrality in the kidnapping of Davis from Mexican soil. Davis had not stayed on Mexican soil; his guerrilla needlings had festered. By the autumn of 1863, Bee in his growing jumpiness had begun to fancy that Davis and his *renegados* and his bandit recruits were a large threat to the Confederate position on the Rio Grande.

At this juncture Juan Nepomuceno Cortina, that bad penny of the border, came back. He appeared suddenly at Matamoros with an important official position as second in command to Manuel Ruiz, Military Governor of Tamaulipas. Ruiz was a *Juarista:* so was Cortina if that was profitable, and it was. At the time, the fortunes of President Benito Juárez were at a low ebb. The French invasion had forced him and his cabinet from the capital and driven them to refuge in the northern provinces. Though the wily Cortina had no intention of ever being trapped with a loser, he still enjoyed adherence to the *Juarista* cause: it had, after all, rewarded him. He was *General* Cortina. Yet his friends were happy to note that he was the same winsome Cheno. He entered without delay into the fomentations the border expected of him.

Whether it was through the Union bribes of the *renegado* Davis, or through the Don Coyote charms of the newly returned Cortina, or whether it was an act totally unrelated to money from Davis or admiration for Cheno, a Texas-Mexican in command of one of Bee's militia companies suddenly mutinied and put the final jumpy touches to Bee's anxiety.

On October 26, Duff's cavalry units and the artillery battery were departing from the Rio Grande. To protect Brownsville, the army stores and magazine at Fort Brown, the cotton yard on the levee and the future of the Confederacy's border trade, Bee found himself left in town with precisely nineteen soldiers. To augment this forlorn guard, Bee ordered a militia unit which had been stationed at the mouth of the river and which had "done good service" to report without delay to Brownsville. This militia was a company of sixty Texas-Mexican recruits under command of Captain Adrian Vidal, who happened to be the stepson of one of Bee's supply contractors, Mifflin Kenedy. Neither Captain Vidal nor his company reported. Toward evening Bee sent Vidal a renewed order for immediate compliance, carried by two dispatch riders. While he awaited their return, Bee was informed "confidentially" that he was to be "attacked during the night by men from below, consisting of Vidal's company and renegades and deserters from Matamoros." A half hour later, one of the dispatch riders got back, shot through the face by a volley from Vidal's men. The other rider had been killed. Fearing the worst, Bee called out his nineteen troopers, alerted the Brownsville home guard and dispatched an urgent recall to Duff's cavalry which had encamped for the night on the Palo Alto prairie some ten miles north.[68]

Whatever Vidal's intentions may have been earlier in the day, he did not attempt the sack of Brownsville. Probably nervous over the escape of the wounded dispatch rider and the alarm he would raise, Vidal by-passed the town and led his troop into Ramireño, a rancho in the next bend of the river. As if he felt called upon to display qualifications for the new rank of quite a dangerous fellow, Vidal gratuitously hanged two men he captured at Ramireño, then gingerly stepped to sanctuary across the Rio Grande.[69] If he had any idea of imitating the pattern already created by Cortina, Vidal was a tinhorn. He had neither Cheno's guile nor Cheno's luck. Adrian Vidal was executed two years later for treachery in yet another army and his turncoat's shame was a sorrow to his family.[70]

On October 28, 1863, Bee reported:

I am confident that it was Vidal's determination to attack and plunder Brownsville, and I also believe that there existed a plan to aid the movement with the renegades and disaffected on both sides of the river, and that the plan was frustrated by the impetuosity of Vidal, who mistook by one day the departure of Duff's command. . . .

Under all these circumstances, I have taken the responsibility of retaining the companies of the Thirty-third ordered to the interior, and I shall keep them here until I hear from the general commanding.[71]

While the general commanding was using cornbread for brains and the brigadier on the Rio Grande tilting at wraiths of commotion, the Yankees arrived.

They came late in the gray afternoon of the first of November, riding a Gulf storm. Twenty-six transports[72] carrying 6998 Union troops[73] nosed in for the passage between Padre Island and Brazos Santiago. The roiled channel to the anchorage behind Brazos was too rough for navigation. The deserted look of the wind-lashed dunes in the dying light brought small comfort to assault troops waiting on heaving decks. They waited through the pitching blackness of the night; next day the storm held. At noon a landing boat managed to put a drenched and shaken party ashore to raise the Stars and Stripes on Brazos Santiago, but it was not until November 3 that troop units began to make their ways to the beach. Heavy seas pounded four transport vessels to distress. Landing boats capsized in the lunging surf. The "terrible coast" of Old Fuss and Feathers Scott retained its character. Handfuls of draggled troops stumbled from the water in defenseless disorder and not a dry round of ammunition came ashore. Horses and artillery were brought to the beach with immense difficulty. The sodden landing dragged on for three days.[74]

Weather was the only enemy to oppose it. Working with that weather, a hundred well-led men could have pushed the landing back into the sea. At that hour the Confederacy might have had a John Salmon Ford on its Rio Bravo; it found itself with a Hamilton Prioleau Bee.

About three o'clock in the morning of November 2, an express from the mouth of the river informed Bee of enemy ships lying off the Brazos bar. Before daylight he sent out two cavalry details of fifteen men each, one to scout from the mouth of the river, the other to patrol the vicinity of Point Isabel, to spy out the enemy strength and movement. Bee himself chose to remain in Brownsville, forming his estimate of events by rumor and report.[75]

He had his orders from Magruder. In case of an enemy landing in force, he must evacuate Brownsville and he must not allow military supplies or cotton to fall into enemy hands. During the day of November 2, while he waited for couriers and news from the coast, he issued orders in preparation for a retreat and set about organizing a wagon train for moving the quartermaster's stores from Fort Brown.[76] Somewhat vague arrangements seem to have been made for a steamer to ferry the contents of the vast cotton yard—thousands of bales stacked on the levee at a bend of the river on the upper edge of town —to safety at Matamoros.[77] That evening Bee received mistaken reports that a huge enemy force had already effected a landing on Brazos Island.

During the morning of November 3, while dribbles of Union troops were struggling through the surf with their powder wet, bug-eyed couriers came galloping to Bee with reports of Union cavalry crossings at the Boca Chica ford, of enemy sweeps into the Palo Alto prairie behind Point Isabel.[78] To the sound of blowing bugles and the long rolling of drums, rumor leaped through the town of Brownsville. Ten thousand drunken Negro troops were moving on the city. They had been seen three miles from town. They were led by E. J. Davis. He was coming to pillage and burn and put the town to the sword in retaliation for the hanging of Montgomery.[79]

A nervous tension which had been mounting in Bee for some time suddenly snapped. He lost his head. He cut short the loading of his supply train and at noon sent forty-five wagons hurrying out the road north from town. He dumped his siege guns into the river.[80] He ordered the destruction by fire of the military installations and remaining supplies at Fort Brown. Realizing that only a small part of the cotton had been moved to Mexico, he ordered torches thrown into the long rows of bales in the cotton yard. Then he mounted his horse and led his troopers to join the wagon train in hasty retreat from the rumored Union horde, abandoning the town of Brownsville to the flames he had set and the citizens to the panic he had caused. Bee was three days out on the Wild Horse Desert, almost to the Santa Gertrudis, before enemy soldiers marched under the pall of smoke from burning cotton and came into the alarm-glutted streets of Brownsville.[81]

The fires got out of hand before the general got out of town. Growing flame and wild rumor fanned a frantic reaction from the river-conscious border folk of Brownsville. They all made for a haven in Matamoros.

By a contagion of mob impulse, the streets leading to the ferry came alive with householders carrying possessions in their arms, trying to find a carriage, a wagon, any conveyance including a wheelbarrow, to move household valuables to the ferry. The end of the street which formed a cut sloping down the river bank to the ferry head was quickly choked not only with crowds trying to get themselves and their families across the river, but with a thickening clutter of clothes, bedding, trunks, musical instruments, bric-a-brac, furniture. In the melee to use the ferry, men had to force by threat of pointed guns a passage for women and children to the safety of the other river bank.[82] Owners of leaky river skiffs charged five dollars in gold for every passenger they carried, and there were not enough skiffs. The piles of household gear became a nearly impassable mass of goods in the cut above the ferry landing.

During this hysteria the flames at Fort Brown, whipped by the same winds dealing misery to the Union landing on the coast, caught at the roof of a building holding eight thousand pounds of condemned gunpowder purposely left by the Confederate retreat. It exploded with a sudden great roar and knocking concussion. A scantling nine feet long hurtled across the river and through the gable end of the Mexican customhouse. The force of the explosion shot firebrands high into the air and showered them down into the town. Buildings fronting on the river back of the ferry, among them the offices of M. Kenedy & Co., caught fire; so did the inflammable clutter of refugee goods on the river bank. Before the fires died, Fort Brown was destroyed, two city blocks were badly burned and the valuables the townsfolk had lugged to the ferry were mounds of ashes and blackened iron debris from bedsprings, stoves, pianos, sewing machines. As night came, the cotton on the levee upriver burned with a red glow under massive billows of acrid smoke.[83]

Darkness brought the murderous and drunken riffraff of the border from both sides of the river to sack and riot and howl unchecked through the streets of Brownsville. "Men were shot down in their homes, in their yards, and on the streets. . . . Stores were looted, residences plundered and it will never be known the amount of property carried away or destroyed or the number of lives sacrificed on that fatal day."[84]

Order was only partially restored by the time Major General Nathaniel P. Banks brought his Union forces into town on the sixth of November, without resistance. Brownsville was immediately placed under martial law, enforced by troops under the command of Major General N.J.T. Dana, and the town, with most of its Confederates "visiting" in Matamoros, settled itself to life and commerce under Yankee occupation. Some citizens, including Mayor Dye, took the oath of allegiance.[85] There were many border cases and border thoughts and border people in a border town like Brownsville where a border was signified by the width of a narrow muddy river.

Over in the garrison of Matamoros, the border character named Cortina was elevating himself to a new niche. Since his return to the Rio Grande, he had found occasion to make certain arrangements with a pair of pro-French Imperialist conspirators engaged in a plot to usurp the governorship of Manuel Ruiz. During the confusion at Brownsville following the departure of Bee, one of the conspirators, José María Cobos, recruited an insurrectionary gang. Upon the arrival of the Union troops, Cobos led his force across the river to join with his co-conspirator, Romulo Vila, at Matamoros. The insurrection, with Cortina's aid, overthrew the Ruiz government in a quick coup on November 6. On the morning of the seventh, Cobos and Vila ordered ex-Governor Ruiz shot. When the order was conveyed to Cortina, he made a startling reply. "No," he told the two successful conspirators. "You first—"[86] After a firing squad attended to Cobos and Vila, Cortina ordered Ruiz released from prison. But the engaging Cheno used the power all this magnanimity gave him not to restore his commander, Ruiz, but to "pronounce" in favor of the out-of-office *Rojo* governor, Jesús de la Serna, who lived in southern Tamaulipas. While the border awaited de la Serna's arrival and while the deposed Ruiz sought redress from the Juárez government, General Juan Nepomuceno Cortina acted as governor of the state. He enjoyed his work.[87]

The very great discomfiture of Texans at the hands of the invading *yanquis* added a piquancy to Cortina's enjoyment. One of his first official acts displayed his acute appreciation for the flavor of power. On November 9, General Banks over in Brownsville reported to General-in-Chief Halleck:

Affairs are quiet in Matamoros. Governor Ruiz is in Brownsville, Cortinas is in power, and messengers have been dispatched for Governor Serna, who resides 200 miles distant. The friendship of the Cortinas party for the American government has been signally manifested by his placing three Rio Grande steamers on this side of the river under our control. One of these, the *Matamoros,* is the only boat that can cross the bar.[88]

Flying the Mexican flag, under Mexican "ownership," the *Matamoros,* the *Mustang* and the *James Hale* were under the proper jurisdiction of Acting Governor Cortina, and his pleasure in turning them over to the enemies of *los diablos tejanos,* his pleasure in friendship "for the American government," must have been accompanied by at least one horselaugh.

The grateful General Dana, in command of all Union troops on the Rio Grande after the departure of General Banks, put the three steamboats of M. Kenedy & Co. under his own orders and soon had them at work hauling his troops and supplies.[89]

The Union invasion of the Rio Grande put Richard King, his ranch, his cotton and contracting affairs, his steamboats, everything he had including his life, into jeopardy.

Captain King and his family — including the ailing Reverend Hiram Chamberlain who at the age of sixty-six was holding a commission as chaplain in a Confederate border regiment[90]—were at the Santa Gertrudis during the debacle at Brownsville. Bee and his supply train arrived at the ranch on November 8; King's anxiety over the news Bee brought is easy to imagine. It is not improbable that King expressed himself to Bee at the time in some straight riverfront language.

On the way north, Bee's cavalry had been "intercepting and turning back all trains loaded with cotton; destroying by fire, from each load, a sufficient number of bales to enable the teams to cross the sand with the balance."[91] The big hurry "to cross the sands" before being caught by the rumored Yankee hordes resulted in a foolish and useless destruction of much cotton on the road. To protect the valuable bales, brought so far at such pains, some train bosses hid wagons in the lonely chaparral.[92] Many made caches of bales near the roadside, and left them. A great stream of half-empty cotton wagons—and of outraged profanity from mule poppers—moved back into the Santa Gertrudis for several days.

By November 12, Bee had pulled himself together and was writing in a report:

I propose to march in three days for Rio Grande City with all the available force I can gather.

I think a demonstration on the river essential at this time, to show that we do not intend to abandon that line, to encourage our friends, and punish, or at most keep quiet, our enemies. It will also serve to make safe the large trains of cotton now *en route* for Laredo.

I shall hold my position on the Rio Grande as long as it may be prudent —certainly until I am forced away by the Yankees.

I trust that recent events will induce the general to save every bale of cotton possible for the Government.

The confusion here is over, and the trains are all *en route* for Laredo and Eagle Pass.[93]

Down at Rio Grande City on that same day, November 12, a dispatch was being addressed to General Bee:

On arriving at this place, I found a large amount of cotton, public and private, coming here and to Roma, and, as I could not attend to it at both points, I sent out parties to bring all in here, and made arrangements with Don Rafael López, of Camargo, to receive it, pay duties on the other side, and forward it as fast as possible to Matamoros. As soon as possible I will report to you in full what I have done in the matter. I have also sent what Government stores I could from here to San Antonio and Laredo.

Of the population on the Rio Grande, there are but very few who will not use all arms we give them against us [Benavides here concurs with Bee's fears of disaffection amongst Texas-Mexicans], and those few I will soon have with me.

In all things be assured that I will do to the best of my ability. I shall leave to prospect on the movements of the enemy as soon as I have got the cotton and public property in safety.

I have with me 120 men, who can be relied on to the last.

I have the honor to be, very respectfully, your obedient servant,

SANTOS BENAVIDES
Major Thirty-third Texas Cavalry, Commanding[94]

A few months later, Magruder would be writing the Commanding General E. Kirby Smith at Trans-Mississippi headquarters to tell him:

Colonel Benavides has stood firm, and all his command, on the Rio Grande. I have written him thanks, and authorized him to dispose of 250 bales of cotton for specie with which to pay in part his men, who, General Slaughter informs me, are very poor, and have not been paid in six months.[95]

Union occupation slowed but never halted Confederate commerce across the Rio Grande. The measure to have ended it decisively would have been a real blockade of the neutral flag vessels plying from the neutral waters off the Bagdad beach, but this drastic step was one the Lincoln government could not afford to take. With the port at the mouth of the river still open to neutral shipping, the principal effect of the Union presence on the Lower Rio Grande was simply a diversion of the cotton trains westward to Laredo and Eagle Pass for a crossing to Mexico farther up the river beyond the reach of Union capture. Once upon Mexican soil, cotton moved without Union interference through the market at Matamoros, to the ships at Bagdad. In the first panic following the Union capture of Brownsville, the market at Matamoros suffered a sharp slump; two weeks after the arrival of Union troops, on November 21, cotton sold at Matamoros for twenty-eight cents a pound with few buyers.[96] The forced diversion of wagon trains to crossings upriver lengthened the time and added greatly to the costs and difficulties involved in exporting cotton and importing war supplies, but the traffic went on.

Circumstances forged two main keys for the maintenance of that traffic: Santos Benavides who protected the cotton crossings upriver and Richard King who kept the cotton moving in that direction. The Union commander at Brownsville was aware of these keys and tried to destroy them.

Upriver expeditions of Union forces, never large, were never successful. Drought conditions aborted the dispatch of large bodies of troops to the interior, both on the shoaly river and on the parched roads. When Union detachments tried to penetrate far from their base at Brownsville, they were frustrated by their problems of supply and by their ineffectiveness in the face of Benavides' vastly superior mobility coupled with his complete knowledge of every trail and every water hole over every reach of the Wild Horse Desert.

The *renegado* E. J. Davis came into his own when the Union invasion arrived; as a commander of cavalry he was sent upriver to capture Confederate cotton and destroy the rawhide riders who shielded the passage of the cotton trains. General Dana at Brownsville reported on November 21:

Colonel Davis left here this morning with 100 mounted men, two howitzers, 100 infantry in wagons, and 150 men [cavalry] and one howitzer, on the *Mustang.* I instructed him to use his discretion in proceeding as far as Rio Grande City. He expects to move 30 miles a day.[97]

Davis on horseback, with his hundred wagons, never saw Benavides and succeeded in rounding up just eighty-two bales of cotton. John C. Black, the infantry colonel aboard the *Mustang,* had even less luck. He got nothing but a creeping tour of the river. Dana reported it a month later:

The water in the Rio Grande is so low that it cannot be relied upon for supplies, with the means at our disposal. The *Mustang,* recently sent to Roma, 120 miles, could not reach there, but was occupied three weeks in incessant toil in arriving at a point 30 miles below there, and returning, with only 180 men.[98]

The *Mustang's* tedious progress may not have been due entirely to the unreliable waters of the Rio Grande. There were some lighter aspects of war on the border which seemingly escaped the purview of Union visitors. When Colonel Black returned to Brownsville, his report commended the officers of the *Mustang* as "capable and accommodating gentlemen in their line of business"[99]—yet these gentlemen were in the hire of the Mexican "owners" who still operated under orders from a staunch Confederate by the name of Mifflin Kenedy. The *Mustang's* speed while serving Union troops might have been slightly impeded for reasons best known to the gentlemen who were handling the boat. Further, there is little doubt that the capable and accommodating gentlemen were not averse to listening for any military information aboard, which could have been of use to a certain office in Matamoros, and beyond.

In its first month on the border, General Dana's entire force managed to lay hands upon "about 800 bales" of cotton, no very brilliant reward for the pains of a large military expedition. On December 2, Dana wrote his superiors that "2500 bales of cotton have been crossed over the river within the last two weeks," but he added hopefully "that trade is about stopped now this side of Laredo."[100] To stop it further, Dana moved outside the realm of military operations; he hired border thugs and killers to terrorize the cotton roads.[101] In December he wrote the United States vice consul in Monterrey, "I desire to make the road from San Antonio to Eagle Pass and Laredo so perilous that neither Jew nor Gentile will wish to travel it. Please make this known, confidentially only, *to good, true and daring men. I wish to kill, burn, and destroy* all that cannot be taken and secured."[102]

A hundred twenty miles away, across a thirty-mile desert, stood a key station in the Confederate cotton traffic operated by "a rebel agent, who knows all about their trains, and who manages most of them."[103] General Dana had dispatched spies and troops to probe this festering thorn and found "that there is now in the vicinity of King's ranch a body of 150 well-armed and well-mounted Texans ... very much on the alert"—odds very much against Union cavalry, operating from 120 miles away, using jaded Union horses. Dana worried the problem until midnight Christmas Eve; then he wrote to his chief of staff suggesting that the situation could best be faced from a base at Corpus Christi.[104] But as he wrote Union cavalrymen were at the Santa Gertrudis.

Captain James Speed, leading a troop of sixty-odd, about half of them Mexican recruits, had orders to reconnoiter seventy or eighty miles toward "King's ranch." At Las Animas the captain had learned the ranch was temporarily unprotected. The possibility of capturing —or killing—the infamous "rebel agent" was more than he could resist, orders or no orders.[105]

Three days before Christmas, a rider had reined a sweated horse at the ranch headquarters gate. The rider wanted to see Captain King. He was a friend.

"Captain," the friend said when they were alone, "tonight a troop of Yankees are coming to your ranch. I know this. They say they are coming to arrest you. I came to tell you."

The old border grapevine — information gathered by friends from the river, the towns, the lonely roads, the enemy camps — was dependable. The captain had to decide, fast.

He had no force on the ranch to resist a troop of cavalry; he might have had, but that day he was caught without it. Earlier in the year he had helped raise a mounted company of Confederate home guards to patrol the ranches and roads of the vicinity. Composed mostly of his own hard riding *Kineños* and commanded by his own ranch foreman, Captain James Richardson, the company was not large but it was well-mounted and it could fight. The day King needed it most, it was away on other business.

In the circumstances, armed resistance was risky anyway. He thought of his ranch people, his own wife, his children, their grandfather. Henrietta was seven months pregnant; a quick flight from the Santa Gertrudis, over rough and exposed roads with four little children, invited tragedy. On the other hand, his family and all his noncombatant ranch people stood a good chance of being left unmolested in the security of their home, if he himself was away when the enemy came and the ranch offered no resistance to search. It seemed to be a chance he must take.

While the best horse he had was being saddled, Captain King sent for the faithful ranch hand Francisco Alvarado, the man who had built the first rough shacks at the cow camp a decade before.

"*Alal, ven pacá, Francisco,*" the captain said, very quietly. "Francisco, you go and sleep at my house and take care of my family. I have to leave now and I don't know when I can return."

When the captain had spoken to his family, he came out of the house with his black hat pulled down shading his eyes, and he walked to where his horse stood saddled, with the guns.

"You take care of my family," the captain said. His black beard moved as he spoke. The two men who were to ride with him were mounted, waiting. The captain swung to the saddle and his people watched the horsemen ride out the gate. The road they took wound through shadow toward the darkening line where the winter sky met the earth in the south, toward the river.

Francisco Alvarado went into the house of the captain. *La Madama* told him secretly why the *dueño* had gone, and what might happen. She told him to be careful, and to let her know if he saw anything.

Nightfall came. *La Madama* herself placed a cot in the hall where Francisco Alvarado could rest while he watched. It was a long night.

In the silence of dim daybreak many hooves clattered. There were far yells, then the pop of a shot. Francisco Alvarado heard the wooden wall splinter and a bullet whine. Rifles opened fire with a cracking loud rattle. Francisco Alvarado jumped unarmed to the door and threw it open. He stepped into the ghost light on the covered porch in front of the open door and he shouted with the bull strength of his lungs.

"Don't fire on this house! There is a family here—"

A ball smashed into him and he fell dead on the boards of the porch floor. Booted soldiers, their blue coats black in the dawnlight, scuffed across the porch with cocked guns, into the open door. At an officer's command, men lifted up and carried the body of Francisco Alvarado through the door, into the parlor, laid it in front of the fireplace, lit a lamp—and saw they had not killed the man they came for.

Pointing guns, troopers shoved past the white defiant face of the pregnant woman, past the stone gray face of the old man standing ramrod straight and silent at the woman's side. A child cried in another room. The wife and the sons of Francisco Alvarado came to bend down over his body in the lamplight.

Every cranny of the house was searched. Probing sabers ran through the mattresses of the beds. Alien hands did not spare the personal effects in the pregnant woman's room.

Unable to find their man, the troopers turned their search into a ribald plunder of the house where he lived. Men rode horses through all the downstairs. They smashed mirrors, china and windows, and wrecked furniture. They grabbed clothes from trunks, coverings from beds, hauling out what they fancied and could carry.

Horses and mules were rounded up for a drive. All adult males caught on the ranch — four Anglo-Americans and many *Kineños* — were thrown into a prison pen. A lieutenant came to take Hiram Chamberlain.

"You don't want me." There was ice in the eyes of the Rebel from Vermont. "I am an old man of sixty-seven and a minister of the gospel."

"I will speak to the captain," the lieutenant said, backing down. He did not take Hiram Chamberlain.

The raiders held the ranch until Christmas Eve. They left in a sudden great hurry, without loading any captured cotton, when unidentified horsemen were reported in the vicinity. Before the raiders rode away, Hiram Chamberlain was summoned to the Yankee captain.

"You tell King that if one bale of cotton is carried away from here or burned, I will hold him responsible with his life," the leader blustered. "Colonel Davis is in camp at the Bóveda below here and some more troops will be paying you a visit soon. When they do, you are going to think all hell has broke loose —"

The brag was empty. Richardson's company or a part of it arrived at the ranch that night or next morning. Hiram Chamberlain wrote later, "Friends came to our aid."

Day dawned bitter cold to light a sorry Christmas at the Santa Gertrudis. Henrietta King was helped into a coach, with her father and her children. Not knowing where her captain might be or how he fared that day, knowing only the look of the fresh earth over the grave of Francisco Alvarado and the havoc in her house, she felt the wheels begin to move carrying her away. The coach with its outriders took the turn of the road north, away from the border, to the Nueces.

"The disturbances of the time" had come to King's Ranch.[106]

At the home of friends in the town of San Patricio beyond the Nueces, on the twenty-second day of February, 1864, Henrietta King gave birth to a healthy and strong baby boy. Remembering a scene, with the lamplit body of a brave servant stretched on the hearth of her violated house, remembering a soldier who pointed out the place for the foundation stones of that house — perhaps remembering a letter, asking her so long ago if she could feel a soldier's blood circling in her own veins — Henrietta King from childbed flung her own defiance. She named the boy she held in her arms Robert E. Lee King.

As soon as she was able to travel, she went with her father and her five children in a coach over the long road to the safety of the city of San Antonio, to wait there while her captain fought his war and her war to the finish the Lord had in store.[107]

Her captain was not idle. What it had cost him in spirit to ride from his ranch leaving the protection of his family to others, he never said. But that ride to the river marked an arrival of full maturity in the personality of Richard King. A formidableness, by which men ever after remembered him, at this time entered into the look of his eyes and changed the set of his massive 39-year-old shoulders. During the next eighteen months, while the Confederacy died slowly of its accumulating wounds, Rebel Agent King was a rough and tough rider in rough and tough times. The sun burned his face dark so that his pale eyes seemed paler. The black broad-brimmed slouch hat he wore turned gray with dust. The dirt of the roads in the wind coated his scuffed boots, rusted his sweaty clothes, ground into his worn spur leathers, gritted his lengthening black beard. Never averse to broaching a barrel or a bottle, he damped his Wild Horse Desert gullet with whiskey when he found it and the time. He kept the cotton trains rolling past Yankee patrols and brigands, fought thieves that stole his cattle and horses, delivered beef and supplies to Confederate troops, and served for awhile as a private soldier, with blood in his eye, in Richardson's company of black-hatted Rebel centaurs.[108]

It is not known how long he stayed across the river when he rode from the ranch on December 22. It seems likely that he caught up with one of the wagon trains he was operating and that he accompanied it to the border at a point like Rio Grande City, then moved down the Mexican side of the river to the office of Partner Kenedy in Matamoros. He undoubtedly found couriers by which he communicated with his family and his ranch; it is probable that he was not across the river for more than a few days.

There were hopeful plans in the making.

The merchants in the border trade were calling upon the government of Texas, not the Confederacy, to send Rip Ford back to the Rio Grande to clean the Yankees out. Forced diversion of the cotton and war supply trains to such distant upriver crossings as Eagle Pass was expensive as well as dangerous; there was also much bother with officials of the upriver states of Coahuila and especially Nuevo León in arranging the duties and the unmolested passage of goods into and from the State of Tamaulipas.[109] Another unsatisfactory feature of the Union occupation was the lack of the M. Kenedy & Co. steamboats which had been so convenient in carrying cotton downriver and in lightering to the vessels off Bagdad. The Yankees were using these boats for their own purposes[110] and even talking of buying them from their Mexican "owners."[111]

The merchants of Matamoros, who never looked with lack of emotion upon a peso lost, were ready to take measures. They were disgusted with Hamilton Bees and Prince John Magruders. The disgust was felt in Austin. Governor Pendleton Murrah was going to put units of the Frontier Regiment into the field if the Confederate States did not act.[112] The only commander considered capable of driving away the Yankee plague and restoring trade to its former profit was Rip Ford. Prince John was moved to official action.[113] On December 22, while Captain Speed's Union cavalrymen were riding hell-bent in a raid on the Santa Gertrudis, Magruder's adjutant general was composing confidential orders to Colonel Ford:

> You will create the impression among all persons, your men as well as others, that you are coming to Indianola, via Goliad, to meet the enemy, and, after you have left San Antonio, you can strike off to the west. You will be very particular, and you will not let a soul know of your intended movements.[114]

With official indorsement of the "Cavalry of the West" in hand,[115] Ford began a gathering of troops and a shaping of plans. On December 27 he wrote General Magruder from San Antonio: "I have already addressed a communication to Colonel Benavides...When I reach the neighborhood of the Rio Grande, I shall receive reenforcements from the other bank. . . . I shall send Col. H. Clay Davis to organize and have them ready. I shall send Col. E. R. Horde to Captain King's ranch, to procure mules, pack-saddles, &c."[116] News of the Santa Gertrudis raid reached San Antonio. Ford acted without delay. "Companies were forwarded to the Nueces as fast as they were mustered into service" to protect this exposed flank.[117]

Early in January, 1864, commands were changing both at Brownsville and at Matamoros. Dana was moved to Matagorda Bay and Major General Francis J. Herron arrived to take charge of Union forces on the Rio Grande. Across the river, the change of command was noisier and more picturesque: by means of a squeeze play on the politically orphaned *Rojo* Governor de la Serna and by means of a violated agreement and two-day battle with the militarily broken *Juarista* Governor Ruiz, General Juan Nepomuceno Cortina nimbly climbed another rung and named himself Governor of Tamaulipas, a position he held at Matamoros for the next eight months.[118]

South Texas, already gripped by an unrelieved two-year drought, was punished during the winter of 1863-1864 with weeks of record-breaking cold. A series of harsh dry northers racked the prairies and lashed the coastal plains. Temperatures were so low Galveston Bay froze over. In leaving the border, General Dana was almost iced in at Point Isabel. He reported on January 7, "I am detained here by a furious norther, which has prevented any communication with Brazos. I have been waiting now for three days."[119] Bitter cold coupled with unremitting drought curtailed all movement across the Wild Horse Desert; bone-chilling winds, dry camps, and scarcity of grass and browse worked extreme hardship and privation upon men and their beasts.[120]

The weather caused a phenomenon afterward referred to as "The Big Drift." Tens of thousands of cattle from Central and North Texas, with no fences across the open ranges to hold them, put the freezing cold winds to their backs and drifted far south before the blasts of the northers, hunting for warmth and for grass. Immense herds moved unchecked to the shores of the Gulf. A wartime shortage of help made it impossible for owners to find their stock and drive it back home; the drifters stayed unclaimed. They and their increase were destined to multiply vastly the numbers of cattle on the

South Texas ranges and to become a profitable resource to South Texas stockmen at the end of the war; the northers that caused "The Big Drift" were not such ill winds as they seemed at the time. But, during the war winter of 1863-1864, men were unable to foresee any good in gaunted cattle with strange brands drifting into the country, consuming the last stubbles of browned grass, standing around shrunken water holes, on pastures unable to sustain the stock already there.[121] "The Big Drift" brought many cattle to the Santa Gertrudis and further worry to Captain King.

Material aid to Rip Ford for his liberation of the Rio Grande was not promptly delivered. Ford's official correspondence indicates that he had to labor mightily to acquire the meager supply and transport he managed to gather before he left San Antonio.[122] In the middle of February, after six weeks of recruiting, of wangling and wrangling to arm, mount and equip his volunteers, Ford was ready to start south.[123] On the march he was not long in making his militiamen into something like rangers.

Late in February, Ford with a few of his companies pitched camp on the San Fernando Creek not far from headquarters at the Santa Gertrudis. There Ford "found Capt. King serving as a private in Capt. James Richardson's company, . . . He did his duty well, if the testimony of his officers can be taken."[124]

Santiago Richardson, his *Kineños* and their boss—who served with them when he was not with the cotton trains—were busy at the time countering a band of Union irregulars under a Captain Balerio who was in the vicinity gathering beeves to feed Yankees. One of Ford's companies led by one of Ford's old ranger hands, Matt Nolan, joined with Richardson's riders and whipped Balerio out of the country.[125] A little later, two other companies of Ford's troops "had an affair with a body of men who had come in the neighborhood of Capt. King's ranch. Some were killed, and a few were made prisoners. At Paistle ranch they captured about 50 men, many of them Mexicans, who were released under promise of returning to their homes.''[126] Ford kept a station of men near the Santa Gertrudis and with this protection in the area, King was free to spend more of his time at a distance from his ranch, moving the cotton trains and delivering Confederate supplies.

Presumably the original Confederate contract with M. Kenedy & Co. was filled before Bee retreated from Brownsville.[127] When Rip Ford came into the country "Frank Campbell and his partners were authorized to furnish supplies from Mexico," at cost plus twenty-five per cent. Apparently the arrangement was unsuccessful and Richard King was on hand to make an offer. Ford recorded that Campbell and associates "were superseded by King, Kenedy & Co. by order of Maj. Gen. Magruder.''[128] If there was a contract, it has not been preserved. Whatever the terms were, Charles Stillman was a party to the arrangements. In these, King evidently undertook to find cotton and deliver it in Matamoros to pay for the required supplies, mostly subsistence items. Kenedy was in Matamoros, finding supplies and furnishing Ford with vital military information.[129]

King found it immensely difficult to get cotton from the Confederate Cotton Bureau, which was channeling most bales branded CSA to supply regular units at the interior and finding none to spare for a border militia like Ford's. Also, much of the CSA cotton that did cross the river was being grabbed and attached there by merchant creditors of the Confederacy who had previously delivered war goods and had not gotten themselves paid. In this tight, the patriot Stillman called for cotton or else cash in hand. He was not supplying anybody at any risk of losing any money and he backed out—leaving King to whatever device he could contrive to supply Rip Ford.[130] King did it. To find the funds, he had to develop a nose for hidden cotton: he and Ford depended mainly on searching out and collecting and selling the considerable quantities cached and abandoned in the wilderness during Bee's retreat. To keep the bales they got from being attached by the Confederacy's creditors in Matamoros, King probably had to ship cotton privately, under guard, and sell it under his own name as a private operator. He managed somehow to deliver what his friend Ford had to have.[131]

On March 12, 1864, Colonel Santos Benavides, defending cotton trains, whipped and drove back downriver a Union force which had penetrated to Laredo. Rip Ford with several of his companies set out across the Wild Horse Desert to join Benavides and effected a juncture of forces on the river by April 17. Ford wrote, "The country was then suffering from a terrible drought. The passage of troops was almost impossible."[132] From Laredo, Ford marched down to Ringgold Barracks at Rio Grande City, where he established a "Headquarters for the Expeditionary Forces" and mapped his plans to take the lower river from the Yankees. He based these plans on the complete intelligence he gathered concerning the Union positions and troop strength around Brownsville. "Capt. Kenedy sent valuable information; so did other gentlemen."[133] The merchants of Matamoros became pleased enough with Ford's presence to send him some of the aid they had promised.[134] "While at Ringgold Barracks arms were purchased out of the secret service money furnished Col. Ford."[135]

In June, Ford probed downriver as if he were leading a ranger "scout." Moving in the back country he knew so well, he joined with a unit of his command which was camped about twenty-five miles north of the river at a place with the fetching name of Como Se Llama, where there was a dependable well. There his troops, numbering about two hundred, butchered and jerked beef for campaign rations. They loaded it to pack mules, swung the rest of it to their saddles, and moved south toward the river. On June 25, at a rancho called Las Rucias twenty-four miles above Brownsville, Ford made contact with an outpost of about 250 Union troops. He carefully came at them from downriver, interposing between them and their Brownsville base. In the sharp fight that followed, Ford's men behaved exactly like rangers: the Union companies were stormed from their positions and driven across the Rio Grande, with several killed and wounded. In the break for Mexico, Ford took thirty-six prisoners and some wagons and horses. His own losses were three killed and four wounded.[136]

He expected prompt reaction from Brownsville where he knew five thousand troops were stationed. Yet none of them came out to meet his riders in the chaparral. Instead of pressing unduly, Rip Ford went slowly back upriver again and allowed his victory at Las Rucias to sink in on the Union command.

It did. General Herron at Brownsville, busy mostly with building a narrow gauge railroad bed and laying rails from the dock at Brazos Santiago to White Ranch on the river, hoping to ease the thorny problem of transport for supplying his garrison,[137] decided that he must either withdraw his upriver outposts, or else he must be reinforced. Reinforcements were not about to be granted him; he withdrew.

The single fight at Las Rucias shrank the area of Union occupation to the town of Brownsville and the port of Brazos Santiago, and the roads that connected them. Simply by his sharpshooting presence and his carefully spread screen of riders commanded by men who knew the country, Rip Ford chess-played General Herron out of the rest of South Texas—then moved in on him.

Without accurate intelligence of Ford's real strength, feeling only the pressure, Herron prepared to pull out of Brownsville and move his forces toward their threatened supply base on the coast—while Ford's friends on the lower river kept him thoroughly apprised.

John S. Ford

On July 21, Ford led eight hundred men to within eleven miles of Brownsville, had a brush with some of Herron's men and followed them as they fell back toward town. Four days later Ford moved up to the very edge of Brownsville and faced a Union force four times the size of his own. After "a good deal of long taw firing," late in the afternoon Ford withdrew. His approach so alarmed Herron over the safety of his communication with the coast that he ordered Fort Brown evacuated and went into camp eighteen miles downriver.[138]

Not quite nine months after the Union landing that brought panic to Bee, Rip Ford rode into Brownsville unopposed, on July 30, 1864. His entire "Expeditionary Forces" were composed of about twelve hundred mixed volunteers meagerly equipped. Ford himself was ill from the effects of a bad bout with fever—either yellow or typhoid—and during all the later phases of his campaign he had to be "frequently helped to mount his horse."[139] Yet nothing stopped him.

Confederate cotton and war supply traffic was immediately resumed through Brownsville. Wagons swung straight south again, instead of west. "One material object in view, in undertaking the expedition," Ford wrote later, "was the reduction in the price of articles purchased in Matamoros and carried to the Confederate States by way of Eagle Pass, the difference was about fifty per cent in favor of the direct route, by King's Ranch."[140] To facilitate communication with that key point in the operation of the wagon trains, Ford quickly issued orders establishing a military courier service, with stations for changes of mounts, from Brownsville to the Santa Gertrudis.[141]

Rip Ford's arrival in Brownsville brought a grin above the black beard of Richard King. The weather widened that grin: not long after Ford settled to headquarters at Fort Brown, the drought broke. Rains fell in torrents. They washed the gray from the chaparral, turned the tan burned earth to rich wet brown, filled sweetwater sinks and holes and tanks brimming across all the Wild Horse Desert, brought tender shoots of springing green, soaked the dust of the roads to quags of mud and raised the trickle between the banks of the Rio Grande to a wide tawny swirling flow — fit for the churning paddles of loaded steamboats.

The initial confidential orders for the Rio Grande Expedition were "to burn and destroy any steamers on the Rio Grande." In March the Confederate command had ordered Ford to recapture the M. Kenedy & Co. steamers "if possible."[142] On August 9, the *James Hale* was still in Union hands[143] and so was the *Matamoros* a month later.[144] Yet it is evident that the Mexican "owners" did regain possession and use of some or all of M. Kenedy & Co.'s boats by the end of 1864 or early in 1865. Ford recorded later that "the boats reaped an unusually rich financial harvest. But for the services rendered by these boats it would have been a difficult matter to have procured the landing of Confederate supplies at Matamoros upon terms as fair as those granted by M. Kenedy & Co."[145] The Union forces had brought in a few steamboats of their own; in August Ford's men had captured one named the *Ark*.[146]

Working from his Brownsville base, Ford's task was to keep the Yankees pinned downriver and at the same time to keep a sharp but diplomatic eye upon the doings across the river. Rip Ford was the man to do it, yet the Confederate high command showed its esteem for his gifts by sending first one and then another brigadier general to rank him and to take technical command of his troops. The brigadier who stayed, James E. Slaughter, proved brave, inept and unable to cope with Ford's level counsel; in spite of animosity from departmental headquarters and many meddlings, Rip Ford by the respect he commanded on the spot continued to exercise the actual leadership of the border's Confederate units.[147]

After rolling up its unused railroad and stacking its rails, a reduced Union garrison no longer commanded by Herron dug in at Brazos Island and at the old shantytown of Boca del Rio which had acquired a new name, Clarksville. The Yankees clashed with Ford's men in frequent skirmishes, but no major show of strength developed from either side. After a few weeks, a touchy but fairly fixed stalemate set in, with the Rebels using the Brownsville-Matamoros-Bagdad route for trade and the Yankees glowering and plotting from Brazos Island.

Across the river, as usual, the doings were somewhat more elaborate. Ford had arrived to find his old foe Cortina the governor of Tamaulipas, but had encountered from him more co-operation than difficulty in establishing workable arrangements for the passage of Confederate goods. Then, three weeks after Ford rode into Brownsville, a new force had sailed in to knock Cortina's co-operation on the head. French men-of-war landed French marines at Bagdad, to take over the border trade.

By the questionable grace of Napoleon III, a French army and a strong reactionary element in the war-shredded land below the Rio Grande, the Austrian Archduke named Maximilian sat enthroned as the Emperor of Mexico. That country's elected president, Benito Juárez, was a fugitive in the mountains of Durango; though he carried with him the buried hearts of the Mexican people, outwardly his only support during that autumn of 1864 consisted of scattered bands of *guerrilleros,* a few liberal *jefes politicos,* a few exiled intellectuals and a few opportunists like Governor Cortina of Tamaulipas who still found profit in *Juarista* patronage.

As a *Juarista,* Governor Cortina understood the meaning of the French appearance at Bagdad. Imperialist forces of Maximilian, cutting a swathe to the northern borders, had just taken Nuevo León and Coahuila. Tamaulipas was next. A French general named Dupin would soon be moving up with an army from Victoria; the Imperialist Mexican General Mejía would soon be closing in with an army from Monterrey. Governor Cortina understood that as a *Juarista* his days appeared numbered.

Unable to deal with the French commander advancing purposefully from Bagdad and unwilling to deal with the *tejano* commander sitting too-wisely in Brownsville, Cortina made a deal with the *yanqui* commander planted forlornly at Brazos.

Through the willing offices of Leonard Pierce, Jr., United States Consul at Matamoros, the agile Cheno worked out a superbly Cortinesque solution to his problem of escaping subjection from an emperor. It was a veritable flower of the imagination: Cortina would use his Matamoros army to capture Brownsville for the Union and be rewarded with a commission as a brigadier general in the Army of the United States! As a patriot, he reserved the right, of course, to resume his former allegiance to Juárez when winds blew more favorably. The fatheaded commander of Union troops on Brazos, one Colonel Day, entered into the plan and promise of it all; Cortina forthwith sent a brigade of his Mexican troops across the river to Brazos Island, to lure Ford from Brownsville so that the town might be left exposed to attack straight from Matamoros. For several reasons, Ford was not lured and the attack did not develop. After a confused set of marchings, countermarchings, crossings, recrossings, a certain amount of shooting and a great deal of rainy weather and hard feeling, Cortina gave up his plan. In the first place, higher authority in the Union command disapproved of Juan Nepomuceno Cortina as a brigadier general in the United States Army.[148]

On September 22, Cortina made a kind of official peace with Ford when he invited his old antagonist to cross the river for a talk. Ford went, and wrote later that "They talked, and arranged everything."[149] There existed a curious personal regard between these two enemies who tried to kill each other in the field. During Cortina's raids into Texas before the Civil War, Ford had shown Cortina's mother an unfailing courtesy and protection; when Ford was campaigning toward Brownsville in the spring of 1864 and his wife had arrived in Matamoros to await him, Cortina had come to Mrs. Ford gallantly, proffering aid and protection.[150] Meeting face to face on the Mexican bank of the river that day in September, Cortina and Ford expressed a mutual appreciation. They exchanged the *abrazo,* the formal Latin embrace of amity or affection.[151]

Four days later, amidst cheers from the populace, the able General Tomás Mejía entered Matamoros with an army of two thousand Imperialists. Cortina did not fight, he joined. In doing so, he took pains to send messengers to Juárez assuring the president that this acknowledgment of an Emperor was *pro forma* only, and that he would return to his true allegiance when circumstances permitted. One of Cortina's colonels, Servando Canales, with lesser officers and about two hundred men, refused to switch with Cortina and escaped to Brownsville—where they sold their firearms to Rip Ford. Canales and his followers then moved upriver on the Texas side, to recross into Mexico at Guerrero and reorganize as loyal *Juaristas* in the field.[152]

Mejía distrusted Cortina. To try his obedience, he ordered him to clean out Canales. Cortina did, with such vigor that his former colonel never forgave or forgot. Yet this was the only service Cortina was asked to perform for the Emperor. Mejía remained unconvinced. General Cortina was reduced to skulking around the edges of Imperialist power, watching for an opening, biding his time.

With Mejía in control at Matamoros, *Los Algodones* swung into a hectic new high. The Imperialists, seeking revenues for their government, were careful to encourage the cotton trade and the commerce in war supplies. Yankee cotton speculators, rubbing shoulders with merchants of Matamoros, foreign brokers and Confederate agents, joined in the resurgent boom. The muddy streets of Brownsville and Matamoros, and the honky-tonk tent and shack town of Bagdad were crowded with freight wagons. The choppy waters off the Mexican beach were crowded with new numbers of cargo ships. Many of these ships were Yankee-owned, though flying neutral flags. Confederate privateers had by this time made the Stars and Stripes risky colors for commercial shipping, but did not deter Yankee ship owners from a trade in cotton for New England mills.

The mouth of the Rio Grande in late 1864 and early 1865 presented a queer spectacle. Union, Confederate, Imperialist and quasi-*Juarista* armies sat encamped within a few miles of each other, too busy trading to fight. Mars stumbled over the cotton bales and moneybags, and loosed the grip on his sword.

The policy of the Confederate cotton bureau became more confused than ever,[153] but cotton somehow continued to make its way, whether bearing the brand of CSA or that of private ownership, to the holds of the scores of ships plying from Bagdad. The world price of cotton reached astronomical heights which have never been equaled; cotton factors at Matamoros made new fortunes.

During the last months of the Civil War, Richard King was in a position to recoup any losses he may have suffered during the Union occupation of Brownsville, and to make a great deal of money besides. How much he did make, no one knows. He did it buying and selling cotton, supplying Confederate troops, running wagon trains and steamboats. He rode a tide of good fortune during a tragedy of war. He rode it in plain view, unlike many of the border operators around him, and all men understood clearly he was a Rebel who trimmed no loyalty for any expediency's sake. He was as ready to take a risk as he was to take a reward. He took both. The Civil War did two things to Richard King. It gave him one of the most formidable characters on the frontier. And it brought him the big stake, in gold from Matamoros, which enabled him not merely to weather hard times of reconstruction after the war but to make the ranch on the Santa Gertrudis into the great enterprise it finally became.

With the death rattles of the Confederacy plainly audible, with peace rumors raking the nerves of the high-flying speculators at Matamoros, the General-in-Chief of all Union armies, Ulysses S. Grant, in February, 1865, dispatched a personal emissary, Major General Lew Wallace, to Brazos Island to see what might be done to shut off the international intrigue and trade at the Rio Grande. A conference between local Confederate and Union commanders, arranged by Wallace at Point Isabel on March 11, 1865, did nothing to curtail either intrigue or trade on the border, but it did bring a military truce, when the contending parties both agreed that further bloodshed on the far edge of Texas could not much alter the course of larger events.[154]

Wallace's truce was in effect on the ninth of April when the relentless course of those larger events brought the Civil War to an end. Yet—if the firing at the Confederacy's back door was slow to kindle, it was last to quench. Not even Lee's surrender joined to Wallace's truce could keep the inveterately contentious place from another fight.

Early in May there had accumulated at Brownsville a considerable quantity of cotton branded CSA. Yankee speculators cast speculative eyes across the river and persuaded the Union commander at Brazos to attempt the capture of Brownsville and the cotton. The speculators believed that the Rebels, having lost their war and heard the news, would not defend the town and, further, that the Union quartermaster would see fit to sell the captured cotton very cheaply as "perishable contraband," to the profit of all good and victorious Unionists concerned.[155]

The plan took no account of Rip Ford who still sat at Brownsville, caring very little about the fate of CSA cotton but a great deal about any violation of the pledged word of the Wallace truce.

On the afternoon of May 12, 1865, as Ford dined with his superior, General Slaughter, a courier from an advance post came to them with a dispatch reporting sixteen hundred Union troops under Colonel T. H. Barrett on the move from Brazos toward Brownsville.

Ford asked Slaughter: "General, what do you intend to do?"

Slaughter replied: "Retreat."

Ford said: "You can retreat and go to hell if you wish. These men are mine and I am going to fight."[156]

That evening he gathered the force he could — desertions following the news of Lee's surrender had thinned the garrison to about three hundred men. Next morning they mounted and marched down the river. At Palmito Hill that afternoon, Ford found his outpost company skirmishing with the advancing enemy. Before the Confederate troopers executed their carefully given orders for battle deployment, their commander made them a short speech.

"We have whipped them before. We can do it again," Ford said.

The troopers yelled "Hurrah for Old Rip!" and galloped for their stations. From there they layed into the Yankees, who broke and ran. The pursuit lasted seven miles, to the ford of Boca Chica, where Old Rip called his men to a halt.[157]

The last shot in the last battle of the Civil War, May 13, 1865, is said to have been fired by a fourteen-year-old drummer boy, who let fly with a musket at the flash of an exploding shell in the growing dusk on the dunes by Boca Chica.

"Boys," Rip Ford said, "we have done finely. We will let well enough alone, and retire."[158]

IX Sole Owner, Rancho Santa Gertrudis

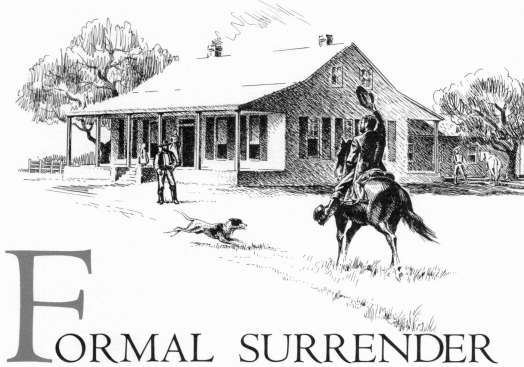

FORMAL SURRENDER

of the Confederacy's Trans-Mississippi army on May 24, 1865, brought a cessation of hostilities in Texas but did not end strife on the Rio Grande. Across the border, the contending forces of Juárez and Maximilian were still locked in a bloody grapple, while in Texas a hated occupation army arrived to administer martial law and Reconstruction. The deep troubles of two nations, one with a war ended and one with a war yet to end, scraped and tangled at each other along the muddy river.

Many Rebel officers, soldiers and government officials hurried toward Mexico bitterly intent upon escaping the rule of victorious Yankees and the rumored personal reprisals that rule might bring. Most of the fugitive, irreconcilable Confederates entering Mexico offered their arms and services as mercenaries to Maximilian, knowing the Union's hostility toward him and hoping to put in another lick against the Yankees yet.[1]

Twisted into the national and international tensions along the Rio Grande were the confusions of the border's war economy. It had fattened on the great boom of *Los Algodones* during the blockade; when that blockade was removed, the whole lower valley of the Rio Grande faced an inevitable comedown. As hostilities ended, considerable quantities of cotton were at the river or in transit toward the border, still seeking the markets of the world through Matamoros; speculators caught with this cotton bent a frantic energy to realize on their investments before the South could grow another crop. Unlike the rest of the Confederacy, the southern tip of Texas was tied to the hard money of Matamoros. If this indicated an escape from the utter ruin caused by the worthless paper currency elsewhere in the South, it no less spelled dependence upon the infirm state of affairs in a Mexico struggling for its life.

Military, political and economic considerations brought the far border of Texas to the attention of the highest authorities in Washington immediately after the surrender of the Confederate armies. Lieutenant General Ulysses S. Grant judged the situation in Texas critical enough to demand the presence of his top cavalry commander, Major General Philip Henry Sheridan, and a force of some 25,000 troops.[2] The display of heavy force was ordered into Texas for several reasons. Prominent among them was a lingering suspicion that the contentious inhabitants of Texas were not yet chastened by events of the war; the truculent "Little Phil" was expected to apply a firm brand of Reconstruction to such Texans as might stand in need of it. He was further expected to prevent Rebels and their arms from crossing into Mexico, to irritate and pressure Maximilian's Imperialists at the border by any means short of war, to encourage and abet the *Juarista* cause at the border by any means short of active aid in the field,[3] and to put the definitive clamp on the yet unstanched cotton trade at the mouth of the Rio Grande.

A strong Union force marched into Brownsville at daybreak on May 30, 1865, to find that the Confederate forces of the area had already been disbanded, either to go home or to Mexico, as they wished. Their arms and ammunition had already been passed across the river, sold to Imperialists. In all of Texas there was little of the former military establishment to take over. Reporting it to Grant, Sheridan called the Trans-Mississippi surrender "for the most part a swindle," and fulminated against the perfidy of Rebels who would "plunder" the Army of the United States of its rightful spoils of war.[4] Neither harsh words for Rebels nor official representations to the Imperialist commander at Matamoros, General Tomás Mejía, brought any Confederate war matériel back across the river. Nor did the Confederate friendship for Maximilian, and the Union ire it aroused, make Reconstruction easier. The war and its aftermath on the border cooked a slumgullion stew of many bad bloods, of Rebels against Yankees, of Imperialists against *Juaristas,* of white men against Negro Union troops, of gringos against "greasers." Brigandage and lawlessness hotly peppered this mixture of many animosities; the Rio Grande seemed never to find an end to its inveterate violence.

Richard King went to Matamoros when the Confederate armies surrendered. Like every other prominent Rebel on the border, he preferred to watch events from a vantage point safely outside jurisdiction of the arriving Union occupation. He had actively supported rebellion throughout the whole course of the war, but when the war ended and the rebellion was clearly lost, it was not in his character to let rancor obscure common sense. He had too much at stake in Texas. Prudently—but conveniently—across the river from Brownsville, he waited to see what amnesty terms the victorious Union would offer.

Richard King's friend Rip Ford, who had been appointed Commissioner of Paroles for the Confederate troops in the area,[5] became the prime factor through which former Confederates received amnesty when the fighting was done. Though he was still ill from the effects of the wasting fever he had caught during his campaign in 1864, Colonel John Salmon Ford made himself as useful at the advent of peace as he had been in war.

Only a few days after Ford had given Union forces a last drubbing at Palmito Hill and retired to Brownsville, Union officers under truce had ridden into town to pay him a call at his home. With the courtesy a professional fighting man feels for his own kind, Ford had treated his visitors cordially, served them an eggnog, and taken them on a tour of Matamoros.[6] His lack of malice, and the respect in which he was held both by his erstwhile enemies and his former comrades-in-arms, made him a natural point of contact where opposing views might meet and have some chance of resolution.

Level heads and generous natures showed themselves both among beaten Rebels and victorious Yankees. When Major General Frederick Steele arrived at Brownsville early in the summer of 1865 to command the Union occupation forces on the border, he sent for Rip Ford. Later Ford wrote:

He [Ford] came to the American side, accompanied by Capt. Kenedy, Capt. King, Maj. Felix Blucher, Mr. Vance and others. They attempted no concealment of their adhesion to the Confederacy and their readiness to renew their adhesion to the Constitution of the United States. Gen. Steele was kind and conciliatory. He said: "My opinion is that the easiest and safest mode to reconstruct a State is to use its representative men in leading the people back to their allegiance." All of the Confederates accepted the situation. They averred that they would observe the terms of parole because honor demanded it. "General, we are now at your service in any matter involving the public good. If you desire information on any subject, couriers to convey dispatches, men to face any danger menacing the country, means of transportation, supplies or any thing in the line of your ordinary duty, we stand ready to respond to your call. We wish it distinctly understood that we reserve our right to act for ourselves in political matters. In that connection we can not be used." The proffered offer of service was accepted. A good understanding was arrived at. In a short time the firm [to] which King & Kenedy belonged was performing their accustomed duty. The promoters of disturbances were ferreted out and arrested. When the District Court convened at Brownsville, after the war, nearly all classes agreed to serve on juries. Captain Kenedy was foreman of two grand juries. . . . The leaven of renewed allegiance had penetrated the masses and borne fruit.[7]

To renew allegiance, the Amnesty Proclamation of the President of the United States made it necessary for a former Confederate to take an oath, an oath to support and defend the Constitution of the United States and to abide by the laws freeing slaves. There were, however, certain classes of Confederates—notably those who had held high office in the government of the Rebellion, those who had left the service of the United States in order to enter the service of the Confederacy, and those who owned taxable property valued at more than $20,000—who were declared ineligible to take the oath. These must make special application for amnesty, have their cases reviewed by proper Union authority, and be pardoned directly by the President of the United States.

As an owner of property valued at considerably more than $20,-000, Richard King found it necessary to apply for presidential pardon. Exactly when this was granted is not on record. There is a letter written by Richard King at Brownsville on September 15, 1865, addressed to Major General Giles S. Smith, commanding at Brownsville, which reads:

General, I beg leave, respectfully to apply to you for possession of my dwelling house, situated on Elizabeth Street in this city, and now, I believe occupied under military authority by a tenant, placed there probably to protect it from injury. As it is not in good repair, I need possession in order to complete the necessary improvements. I have delayed this application until this time, as I wished first to be apprised of the departure of my family from San Antonio, where they have for some time resided, but as I now learn that they are on their return to this place, I desire to make the house habitable for them as soon as possible. It is my intention to resume my residence in Brownsville, as a citizen of the United States, obedient to the law of the land and to the constituted authorities. I say this candidly and frankly, and I am persuaded that you will believe me.

The letter is countersigned "By order of" Major General Steele:

Respectfully referred to W. W. Gamble, Custom House Collector. This property is not in the military authorities, but is abandoned property, and Mr. King comes under the $20,000 clause of the Amnesty Proclamation. Mr. Gamble will take such action in the case as he deems proper and just.[8]

Former Rebel King was not only naturally impatient to have his family back with him on the border again, he had every reason to be anxious for restoration of his rights as a citizen in order to take care of the business affairs that pressed upon him. The formal wording of the letter to General Smith indicates that Captain King had help in drafting it. Whether or not the hand of Rip Ford shows here, it was in fact Ford who paved the way to amnesty for his friend King. His friend was grateful. Something about the way he showed it was divulged for the first time in a letter written to the *San Antonio Express* nearly twenty years later:

After the war closed between the North and South, in 1865, an old and widely known and respectable Texan, who had commanded a Texas regiment in the Confederate Army, returned to his home broken in health and fortune. He was for two years too much prostrated by sickness resulting from the hardships, fatigues and exposures endured in the field, to admit of his prosecuting any business. He had a wife and eight children. When all his scanty means were exhausted, when the rent of the house in which he lived was about to fall due, and when the outlook was as gloomy as it could possibly be, aid came unexpectedly, and from an unknown hand, and the wolf was driven from the thresh-hold. The agent of the landlord came around to say that some arrangements had been made, but of the terms of which he was not at liberty to speak, by which no rent was due, or to be paid in the future; and in a few days a banker called to say a sum of $250 had been deposited with him for the sick Colonel, but that he could not give any information as to who had made the deposit. At the beginning of every succeeding month a similar sum of $250 was placed in the hands of the banker for the invalid Colonel, and this state of things went on with the regularity of clock work for the two years of invalidism and disability. This deed of benevolence was performed by a rich man, . . . Capt. Richard King, . . .

Colonel Rip Ford, now of Austin, was the other party to the transaction, and the details given were derived from the lips of a grateful daughter, in conversation with a daughter of mine, who communicated them to me.[9]

When the Civil War ended, affairs on the Rio Grande rather than on the Santa Gertrudis demanded the immediate attention of both Richard King and Mifflin Kenedy. The ranching business of R. King & Co. seems to have been left in abeyance while the steamboating firm of M. Kenedy & Co. was put in order after four complicated years of border war. Richard King spent most of the first eighteen months after the surrender of the Confederacy at work in Brownsville with Mifflin Kenedy, reorganizing the boat business. During this time, King presumably lived at the refurbished cottage on Elizabeth Street with Henrietta and the children.

King and Kenedy had lost two partners. Sometime before the spring of 1865, Charles Stillman had withdrawn from M. Kenedy & Co. No record makes clear when, why or upon what terms Stillman left the business. A part or all of his interest in the firm had been taken over, sometime during the war, by James Walworth. And at Austin in April of 1865, Walworth had died.

By the terms of his will filed at Austin on April 24, his entire estate was left to the widow, Jane M. Walworth. Walworth's joint holdings with King and Kenedy made an immediate settlement with Mrs. Walworth a prime item of business for the surviving partners. On May 6, 1865, less than two weeks after Walworth's will was filed, King and Kenedy paid Jane M. Walworth $50,000 cash for her husband's interests in both M. Kenedy & Co. and R. King & Co., a settlement in which Mrs. Walworth expressed her "entire satisfaction."[10]

King and Kenedy then set about a complete reorganization of their affairs, first on the river, then on the ranch.

The process of refitting their steamboat company to a profitable post-war operation was a fourfold task: the boats had to be brought out from behind their wartime fronts of Mexican ownership and the devious system of accounting and leakage of profit these fronts had created; new boats had to be bought to make new operations efficient; the firm had to shore itself up against any competition threatening the monopoly which M. Kenedy & Co. had enjoyed; and above all, there was the obvious necessity for good relations with the military administration and the politicians of the Reconstruction regime.

Soon after their arrival at Brownsville, Union occupation authorities seized the *Matamoros, Mustang, James Hale* and another of M. Kenedy & Co.'s steamers called the *Señorita*.[11] Yet King and Kenedy were evidently on friendly enough terms with their former enemies to be able to buy back the vessels and operate them—though after the knocks of the war years there seems to have been little service left in the old boats, and mention of them drops out of record.[12]

For efficient and hence profitable operations on the river, the partners always depended upon especially designed boats which they ordered built at Pittsburgh. Some estimate of King's and Kenedy's financial condition at the end of the war may be made by the fact that even after buying out Walworth's holdings for cash, the partners were able to order four expensive new steamboats, the *Antonio, Eugenia, Tamaulipas* and *Camargo,* and have them on the Rio Grande by late in the summer of 1865. Shortly after her arrival, the *Tamaulipas* was put in charter to the United States Quartermaster;[13] the *Antonio* and *Eugenia* were sold to the Imperialist forces based at Matamoros.[14] King and Kenedy presumably used the new *Camargo* with several of their older vessels to carry on their regular river business until other new steamers could be delivered to the Rio Grande the following year.[15] Early in 1866 the firm bought at least two boats, the *Enterprise* and *El Primero,* to keep competitors from the river;[16] it is certain the partners had several vessels on hand for which their business found little use. King and Kenedy were so successful in hiding their steamboat operations behind various fronts during the years 1863-1866 that it is now nearly impossible to trace the names and the exact number of vessels the partners controlled at the time.[17]

The transportation business in the wake of the war could not have justified the operation of very many boats on the border. Merchants were finding times too uncertain.[18] Aside from the cotton which was moving in diminishing volume through Matamoros to ships off Bagdad, there was little private freight to haul. The United States government's stores and supplies were another matter. Former Confederates King and Kenedy, just as soon as they had their presidential pardons, resumed their rock-bottom long-time business of hauling freight for the United States Army. In accommodations to the quartermaster, they not only improved their standings with the

Union authorities, they kept their boat business out of the red.

The inevitable post-war slump and the final drying up of the cotton boom came to the Rio Grande, not with the end of the Confederacy but with the end of the Imperialist occupation of Tamaulipas, in the summer of 1866. Strong forces working from great distance—from as far away as Washington and Paris—made the Imperialist withdrawal an eventual certainty, but the event which actually precipitated it was a local border affair called the "Battle of El Convoy."

Early in June of 1866, Imperialist commander Mejía informed the merchants of Matamoros that he no longer had money to pay his troops and must ask for a forced loan. The times were difficult: a closing ring of *Juarista* forces around Matamoros had been making the passage of trade toward the interior increasingly hazardous and unprofitable. The merchants protested to Mejía that they were not prosperous enough to furnish the required loan. They suggested that they could help the general's cause with funds if he would provide adequate troops to guard a wagon train on a passage to Monterrey, where goods could be sold and funds raised. Shortly thereafter a train of two hundred loaded wagons escorted by about 1300 Imperialist troops and two pieces of artillery set out for Monterrey. Near Camargo on June 16, 1866, a *Juarista* army swept in upon the train, overwhelmed the convoying troops in a bloody fight, and wildly looted the wagons. The utter rout of Mejía's soldiers wrecked his cause on the border. The loss the merchants suffered put a period to the long wartime boom of the lower Rio Grande. A week after the battle, Mejía and his remaining Imperialists were forced to flee Matamoros; a *Juarista* governor took over the town and the state of Tamaulipas.[19] Mejía—who was a better man than the cause he represented—began a series of retreats southwestward, which ended a

year later on a barren hillside outside the town of Querétaro, where a firing squad shot him down at the side of his inept emperor, Maximilian.

At about the time the Imperialists were leaving Matamoros, the grizzled merchant Charles Stillman, in failing health, was settling his affairs on the border and preparing a move to New York. In the summer of 1866, the veteran operator "Don Carlos," whose ledgers had indexed so much of the border's early story and whose long labors with the clink of coin and rustle of paper had shaped so much commercial history in such a contentious time and place, left Brownsville on the Rio Grande to live out his days at Cornwall-on-the-Hudson. He carried away much money and many memories. His money from the border developed the National City Bank of New York and other varied enterprises.[20] His memories must often have warmed him. The ships he owned brought him, in their ballast, ebony chunks cut from the brush thickets of the Rio Grande; he burned them upon the hearth of a gray mansion, remembering in his old age the sun on a far river.[21]

That same summer of 1866, King and Kenedy accomplished an entire reorganization of their steamboat business to adjust it to the withdrawal of Partner Stillman, to the death of Partner Walworth and to post-war conditions in the border's commerce.

The firm took a new name: KING, KENEDY & CO. With a capital stock set at $250,000, its ownership was divided thus: one fourth each to Richard King and Mifflin Kenedy; one eighth each to two steamboat captains working for the firm, Robert Dalzell and Joseph Cooper—Dalzell was Mifflin Kenedy's stepson-in-law through marriage to Louisa Vidal; and one twelfth each to three citizens on the border, all former associates of Charles Stillman, whom King and Kenedy had reasons for bringing into the firm. These were Francisco Ytúrria, banker and friend of King and Kenedy and one of their fronts during the wartime operation of the boats; Jeremiah Galvan, who in the course of the war had dealt with both Yankees and Rebels and who after the war had by his Union connections become County Judge of Cameron County; and a prosperous merchant by the name of Artemus Brown. Mifflin Kenedy assumed the active management and main burden of operating the reorganized firm.[22]

Contrary to the emphasis implied by the new name of King, Kenedy & Co., the 1866 reorganization of the steamboat business marked the beginning of the end of Richard King's active interest in it. After 1866 his participation in the affairs of the firm was little more than a watchful salvage of his investment. His heart was in ranching, not steamboating. All his actions suggest that he sensed the arrival of a new economy and understood that the days of profit and importance for riverboats were waning.

Yet there were several years of river business still before him. To guard his investment, he joined with his partners in trying to sustain and prolong the monopoly M. Kenedy & Co. had previously enjoyed. This led King, Kenedy & Co. into a fight against the arrival of any railroad which would compete with the boats. It was a fight doomed to defeat: it was against the grain of the times.

The first threat of rail competition appeared in the not very formidable shape of a narrow gauge military railway laid down in 1865 by order of General Sheridan to speed movement of supplies from the sea anchorage at Brazos to the riverboat terminal at White Ranch.[23] In effect, this little stub line of rails took the place of King, Kenedy & Co.'s "outside" boat; the competitive possibilities were not lost upon rivermen.

When the Army decided in 1866 that its railroad was no longer necessary to border military operations and put it up for sale, Kenedy and King were interested enough to offer $60,000 for it, but were outbid. A firm of outsiders, West & Chenery—who offered $108,-

ooo, with a cash payment of $10,800 down—came into possession of the line.[24] Messrs. West and Chenery had not reckoned with monopolists Kenedy and King, who owned the terminal facilities at White Ranch, controlled the steamers for handling freight from there, and held part title—through a purchase from the estate of James Walworth—to the land upon which the railway's Brazos Santiago terminal was built.[25] West and Chenery found themselves the disgruntled owners of a stub line with no place to go, and turned their dead-end purchase back to the government.[26] Any further threat of competition from Sheridan's railroad ended when it was destroyed by a hurricane in 1867.[27]

The military railway to White Ranch was a temporary expedience; Brownsville expected a better answer to its problem of receiving freight overland directly from the port of Brazos Santiago. When citizens broached the subject of bringing in a better equipped line by a better route, King and Kenedy managed to find sufficient support in the Texas legislature to acquire a charter, dated October 1, 1866, granting exclusive rights for the building of a railway from Brazos Santiago or Point Isabel into Brownsville.[28]

There is small evidence that the monopolists intended the building of a rail line. They were only forestalling any threat to the freight rates they charged on their riverboats. Kenedy and King both took pains to buy certain tracts of land in the Espíritu Santo grant over which a right-of-way would reach toward Brownsville,[29] but nothing else was done.

This failure to act brought heated criticism in the Texas Republican press which referred to King, Kenedy & Co. and its supporters like Stephen Powers as the "Sesesh Clique," whose loyalty to the Union had "the shortest history that ever was penned." Yet hostile Reconstructionists were by no means the only enemies of the monopoly King and Kenedy found themselves bucking to maintain. A bloc of veteran border merchants, headed by H. E. Woodhouse of Brownsville, bitterly assailed the high freight rates charged by King, Kenedy & Co.'s steamers, and demanded more than a paper railroad to relieve the border from the grip of a monopoly "incompatible with the public interest."[30]

The clamor was heard finally in Austin. In 1870 the legislature revoked King and Kenedy's charter and granted it to a group of "anti-monopolists," headed by Simón Celaya, wealthy businessman and Spanish vice-consul at Brownsville, who organized as the Rio Grande Railroad Co., built twenty-two and a half miles of off-gauge 42-inch tracks from a dock at Point Isabel to a station in Brownsville and had cars operating over the line by 1871.[31]

Kenedy, backed by King, then brought two obstructive lawsuits against the Rio Grande Railroad Co., one to prohibit it from entering the city limits of Brownsville,[32] and another suing against the line's use of lands owned by Kenedy and King on the Espíritu Santo grant. In the course of his court fight against the railroad Mifflin Kenedy grew heated. The staid Kenedy, not given to extravagance in language, indignantly referred to the Rio Grande Railroad Co. as a "fifth class one pilon dog power railroad."[33] He and King lost suits in court; they also secured a judgment. But neither their litigation nor the political influence they had tried to muster, nor any other tactic, could forestall the inevitable end of a monopoly which in fact did not serve the changing times.

During the half decade between King and Kenedy's reorganization of their steamboat business and the advent of the wheezy little iron horse on the tracks of the Rio Grande Railroad Co., the affairs of King, Kenedy & Co. were in a more or less chronic decline. By June of 1867, the month of Maximilian's demise at Querétaro, a trade slump had brought business on the Rio Grande to a nearly complete standstill. All but one of King, Kenedy & Co.'s steamers were tied up, idle.[34] Four months later the border suffered a blow which put finishing touches to its already well-developed postwar depression. A hurricane roared in from the Gulf and ripped at Brownsville and Matamoros, causing immense damage to both towns. Wind and water destroyed Bagdad and Clarksville, knocked flat most of the buildings at Brazos Santiago and Point Isabel, destroyed the military railroad, the terminal at White Ranch, and sank four steamers, the *Antonio, Enterprise, El Primero* and *Camargo.* The whole economy of the lower Rio Grande staggered.[35]

Richard King seems to have viewed the damage as a clear signal to quit the river, to devote himself to the greater promise of the ranch. At the time of the storm he and his family had already moved back to the Santa Gertrudis. Mifflin Kenedy was soon convinced of his partner King's acumen. By the fall of 1868 Kenedy had put his son-in-law Dalzell in charge of the boats, and become a rancher himself.[36]

The firm's steamers went on hauling the border's trade goods, King and Kenedy continued as freighting contractors and suppliers for the United States Army units in the area,[37] but the increasing vagaries of the always undependable Rio Grande, and the advent of the iron rails, spelled eventual doom for the boats. Faced with the dwindling away of a business which had seen golden days but saw them no longer, the directors of King, Kenedy & Co. met on May 5, 1874, to decide the fate of the firm. Richard King and Mifflin Kenedy sold out, on terms now unknown. Captain William Kelly, one of the company's most able skippers, took over the business, financed by a bloc of merchants still willing to venture on future operations of the firm's equipment. Kelly's investors were H. E. Woodhouse and Francisco Armendaiz, both prominent in the Rio Grande Railroad Co.; José San Roman, a wealthy mercantile operator in the Rio Grande trade; and two stockholders of the liquidated

King, Kenedy & Co., Francisco Ytúrria and Jeremiah Galvan.[38]

The fleet of steamboats which had in earlier days played a great rôle in the economic life of the border finally dwindled to one small steamer named the *Bessie,* whose trips up and down the shallowing Rio Grande furnished little more than a living to her Captain Kelly. In 1903, even the *Bessie* ceased to run. Another age had arrived on the border.[39]

In 1866, when the new steamboating firm of King, Kenedy & Co. had been set in order, the two partners turned their attention to the future of their very large property with headquarters on the Santa Gertrudis. The bookkeeping in the ranch account books could indicate only the roughest approximation of the actual value of R. King & Co. Its assets were of a most involved nature, consisting of undivided half-interests in a sprawling set of titles to numerous parcels of land totaling more than 146,000 acres,[40] in an actually unknown and constantly changing number of many kinds of livestock of fluctuating value, in an unaccounted accretion of land improvements and ranch buildings, and in debits or credits from old and new side ventures of various kinds connected with livestock and land trading.

King and Kenedy could only guess at what each of them owned. For two partners devoted to an efficient control of what they owned and what they owed, it was no satisfactory state of affairs. Considering the difficulties another death in the firm could bring to the ranch operation, when all its undivided half-interests would have to be evaluated and separated for the sake of the two families involved as heirs, King and Kenedy came to the conclusion that a careful inventory of their ranch was immediately in order. Looking toward the future, they also considered the sound business advantages that might mutually accrue to them through a friendly division of the complicated holdings before they became inextricable.

They drew up and signed an inventory of R. King & Co.'s properties on November 5, 1867, stating that the purpose of this indenture was to make between them "a legal and effective release and transfer each to the other, so as to vest in each of the said parties, clearly and distinctly an undivided half in and to all such partnership property, and to declare and establish their respective rights."[41]

With these rights listed and agreed to, the way was cleared for separation of the two partners' shares in their ranching enterprise, a separation which was evidently already decided upon, for at the same time, November 5, 1867, in a "Partnership Agreement Between King and Kenedy," they signed a plan for the division of their herds:

The cattle shall be gradually gathered and driven to the rancho at Santa Gertrudis or any other convenient rancho . . . belonging to the firm and there divided as fast as collected by each partner . . . taking an animal alternately and placing his own brand thereon, and so continuing until all of said cows have been gathered: the horses, mules, jacks and jennets shall be divided by taking the manadas and remudas two at a time as nearly as possible of equal value and allotting them to the respective parties who shall draw lots for the first choice . . . ; the sheep, goats and other stock shall be divided into two lots of each kind of equal value and the parties shall draw lots for the first choice; provided also that it is distinctly understood that neither party shall use any of the original or present brands of the stock belonging to the partnership, as his own after such division, but shall have a new and distinct brand to be put on his share respectively at the time of the division . . .[42]

Six months later, on May 31, 1868, the partners signed an instrument entitled "Articles of Agreement and Settlement Between R. King and M. Kenedy," setting forth procedures they agreed to follow in the equitable division of all land and other assets held jointly in R. King & Co.[43]

Three days after the "Articles of Agreement" Mifflin Kenedy signed the papers by which he purchased the land necessary for his own independent ranching establishment. This was the twenty-six leagues of the Laureles grant for which Kenedy received a warranty deed from Cornelius Stillman, brother of Charles, on June 3, 1868. In addition to the down payment of an unstated consideration, the terms of sale called for the making of three notes "each for the sum of 2061 pounds, 17 shillings and 4 pence, payable (1) one, (2) two and (3) three years after date" by Kenedy.[44] The British exchange may or may not indicate where Kenedy had banked and held some of his wartime profits.

Along with their decision to divide their ranch holdings, King and Kenedy also decided to begin fencing the properties that would comprise their separate establishments.

Neither King nor Kenedy were ever exponents of the open range or free grass style of ranching. From their beginnings as stockmen, they believed that an efficient operation consisted in complete control of the water and grass on the land where their herds were pastured. The only way to arrive at control was to own the land; the only practical way to maintain control was to enclose what was owned. A fenced range made a livestock breeding program possible by controlling the animals in the enclosure and by keeping out strays. In a land where lawlessness was chronic, a fence was also legal notice to trespassers, thieves and squatters.

There were few fenced lands at the time. Before 1874 when barbed wire came on the market, the fencing of any large area — especially in a region without timber or even any stone for fencing material — was not only difficult but immensely expensive. Disregarding the difficulties and having resources that fortunately enabled them to cope with the expense, both Kenedy and King began in 1868 to build fence, of creosoted cypress posts and hard pine planks which were brought on order by ship from Louisiana and hauled out by wagon to the Santa Gertrudis and the Laureles ranches.[45]

Before the end of the year, Mifflin Kenedy's fence had created a milestone in the development of the livestock ranching industry. By completing thirty miles of heavy post and three-plank fencing across the throat of the peninsula which formed the Laureles grant, Kenedy effectively enclosed the 131,000 acres of his new purchase and became the owner of the first fenced range of any real size west of the Mississippi.[46]

The Santa Gertrudis lands were not conveniently bounded on two sides by the waters of the Laguna Madre, and to enclose inland pastures was a project considerably more extensive and expensive than Kenedy had found on his peninsula. Nevertheless, by the end of 1868, King had enclosed a tract around the Santa Gertrudis headquarters.[47] The partners were ready to divide their joint holdings and become the separate owners of neighboring ranches.

The roundups by which the livestock were divided began early in January of 1869 and were finished on November 11 of that year. More than a hundred vaqueros were employed in combing the ranges. Mifflin Kenedy said later, "There were branded for me at the Rancho de Los Laureles, 25,000 head of cattle. There were branded for Captain R. King at Rancho Santa Gertrudis, up to the 11th of November 1869, 23,664 head of cattle. At this time, finding the expense to be very great, Captain King and myself made an agreement that he would receive the balance of the cattle on the prairie (belonging to the firm and not gathered) at 10,000 head, this making a total of 58,664 head of cattle on hand November 11, 1869, belonging to the firm of R. King & Co. We had on hand on November 11, 1869, 4400 head of horse stock."[48]

It was 1873 before King and Kenedy had delivered to each other's ranches the last odds and ends of the divided properties, but the formal period of division may be dated from the "Articles of Agreement and Settlement" of May 31, 1868, to the "Agreement and Final Settlement of Affairs of R. King & Co."* signed February 26, 1870, and filed at the Nueces County Court House on September 21, 1870.

The text of the "Agreement and Final Settlement" indicates not only the diversity of the real estate King and Kenedy had acquired during more than twenty years of business on the border, it shows how the two friends traded so that they might split their holdings evenly and at the same time each maintain property that best fitted separate preferences and operations in the future. In return for King's interests in six parcels of Brownsville town property and three tracts of pasture land unrelated to the Santa Gertrudis ranching operation, Kenedy traded King all the Santa Gertrudis as a working unit, with one parcel of Corpus Christi town property and some odd Rio Grande river frontage thrown in to equalize the totals in the split.

When the livestock and the land had been divided, and the cash debits and credits in the R. King & Co. account books—all finished and unfinished contracts, bad debts and "sundries" including the original costs of two slaves who had worked on the ranch before the war—had been adjusted, balanced and dealt two ways, neighbors King and Kenedy began the development of their separate ranches. The division of a complicated partnership, touching intimately at the self-interests of both men, cast no hint of reserve upon the continuing close association of Richard King and Mifflin Kenedy, or upon the regard in which they held each other. Decades later, the aged Mifflin Kenedy would tell a small grandson of Richard King's, "Your grandfather and I had lots of fights. Always on the same side."[49]

After seventeen eventful years of ranching in partnerships, Richard King became the sole owner of the Santa Gertrudis. According

* The complete text of this document is printed in Appendix VII.

to the terms by which he and Kenedy divided the livestock of R. King & Co., a new brand was required of each partner for the counterbranding of the sorted herds. Mifflin Kenedy chose for his own mark the Laurel Leaf *Ł* befitting his Rancho Laureles. Richard King used as the sign and symbol of his new sole ownership a cleancut, simple mark destined for enduring fame, the Running W.

The earliest official registration of the *W* was entered thus: "The State of Texas, County of Nueces. Be it Remembered that on the Ninth day of February A. D. 1869, Richard King having deposited his Brand and Ear Marks for Horses & Cattle as described and laid down in the Margin hereof, the same was and is hereby duly Recorded, in Book B for the Registry of Brands in said Nueces County on page 181. Witness my Official Signature at office in Corpus Christi, the day and date above written. Joseph FitzSimmons, Clk C. C. N. Co."*

The exact date of King's first use of the *W* has not been determined. Undoubtedly he burned it on any stock he acquired personally after the decision to dissolve the partnership, probably beginning in late 1867 or early 1868.[50]

Some measure of the difference between the Anglo and the Latin mind is indicated by the name each race has given to the *W*. In English it is called rather literally a Running W; in Spanish it is named with more imagination the *Viborita*, the Little Snake. Whether the *W* had its origin north or south of the Rio Grande is a question that has not been answered. Though Mexican stock brands are usually characterized by a certain crabbed intricacy, it is by no means impossible to find among them dramatically simple designs; moreover, the flourish of a mark to represent a wriggling snake, with its implication of *Cuidado*, don't tread on me, is worthy of the Mexican imagination and its preoccupation with an ancient serpent image,

* See Appendix V for reproduction of this registration.

which is even enfigured on the national flag. On the other hand, there are solid grounds for believing in a plainer Texan origin of the Running W. There are versions of a W, both rounded and angular, with appendages and without, in many Texas county brand registries. And it may be that Captain King did not arrive at his brand by any W or by any Little Snake at all, but by a letter M. When he bought the land and livestock of William Mann's estate in 1862, three of Mann's brands came with the purchase. One of these was M A N, another was his initial M, and the third was a variant of that initial, ᶯᶯ.[51] Captain King, already owner of ᶯᶯ, may have simply inverted it to create the ᗯ which became his distinctive mark.*

There were clear reasons for adopting it; it was open-spaced, unmarred by the juncture or crossing of any lines which in a brand causes a deep spot in the burn, invites screw worms and heals widened and blurred. The ᗯ also had the advantage of being an unusually neat figure to shape with a running iron when a stamp iron was not handy. The four straight lines could be evenly joined by using the side of the semicircular hook at the end of the iron to stamp the uniform curves that finished the design. And in its single-line simplicity, the brand made a shape which was exceedingly hard to alter or deface by any subsequent reburning. Beyond such practical considerations, the ᗯ was good-looking. Burned on a living flank and healed on a living hide, it lost the rigid geometry of the iron, to become a W that really ran and a Little Snake alive. It immediately took its place at the top of every list of the many stock brands worn by Richard King's many herds.[52]

The five-year period between the end of the Civil War and the opening of the 1870's was one of transition and readjustment at the ranch on the Santa Gertrudis. King and Kenedy sold some cattle and

* For a reproduction of Richard King's newspaper advertisement listing his brands see page 270.

they operated some hide and tallow works to thin out their scrub stock in the years immediately following the war,[53] but they pursued no extensive marketing of the livestock on their overstocked pastures until the division of the herds was accomplished, and each partner had a free hand.[54]

Former steamboat captains King and Kenedy chose a wise time to clear decks for the future. During the first postwar years, a number of economic forces were at work which, joining together, were destined to open an immense new market and bring immense new wealth to the owners of the grasslands in South Texas.

Fortune had planted Richard King astride a Cotton Road during a war, to his great profit. Now a fate of King's own making planted him, to his much greater profit, firmly at the fountainhead which was to provide a nation with beef and to stock half a continent with breed herds.

War had brought a dearth of beef to the densely populated states of the North and Middle West; the same war had brought an almost incredible increase of untended cattle to the prairies of Texas. In a hectic surge which the war had pent up, rail lines were reaching westward on their competitive ways to the Pacific, bringing the great markets and the great grasslands of the nation closer to each other. At the same time, in hub cities like Chicago, St. Louis, Kansas City, bustling stockyards and packing plants were springing up — a newborn industry — putting beef within reach of the urban worker's purse and, to supply that beef, offering prices that called out along the iron rails into Kansas and across the dust trails far south to Texas, where there stood cattle by the scores of hundreds of thousands — and men who knew how to drive them. A five-dollar steer in Reconstruction-ridden Texas was a twenty- to forty-dollar steer in Chicago, if you could get him there. By the early summer of 1866, big herds of Texas cattle were strung out on trails toward Kansas, toward beckoning, promising, profitable markets in the North.

During the fifteen years since Richard King had pioneered with an idea at a cow camp in the wilderness, ranching had become the prime economic resource and promise of Texas. In another fifteen years, with the ranges to the Rocky Mountains being cleared of buffalo and Indians and being served by railroads, ranching would produce a Cattle Kingdom, complete with song and story.[55]

Richard King faced the stormiest decade of his life the morning in 1870 he first rode out upon his pastures as sole owner, Rancho Santa Gertrudis. He would not only be working at the sometimes complicated advice of his remembered mentor, *"Buy land and never sell,"* he would not only be sending scores of thousands of cattle on long trails north, playing a large rôle on the huge stage outspread around the cradle he had helped to create for the livestock industry; he would also be bitterly embattled to protect his property and guard his life.

X "He Thinks He Can Defend Himself"

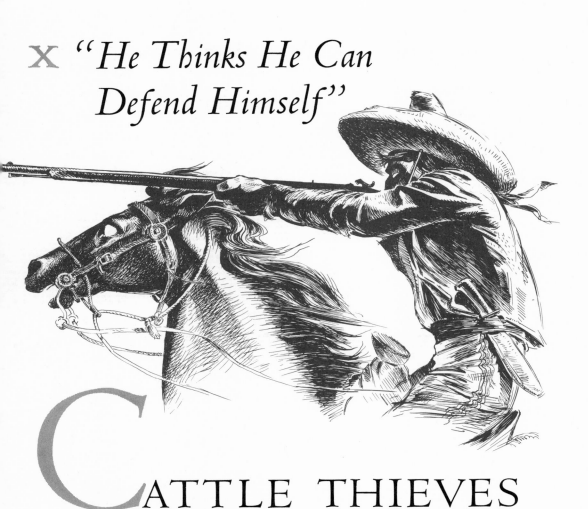

CATTLE THIEVES

began to plague the ranges of Southwest Texas immediately after the end of the Civil War. The stealing began as a consequence of the severe winter of 1863-1864, when huge numbers of strayed cattle from north of the Nueces drifted before the punishing winds into the south tip of Texas. Owners could do little toward recovery of this stock; most of it was left unclaimed, untended, bearing its increase. Uncounted thousands of cattle so far from home ranges and so close to an international boundary were an open invitation to theft; a traffic in stolen livestock sprang up. Any foot-loose horse-man could drive cattle wearing any Texas brand across the river into Mexico and get two to four dollars cash for a cow that cost nothing but the effort to deliver it. Scattered thievery soon became whole-sale depredation. A spawn of border ruffians, operating mostly from lairs south of the Rio Grande, began to raid and terrorize the ranches of the border country as far north as the Nueces.[1]

The risk was very small. Texas suffered a sorry lack of means to enforce law and to put down the disorder that followed in the wake of a ruinous war. The Texas Rangers were disbanded, abolished by order of the Reconstruction regime.[2] Local law administrators were powerless to provide peace officers who would even attempt to cope with the brigands adrift along both banks of the convenient river.[3] The only real presence or semblance of force against unbridled bor-der lawlessness were garrisons of United States troops. And, as Rip Ford wrote later, "It might have been that the powers of govern-ment remembered the course of Texas during the Civil War, and left her to take care of herself in the emergency brought about by Mexi-can raiders."[4]

To this sorry lack of means for the enforcement of law in Texas there was joined a cynical lack of interest on the part of Mexican authorities in stopping thieves from bringing stolen Texas cattle to Mexico.[5] The old hatreds and mistrusts between the two races were still alive and needed only a little fanning to burst again into flame.

Plunder of the ranches along the Texas side of the river soon assumed the guise of race war. The operations of the brown-faced marauders were so surprisingly successful they were soon bragging, "The *Gringos* are raising cows for me."[6] They justified themselves, if they had any qualms, by saying that the cattle and everything else between the Nueces and the Rio Grande originally belonged to Mexicans, that they had every right to take back their own. They called the cattle they stole "Nanita's" cattle, meaning "grandma's."[7] Grandma's cattle brought quick cash money.

It was a situation which could hardly be improved upon as a background for new operations by the border's own badman, Juan Nepomuceno Cortina. Sniffing the troubled air with his Don Coyote nose, he inevitably reappeared. Back in 1859, Rip Ford's rangers had brought Cortina's personal war with Texans to a jolting halt. In 1861 Santos Benavides' Confederate cavalrymen had forcibly stopped Cortina again. When the wily Cheno returned to the border he came well-equipped and there was nothing to stop him.

He returned as Brigadier General Juan Nepomuceno Cortina, Commander of the Line of the Bravo, with the power to make or unmake governors "at his pleasure."[8] Many of his old lieutenants were busily engaged in supplying Texan beef to Mexico at cut-rate prices. It was no trouble to deal himself in on this profitable enterprise. As a suit against the Mexican government would later say, cattle theft was "coterminous" with his presence and authority.[9]

At only one point was there anything approaching a cessation. Enjoying a position of official responsibility in the army of the Republic of Mexico, Cortina chose to manifest a rather delayed desire for respectability on the left bank of the river. He communicated this desire to leading citizens of Brownsville, who even believed him and took steps.

By a deal through Mifflin Kenedy with the prominent lawyer and politician Stephen Powers, Cortina sought pardon for past offenses in Texas. In return for such a pardon he promised to use all the power at his command — and it was considerable — for the suppression of the brigandage rampant on the border. In 1871, Powers actually got a bill passed through the State Senate to pardon Cortina, but the action brought such an explosive uproar that the bill was "postponed indefinitely" by the House.[10]

Smarting with this rebuff from the ungrateful Texans, Cortina gave his old hatred full rein and summoned up his ripe talent for the raising of border strife. As Commander of the Line of the Bravo, he set about supervising and improving on the spoliation his compatriots were practicing over the river. A Brownsville grand jury in 1872 called Cortina a criminal occupying "the double position of ranking officer of the Mexican Army upon the Line of the Bravo, and ranking cow and horse thief on both frontiers."[11]

There is no proof that Cortina himself stole Texas livestock. He only handled and received it. Using his official position for the subornation of all local Mexican authority along the river, he organized the raiding forays into Texas and protected the raiders from any punishment or any inconvenience at the hands of the Mexican law. Using his official position further, Cortina appropriated such stolen stock as he fancied or bought it at his own price. Testimony given under oath repeatedly stated that Cortina stocked four ranches in Tamaulipas mainly with cows and horses stolen from Texas. It was proved that he filled beef contracts for the Cuban market with cattle he ordered his bravos to steal in Texas and deliver to waiting ships. The Commander of the Line of the Bravo got rich.[12]

The raiding of Texas ranches and the theft of almost incredible numbers of Texas livestock, which Cortina brought to a climax of viciousness in 1875, was continuous from 1865 until 1878. In the years when the raiding was at its height, Texas stockmen estimated that as many as 200,000 head of their cattle were stolen annually. By 1875, there remained in the region between the Rio Grande and the Nueces only one third to one fourth the number of cattle there had been in 1866.[13]

The raiding was often accompanied by brutal murder. Isolated ranchmen had no recourse, no protection but that which they could furnish themselves. "Old and young were subjected to every form of outrage and torture, dragged at the hooves of horses, burned and flayed alive, shot to death or cut to pieces with knives, their homes and ranches looted and destroyed."[14] Defenseless travelers were ambushed; the roads over the lonely prairies became too dangerous to travel without armed escorts.[15]

Not all the thieves drove away the stock they stole. Gangs of hide-peelers killed cattle on the range, skinned them, and hauled the hides to market—a thievery practiced with greater dispatch, if less profit, than delivering herds of cattle on the hoof. Hide-peelers displayed unspeakable cruelty in their operations. Many of them used the *media luna,* a scythe-like knife in the shape of a half-moon mounted on a long shaft, handled from horseback to hamstring cattle. The knocked-down animals were sometimes skinned while still alive. Ranchers pursuing hide-peelers would come upon suckling calves bawling by their mothers' raw carcasses still warm and jerking with signs of life.[16]

A resident on the Rio Grande described the plight of Texas stockmen and the intimidation of the whole region at about the time Cortina began to make the raids more frequent and more punishing:

It may be wondered that the inhabitants of the District, over twenty thousand, cannot prevent Mexican thieves from making raids on them, particularly as there are three Military Posts within the District. The wonder will cease when it is known that the Posts are all on the Rio Grande and over 100 miles from each other, that the garrisons are composed almost entirely of infantry and that the few cavalry on hand seldom go out scouting. It must also be borne in mind that the District wherein the cattle stealing is carried on is almost entirely settled by Mexicans, that outside of the towns there is hardly one American to 100 Mexicans. A few of the Mexicans can be depended on, but the majority, if they are not participators themselves in the stealing, aid and abet the thieves and never give information which may lead to their capture and conviction. The good and well disposed Mexicans dare not inform against the thieves, as they fear that these might at any time thereafter organize a band to destroy their ranchos or murder them. How long are we to suffer our property to be taken from us with impunity and without redress, and how long will our State and general Governments tolerate the invasion of our soil by the people of a neighboring Republic? Present appearances would indicate that we must suffer as long as we have a head of cattle to be taken from us and that our soil will be trodden down by armed bands of Mexicans as long as they please.[17]

In the midst of this trouble, rancher Richard King was no novice at defending himself. He fought the gangs of spoilers by every means he could muster, from firearms to political pressures, but the thieving was so stealthy and endless, the raiding so malign, it threatened the survival of his ranch.

From a postwar roundup of stock on the Santa Gertrudis in 1866, R. King & Co. had estimated it owned 84,000 head of cattle. Yet at the division of the property in 1869, King and Kenedy managed to gather just 48,664 cattle which, added to an estimated 10,000 head ungathered, made a total of 58,664. This startling decrease, after three years in which few cattle were sold and in which an undisturbed breed herd would ordinarily double in size, was some indication of the plunder in progress even before Cortina fanned the raiding to its full fury. During the next period of three years, from 1869 to 1872, Richard King claimed loss by theft of 33,827 head of cattle.*

Losses like these came in spite of constant vigilance. Since its first establishment, the ranch on the Santa Gertrudis had been forced to maintain its own defense. A band of *Kineños* commanded by their foreman, Captain James Richardson, had stood guard against thieves for years. There was nothing new in keeping the brass cannon at headquarters loaded or in manning the lookout atop the commissary, high on the rise in the prairie. As the livestock thefts increased regardless of his vaquero patrols, King bought "some thirty stands of Henry rifles and a supply of ammunition."[18] He hired extra riders,

*See Appendix VIII.

probably as many as a dozen, who were handy with the Henrys. And while foreman Richardson and his riders patrolled, King built fence. A visitor to the ranch in 1872 said that Captain King "calculated that it would cost $50,000 to fence his ranch, and that he would be repaid in one year by the prevention of these thefts and proceeded to fence his ranch, . . . and has now built 31 or 32 miles and has 8 or 9 miles now under way. This is directly a preventative against theft. Guard stations to be placed on each of the four sides of this enclosure."[19]

Direct action, in trying to keep thieves off his ranch and in fighting them with guns when they came anyway, was not enough. King paid agents along the Rio Grande and even in Mexico to spot stolen cattle bearing his brand. He hired men to ride after this stock to try to bring it back.[20] He found that once the cattle had crossed the river attempts at recovery were futile.

A deposition made under oath by Richard King in 1870 throws vivid light on the conditions in Mexico which encouraged rather than punished thievery and made the return of stolen stock impossible. On October 10, 1869, at the Miller Hotel in Brownsville, King was called upon by one Pedro Hinojosa, a general under half pay in the Mexican Army, lately Minister of War in the cabinet of Benito Juárez, and at the time of his call enjoying a sinecure as First Alcalde of Matamoros. Hinojosa came to say that there were several thousand head of stolen Texas cattle being held near Matamoros, many of them wearing King's brand; Hinojosa came to inquire about buying King's cattle. Reminding him that the stock was already beyond recovery, Hinojosa asked King for a price. Anxious to probe at this knavery King asked for an offer. Hinojosa said that he would give $1000 for the yet uncounted stolen stock in King's brand. No rewriting of King's deposition can improve upon the dry legal verbiage in setting forth the remainder of the interview:

... deponent then considered that should he sell his brands in Mexico the purchaser could claim all other cattle that might afterwards be found there, declined to sell but inquired how he, Hinojosa, could get them from the thieves, to which he replied, by his own order; deponent then for the first time recollected that said Hinojosa was an alcalde at Matamoros, and this put him upon further inquiry, as his business to Brownsville was to endeavor to find some way to stop the wholesale stealing which was ruining the stockmen of Texas; deponent then said in reply to said Hinojosa, that if his order was good for himself, it was also good for deponent; and after further conversation in the matter, finally asked him directly to grant an order to put him in possession of his own property; that after several excuses and some hesitation, said Hinojosa finally declined to grant any order, alleging among many other things that it was what no alcalde had done, and gave as his reason that he would not be sustained by other authorities or by the people; deponent then asked him if his own powers were not sufficient, irrespective of any other authority, to enforce his own orders, which he admitted under the laws was so, but from the state of the country the practice was very different ... after a general conversation in these matters, in which said Hinojosa was candid and showed no hesitation in his suggestions or replies, deponent again reverted to the order for the reclamation of his cattle in hopes to get them back if possible, but could not get even the proffer of assistance; deponent then called the attention of said Hinojosa to the inconsistency of his order being good for himself but not for deponent, to which he only laughed and shrugged his shoulders, which deponent interpreted to mean, that he ought to be sufficiently understood as acting in other interests, without being questioned upon the subject.[21]

Facing conditions like these, ranchmen on the north bank of the river banded together in 1870 as the Stock Raisers Association of Western Texas, to help each other gun for thieves, to find and return each other's stolen stock, to prosecute in court every criminal that could be caught, and to bring pressure on the state and national governments for protection. Mifflin Kenedy presided over the first meeting; he and King not only supported but led the activities of the organization.[22] Among these was the advertisement of the stock-men's registered brands in the local newspapers, so that the legal owners of cattle wearing such brands might be unmistakable. The list of brands used by Richard King, always headed by the ᙡ and followed by a long array of brands he held by purchase, appeared regularly.[23]

In 1869, official hide and cattle inspectors appointed by the Army post commanders on the Rio Grande were authorized to examine all cattle and hides in the commerce crossing the river.[24] The inspectors gathered facts and figures, but were armed with no power whatever to check the traffic they daily observed. A too earnest pursuit of their duties proved unhealthy for reasons clearly discernable in a typical Matamoros hide yard dealer's instructions to his help: "Shoot the first damned gringo son of a bitch who comes here and attempts to look at a hide."[25]

When the thievery increased rather than diminished, and especially when it became clear that there was some connection between the official Mexican Commander of the Line of the Bravo and the depredation north of the Bravo, United States Army details were at times ordered into the field to pursue reported raiders. As usual, regulation soldiers on limited scouts were incapable of countering the non-regulation elusiveness of brush riding bandits.[26] What the border needed, and missed sorely, was a troop of Texas Rangers.

The plundered stockmen, nearly all of them former Rebels, made every representation to the Unionist authorities in Austin for a re-establishment of the rangers, to no avail. In 1869, the former *renegado* E.J. Davis, who had become governor of Texas in an election rigged by the carpetbagging general in command of the state, did set up an organization intended to replace the rangers, called the Texas State Police. There were some good men in its muster, but it was soon

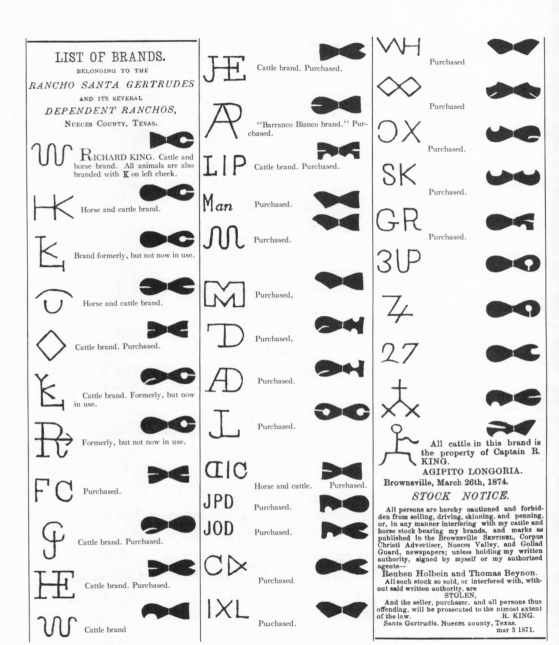

LIST OF BRANDS.

BELONGING TO THE

RANCHO SANTA GERTRUDES

AND ITS SEVERAL

DEPENDENT RANCHOS,

NUECES COUNTY, TEXAS.

RICHARD KING. Cattle and horse brand. All animals are also branded with **K** on left cheek.

Horse and cattle brand.

Brand formerly, but not now in use.

Horse and cattle brand.

Cattle brand. Purchased.

Cattle brand. Formerly, but now in use.

Formerly, but not now in use.

Purchased.

Cattle brand. Purchased.

Cattle brand. Purchased.

Cattle brand

Cattle brand. Purchased.

"Barranco Blanco brand." Purchased.

Cattle brand. Purchased.

Purchased.

Purchased.

Purchased,

Purchased,

Purchased.

Purchased.

Horse and cattle. Purchased.

Purchased.

Purchased.

Purchased.

Purchased.

Horse and cattle. Purchased.

Purchased.

Purchased.

Purchased.

Purchased.

Purchased.

Purchased.

Purchased.

Purchased.

Purchased.

All cattle in this brand is the property of Captain R. KING.

AGIPITO LONGORIA.

Brownsville, March 26th, 1874.

STOCK NOTICE.

All persons are hereby cautioned and forbidden from selling, driving, skinning, and penning, or, in any manner interfering with my cattle and horse stock bearing my brands, and marks as published in the Brownsville SENTINEL, Corpus Christi Advertiser, Nueces Valley, and Goliad Guard, newspapers; unless holding my written authority, signed by myself or my authorized agents—

Reuben Holbein and Thomas Beynon.

All such stock so sold, or interfered with, without said written authority, are

STOLEN,

And the seller, purchaser, and all persons thus offending, will be prosecuted to the utmost extent of the law. R. KING.

Santa Gertrudis, Nueces county, Texas.

mar 3 1871.

generally despised as an officious tool used to enforce radical Republican political edicts while criminal outlawry went unpunished on the frontier.[27]

In the midst of an unavailing fight for protection against cow thieves and raiders, Richard King was in business, ranching on a booming big scale, and to conduct that business he had to travel constantly. The roads between Corpus Christi and Brownsville were death traps and travelers preferred not to tempt death by traveling alone. On his trips away from the ranch King went armed and took armed men with him, ordinarily a driver when he traveled by coach, and four or five vaqueros. In an age of gunmen and fancy gunplay, it is interesting to note that the owner of the Santa Gertrudis carried no flashing six-shooter but a shotgun loaded with buckshot.[28] When he needed to shoot, he wanted results. As for the men he took with him, the legends of a later time recounting how Captain King rode with a cavalcade of "private rangers" or "a hundred guards" are somewhat exaggerated. King always kept careful expense accounts of his travels and entered them in his books. Tallying the expenses on the road, he usually named the hands he took with him; these seldom totaled more than half a dozen. There were many occasions when he traveled alone. Entries for a trip to Corpus Christi made in February of 1869 are typical: he kept tab on his own expenses and those of Usario Ilirano, Eluterio Mantavo, Guadalupe Divido, Franco Villanueva and P. Flores—not neglecting an item of "$7.50, whiskey for hands."[29]

King had learned long before that safety on the road consisted not so much in armament as in speed. Probably taking his cue from the military courier service Rip Ford maintained between Brownsville and the Santa Gertrudis in 1864, King sometime during or immediately after the war set up stage camps for his own use at roughly twenty-mile intervals along the length of the road from the ranch to Brownsville. He stocked each guarded camp corral with fast horses and strong mules; when he needed speed, it was there, in relays. Richard King said later, "I had to travel fast. My life depended on it."[30]

At times he found it necessary to transport large amounts of currency. There were occasions when he had with him as much as $50,-000, for payrolls and for buying land. To hide the money, he had a steel box built inside his road coach. The existence of this box was known only to Henrietta King and to Reuben Holbein, the ranch office manager. The box was never robbed nor, in spite of several attempts, was King ever successfully ambushed.[31]

The losses of the stock raisers of western Texas and the state of siege under which they lived finally came to the attention of the government in Washington. Under a joint resolution of Congress approved by President Grant on May 7, 1872, six thousand dollars were appropriated to send a United States Commission to Texas for the purpose of investigating and reporting upon the alleged disorders. The commissioners appointed were able citizens from the East, Thomas P. Robb, Richard H. Savage and J. J. Mead. They arrived on the Rio Grande in July of 1872 and traveled from Point Isabel to Rio Grande City with their eyes and their ears open, taking formal depositions and recording sworn testimony in public sessions from July 30 until October 3. Upon their return to Washington, the commissioners submitted a strong report to Congress, a report bringing to public attention a vast body of testimony from hundreds of eye-witnesses and property owners, documenting in detail and beyond any cavil the outrages and losses being suffered by United States citizens at the hands of raiders from south of the Rio Grande.[32] Nothing was done about it.

While the commissioners were holding sessions, border citizens were hopeful. Men who could and did name the names of thieves and murderers risked their lives to testify in spite of the threats made against them. The daily testimony came from every kind of border citizen and range man, from illiterate vaqueros, from hard-faced hide inspectors, from gun-toting owners of ranches, and the testimony all carried the same burden: the south tip of Texas was being robbed blind without recourse.[33]

Richard King had personal knowledge not only of the thievery but of the violence that went with it. In the witness chair himself before commissioners on August 26, 1872, the owner of the ranch on the Santa Gertrudis testified:

Question. What is the condition of this frontier, as to the security of life and property?

Answer. There is none whatever for life or property. Armed bands of Mexicans are roaming over the country daily in large numbers committing depredations, . . . I have been threatened and followed often; I have received letters showing threats to burn my property. I am obliged to travel with an escort of five or ten armed men.

On 31 July, 1872, I left Corpus Christi, in company with George Evans, my driver, and Franz Specht for the purpose of appearing before this Commission. At a point six miles east of my ranch, on the Corpus Christi road, at a place called San Fernando Creek, at about 8 o'clock in the evening, twenty-five or thirty shots were fired into the ambulance in which I was riding, killing Franz Specht. It was quite dark, and we saw no one. I do not know who my assassins were, but to the best of my knowledge and belief, they were a party of Mexicans, eight or ten in number. I saw on that evening five Mexicans cross the road, on which I was traveling. I have been obliged, for a number of years, to keep quite a number of men, for my protection, at my expense, around my ranch; and in traveling I am obliged to have an escort of those men. Citizens of this frontier are obliged to travel armed always in self defense.[34]

Franz Specht was a traveler from Corpus Christi who had by chance asked for a ride to Brownsville.[35] A $600 reward posted by the governor of Texas failed to bring any information to identify the assassins who in gunning for Richard King killed the luckless stranger sitting at his side.[36]

Important portions of the testimony taken by the United States Commissioners related to the rôle of General Juan Nepomuceno Cortina as the chief instigator and organizer of the traffic in stolen livestock. Too many witnesses gave testimony too specific for the commissioners to doubt that the Commander of the Line of the Bravo was behind much of the mischief. Testimony like that of a former Mexican soldier, Apolinario Hernandez, who signed his name with an X, was entirely typical:

Question. Were you at a three days' frolic at Cortina's ranch, Canelo, in June 1872?

Answer. I was at the bull-slinging feast, and also helped to round up or herd together a lot of cattle. There were about two thousand got up. I did not see all Cortina had. I saw represented in this number, say two hundred different Texan brands. We only gathered up the cattle near the water-holes. The Texan cattle were mostly cows, calves and heifers. Cortina habitually sold the steers for butchering. I saw the following brands, viz: Parker and Hale, E. Dougherty, King and Kenedy, Veras Brothers, and various other brands. . . .

Question. Have you ever heard, in your service, Cortina order or request, or direct any one to go and get cattle from Texas?

Answer. Not to his soldiers but to other people such as the Holiguines Brothers, and others who had his confidence. He usually advised them to bring in all that were foreign. He told them to go and steal openly in Texas. The most skillful thief usually holds a high place in Cortina's confidence and esteem. Sabos Garcia was the leading man in this business, and was high in Cortina's confidence. I have seen them consulting.

Question. Who are the principal agents of Cortina in his cattle thieving operations?

Answer. Sabos Garcia, Segundo Garza, Holiguines Brothers (Andres and Esminargildo), Perales Brothers (Sylverio and Pedro), Antonio Belangel, Francisco Villareal, Juan Garcia, Librado—Lugo Brothers (now dead), Jurado (now dead), these are men who operated on the river below the Bolsa (say sixty miles of the river line). There are other robber chiefs who operate alone, and make no acknowledgment of Cortina's power. . . . The Lugo Brothers, and Jurado, mentioned above, were killed on account of being in arms against the government and not on account of their Texan depredations.[37]

The information gathered at the commissioners' public hearings aroused official indignation on the other side of the river. A by-product of the warring along the Rio Grande was a paper war over whether there were any such criminal doings as reported and, if there were, who caused them. Not to be outdone by the United States, the Mexican government appointed a commission of its own. The report it prepared naturally claimed that Mexican ranchers in Texas were being heartlessly victimized by Texan thieves but troubled itself little with specific testimony signed and sworn to in support of the charges. The Mexican report reached the enlightened conclusion that "society in Texas" was "utterly demoralized and corrupt" and that the corruption had "spread its pernicious influence to the regions of the Bravo and the Nueces." It did not neglect to mention as an example of pernicious corruption in Texas a rancher by the name of Richard King who was accused, without adducing testimony to back the accusation, of branding calves that belonged to his neighbors' cows.[38]

The paper war with border thieves was by no means ended in the blast and counterblast released in the reports of the United States and of the Mexican Commissions of 1872. In 1875, a Permanent Committee of Brownsville citizens prepared and printed an exhaustive account of the depredations suffered at the hands of Mexican thieves and bandits;[39] a Congressional Committee of the 44th Congress in 1876 drew up an even longer list of specific murders, burnings, losses, thefts to which the south tip of Texas had been subjected.[40] Yet all this documentation produced little more than prime source material for the writing of history in a later day. At the time, the reports brought no comfort and very little direct aid to the ravaged citizens above the Line of the Bravo.

In 1872, Cortina's *jefe*, President Benito Juárez, died of a stroke. When his successor to the presidency, Sebastián Lerdo de Tejada, assumed power Cortina was relieved of his post as Commander of the Line of the Bravo. Yet the crafty and by now rich and arrogant Cheno maintained himself as the actual if not the official Mexican military power on the border for almost four more years. Ordered to Mexico City by President Lerdo, Cortina resigned his commission as a general and refused to obey his president. When Lerdo managed to arrest this border troublemaker and bring him to the capital, Cortina escaped custody, returned to his own private army on the border, defied the government of Mexico by "pronouncing" for an opponent of Lerdo's, Porfirio Díaz, and in a kind of desperate defiance brought depredations in Texas to their highest tide.[41]

The Wild Horse Desert suffered mightily again, in its old phrase, "the disturbances of the time." In 1875, many of its ranches were again deserted; many of its rancheros had again moved to town to protect themselves and their families. In the words of the report to the 44th Congress, "the question with the people has become one of existence, not of pecuniary loss."[42]

Among the citizens who did not move to town, who chose to stay on their ranches with their families and to fight the raiders as they came, were Richard King at the Santa Gertrudis and Mifflin Kenedy at the Laureles.

In recounting the situation Rip Ford wrote later that Mifflin Kenedy was "less exposed to the vengeful feelings of the raiding

Mexicans" through the influence of his wife, Petra Vela Kenedy, who "did not meet any of the bandits, but . . . could reach them through others."[43] Whether or not this was so, Kenedy was president of the Stock Raisers Association of Western Texas and active in every countermeasure that could be taken against the thieves.

Richard King's status with the bandits was unmitigated by any "influence" in his favor. Furthermore, his prominence in the fight against lawlessness had long since made him an object of "peculiar enmity."[44] Cortina had sworn to capture and to hang the owner of the ranch on the Santa Gertrudis and more than once tried to ambush him. The black-bearded Captain King fought back with everything he had. When John S. McCampbell of Corpus Christi, who in 1873 had abandoned his practice of law because of the dangers of travel to attend the courts, was asked about King at his isolated ranch, McCampbell replied with a clear note of doubt: "He thinks he can defend himself."[45]

His defenses and his *Kineños* had met the test of fire. On February 12 or 13, 1875, "a large herd of horses was taken from Captain King's ranch, or from about there, and several of his men were killed."[46] There is record now of only one occasion, less than a month later, when his ranch was so besieged that its defense was a doubt in Richard King's own mind. On March 20, 1875, an Army telegram from the Department of Texas was relayed by General W. T. Sherman to Secretary of War Belknap:

THE COUNTRY BETWEEN CORPUS CHRISTI AND THE RIO GRANDE IS IN A STATE OF CONFUSION AND WAR, AND IS FULL OF ARMED BANDS OF MEXICANS, ROBBING AND DEVASTATING THE WHOLE SECTION. FIVE RANCHES HAVE BEEN BURNED AND SEVERAL PEOPLE KILLED AND WOUNDED. WIRES CUT BETWEEN CORPUS CHRISTI AND BROWNSVILLE. A COURIER SENT FROM KING'S RANCH BRINGS INTELLIGENCE THAT THEY ARE SURROUNDED BY A LARGE PARTY OF MEXICANS, AND ASK FOR AID.[47]

Beyond the one communication there is no further record of this climax to Richard King's war with bandits. The only certainty is that the ranch received no help from the Army. A border tale relates that the raiders attacked and were given a good beating, that some were killed, others captured and hanged by *Kineños*.[48] In the absence of any documentation beyond the Army message, it seems more likely that the raiders themselves thought Richard King could defend himself and that they melted away.

While the Santa Gertrudis was being threatened in that month of March, 1875, a band of fifty heavily armed Mexicans, with some of Cortina's bravos identified amongst them, perpetrated a sordid raid on the hamlet of Nuecestown, twelve miles from Corpus Christi. They hanged one man, killed another, wounded two, stripped and tortured a number of prisoners caught on the outskirts of Corpus Christi.[49] The depravity of the raiders and their penetration more than a hundred and sixty miles north of the Rio Grande aroused wild alarm along the Nueces and resulted in the raising of several so-called "Minute Companies" which proceeded to outdo the brutality of the raiders, hanging and killing innocent Mexicans who lived in the vicinity, looting and burning houses, bringing the whole area to the verge of mob rule.[50]

At this high tide of violence, a belated, infinitely welcome help was on its way to the border.

In January of 1874, Governor Richard Coke, elected by the people of Texas and not by the ballot stuffing of Carpetbaggers, had taken the reins of office from E. J. Davis. A Democratic legislature had already abolished the Texas State Police; late in 1874, the Texas Rangers had been re-established, to the relief of every decent citizen in every frontier county of the state. In the spring of 1875, an extraordinary officer by the name of L.H. McNelly, former Rebel, one of the few men with a fine record in the Texas State Police, was

commissioned as a captain of Texas Rangers to enlist a company for special duty on the lower Rio Grande.[51]

On April 18, 1875, authorities at Austin received a telegram from Sheriff John McClane of Nueces County:

IS CAPT MCNELLY COMING. WE ARE IN TROUBLE. FIVE RANCHES BURNED BY DISGUISED MEN NEAR LA PARRA LAST WEEK. ANSWER.[52]

Captain McNelly came, disbanded the "Minute Companies," made short work of the villainous excesses of "disguised men," then late in May led his rangers south to Brownsville.

His arrival there coincided with a burst of activity on the part of cattle thieves in the area. Their chieftain Cortina happened to be gathering livestock in Texas to fill a contract for the delivery of 3500 beeves to Spanish army garrisons in Cuba. A ship was waiting at Bagdad; Cortina was watching it load.[53]

McNelly hit like a bolt of lightning from a clear sky. Early in the morning of June 12, on the Palo Alto prairie fourteen miles north of Brownsville, the ranger captain with twenty-two of his men struck a band of about a dozen bandits driving three hundred stolen cattle toward the river. In the blazing fight one ranger was killed; not one of the thieves got away alive. Next day the bandits' dead bodies were hauled in and dumped on the market square in Brownsville. As a public notice, it was a statement bandits could understand, published in their own language. The bodies were quickly identified as some of Cortina's more notorious bravos; the display aroused a great wrath across the river. And after ten long years of banditry unpunished, the dead bodies left for relatives to claim on the market square of Brownsville that day in June aroused an entirely unaccustomed caution on the part of men who made their living stealing cattle.[54]

The 31-year-old Leander H. McNelly was a leader exactly formed for the work he found on the border. With less than fifty men, in less than a year, he broke the back of a long war with hundreds of organized brigands. He burned himself out at it, dying young from the tuberculosis his life of exposure and hardship brought him. But while he lasted—there were never any like him.

He had a soft voice, an even temper and a cold steel disdain for personal danger. Beneath this unassailable cool steadiness burned a flame that made him a brilliant leader, a fire that warmed the hearts of the men he led, that kindled them with respect for him in camp, with emulation for him in a fight. The men he enlisted to follow him were all young and they did not stay unless they were daring. There were only a handful of Texans; their captain preferred to recruit from backgrounds remote from any locale of ranger duty. The basic requirements for service were unflinching bravery and disregard of hardship; skill with firearms and horses came next. McNelly was a demanding master who made his demands by example. The western frontier seems not to have had at any time a more fearless band of disciplined fighters than McNelly's border company of Texas Rangers.[55]

The only way McNelly could catch bandits—he never had more than forty rangers to patrol the whole area—was to be in the right place at the right time. To be there, it was necessary to have advance information and the only way to get that information was from spies or captives. McNelly used both.

The bandits had their informers among the rancheros in Texas. Fighting fire with fire, McNelly set about acquiring spies among the bandits in Mexico. He said, "I made inquiry about the character of the men who composed the various bands on the opposite bank and I found they were organized into bands of fifteen or twenty or thirty, . . . I made inquiries into the personal character and reputation of the individuals of the bands and I selected those whom I knew to be tricky." To these tricky ones McNelly offered more money than they could make by raiding, a regular salary of sixty dollars a month plus additional rewards depending on the number of thieves identified with any foray for which the spy furnished advance information. McNelly said he found the informers "reliable and trustworthy. I did not propose to interfere with their own individual stealing at all. I gave them liberty, when I was not there in their neighborhood, to cross over with their friends, and get cattle and return again."[56] The money required to pay these spies was clearly outside any ranger service budget; some of the members of the Stock Raisers Association were furnishing McNelly with a war chest. At the time, Richard King was supplying the rangers with beef.[57] He doubtless supplied more, including his own network of informers and contacts with border characters whom McNelly could trust.

McNelly also got information from the thieves he captured. Fighting ruthless enemies, McNelly used ruthless methods. Among the recruits he took into his company was a strange figure named Jesús Sandobal, who from his knowledge of the language and of the country was given charge of forcing information from prisoners. Sandobal often hung them afterwards. His cruelty stemmed from vengeance: the ranch he owned in Texas had been destroyed and his wife and daughter violated by raiders. McNelly used "Casuse" Sandobal as a harsh instrument in a harsh operation. The border war with cow bandits was at no time, on either side, a tournament of chivalry.[58]

For five months following the fight on the Palo Alto prairie the rangers had no major encounter with any big band of raiders. During that time McNelly's men caught scattered thieves and recovered herds of stolen livestock north of the river, while McNelly entertained the growing conviction that the only way to end the border's trouble was to hit the heart of the matter: to strike with full force *south* of the river.

Through his spies McNelly learned that the principal lair of the organized brigands was a fortified ranch called Las Cuevas belonging to a General Juan Flores, located in the brush three miles south of the river, twelve miles below Rio Grande City and Ringgold Barracks. The proximity of Las Cuevas to a post of newly arrived troopers belonging to the Eighth Cavalry at Ringgold suggested an augury for the operation McNelly began to plan. He lost no opportunity to meet Army officers and to work at an Army promise for cooperation with a ranger thrust across the Rio Grande—where it would do the most good. Though the Army was hampered by its usual instructions not to violate neutrality by pursuing bandits into Mexico, field officers stationed on the border lent the ranger captain a sympathetic ear.

Early in November, McNelly learned that Las Cuevas was to be the gathering point of 18,000 head of Texas cattle which Mexican traffickers in stolen livestock had contracted to deliver to purchasers in Monterrey within ninety days. He made this information known to the Army; on November 12, McNelly had seen the commander at Ringgold, Major A.J. Alexander, and had gotten a promise from him that he would "instruct his men to follow raiders wherever I will go." Alexander's promise was backed by a similar commitment from his superior in command at Brownsville, Colonel Potter. Sharpened with this prospect and alerted for the expected raiders bringing stolen herds south toward Las Cuevas, McNelly took the field planning to pursue the raiders into Mexico, when necessary, and to wipe them out with United States Army help.[59]

Events did not conform to McNelly's plans.

While he and his men were in the brush near Edinburg[60] fifty-five miles downriver late in the afternoon of November 17, a scouting company of the Eighth Cavalry found a gang of bandits chousing a herd of cattle into Mexico at the Las Cuevas crossing. In the firing, two thieves were killed and another wounded, but the troopers did not cross the river in pursuit. Instead, they made camp on the Texas river bank, to await further orders.

No dispatch rider was needed. That evening the old wilderness warfare on the remote Rio Grande partook of a new time: a telegraph line now ran along the river close by the cavalry camp. A field telegrapher was soon in communication with Ringgold Barracks and Fort Brown. And the wires went on to Washington.

During the night, Colonel Potter at Brownsville ordered Major Alexander at Ringgold to reinforce and to assume command of the encamped troops at the Las Cuevas crossing; at dawn another cavalry unit came from downriver and joined the force.

There were at least a hundred troopers perched on the river bank doing nothing when Captain McNelly, riding alone, came into the camp at noon on November 18. He quietly announced he intended to go into Mexico after the stolen cattle as soon as his rangers arrived, and he dispatched a messenger for them. They rode the fifty-five miles to the Las Cuevas crossing in five hours.

The telegraph wires had already tangled the troops with Army red tape and with second thoughts on the part of the command. When McNelly asked the senior officer present on the river bank, Major Clendenin, for troops to go with the rangers into Mexico, the request was refused, though Clendenin said, "If you are determined to cross, we will cover your return." Knowing the odds his rangers faced on the other side of the river, McNelly replied "that not one of us could get back alive without the aid of their troops."

McNelly shoved off that night. Five men swam their horses to the other bank; the others, including McNelly, crossed three at a time in a leaky Mexican scow. At four o'clock in the morning on November 19, the ranger company stood gathered in the dark on the Mexican side of the Rio Grande: thirty men, five mounted, each man carrying only pistol and rifle, with forty rounds of ammunition for each weapon, and a little broiled goat meat prepared before the crossing. With this force McNelly expected to attack a fortified ranch he knew was defended by at least ten times his own number. He expected no quarter from them and he expected to give none. He took the risk believing that his action would bring the United States Army into Mexico and into decisive war against the brigands.

Standing in the dark before daybreak he said, "Boys, the pilot tells me that Las Cuevas Ranch is picketed in with high posts set in the ground with bars for a gate. We will march single file as the cow-trail is not wide enough for you to go in twos. The mounted men will go first, and when we get to the ranch the bars will be let down and I want the five men on horses to dash through the ranch yelling and shooting to attract attention and the rest of us will close in behind and do the best we can. Kill all you see except old men, women and children. These are my orders and I want them obeyed to the letter."

At first dawn they arrived before the heavy picket posts they thought enclosed Las Cuevas. McNelly inspected his little invasion force in the dim light. "Boys," he said, "I like your looks all right —you are the palest set of men I ever looked at. That is a sign you are going to do good fighting. In the Confederate army I noticed that just before battle all men get pale."

Gate bars were let down. The rangers charged in yelling and shooting, killing four men surprised while chopping wood for breakfast fires. In the growing light, the guide suddenly told McNelly that he had made a mistake, that he was in the wrong rancho, that this was a place called the Cachattus, that the Las Cuevas headquarters was a half mile up the trail.

By the time the rangers had made their way on to Las Cuevas

itself, more than two hundred mounted Mexican soldiers were dashing into the stronghold, stirred up by the shooting they had heard at the outlying rancho. McNelly formed a line and opened fire but soon decided to withdraw. "Our surprise is gone," he explained. "It would be suicide to charge them with only thirty men. We will go back to the river."

At the river's edge, McNelly had no thought of recrossing to the Texas side. Posting two pickets in the brush, he hid the rest of his men under the cover of the river bank, hoping the Mexicans would come in pursuit — and still hoping to bring United States cavalrymen into Mexico for a fight.

The bandits were not long in coming. About twenty-five horsemen dashed from the brush expecting to catch their enemies swimming the river. The rangers charged up from the river bank and opened fire, advancing. After a hot exchange the horsemen wheeled back into the thickets. They left a dead man on the open field. When the rangers moved up firing to where he lay they found they had killed the bandit chief himself, the *dueño* of Las Cuevas, General Juan Flores. McNelly tucked Flores' gold- and silver-plated pistol into his own belt and ordered the rangers back to the cover of the river bank.

Meanwhile, Captain Randlett of D Company, Eighth Cavalry, had crossed the river with forty troopers. At the beginning of the action McNelly had shouted across the river — in carefully exaggerated distress — while his men were charging up the river bank and out of sight, "Randlett, for God's sake come over and help us!" Randlett had decided that the rangers were "in danger of annihilation" and had come over to keep the Army's promise.

When the rangers got back to the river and found Randlett with his troopers ready on the Mexican side, McNelly tried to persuade Randlett to go with him to assault the ranch. The Army captain replied he was not unwilling to stay on the Mexican river bank until his commander, Major Alexander, arrived on the other side and could give orders, but he refused to consider McNelly's proposal for a move inland.

They did not find it necessary to leave the river to find a fight. The enemy returned in force to avenge the death of Flores. At intervals from eleven that morning until nearly five that afternoon, the Mexicans came charging. Each time the rangers and the troopers beat them back.

At five o'clock, Mexicans suddenly appeared with a white flag of truce. They presented a note which was interpreted at great variance by Randlett and by McNelly in separate reports later.

Randlett said the truce proposal promised that the stolen cattle would be returned to Ringgold next day, that every effort would be made to arrest the thieves, that a withdrawal of American troops was requested. McNelly said the note as written demanded that the troops vacate Mexico—and only promised to consider any Texan complaint afterwards. He said that Randlett was ready to agree to such terms but that he, McNelly, refused to leave Mexico until the stolen cattle and the thieves were brought to him. The Mexicans then asked a cessation of hostilities for the night. When this was arranged, McNelly and Randlett moved back to the river bank. It was dusk; Alexander had arrived at the campfires across the river. He ordered Randlett and his troopers out of Mexico immediately.

As night came on, the handful of Texas Rangers stood alone in Mexico, and stayed alone. An overwhelming force of brigands and soldiers enveloped them. Yet with the bearing of a man who led a fire-eating regiment, not a company of thirty, McNelly in the truce arrangements had agreed to give the enemy "an hour's notice before I commenced active operations." In the dark of the long night he had his men dig a trench by the river bank.

The next morning, November 20, the wires on the poles along the other side of the river made a high hum. The affair at Las Cuevas had reached Washington. Through channels, Colonel Potter at Fort Brown received orders which he relayed to Major Alexander, "Commdg. in the Front":

ADVISE CAPT MC NELLY TO RETURN AT ONCE TO THIS SIDE OF THE RIVER. INFORM HIM THAT YOU ARE DIRECTED NOT TO SUPPORT HIM IN ANY WAY WHILE HE REMAINS ON THE MEXICAN TERRITORY. IF MCNELLY IS ATTACKED BY MEXICAN FORCES ON MEXICAN SOIL DO NOT RENDER HIM ANY ASSIST-ANCE. KEEP YOUR FORCES IN THE POSITION YOU NOW HOLD AND AWAIT FURTHER ORDERS. LET ME KNOW WHETHER MCNELLY ACTS UPON YOUR ADVICE AND RETURNS.

The clatter of the telegraphers reached past the Army, into the State Department. The United States Consul at Matamoros was wiring the United States Commercial Agent of Camargo, standing in readiness at Ringgold:

I UNDERSTAND MC NELLY IS SURROUNDED AND TREATING FOR TERMS OF SURRENDER. IF SO GO TO HIM IMMEDIATELY AND ADVISE HIM TO SURRENDER TO THE MEXICAN FEDERAL AUTHORITIES AND THEN YOU GO WITH HIM TO THIS CITY TO SEE THAT NOTHING HAPPENS ON THE WAY. INSTRUCTIONS HAVE BEEN SENT FROM HERE TO AUTHORITIES IN CAMARGO TO ALLOW YOU TO ACT IN THE MATTER. ANSWER.

Copies of both these communications, accompanied by every official pressure, were hurried across the river to save the "doomed" rangers.

At four o'clock that afternoon, McNelly notified the Mexicans, according to his truce agreement to give one hour's advance warning, that he was *advancing to attack* unless his demands were met. He demanded the delivery of the stolen cattle and the thieves who stole them, with no legal dodges nor any excuses for delay. The ruffians facing this man with the lethal eyes, this *hombre de verdad,* gave in. They agreed to deliver to Rio Grande City at ten o'clock the next morning all the stolen stock that could be rounded up and all the thieves that could be caught. With that promise, McNelly withdrew — "reserving the right, if I saw proper, to go to Camargo and take the cattle."

The next morning McNelly took ten rangers to Rio Grande City to get the cattle; he was fairly certain he would get no thieves. Instead of cattle, he got a note. The *jefe* in Camargo wrote: "Because of excessive work on hand, I do not send you the cattle today, but early tomorrow morning. . . ." McNelly wrote a note in return, which ended: "As the Commanding Officer of the United States forces is here awaiting your action in this matter, I would be glad if you would inform me of the earliest hour at which you can deliver these cattle and any of the thieves you may have apprehended."

The Commanding Officer was not "awaiting" and would have done nothing about it if he had been. But McNelly's acute mention of the United States Army was not lost upon the *jefe* in Camargo, who forthwith changed the schedule of his excessive work on hand. He wrote a note informing McNelly that the cattle would be delivered at three o'clock that afternoon.

Seventy-five stolen cattle close-herded by twenty-five Mexicans armed with Winchesters and pistols came to the river's edge at three. McNelly with his ten men, armed, had come over on the ferry to meet them. McNelly asked the drovers to put the cattle on the Texas side, as agreed. The *caporal* refused, saying it was impossible until the cattle "were inspected." McNelly told his interpreter to tell the *caporal* that the cattle were stolen from Texas without being inspected and they were going back that way. The *caporal* said no. McNelly rapped out an order. The startled drovers were instantly looking down the barrels of the rangers' cocked guns. One of the men holding one of the cocked guns said later that McNelly told the interpreter "to tell the son-of-a-bitch that if he didn't deliver the cattle across the river in less than five minutes he would kill all of them, and he would have done it too, for he had his red feather raised. If you ever saw cattle put across the river in a hurry those Mexicans did it—"

In the herd that came back at last, after the long years in which herds moved only one way, there were thirty-five head of cattle wearing the brand of Richard King. McNelly thought his good friend might be glad to see them; the next day, four sharp young ranger blades—George Durham, Ed Pitts, W.L. Rudd and Bill Callicott—volunteered to drive Captain King's cattle home. Callicott told how it was:

We reached Santa Gertrudis Ranch without losing a cow. We got there about 3 P.M. and sent the old Captain word that Captain McNelly had sent him some cattle from Mexico. Captain King came to us and said, "Well, boys, I am glad to see you. From the reports at one time I didn't think any of you would ever get back to Texas. How many men did the Captain have with him over in Mexico?"

We told him.

"What! only thirty men to invade Mexico with!"

"Yes, sir," we said.

"Were you mounted or on foot?"

We told him five were mounted and the rest on foot.

"And all afoot but five! And the ranches you attacked were Las Cuevas and Cachattus. Those are the two worst ranches in Mexico. They are headquarters for all the cow-thievin' bandits who steal from this side of the river. I know all about Las Cuevas, know when it was started. It was settled by General Juan Flores and I understand he still owns it—"

"No, Captain," we said. "The other fellow owns it—we killed the General." Then we told him all about it.

"Well," replied Captain King, "I am glad you all got back alive. It was reported that you were surrounded, cut off from forage and water, that it would be a second Alamo with you, that you would have to surrender."

"No, sir," we said, "the Captain told us when we went over that he wouldn't have any surrender. It would be death or victory or all get out together the best we could, and he meant what he said."

"That was a daring trip," said Captain King. "There is not another man in the world who could invade a foreign country with that number of men and all get back alive. Captain McNelly is the first man that ever got stolen cattle out of Mexico. Out of thousands of head I have had stolen these are the only ones I ever got back, and I think more of them than of any five hundred head I have."

He told a ranch hand to tell his boss to come with ropes, a saw, and two men. When the boss came he told him about the cattle and where they came from. He told him to saw off the right horn of each cow and turn them all on the big range for the rest of their lives. The old Captain stood at the gate and saw the work done, and then he told the boss to open the gate and let them go free as long as they lived. He wanted these thirty-five cattle to spend the rest of their days in peace.

Captain King invited us to go up to the house, but we told him we were too dirty to go where there were ladies—we hadn't changed clothes in ten days. Then he told us to take our guns and pistols and go to a room over the warehouse. There we found plenty of nice clean blankets, pillows, chairs, table, wash bowl, towels, water, candles, matches—everything nice enough for a St. Louis drummer. We made our pallets and about dark our supper came—ham and eggs, butter, cakes, pies, in fact, everything good to eat with plenty of fresh buttermilk and coffee. Captain King's two daughters who had just graduated from some school in Kentucky sent up two big poundcakes tagged

COMPLIMENTS OF THE TWO MISS KINGS
TO
THE MCNELLY RANGERS[61]

The McNelly rangers brought an abrupt change of demeanor to the outlawry on the border. The stealing of cattle from Texas, formerly such an attractive pursuit, lost its appeal. It began to be dangerous. Though the raiding continued for another three years, it became desultory and increasingly furtive. The wholesale depredation ceased, the outrageous open traffic in stolen livestock came to an end with the affair at Las Cuevas. The raffish practitioners of border banditry and the purveyors of border race hate lacked the guts to hunt a fight with men like L. H. McNelly and his rangers. When the rangers hunted them, they quit.

Meanwhile there were less direct but larger reasons for the ebbing of the tide of lawlessness. Revolution swept Mexico early in 1876; this uprising against the government of Lerdo, led by an astute and tough young general, Porfirio Díaz, recruited much of the border riffraff and led it away as soldiery in campaigns to the south. Like many of his countrymen, Díaz organized and laid the groundwork for his revolution during an exile in Brownsville. Unlike any of the others, Porfirio Díaz within a year created a force that pushed to the capital itself and placed its chieftain in a power destined to grow to an iron grip which would shape the history of Mexico for more than three decades. While Díaz was still in Brownsville needing money for the inception of his revolt, American citizens there lent him funds in return for a promise: to remove the "ranking cow and horse thief," General Cortina, from his troublemaking on the border.[62]

When the time came, Díaz took care of the situation with an expert touch. Though Cortina had pronounced early in his favor and though he had led the cavalry in Díaz's capture of Matamoros on April 2, 1876, Díaz passed over Cortina in choosing a commander for the Line of the Bravo and placed Cortina's former colonel, General Servando Canales, in command. Canales had never forgiven Cortina for the vicious beating Cortina had inflicted upon his little band of *Juaristas* at the Imperialist Mejía's orders in 1864. Canales finally had his day. He arrested Cortina on a charge of disobedience and condemned him to death. The magnanimous President Díaz forestalled the execution of his loyal aide Cortina by sending for him, requiring him to live in the capital, keeping him under surveillance and out of mischief for the rest of his natural life.[63] It was a squeeze play with a rougher squeeze than the wily Cheno himself had ever contrived, or could ever combat. By it, according to his promise, Díaz rid the Rio Grande of the bloodiest, most engaging ruffian it ever raised.

At about the same time, government policy in Washington became belatedly aggressive in the use of troops on the border. In June, 1877, Secretary of War McCrary was writing to General W. T. Sherman that it was the new President Hayes' desire to put an end to the trouble: "You will, therefore, direct General Ord [commanding the Department of Texas] that in case the lawless incursions continue he will be at liberty . . . when in pursuit of a band of marauders . . . to follow them across the Rio Grande, and to overtake and punish them, as well as retake stolen property taken from our citizens."[64]

This policy, joined to the policing of Southwest Texas by the rangers and coupled with an entirely new policing of Northeast Mexico by the iron-handed Díaz's *rurales* who stood brigands against a wall and summarily shot them down, quelled the incursions for good.

The man who had been the most effective single factor in that quelling died of consumption he had contracted in the line of duty, on September 4, 1877, at Burton, Washington County. Texas treated him shabbily. When he was too sick to ride, the adjutant general at Austin simply reorganized McNelly's company, omitting his name from the roster and appointing a new captain in his place, with no compensation to the dying man, who left a wife and two children.[65]

Richard King upon at least two occasions had sent the McNelly rangers a cash bonus as a token of his esteem for their work.[66] There is no record that he aided the ranger captain in his final illness or helped the widow later, but it was Richard King who had a decent monument of granite erected over the resting place of brave Leander H. McNelly.[67]

The commander of the reorganized company was Captain Lee Hall, another able leader. His rangers were in Southwest Texas to stay until they were no longer needed, until the administration of law by local agencies of government made the citizens secure.[68] The cooperation maintained between these rangers and the owner of the King ranch shows in such notes as the one written from San Diego, thirty miles northeast of the Santa Gertrudis, on April 15, 1880:

Dear Capt.

This will be handed to you by Pavlin [Pablino] Coy the man of whom I spoke to you and Mr. Fitch as an outside person—to work up the cases of *horse skinning* below you. Instruct him fully as to what you wish done and I am satisfied he will do it. Keep him so long as you see fit.

Truly your friend,

Lee Hall[69]

By that time there were United States soldiers encamped in the area. King had given the government a tract of land in the San Leandro grant, near San Diego, for the use of the military; a detachment of cavalry troopers was stationed there.[70]

And by that time, some of McNelly's young veterans—George Durham, George Talley, L.L. Wright—had left the rangers to work for Richard King on the ranch. In 1882, McNelly's sergeant and Hall's lieutenant, intrepid John B. Armstrong, with some of the most iron-nerved exploits in ranger history to his credit, became Richard King's ranching neighbor and strong friend at the La Barreta grant.[71]

The old days of unprotected isolation at the Santa Gertrudis faded gradually away. An era of security, of law and order, began to emerge as the decade of the 1870's drew to a close. Richard King's unremitting, bitter fight to punish violence had made him a special target for the hatred of those who made their living by violence. They had tried to kill him. He had been not only a special target, the size of his property had made him a large target. He was often hit. When the depredations came to an end, he had suffered live-stock losses totaling well over a million dollars. Losses to R. King & Co. from August 20, 1866, to November 11, 1869, were estimated at $2,003,040. In 1872 Richard King petitioned against the Mexican government for losses from the time he took over as "sole owner" of the agostadero Santa Gertrudis.* Again, in 1926, his heirs would press the claim.[72]

In testimony before a Congressional committee of investigation on January 24, 1876, Captain McNelly had said, "My position, in command of a company of troops, I do not consider half so hazard-ous as that of those men living on ranches."[73] In view of McNelly's own performance, he may have been stretching the ranchmen's haz-ards a little, but the hazards were there. And they were all in the day's work. The fight with the "cow-thievin' bandits" was only one phase of a ranchman's toil. The black-bearded ranchman at the Santa Gertrudis not only thought he could defend himself, while busy at it he became "the great cattle King of Texas."

*See Appendix VIII.

XI "This Mammoth Rancho"

CAPTAIN KING
could not have chosen a more profitable time to become an independent ranch proprietor than the spring of 1870. It was the first great "banner year" of the Texas cattle drives to northern markets. Trails were already well beaten; points of commercial contact between northern buyers and Texan drovers were already in smooth operation. The Kansas Pacific could shunt cars by the hundreds alongside the chutes leading from the big sprawl of cattle pens already

built at booming Abilene. For the three seasons since 1867, long trains had been carrying bawling, horn-clashing loads eastward across the plains to the Missouri and beyond, to growing packing plants providing growing cities with growing volumes of meat to eat.[1]

It was about eleven hundred miles from the Santa Gertrudis head-quarters to the railroad sidings in Kansas and the cattle had to walk. Captain King owned a breed that could do it. His strong-legged Longhorns, with a vitality shaped by generations of survival in un-fenced wilderness, could be driven ten or twelve miles a day for a hundred unremitting days and more, through heat or cold or drouth or deluge, across mountain or plain or unbridged river — and arrive thriving.[2]

The way was clear and the price was up in 1870. Stockmen in South Texas were affectionately referring to three-year-old steers as "roaming $20 gold pieces." A beef steer worth $11 in Texas brought $20 from a northern buyer at Abilene, who got at least $31.50 for his buy at the stockyards in Chicago.[3] Three hundred thousand head of western cattle, at least 95 percent of them from Texas, made their ways to the northern markets in 1870.[4]

The early dream of ranchman King, of building great herds until there should come a time of great markets, was in prospect of ful-fillment the day in February, 1870, when he signed the "Agreement and Final Settlement of Affairs of R. King & Co." Though ranch account books show that R. King & Co. had sold several thousand head of cattle in the period from 1866 to 1869, and though the part-ners were operating two or more rendering plants to dispose of scrub stock in the hide and tallow trade that flourished along the Texas coast in the postwar years, King and Kenedy had marketed only an inconsiderable fraction of their marketable stock.[5] King had at least 33,000 head of cattle on his own Santa Gertrudis in the spring of 1870; and from November 11, 1869, to August 28, 1872, he sold at least 13,500 beeves at excellent prices.[6] Most of them were driven up the long way to the cars in Kansas.

The horseback men who moved cattle north through the hardships of so many miles became known in history as trail drivers.[7] Yet while this history was being made, the word "trail" and the word "driver" were not to be found in the account books at the Santa Gertrudis. Captain King put his cattle on the "road" and the men he hired to move them on that road were called KANSAS MEN.[8]

Precisely when he sent his first herd to the northern market is not known. There is an old King Ranch story that he himself led his drovers with a thousand beef steers to St. Louis in 1869.[9] In view of the important business at hand all that year, with the roundup and division of R. King & Co.'s livestock, it is unlikely that he chose to be absent from the Santa Gertrudis for the months required to make such a drive. More probably he went by steamboat to St. Louis, met his herd when it arrived, and himself arranged its sale.

Whether or not he sold steers at St. Louis in 1869, it is certain that he was busy with his Kansas Men in the spring of 1870. He sent cattle to Abilene; they made money. His large operations in moving Texas beef to northern markets began that year.[10]

The great success of the 1870 season caused western stockmen to send a flood of 700,000 head of cattle toward the northern market in 1871.[11] Buyers could not handle the vast numbers of cattle offered for sale. As a consequence, half the stock from Texas had to be wintered in Kansas, unbought, at a loss to the owners. Yet King had another good season. At Abilene during the month of August, personally supervising his sales he suffered no losses in the glut of the market.[12]

Only half as many cattle, some 350,000, took the road north in 1872. While buyers were offering generally higher prices, a new trend was noticed in the market. There was less demand for mere volume. The great stockyards at Chicago, Kansas City, St. Louis and the East were paying premiums for beef of a better quality than the flood of scrub stock driven up from Texas. That year the Middle West produced a bumper crop of corn; farmers bought Texas steers to fatten for market. The stock feeders made a whole new outlet for dealers in the grass-fed Texas cattle, and a feeder industry to provide the markets with heavier cuts of beef began to develop.[13]

Though Longhorns from Texas were firmly fleshed and dressed out surprisingly well when fed with grain, their rawboned sinewy frames did not produce the choice grades of beef. Captain King from his beginnings as a rancher had been interested in improving the quality of his livestock. By selecting the heaviest and strongest cows and the best bulls he could find in the range stock available to him in South Texas, and earlier in Mexico, he had noticeably improved the size and meat qualities of his Longhorn herds. He was interested in improving them further. While he realized that no cultivated stock like that bred and tended in a cow lot could ever endure the punishment of a drive to Kansas, he was working for a day when a railroad would carry finer cattle all the way to market. Late in 1872 or early in 1873, King imported from Kentucky a hundred Durhams, a large proportion of which were bulls for use with a selected herd of his range cows.[14] With them he hoped to begin an improvement of his stock, just as he had already done successfully by using American blooded stallions on his mustang range mares. An item in the February 1, 1873, *Corpus Christi Gazette* indicates how heavily King was investing in the future of his ranch — this at a time when Cortina's raiders were scourging the land and the Robb commissioners were reporting the plight of South Texas ranchmen:

We understand that Capt. King's improved stock, lately imported, are doing finely. This enterprising gentleman, during the late cold spell, had snugly in his Rancho stable, not less than forty thousand dollars worth of the most valuable kind of blooded animals, consisting of proof jacks, durham bulls and cows, American stallions, mares, etc. Also a large number of horses and mules, intended for use on the Rancho when the season fully opens for cattle operations. The building of his pasture fence is being pushed vigorously forward. The future of his stock interests depends solely upon the amount of land pastured, and we hope the Captain's efforts will be crowned with success, as have been those of Capt. M. Kenedy in a similar great enterprise.[15]

By the very nature of his work, a stockman was a speculator. Running a ranch could never be "business as usual;" there was no norm to which "usual" could be pegged. Each season was a differing blend of compounded elements involving weather, grass, herd welfare and the human judgment required to make a successful recipe from the season's own variable measures. To the uncertainties at the ranch were added another set of uncertainties at market. Each season's livestock prices were a series of tangled factors of timing in the shifting scales of supply and demand. One factor unforeseen could measure the difference between a stockman's profit and his ruin.

In the year 1873, ranching on the western grasslands suffered its first harsh setback. On September 19, the "Black Friday" panic in Wall Street struck suddenly at the money market of the nation. In the quick tightening of credits and the plunge of prices, the beef market collapsed and many western stockmen caught in the midst of a season with obligations they could not meet were ruined. The market did not recover for two years; until it did, there were hard times on the cattle ranges.[16]

Captain King managed to sell his 1873 herds before the crash in September.[17] During that month he was taking a decisive step in the expansion of his ranch, acquiring title to an interest in a tract of land in the San Juan de Carricitos grant, which would later become a great southern section of his property. The road from the Santa Gertrudis to Brownsville led across the huge area of the Carricitos; one of King's stage camps was at an old water hole and rancho there, El Sauz; he had camped at the place hundreds of times. Though the Carricitos was in the region travelers called "the sands," King had noted how it grew nutritious grasses even in dry times. He had asked his lawyer Stephen Powers to begin buying titles in the Carricitos. The first deed came to him on September 13, 1873.[18]

In the hard year of 1874, King adapted his ranching operation to the conditions of the straitened market and managed to weather the depression. He shifted his attention from the sale of beef to the operation of his hide and tallow works,[19] to the sale of his horse and mule stock and to the marketing of wool from his sheep flocks. Nueces and Duval counties were then the leading wool producers in Texas. There were half a million to a million sheep in the region; wagons piled high with wool sacks often crowded the streets of Corpus Christi. King devoted a large corner of the Santa Gertrudis tract to his sheep and tided his ranch over until the beef market grew firm again.[20] In December, 1874, Mifflin Kenedy over at his Laureles was having the glooms over the prospects and was writing to his lawyer Stephen Powers: "I regret now that I built a pannel of fence or ever saw a ranch, but it is too late now for regrets and I must make the most of the elephant."[21]

King seems to have suffered no such regrets. He went on building his ranch. How big he had already built it was copiously recorded by a visiting reporter from the *Corpus Christi Gazette*, February 7, 1874:

The main rancho, Santa Gertrudis, is situated on a high hill between the Santa Gertrudis and San Fernando creeks. A tower or lookout, erected on the top of a large brick warehouse, commands an extended view, the eye taking in at one glance a scope of country for twenty miles around. The sight is delightful, combining the pleasant with the picturesque. On this hill the Captain has erected a large and commodious dwelling with the necessary out-houses. He has also a stable built for the use of his rancho, capable of accommodating from fifty to sixty head of animals at a time. The houses for his vaqueros are constructed with a view to comfort and durability, at a respectful distance from the main house. A neat and substantial picket fence encloses several acres of Bermuda grass; its appearance in Spring resembling a well cultivated park, interspersed here and there with beautiful shade trees. Several immense brick cisterns furnish an abundance of water for the residents of the rancho, while the stock is supplied from tanks and the adjacent creeks.

Efforts have been made to establish an artesian well in the immediate vicinity of the dwelling. Considerable money was expended in this venture, and the well sunk to a depth of one hundred ten feet, with fair prospects of final success, when the contractor departed on business connected with the affair, and his memory being remarkably poor, he forgot to return.

The Captain has endeavored to so arrange his matters as to render himself entirely independent of all the annoyances connected with the successful operation of so large a rancho at so great a distance from a City, and has furnished himself with all the modern appliances of a well regulated farm. The work prosecuted under his own supervision and from the forging of a horse-shoe nail to the erection of a first class house, can all be accomplished by those living upon the rancho. Upwards of one hundred men are constantly employed in looking after the various interests of the immense hacienda.

The Santa Gertrudis contains 78,225 acres, and originally was an old Spanish grant, the title from the Spanish Government running back through a long series of years. Of this tract about 65,000 acres are under fence, embracing within its folds grazing lands and unsurpassed in the known world for its abundance in producing and in point of quality. An almost impenetrable belt of mesquite timber borders both sides of the Santa Gertrudis creek, within the pasture, extending for a distance of twelve or fifteen miles, and abounds in wild game—deer and turkeys predominating in numbers.

In construction of the pasture fence great care was evidenced in the selection in both posts and lumber. Like the pasture fence of Captain Kenedy, wire and lumber have both been brought into requisition. The entire fence is forty miles in length, a portion of which is constructed of first class heart pine planks, sawed in accordance with orders to a special size, say twenty-four feet in length by six inches wide and one and a quarter inches thickness. The posts used are mesquite, the majority of which are from ten to fourteen inches in diameter, calculated to last a lifetime. In building the lumber portion of the fence, three planks are used, and are firmly fastened to the posts with wrought iron spikes manufactured for the purpose; the posts being set in the ground three and a half feet. The wire portion of the fence consists of three No. 9 galvanized iron wires, fastened to the posts with a wrought iron pin, so made as to securely fasten the wire on being driven into the posts. Above these wires and along the tip of the posts, is nailed a board of the same description as those used in building the lumber fence. This fence is perfectly secure, and it is more than useless for stock to attempt to either get in or out. This pasture is mainly intended for the pasture of beef cattle, horses, mules and imported stock. Another fence within the main pasture, is now being erected, with a view to the better and easier handling of stock intended for immediate sale. The pens used for working stock are constructed of the very best material, and are large and accommodating in their makeup.

The gates of the pasture are guarded by men employed for that express purpose, and for whom are erected comfortable quarters. There are six gates, distributed as follows: One on the road to the City, one on the road leading to Brownsville, one at the Escondidas, one at the Borregas, one at Las Conchas, and one at Los Indios. These openings have all been left with a view to confer the greatest accommodation possible to all concerned.

In addition to his landed interest embraced in the Santa Gertrudis tract, Capt. King has added thereto the Rincon de Santa Gertrudis, containing 15,500 acres; 33,631 acres on the Agua Dulce, controlling magnificent watering places and grazing lands; 13,284 acres on Padre Island; 15,000 acres on the Saus creek; Two leagues at San Diego, and by a recent purchase of the Loma Alto and dependent ranchos, 25 leagues, out of an original Spanish grant of 106 leagues, known as the San Juan de Carricitas. The whole of this immense scope of country consists of the finest of the pasture lands in Western Texas, and must some future day be of almost an incalculable value.

The stock of the rancho consists mainly of cattle, horses and sheep, although a great number of jacks and jennets, goats and hogs are included in the grand total. The cattle stock number about 50,000, out of which are branded annually 15,000 head of calves. Great efforts have been made by Capt. King to introduce a fine breed of cattle, in which we believe he has succeeded, his last importation having been weathered the past Fall and Winter in remarkable condition, now being thoroughly acclimated and out of danger.

Next come the horse stock, consisting of mares, colts, mules, jacks and horses, numbering about 6,000 head, out of which, in favorable seasons, are branded from fourteen to fifteen hundred head of colts. Like the cattle stock, large sums of money have been expended in the introduction of fine stallions and jacks, until the stock has attained to a degree of fineness unsurpassed in this portion of Texas.

The sheep stock numbering thirty thousand head improved Merino, yielding an average of four pounds of wool per head. In this as in his other stock, the owner has spared no pains nor means; to improve the texture and staple of their fleeces and increase the size of their bodies has been his great aim, which frequent importations of fine bucks amply testify. His main sheep rancho is Borregas, taking its name from the stock most frequenting that range. From here the stock are distributed to best suit the grazing grounds. This stock has for a number of years been in charge of Captain J. S. Greer, who has taken great pains and pride in their successful culture.

The last but not the least of the stock of this rancho consists of an unknown number of hogs. Five years ago 1,000 head were purchased and turned loose upon the range, since which time but few have been slaughtered or molested in any manner. They will probably now number between six and seven thousand head. A packery, two miles above the rancho, for the slaughtering of surplus and rough stock, furnishes them with the food obtained in the thickets, an abundance to keep them continually in a fat, sleek condition.

Many other interesting facts in connection with the rancho could be mentioned; but sufficient has already been said to convey an adequate idea of the proportions of this mammoth rancho, and the indomitable energy of its owner, and at the same time enable our readers to form a partial estimate of the wealth of Western Texas.[22]

With such an establishment as this, King was ready for the rising markets that followed the low point of 1873-1874. In the subsequent ten years, cattle ranching grew steadily into the dimensions of a boom which did not burst until 1885. Huge areas of untenanted wilderness became livestock ranges. Texas cattle not only went to the northern markets as beef but also became the breed stock for ranches springing everywhere in the West. Great herds of Longhorns no longer stopped in Kansas for the cars, but moved on, as stockers to the grasslands of Nebraska, the Dakotas, Colorado, New Mexico, Wyoming, Montana, the Rockies and beyond.[23]

In the spring of 1875, at the very time when the Santa Gertrudis was besieged by bandits, Captain King sent thousands of cattle to the northern markets. On January 31, 1876, Captain Kenedy was writing to Lawyer Powers that Captain King was "busy getting thirty thousand head of cattle on the road to Kansas."[24] Later that year, on October 5, the *Galveston News* reported King's return from his sales in the North and the East: "Richard King of Santa Gertrudis, the great cattle King of Texas, is at the Washington."

The business of the cattle King in marketing his stock was surprisingly efficient and watchfully administered. King selected his beef herds carefully, put skillful men in charge of them and remained in frequent communication with each group, by letter and by telegraph, during all their progress north. He knew how his cattle were faring on the road. He knew the state of the market. He traveled to meet his herds at the point of contact with their northern buyers. The acceptance or rejection of a price was most often his own decision.

The herds for the long road were usually gathered late in February or early in March when the grass in South Texas was far enough along for cattle to begin fattening on it. The drives were timed so that the herds, grazing on the way, moved northward with advancing spring. The King cattle were ordinarily driven to Abilene, though herds were occasionally turned eastward into Missouri for loading at Sedalia and delivery at St. Louis. In 1873, a railhead of the Missouri, Kansas & Texas reached Denison, Texas, on the Red River, which was sometimes the point of delivery; and after 1875, the sidings at Dodge City west of Abilene were often the terminal of the King Ranch drives.

A herd for the road varied in size, but it was usually within the limits of a thousand to four thousand head. Too many cattle moving together cannot do well. Big herds were often strung out to move in separate sections for better forage and more efficient handling. Half-wild on their native ranges, the tough and snuffy Longhorns were touchy to handle even after they became accustomed to the daily drive and were trail broken.[25]

A herd boss was in charge of the whole operation, in command of the men and the outfit needed to deliver the cattle to their destination. If the herd were large, the boss appointed a foreman for each separately moving section. A road herd of three thousand cattle was ordinarily handled by about ten cowboys, a cook who had charge of a team and wagon carrying camp provisions and bedrolls, and a wrangler who herded the *remuda* of mounts required by the cowboys, about six horses to a man. Such an outfit was usually on the road from early spring to late summer. Buyers met the herd boss upon arrival in the vicinity of the railroad loading pens, looked over the stock and struck a bargain after what was often a considerable and protracted dickering. Then the cattle were turned over to the drovers of the buyer or his agent and the Kansas Men from Texas returned to their home ranges in the fall, either by horseback as they came or, if their boss had sold the road outfit, roundabout by train, steamboat and stage.

Most herd bosses (called trail bosses later) worked for wages as employees of ranchmen sending cattle to market—though buyers often came to Texas, purchased a herd and hired an outfit to move the cattle north. In any case, a herd boss kept the road accounts for the owner of the cattle, disbursed expenses while in transit, directed the hands, was responsible for safe delivery of the stock, and often acted as the owner's agent in the sale of the cattle at destination.

Captain King usually put his cattle on the road using a different business plan. Instead of hiring bosses for wages, he made them contractors and profit-sharing partners. Most of his herd bosses were employees in other capacities; Thomas Beynon, John Fitch and James Bryden were ranch foremen. On the road, heading an outfit of Kansas Men and a herd of King Ranch cattle, they were partners in the enterprise rather than employees.

When a herd had been gathered, branded and tallied for the road, a King herd boss signed a contract which made him the actual owner of the cattle and the outfit that went with them, and further made him the actual employer of all hands, responsible for wages and provisions during the drive, though King furnished him on account the cash required for such expenses. The boss bought the herd by signing a note both for the value of the road outfit (horses, wagons and other equipment) and for the value of the cattle at their current price in Texas, payable to King upon sale of the herd to northern buyers. The partnership arrangement of the contract consisted in a split of the profits, which was the difference, after road expenses, between the price the herd boss paid King by note at the Santa Gertrudis and the price the boss got for the cattle in Kansas. By these terms King not only protected himself to the amount of the herd's value on the range before it left the Santa Gertrudis, he also gave his herd boss a chance for profit far beyond the ordinary wages paid for such work, which were about $100 a month.

To aid in making contacts with buyers offering the highest prices and to keep himself constantly informed on the trend of the market, Captain King employed a livestock broker and agent named James H. Stevens. King's comings and goings to the markets in the Kansas cow towns, and to St. Louis, Kansas City or Chicago, were largely determined by the information and advice Stevens furnished. King's herd bosses, working with the astute captain and the knowledgeable Stevens, were practically guaranteed rewards for delivering "their" cattle at the end of the long road north.

A picture of the business mechanism by which Captain King so successfully marketed scores of thousands of cattle can be revealed by one example showing that mechanism at work, by one set of documents showing exactly how one herd was moved from the Santa Gertrudis to the northern market.[26]

In January of 1875, King's foreman at the Agua Dulce, Captain John Fitch, agreed to boss one of the drives when spring came. King could pick a man for a job: Fitch was both a good man and a good stockman—his captain's title came from his service with Rip Ford in the Confederate campaign on the Rio Grande.

During February and early March, Fitch was busy with fourteen cow hands gathering stock from King's range. When the drive was brought together, branded and tallied for the road, there were counted 4737 head of beef cattle ready to move. They were divided into four herds which were to travel as separate units, each with a foreman, the necessary hands, a cook, a wagon and a *remuda*.

Before any of the papers were signed, Fitch asked a friend named A. C. Allen into the partnership agreement for the drive and this was evidently agreeable to King. On March 12 a contract was drawn up and signed by King, Fitch and Allen.* King agreed to furnish 4737 head of cattle for which Fitch and Allen agreed to pay King $12 a

* See Appendix IX for a facsimile reproduction of this contract.

head; the profit, "if any," to be made from driving these cattle to "a market in The State of Kansas, or the State of Texas" was to be divided, after the payment of all expenses incurred by the drive, one half to King and the other half to Fitch and Allen, "share and share alike." The same day, "in consideration of One dollar coin," a bill of sale conveyed title to the livestock from King to Fitch and Allen; actually, John Fitch signed a note for which the following receipt was made:

Rancho Santa Gertrudis, Nueces County Texas
March 12th, 1875

John Fitch Esq.

Bought of Rich'd King

		$	Currency
4737	head of Beef Cattle	$ 12.	$56,844.00
137	do " Horses	$ 27.	3,699.00
9	do " mules	$ 27.	243.00
3	do " mares with 1 colt	$ 27.	81.00
4	light 2 horse wagons & harness . . .	$ 130.	520.00
	Cash advanced you $800 Silver	.08 [8%]	864.00
	Total Dollars . . .		$62,251.00

Received payment from John Fitch this 12th day of March 1875, his note payable on demand to my order for Sixty two thousand two hundred and fifty one Dollars in U. S. Currency in full of the above account.

(Signed in Duplicate, both as originals.)

R. King

The expenses of the roundup camp, for supplies and wages while the herd was being gathered, were itemized and entered in account with R. King: these were to be included in the total expenses of the drive. Then Fitch hired the hands and appointed as herd foremen King Hinnant, Theodore Byington, William Allen and Willis B. Moore, at salaries of $108 a month. Under the four foremen, a total of 43 men were entered on the payrolls before the drive was accomplished. Twenty-three of these men were vaqueros with Latin names; twenty were Anglo cowboys; their pay per month ranged from $43.20 for top hands to $32.40 for cooks down to $25 for horse wranglers and common hands. They were all required to furnish their own saddles, bridles, blankets, pistols, spurs, leathers, clothes and bedrolls; and they had to buy their own soap, medicine, whiskey, tobacco and ammunition if they wanted such. Their employers furnished them with the horses to ride, and with the victuals at the cook's wagon: beans, bacon, rice, coffee, bread, molasses, pickles, and later as they traveled into certain areas, fresh vegetables, chicken, butter and milk. On the road, beef was to be driven, not eaten.

The day after Fitch and Allen signed the contract, the drive began moving out from Santa Gertrudis in four separated herds, each with something less than 1200 head of cattle, a *remuda* of thirty-odd horses, a cook and mule-drawn wagon, and the hands. They rode at assigned stations around the herd; the foreman leading off with the wagon following; the wrangler herding the *remuda* close-by; a top hand at each side of the forward point of the moving herd; a little ahead of the center of the herd at each side, the "swings;" farther back, the "flanks;" and in the dust bringing up the rear, the "drags."

Next day, on March 14, at Vaughn's Crossing on the Nueces, one of the herds lost twenty-seven head of cattle when they stampeded before crossing the river. In all subsequent accounting of the drive, the total was placed at 4710 instead of 4737 head; the stampeded animals were not written off as losses but simply as returns to King's range where they made their ways after breaking from the herd.

After this flurry, the cattle settled gradually to the routine of being driven ten or twelve miles a day and being held together as a herd on the bed grounds each night, close by the camp where the men not on watch slept in their "suggans" by the wagon. Scouting out ahead,

John Fitch advised on routes and watering places and was in frequent touch with his four foremen. He carried with him a little tan leather daybook. In it he kept meticulous accounts of the expenses he and his outfits were incurring day by day. On April 2, Fitch was buying half a bushel of salt for seventy-five cents and paying two dollars for "Ferage at Austin." On April 17, he had made his way north to Waco where he was buying two pounds of onions for twenty-five cents, buying a "curie comb 25 ct." and spending $3.50 on the repair of a wagon.

The four herds gradually strung out and away from each other. On May 26, one of them was still at Waco, delayed by high water on the Brazos. That day a top hand with this herd, John B. Morgan, was writing from Waco to his chum in one of the King herds farther north:

Friend Frank

It is raining like hell and we cannot travel so I thought I would drop you a few lines to let you know how the old thing worked we found the lost Cattle and Sold them I caught hell for a couple of days we had to do all the work alone for the hands we got were green as goose ————— Everything looks gay and festive here lots of ———— arrived night before last By Rail two fine houses to be established. No news from home

Your Friend
John B Morgan

Meanwhile, back at the Santa Gertrudis on April 10, Captain King was dictating a letter to Reuben Holbein, addressed to John Fitch at Fort Worth:

Dear Sir:

I am in receipt of a letter from Mr. J.H.Stevens, at Concrete, March 30th last, advising that the cattle had all passed up and moving along smoothly except the loss of a few head in the San Antonio river. I am glad to hear news so favorable, and trust that I may continue to hear such to the end, not alone for my individual benefit, but that of your own and Mr. Allens: Sincerely trusting that all well in the future in which I am prepared to assist, and desirous of promoting. Having heard that you lost your Memo book, I send you list of Banks & Bankers as well as friends of mine and Stock dealers Viz:

Bankers — Swenson Perkins & Co. New York, N. Y.
    do   Perkins Swenson & Co. New Orleans, La.
    do   Mechanics Bank   St. Louis, Mo.
Stock dealers, Adams, Burke & Co. Union Stock Yards, Chicago, Ill.
    do   Joseph Mullhall   Saint Louis, Mo.

Use telegraph freely before delivery of stock and taking any checks or drafts, and beware of counterfeits should you take currency.

You are aware of my necessity for money, and I hope you will be enabled to sell speedily, and without any sacrifice and remit me as speedily as you possibly can to either of the mentioned banks preferring that of Swenson, Perkins & Co. New York, being first assured that your draft will be paid.

I hope Mr. Stevens will remain, and give you his good advice and council.

I shall be much pleased to hear from you and Mr. Stevens at every opportunity.

> Yours very truly
> R. King
> per Reuben Holbein

Three days later, on April 13 at Flatonia, Texas, agent James H. Stevens also wrote Fitch at Fort Worth—and mentioned news of the banditry that had been occupying Captain King's direct attention at the ranch:

Mr. John Fitch

Esteemed friend & Sir. I leave to-night for Kan. May come out from Denison to see you if I find any buyers. Jim Reed sold at Austin for $20 currency. The Book you left at York Town Ed Lott will send it up by Fant. I suppose you will have heard of the Mexican Raid. 60 men came as far as Nueces Town, took horses & robbed one store of $2500 and left, hurt no one as far as heard from. My regards to Boys and accept good wishes of

> J.H. Stevens

On the way to Fort Worth, Fitch had trouble with his partner, A. C. Allen, over an unauthorized deal Allen tried to make in some horse stock belonging to Captain King. Allen's misconduct can only be inferred from the consequences it brought and from the following letter:

Santa Gertrudis, Nueces Co., Texas, April 17th, 1875

Mr. John Fitch
Fort Worth, Tarrant Co., Texas

Dear Sir:

I am in receipt of your favors of 3rd, & 6th instants, and duly note contents. I am really much surprised at Mr. Allens acts, and if your report be true, he has certainly practiced deception, and deceived yourself, Mr. Holbein, and myself. He has no right or authority to bargain or sell the cattle to any person without first consulting you and getting your approval and sanction. It was distinctly understood, that the Burke and Rider horses were purchased for my account, and for which purchase Mr. Holbein advanced him the money. Mr. Burke & Rider so understood it at the time, and now so understand it, as also Mr. Holbein; if it is otherwise, then Allen is guilty of procuring money under false pretenses, and in consequence will bear watching, which I regret to say.

You have all the authority to protect the property, and study your own interest, and which you must not fail to exercise to the utmost extent of the law.

Should Mr. Allen act in bad faith or dishonesty, or attempt to do so: Consult good legal talent wherever necessary. You have full authority to give bond and security in my name. I shall await your reply with great anxiety regarding matters in general, and your movements in particular in which you will not fail to post me fully, by letter and by telegram: the latter of which you will use freely, Should anything go wrong, so I can come to your rescue if necessary.

Regarding the Burke horses, it may be better as you say—to leave them until final settlement. I do sincerely hope, however, that all will work smoothly, and that you will have no trouble.

Should it be necessary for you to take legal proceedings to protect the Cattle from loss, waste or sacrifice in any manner—do so promptly, quietly and understandingly, keeping your own council. You can however, consult with Mr. Stevens confidentially in all matters.

All well and quiet here at present

Yours very truly
R. King
per Reuben Holbein

P.S. I wrote you on 8th inst. to Fort Worth. When you write don't fail to inform me where to address you. Sell as speedily as possible, and remit me all the funds you can, to Swenson, Perkins & Co. 80 Wall Street, New York, N.Y.

R. K.
per R. H.

Allen was on his way out of the Fitch partnership contract and Stevens was on his way in, though he did not know it yet. On April 20, Stevens at Kansas City wrote Fitch at Fort Worth:

Dear Sir

I have been up three days find the market much less than I expected it will not reach more than 125,000 head of all grades if meet a chance to sell for a fair price say $18.00 without too much cutting sell, though I think prices will rule firm up here. Indian agent fort sill here, he does not buy beef cattle wants cows, about ½ of the drive is sold under contract leaving a pretty fair thing for balance—if Allen wants to sell buy him. I did not make known to him any thing. Don't hurry at all—make a study move as I know you will do without any suggestions from me. Wintered cattle are selling 3 to 4 cents now in yards though not many are selling or offering. They bring by weight 25 or 27 dollars. I am told grass is starting fine about the Great Bend. I may come down in a few days and see what is going on around Denison. They are having some excitement west with Mexican Raiders. Can't tell where it will end. Regards to the Boys & accept the good wishes of yours truly

J. H. Stevens

Still at Fort Worth more than three weeks later, Fitch had settled his difficulty with Allen by removing him from the partnership and replacing him by Stevens whose name Fitch signed to the following agreement:

Fort Worth, Tarrant Co., Texas
May 15th 1875

This is to certify that I have this day purchased and received the Entire interest of A.C. Allen it being the one fourth interest of the profits of 4586 head of Beef Cattle. One hundred head being sold at Fort Worth May 4th 1875 leaving 4486 head of cattle on hand up to date. Said cattle valued at $12.00 per head at Rancho Santa Gertrudis Nueces County Texas from where they were driven and A.C. Allen to receive $16.00 per head in consideration of his interest to be paid upon sale of said cattle less amt. of driving up to date. Also to certify that this releases said A.C. Allen from all responsibility from this date pertaining to said Cattle together with 92 head of horse stock, cattle and horses branded thus: ᗯ

Signed: J. H. Stevens
by John Fitch

Witness: D. McKenzie

By the end of May, Fitch had moved on with the remaining 4486 head of cattle and was being addressed at Bolivar, about fifty miles north of Fort Worth. Sheriff John McClane of Nueces County was at the Santa Gertrudis and writing to Fitch, "Old Cap is in the finest humor all goes well Mrs. K starts to St. Louis this week." The arrival of Ranger Captain McNelly may have had a good deal to do with Captain King's humor — two weeks later McNelly would be wiping out the band of Cortina thieves in the fight on the Palo Alto prairie.

By the end of June, Fitch was at Gainesville holding his cattle on pasture nearby, evidently at the advice of his new partner and market expert James Stevens, who was angling for a buyer at the Denison railhead and considering the advantages of selling the cattle there without the necessity of driving them more than four hundred miles farther north to the Abilene market. On the last day of June Stevens wrote from Denison:

Mr. John Fitch, Cattleman
Gainesville, Texas
    Esteemed friend & Sir:
I leave to day for up country. Will try to look through all the herds for
〜 & C   I found one steer here yesterday being shipped [was] one of
ours. Had a letter from Allen he says he found all the lost cattle and sold
them. I will keep the letter & file with the papers when I return. Buy what
salt you need for a couple of weeks, I have bought 50 barrels here will send
it out when I can find wagons. Get it cheaper here. Give them all of the
room & quiet handling you can. Will bring a man to buy them when I
come back. Could not trade with Ellis & Lane had them on the point they
saw I would close they took it back quick.
Marshall says they will make us plenty of Money over the price by holding
but we will be satisfied with less & sell first chance If mr. Myers comes show
him around well and treat him white but don't close anything until I see you
Except it be all cash up. Knowing you to be always on the "cuidado"
                 I am   Yrs truly
                       J. H. Stevens

    As July wore on, with Fitch on the *cuidado* and Stevens still look-
ing for a buyer, their cattle stayed at pasture near Gainesville—un-
sold. It was no situation to please Captain King who in June had
instructed Reuben Holbein to write Fitch that

you are the owner of the stock to sell where you please, a portion, or all of
them; that you must place to his [King's] credit with Swenson, Perkins &
Co., 80 Wall Street New York, $20,000 by the last of July at the furtherest;
that you must not hold too long and act according to your own good judgment in the matter, delays are dangerous, and quick sales & small profits
are preferred.
    About trading the horses, and as you have charge of both horses & cattle
act as you deem best except that you have some 〜 horses of his own
raising that are valuable, which he would like to have returned, unless a good
Sale could be made of them. As to Mr. Stevens, he is under your orders, and
you are the judge in all matters. Write immediately and fully, particularly
about money matters; and at what point or place a telegram would reach you.

The cattle were sold at Denison on July 21 at an average of $18.44 a head, to the livestock brokers Bulkley & Powers of Leavenworth, Kansas. Five days later when Fitch had gone back to the herds, a note came addressed: "Mr. John Fitch, at Camp near Gainesville, Texas, Camp on Spring Creek." The note read:

Denison, Texas, July 26th, 1875

Mr. John Fitch   Capt. King here & says for you to come in right away.

Yrs truly

J. H. Stevens

The cattle King of Texas had come to put the clincher on the deal. He stayed in Denison until August 8, when he wrote to Fitch, who was back with the herds near Gainesville waiting to deliver to Bulkley & Powers, "you will have all Drafts made out in your own name for the Cattle you sold."

It was more than a month before the cattle had been turned over to the buyers, though most of the Fitch Kansas Men were paid off and sent home by late in August. Drafts from Bulkley & Powers were being paid by September 15. By that time Captain King was at Danville, Kentucky, Fitch was preparing to move the road outfit back to the Santa Gertrudis — because of the good horse stock King did not want to sell at prices offered in Denison — and Stevens was in Denison cleaning up the last of the business concerning the drive. On September 17 Stevens wrote Fitch:

Esteemed friend and Sir, please find inclosed acknowledgment of Deposit in Mechanics Bank St. Louis for $20,000. I left camp last Sunday 12 o'clk. All the boys well. Cattle a few head short on count but were near on range. Powers & Bulkley have sold to Maj Mabry ½ interest in the whole thing so you see we will get all of our money by 10th of Oct. if not earlier. I wrote the Capt. full particulars. Flies still giving some trouble. I will sell all the horses not needed to take hands home to Mabry & Bulkley for $30.00 unless otherwise instructed. They are going to winter over ½ of the cattle Either in the Nation or on Wichita. I have sent $8000.00 Dollars to N.Y.

to Capt's credit as from you also. I was left in somewhat of an awkward condition here. Drafts all made payable to you & no authority to use your name or assign for you. I took all the chances, knowing they were not acquainted with your signature. I used and came out alright but the chances were against me in the matter. Why don't you write & let us know what you are doing & how you are getting along & when you expect to start. Stiff norther blowing now. Think we will have an early fall. Expect Capt. here in a few days. I have had 3 chills since Monday on arriving here. My regards to R. Holbein & accept the good wishes of Yrs truly

J. H. Stevens

The enclosure in this letter read:

THE MECHANICS BANK

Mr. John Fitch   St. Louis 9/15-1875
     Denison, Texas
        Dear Sir:
              Your favor 11th inst is received with inclosures as stated to credit Capt. R. King, as you direct
                 Yours respectfully
                 Geo. T. Hulse—Cashier
Inclose for collection,
    Have also rec'd draft of ten thousand dollars from Martin Bank, Kansas City, sent on your account for credit Capt. King. I have advised Capt. King at Danville, Ky. of these credits.

The final balance for the whole venture was made in the office at the Santa Gertrudis headquarters on November 27, about the time McNelly's four rangers arrived with the cattle brought back from Las Cuevas. Accounts were turned in for the settlements which had been made with each of the 47 Kansas Men employees, with due attention to such minutiae as "Henry Wooten—leggins $6.00, pills 25 cents, whiskey and quinine $1.00." The wages paid all hands amounted to $7316.78. All other expenses, including the item of "Oct 26 4 pr. Boots *Premium to Fattest Herd*," came to $3574.52, so that the total cost of the drive was $10,891.30. The share of A. C.

Allen, according to the agreement he had made when relinquishing his partnership at Fort Worth, was computed at $2573.71, paid and listed against the total profit of the venture. A final recapitulation was drawn up in this form:

TOTAL SALE OF THE CATTLE

May 4	Sold to W. A. Day		100 head	$25	$2,500.00
"	" " " "		4	"	54.00
"	" By A. C. Allen		48	"	885.59
July 21	" to Bulkley & Powers		4478 head		82,618.60
Aug. 25	" " Deister		1 head		14.00
Oct. 21	" For Provisions		1	"	12.00
	Total		4632	"	
	Lost & Died		78	"	
	Total		4710	" Gross Proc.	$86,084.19

Gross		$86,084.19
Less cost of cattle	$56,520.00	
Less Expenses	10,891.30	
Less A. C. Allen share	2,573.71	69,985.01
	Net Profit	$16,099.18

Distributed as follows

Rich. King	⅓ is	$5366.40
John Fitch	⅓ is	5366.39
Jas. H. Stevens	⅓ is	5366.39
		$16,099.18

It is interesting to note that instead of taking half the net profit to which the contract agreement entitled him, King ordered the profits split equally three ways, sharing alike with his two friends for their work in the venture. The settlement for the horse stock used in the road outfit showed an additional earning of $62.67 for each of the three partners.

King's own proceeds from the sale of 4710 head of his beef cattle were $56,520.00 plus $5366.40 or $61,886.40 — minus the cost of breeding and raising the stock, which could hardly have exceeded two dollars a head.

Captain King clearly made $50,000 net profit from the drive.[27]

This venture, which he repeated scores of times—with as many variations—through the booming years of the 1870's and the first half of the next decade, has been presented here in detail not only to demonstrate exactly how King made the money that made his ranch an "empire," but also to show the business, the managerial and commercial activity actually required to move a herd of cattle from Texas to the northern market. This is a prime aspect of the famed Trail Drives for which little documentation has survived and for which history has evinced only a minor interest. The romance of the great herds moving north across the great plains, the adventure of fighting stampedes and Indians on the trail, the excitements of rioting in the saloons and bawdy houses at cow towns, the outdoor hardihood, the faithfulness, the skill of the horseback men who suffered every hardship to keep the herds moving north, these have been the subjects of a literature, but they have obscured the business basis for the enormous trade which in the thirty years following the Civil War sent 9,800,000 cattle, 1,000,000 horses and 35,000 men up the trail from Texas.[28]

The Santa Gertrudis was not merely the headquarters of a flourishing livestock enterprise, it was a home place. Richard and Henrietta King lived there, with three daughters, Nettie, Ella and Alice, and two sons, Richard and Lee. The "Old Cap" as Sheriff McClane and the Rangers called him—behind his back—was not merely the hard-driving, far-traveling, formidable *patrón* of a big spread, he was the head of a family to whom he signed his letters, "my love to all of Pets from Papa."[29]

Buried memories of his own boyhood, of hunger not only for bread but for affection, for family ties, were never a part of his conversation but were always a part of his conduct within the circle of the family he brought to being. The boss of the Santa Gertrudis, peremptory to others, evinced a quiet deference both for the wishes and for the opinions of his wife whom he not only greatly loved but very greatly respected. Toward his children he was tender. A natural desire to provide for them all that he himself had been denied made him a highly indulgent father. A granddaughter said, "The Captain did spoil his children."[30] He had no intention of spoiling them; he only liked to see them happy.

Their mother, who considered self-denial a cardinal Christian virtue and ostentation a cardinal social sin, did much to keep the captain's indulgence of his children within bounds.

Henrietta King's dislike for indulgence and for display was clearly exemplified by what she did with the diamond earrings her captain once brought her as a present. She could not forego the indulgence of possessing for herself the beauty or value of the gift and its meaning as a token of her husband's affection; she wore the earrings—after she had a jeweler cover the diamonds with dark enamel, to avoid the vanity of their display.[31]

Henrietta King was not Spartan; she was Presbyterian. She was mistress of a home in which there was no stint of comfort, good living, even luxury. In that home she presided over a hospitality which was both gracious and openhanded. But she would not countenance any vainglorious parade of the material blessings the Lord vouchsafed His servants.

By 1867, when the ranch was re-established as the King family home after the wartime sojourn at San Antonio and the postwar stay at the cottage in Brownsville, the frame house on the rise above the creek had been remodeled, enlarged, repainted, refurbished. A second story to provide new rooms for the growing children had been added to the main living quarters; a servant named Ann Brown was employed as housekeeper. Close-by the living quarters, the brick kitchen and dining room were enlarged to accommodate increasing numbers of guests at the table of the increasingly famed Rancho Santa Gertrudis; a cook named Lloyd Toasten presided over the big wood-burning range in the kitchen. A governess from Virginia, Mrs. McGuire, and a tutor, entered on the payrolls as "Professor Allen," helped Mrs. King with the children. At various times the isolated ranch also employed its own physicians.

The King children were not the only young members of the household: Henrietta's half brothers lived at the ranch. The Reverend Hiram Chamberlain, long ailing, had died at Brownsville on the first of November, 1866, "exchanging his life of labors for his eternal rest."[32] His widow had gone East to live, taking her daughter Adelia and her youngest son Edwin, while the other Chamberlain boys, Hiram Jr., Bland and Willie, had come to live at the Santa Gertrudis and work for Captain King. Edwin soon afterwards joined his brothers. All the Chamberlain boys were a lively part of the King household; the captain often grinned referring to his children's "half-uncles."[33] Of the four boys, only Bland—who was eighteen when his father died and who had worked for Captain King since he was twelve—was to live all his life as an employee on the Santa Gertrudis.

Mrs. King and the children were not constantly at the ranch. They traveled each year, accompanying the captain on a business trip or else meeting him in cities like Galveston, San Antonio, New Orleans and St. Louis, during his shuttles between deals with livestock traders. The Kings had a memorable trip to Kentucky in 1867; the captain bought blooded stallions to ship to Texas, while Mrs. King and the children vacationed at Kentucky Springs. Then the whole family went on to Virginia, to pay their respects to their old friend, the president of Washington College at Lexington, Robert E. Lee.

Proudly Richard and Henrietta King took their four-year-old son to see the great man for whom he was named. The care with which Mrs. King had scrubbed and combed and dressed her little Lee may be imagined. As Mrs. King always told the story later, General Lee paid a most gracious attention to his small namesake — and in particular, commented on the fine new suit Robert E. Lee King was wearing for the occasion. The august gray general looked smiling at the little boy and said that he liked the suit very much. All but the color. Mrs. King then realized it. She had dressed little Lee in blue.[34]

In 1870 Nettie King was fifteen and ready for schooling beyond that afforded by the tutor at the ranch. That year Mrs. King took her oldest daughter to Danville, Kentucky, and enrolled her at Henderson Female Institute, a solidly Presbyterian girls' school, near the solidly Presbyterian Centre College which had been attended by her "half-uncle," Hiram. In 1871 or 1872, Ella King was also enrolled at Henderson. The King girls, joined by their young sister Alice in 1874, attended the school in Danville until the close of the spring term in 1875, when Nettie either graduated or decided she had schooling enough. The King girls were at the ranch that fall — it was when they made the poundcakes for the four hungry young rangers.

The next year, Mrs. King transferred Ella and Alice to a girls' school more conveniently situated for traveling to and from South Texas, and nearer home, Mrs. Cuthbert's Seminary at St. Louis. All the Kings seemed to grow increasingly fond of St. Louis as a sort of headquarters when they were away from the ranch. They became familiar figures at the Southern Hotel, where they usually took rooms, and they had many friends. Mrs. King and Nettie made frequent and sometimes prolonged visits to be near Ella and Alice at Mrs. Cuthbert's; Captain King found numerous occasions to be in St. Louis on business and to see his daughters. He always arrived with gifts. As a granddaughter said, "He would bring all those diamond things."[35]

The ties with Kentucky were not broken when the girls went to school at St. Louis. In the fall of 1875, Richard King II, fifteen years old, entered Centre College. This was the important business which had taken Captain King to Danville while Fitch and Stevens delivered cattle at Denison in September.

Young Richard attended Centre for the next three years and graduated there in the Class of 1878. The captain sent his eldest son to college in high style. While he was at school the handsome and rollicky Richard II from the big rancho in Texas had his own carriage and manservant — he cut quite a swathe on the campus and in town.

When the time came, young Lee King also went to Centre, enrolling the year after his brother graduated. Lee, who loved most to learn the skills of the *Kineños,* to work in the cow camps, to hunt alone, to ride the solitudes of the ranch, was a far quieter and more serious boy than his elder brother Richard. He cut no swathe at Danville and chose not to graduate at Centre but to finish his schooling with commercial courses at a business college in St. Louis, where he could learn technical methods of accounting to use in his father's business.

All the King children spent their school vacations at the ranch where they found a life that attracted and interested them, though the two youngest children appear to have liked it best. Alice called the Santa Gertrudis "Home, Sweet Home." Lee's letters were shaded with nostalgic desire to be back in the midst of the ranch activities he loved. The King girls and boys had their own horses to ride. They knew the yearly cycle of the ranch operations, the roundups, the gatherings of the great drives. Traveling to and from the ranch, they were thoroughly familiar with the dangers of the roads, the bumping long coach trips, the circling outriders ready with their guns at every twist and dip and rise of the wheel marks through the silent, heat-dazzled prairies. During the early part of the 1870's, the family made annual expeditions to San Antonio for ranch supplies. Decades later Alice could remember the campfires by the road at night, the guard of armed *Kineños:* she remembered the rumble of the moving wheels of the King ranch wagon train, paced by the statuesque outriders sweeping through high grass, on fast horses with manes and tails flowing.[36]

The vivid lineaments of the cattle King of Texas, the "Old Cap" who kept things moving, were known from the Brownsville saloon of Celestin Jagou to the New York bank of Swenson, Perkins. More than sixty-five years later, the aged cow hand Jack Kivlin remembered the captain on the steps of the San Patricio County Courthouse. "He was a very noticeable looking man," Kivlin said.[37]

The tip of Richard King's black beard touched the second button of his shirt. He wore a wide-brimmed black hat strongly reminiscent of Rebel cavalry, a black string tie with the knot hidden under the beard and the ends of the rusty silk usually askew. Arcing across his vest front hung a heavy gold chain which disappeared into a pocket where he carried a watch the size of a big thick biscuit. His muscular and square-built body, height five feet eleven, weight one hundred eighty, was usually clothed in dark broadcloth coat and wrinkled pants that did not match. He went shod in the scuffed boots of a cowman no stranger to a corral. It was well known that when the captain appeared with one pants leg in and one pants leg out of his boot tops, the barometer was falling, the storm was on its way and "everybody better watch out."[38] At times in town he was spruced up and polished, though the effect was transitory; he had little talent for staying unmussed.[39] At St. Louis he once chided his daughter Alice about being ashamed of his rough appearance.

He walked with a slight limp. It was a characteristic which gave him a name: his vaqueros sometimes called him, being carefully out of his hearing, *El Cojo,* The Lame One. There are two stories about the origin of the lameness. One says that his leg was broken by being caught in a moving anchor chain during his steamboat days, that the break healed crooked. The other and less likely tale says that the limp was the result of a bullet wound in the leg suffered during an ambush on the road to Brownsville.[40]

There was another noticeable mark upon him. His left nostril was somewhat misshapen. This was no memento of a riverman's brawl but a scar from an inglorious encounter with a parrot which he had once brought home to Mrs. King. The bird had bitten the captain on the nose; it had healed with the nostril awry.[41]

As the 1870's advanced, the captain's appearance and manner bespoke the ranchman he had become. In one regard he did retain an old mark of his life on the river. He still liked to participate in a good solid fist fight and he looked for one once in a while — always at a safe distance from the strictures such a performance would evoke from his wife and usually while he was partaking of the "Rose Bud Whiskey" which was an item entered regularly on the captain's personal account in the ranch's books. Up to the last few years of his life, the captain never lost his knack with his fists. Some of his vaqueros liked knives, many of his riders were handy at a quick draw with a pistol, but the captain appears never to have acquired any taste for the use of such tools. He liked bare knucks. George Durham, one of McNelly's men who became a King man, told his son Ed that the captain hired a tough Irishman whose main duty was to fight with the captain when he was in the mood.[42] Back in the 1850's, Kenedy had seen his partner King lay into a big Army sergeant who was bragging in a saloon that he had a nice game: he was receiving M. Kenedy & Co. supplies for the quartermaster, jacking the price on the post books and keeping the difference. When fists had finished flying, the sergeant with more than one of his friends from the post had to be helped out the saloon door.[43] Twenty years later King could still connect. An old trail driver named Branch Isbell told Frank Dobie in 1925 that "King was a rough old devil. One time a man named Kelley who was working for him said: 'Captain King, if you were not such a rich man and a captain, you wouldn't cuss me as you do.' 'Damn you,' King replied, jerking off his hat, 'forget the riches and the captain title and let's fight.' The two fought for half an hour in a slaughterhouse where they mingled their blood with that of the cattle. Then they shook hands in mutual admiration."[44]

This streak of animal pugnacity in the captain's character was ordinarily kept well submerged. When fists were out of order, he had no difficulty in shaping his conduct for the occasion. The formidable force that emanated from his presence, the habit of command, made him peremptory in his ordering of affairs at the ranch; growing from this habit, a brusque self-confidence invaded his talk, causing even his best friend Kenedy to remember that King was "violently opinionated."[45]

But King's ego was not the bullying kind. It was never sullen, never withdrawn behind protective walls. It stood in the open, ready for all comers — and the same force that could make him domineering reached out more often to reveal a natural geniality in his cast of mind. An Army lieutenant introduced to King aboard a New Orleans steamer bound for the border remembered many years later how he had enjoyed the hearty company of the "great cattleman" during the voyage — at the same time recalling that Captain King "had a way of looking at a man that seemed to penetrate his thoughts."[46]

Yet a visitor to the ranch might be awakened from siesta to see the "great cattleman" carefully tiptoeing in his sock feet into the visitor's room to bring him a glass of cool lemonade.[47] The "violently opinionated" King would drop all other business to spring a *Kineño* from jail, to help a friend in trouble. Wherever he went, he was an easy touch for a hard luck story. His regret was genuine—and partook of surprise—when he felt compelled to say that a man he knew might "bear watching." He derived the same pleasure from giving a young tramp a job as he did in providing an Episcopal bishop with a comfortable carriage for a journey to Brownsville.[48] The force that activated him sprang from no lonely egoism but from the warmth he found reflected from humankind, from joys in human company, from loyalties men evoked in him and loyalties he evoked in them. He ordered his doings by the dictates of those loyalties. He had his full quota of human faults but unfaithfulness was not among them.

No strong man is without his enemies, just as no successful man is without his detractors. Captain King was both strong and successful. Men opposed him and men envied him. Any large accomplishment—let it be the building of a rich city or the writing of a good sonnet—sets into motion a chain of legends and lies amongst the neighbors. Legends ordinarily seem to be folkways of expressing interest or admiration; lies ordinarily are personal ways of venting malice. As the ranch on the Santa Gertrudis grew into a large accomplishment, legends and lies inevitably sprang up around it.

All the while the owner of the Santa Gertrudis was embattled with cow-thieving bandits and during all the years he was putting big herds on the road to Kansas, he was continuously engaged in practicing the advice of his remembered friend: *Buy land and never sell.* Richard King ultimately acquired title to more than 600,000 acres of pasture for his livestock. No part of the story of his accomplishment is fogged with more legend and lie than that phase of his business which relates to the acquisition of land. There are fables in great variety about how King got his land by going out and grabbing it, a robber baron beyond the law.

The truth, as usual, is less picturesque. King's careful legality in the purchase of his first two tracts of ranchland, the Rincón de Santa Gertrudis and the de la Garza Santa Gertrudis, has already been examined in an earlier chapter. His subsequent purchases, of more than sixty tracts, as large as 28,782 acres and as small as 320 acres, display the same care, the same legality. Every land acquisition King ever made was done through lawyers. They transacted the business. They advised King when he had rights to possession.[49] King bought every piece of land he came to own. He sometimes bought one piece again and again to satisfy multiple claimants.

The trouble came and the fables originated from the fact that King with his superior bankroll adamantly pursued an ambition to piece together a great and cohesive property on lands that were a peculiar piece of the earth as far as cadastral title was concerned. Most of the Wild Horse Desert was a giant jigsaw puzzle of Spanish-Mexican land grants. Primitive surveys of these whimsically irregular shapes left many boundary lines inexact. The pieces of the vast jigsaw were ill-cut: sometimes they fitted together too loosely, sometimes they overlapped. Wherever the fit was poor, there was room for contention over who owned what. No prim section lines marked the Wild Horse Desert into a neat and indisputable grid.*

The inexact cut of the pieces was not the only trouble with the jigsaw. There was a worse difficulty. Few pieces of the puzzle had a single owner. The land grants dated from 1770 to 1835 and Latin families were large. Their increase, pyramided for three or four generations, created amazing numbers of descendants from the original grantees. These descendants were the heirs to the land grants, and their legacies had only in uncommon cases been divided: with few exceptions, these multiple heirs held undivided interests in the lands of their fathers, grandfathers, great-grandfathers. Each undivided interest owned by an individual heir was called a *derecho*, literally, a

*See map, Appendix I.

"right."[50] To buy title to a land grant was to buy up all the *derechos* from the scattered heirs. Rarely did *derecho* holders live upon and put to use the land in which they held rather abstract fragments of ownership; some idea of the difficulties involved in a land purchase under such circumstances may be imagined from the fact that in 1879 King's lawyers were dealing with more than sixty-five heirs holding or claiming *derechos* in the vast area of the San Juan de Carricitos grant which King was trying to finish buying.[51]

To further complicate the problems of multiple ownership in the Spanish-Mexican land titles, there were the certificates for small blocks of land, usually in units of 640 acres, issued by the Republic of Texas and the Land Office of the State of Texas, which were often indicated within or overlapping the older grants. The small blocks were seldom tenanted or improved by certificate holders unless the land happened to be well watered or tillable, but whether used or not these parcels gave rise to conflicting claims which had to be satisfied by purchase or in the courts before title to any larger tract was clear.

To put together some 600,000 acres of working ranch from so many poorly fitted pieces of the giant jigsaw was the necessarily patient feat of Captain King's lawyers working in their offices and, when that did not suffice, in the courts. King had the money and the unbending will to pursue title to a piece of land until he got it; with his resources he had the undeniably final advantage. Die-hard squabbles with *derecho* hold-outs were inevitable, and King had them.

The lawyer-historian Harbert Davenport, who has practiced law in Brownsville for more than forty years, cuts through the hearsay in the fable of the robber baron and comes to the kernel of the truth:

Captain King seldom bought a tract of King land at a single purchase. He bought from heirs or assigns of the original grantees who wished to sell. It was not often that these were other than undivided interests. Captain King would avail himself of the title thus acquired to take possession of the land and bought outstanding *derechos* of other heirs or assigns as such were offered for sale. He never refused to buy from any true owner at the standard price for those years.[52]

From the year 1870 on, King had a standing order with his lawyers to buy *derechos* in certain land grants and to buy up titles to desirably located odds and ends patented under certificates issued by the Republic or the State of Texas. To enter into a chronological list of each parcel thus acquired, and to try to set forth the date of each confirmation of title, leads into the labyrinthine maze of the Abstracts of Title to the manifold properties of the King Ranch, on record in the court houses of the counties where the lands are located. Richard King in his lifetime acquired title to the following adjacent grants forming one great shape of pastureland: Rincón de Santa Gertrudis, de la Garza Santa Gertrudis, Los Sauces, Rincón del Grullo, La Bóveda, El Pasadizo, Miguel Gutiérrez Santa Gertrudis and Paso Ancho de Abajo. North of this central unit of the ranch, and not contiguous, King owned titles in the grants of San Leandro and Agua Dulce, with parts of the San Antonio de Agua Dulce, Casa Blanca and Los Preseños. Some fifty miles south of the Santa Gertrudis headquarters ran the northern boundary of a third separate unit of the ranch, the lands in the San Juan de Carricitos. By 1884, ninety miles of fence built on the Carricitos did not entirely enclose what King had acquired there. In 1885, the total area of the entire ranching property was 614,140 acres, "more or less."*

The expenses involved in the purchase of title to any one of the many pieces of the jigsaw, from the buying of the first undivided interest through the final paying off of all *derechos,* cannot be accurately computed. Added to the difficulties of land acquisition under the legal maze of Spanish, Mexican and Texan land laws were the prob-

* See Appendix X.

lems Richard King faced because of partnership entanglements. These difficulties are clearly indicated by reviewing, for example, the first land purchase, the Rincón de Santa Gertrudis. Compared to most of the grants comprising the ranch, the Rincón had a title which was easy and cheap to acquire. In 1853, King paid the heirs of Juan Mendiola $300 for the entire wilderness tract of 15,498 acres, or 1.93 cents an acre.[53] This is by no means what King finally spent for the Rincón title.

A few months after he bought the land from the Mendiolas he sold a half undivided interest to his partner Legs Lewis for $2000.[54] It is likely that this consideration was a side trade in which little or no actual cash changed hands. If King did receive the money it was still a transaction without profit, for when Lewis died, King was compelled to buy back at auction the half interest in the tract for $1575.00 and other costs.[55] His friend Major W.W. Chapman was a partner in the purchase, but he was ordered to California by the Army and was unable to comply with his partnership obligations, so that King found it necessary to pay the full amount of the note, plus interest, to Lewis' estate. King was tardy in payment. The principal and interest, added to the cost of having the Rincón accurately surveyed in 1853, and to the lawyers' fees and filing costs, must have amounted approximately to the $2000 King originally charged Lewis. So far, King was about even, at least on paper, with his start when he bought the whole tract for $300.

Then in 1860 the Rincón became a part of R. King & Co.'s holdings; upon the death of James Walworth it was necessary for the two surviving partners to buy back Walworth's one-fourth interest. A part of the $50,000 paid Mrs. Walworth was spent to retrieve title to this one piece of land, which represented approximately one ninth of the acreage owned by R.King & Co. at the time[56] and must be entered into the total costs of the Rincón title.

In 1868, the District Court of Nueces County rendered judgment in Confirmation of Title to the Rincón de Santa Gertrudis grant.[57] For this, King and Kenedy paid court costs and attorneys' fees in an unknown amount. Upon the division of R.King & Co. properties in 1870, title to the Rincón passed to King as sole owner — but he was not yet finished with paying for it.

In 1879, Helen B. Chapman, widow of Major W.W. Chapman who had died in 1859, brought suit against Richard King alleging that she was the owner of an undivided half interest in the Rincón by reason of a deed she had found among her husband's papers, dated April 25, 1856, conveying such interest from King to Chapman. At court King testified that Chapman had paid no part of the note due the Lewis estate and that Chapman soon after departure for California had sent King a release from the partnership agreement but that this paper had been destroyed during the Civil War. The deed held up in court. The outcome of the suit was a judgment in 1883 against Richard King for $5811.75 plus costs awarded John Rankin, executor of the estate of Helen B. Chapman, deceased. King paid the judgment.[58]

Exactly thirty years after making his initial payment for the Rincón, King stood as uncontested sole owner of the tract.[59]

Buying *derechos*, building fence, breeding livestock, fighting bandits, delivering huge herds of Longhorns to northern markets, the indefatigable big boss on the Santa Gertrudis found time for other business. His old practice of turning a profit by a joint venture, which he had pursued in his steamboating days, he continued when he became a cattleman. He was not only a partner in beef contracting and livestock brokerage firms like Broll, Paschal & King; King & Glaevecke; King & Plato;[60] he also owned an interest in the *Corpus Christi Free Press*.[61] In 1877, the same year he became a newspaper owner, he ordered ice-making machinery from Crane & Co. at Chicago and by June 1, 1878, he had built and set in operation the first ice plant at Brownsville. The next year, he established another at Corpus Christi. Loaded refrigerator cars had moved on rails from the slaughterhouse at Denison, Texas, as early as 1873;[62] King's ice-making clearly stemmed from his interest in the refrigeration of the meat products from his ranch.

The business of transportation never ceased to concern the former steamboater. In a fit of impatience over the poor service it displayed, King bought the mail and stage line which ran from Corpus Christi to Laredo and from Brownsville to San Antonio; he was its watchful proprietor for about a decade before railroads arrived to serve the area. King improved the stage line with such new equipment and fast horses that it maintained a dependable schedule but, unlike most of its owner's other operations, never managed to make a profit.[63] Anxious for every possible shipping facility to and from his ranch, in 1871 King became a director and strong supporter of the Corpus Christi Navigation Co. whose purpose was to dredge a channel wide and deep enough to make Corpus Christi a real port open to the ocean shipping of the world.[64] This goal was not attained in King's lifetime, though in 1874 the channel became adequate for regular calls by Morgan Line steamers — and when Corpus Christi needed a new wharf for putting cattle and wool aboard these ships, it was King who furnished the money to build what was required.[65]

Above all other businesses stemming from his interests as a ranchman, King was most concerned with a railroad that would bring his South Texas pastures closer to the nation's markets. At Abilene in August of 1871, King was receiving letters from New York concerning his subscription to shares in the International Railroad Co. which was planning to build a line from Fulton, Arkansas, to San Antonio, then to the Mexican border and beyond. With an eye on Laredo as a railhead for his cattle, King bought twenty to thirty thousand dollars worth of stock in the projected International.[66] Then he backed an able and energetic enthusiast, Uriah Lott of Corpus Christi—former employee of King, Kenedy & Co. at Brazos Santiago—in building a connecting railway to the border.

The Corpus Christi, San Diego & Rio Grande Narrow Gauge Railroad Co. was chartered under an act of the Texas legislature in March, 1875, to build and operate a line from Corpus Christi sixty miles west to the hamlet of San Diego, thence about a hundred miles farther west to Laredo. The State lands granted by this act, sixteen sections per mile of track, fell far short of being adequate to finance the project: the land at that time brought only about $100 a section. Private subscriptions for the purchase of corporation stock were painfully slow; the country had not yet recovered from the panic of 1873. Scrounging for money, the admirably determined Lott began construction anyway. King and his friend Kenedy, as chief supporters and financial backers of Lott, kept the track laying alive but progress was tedious, irregular, always in straits for funds. The single locomotive owned by the line as it inched westward was purchased by a subscription from the not easily discouraged King.[67] The rails finally reached Laredo in 1881, after Lott and Kenedy had made a trip to New York and sold the corporation to the builders of the Mexican National Railway, who pushed the line to completion and changed its name to the Texas Mexican Railway.[68]

When the work was done and the service was inaugurated, the company provided a celebration for the original backers of the enterprise. A special train carrying about a hundred citizens of Corpus Christi and vicinity made a two-day junket to Laredo and return. It was known as the "King and Kenedy Excursion." The excursionists were jubilant. "Captains King and Kenedy rode in a private car called the 'Malinche' on the back of a long train, and with plenty to eat and drink a big time was had by all." During the train ride someone poured three gallons of Rose Bud whiskey and twelve quarts of champagne into the lemonade tub. "It was drunk with avidity, and by the time the train reached Peña Station, a state of hilarity manifested itself."[69]

Though the little "Tex-Mex" was certainly no trunk line, it was the first fulfillment of a dream long nourished by Richard King. An unidentified newspaper clipping of the early 1880's reads: "The Tex-Mex railroad is driving ahead pretty rapidly in the cattle business just about this time. Yesterday I saw a train of about 28 cars another with nearly the same number, making in all, say 1800 head shipped by that energetic cattle king of Santa Gertrudis, Captain King, to Abilene. I am informed Capt. King intends to continue right on until he has shipped 6000 more."

The great majority of his herds still walked the dusty roads to Kansas, but the rails reaching into South Texas were promising less toilsome and more profitable tomorrows. Collins Station on the narrow gauge "Tex-Mex" was only twenty miles from headquarters at the Santa Gertrudis — and the whole world had moved nearer.

In the conduct of his constantly expanding enterprise Richard King found his lawyers as necessary as his branding irons. Early in the spring of 1878, Stephen Powers' law partner, Nestor Maxan, a handsome Louisiana French creole, was killed duelling with General Miguel de la Peña of the Mexican army, in "an affair of honor" over the pretty wife of an Army officer stationed at Fort Brown.[70] The scandal of the duel set the whole border talking. The demise of Maxan created a vacancy in the law offices of Stephen Powers which was filled four months later by a young lawyer named James B. Wells.

The 64-year-old Powers met the 28-year-old Wells one day in court at Corpus Christi and was so impressed with the young man that he offered him a partnership. Wells, a Texan born on St. Joseph's Island, had received a law degree at the University of Virginia in

1875. To his excellent education and natural bent for the law was added a warmth, a sympathy, an intuition for the characters of men. He had a gift for making friends. As the junior partner in the Brownsville law firm of Powers & Wells, he immediately made his mark, not only in the legal fraternity but politically in the Democratic party councils of South Texas. By 1880, when he married Miss Pauline J. Kleiber, daughter of a pioneer Brownsville merchant, the affable Jim Wells was one of the promising young men of the border, with a growing circle of friends on both sides of the river.

Stephen Powers' young partner quickly commanded Captain King's warm regard and complete confidence. Not long after Wells' arrival at Brownsville, he was on retainer to buy *derechos* for land King wanted. Wells' probity and legal skill, his knowledge of the Spanish tongue and his understanding rapport with the people who spoke it, gave him a natural rôle in the business affairs of his client King.

When the senior partner of Powers & Wells died in 1882, the mantle he had worn as the border's leading legal light and Democratic party leader fell inevitably upon the capable shoulders of his young partner.[71]

King was deeply affected by the death of Stephen Powers, the counselor through all the years since the steamboat *Colonel Cross* had moved along the river with a young Richard King in the pilothouse. On February 7, 1882, a much older Richard King found an indelible pencil and a piece of paper at the ranch office and wrote in his crowded, rough hand to Jim Wells: "It is with great regret I learn from Capt. M. Kenedy's telegram and your kind letter that my old and true friend Judge Powers has left us which is a great loss to all of us. You must double your energy in all particulars and take his place and stick in all matters which you can fill my dear friend's place. There is not a man in this State, less yourself, misses him more than myself. God bless him and his dear family."[72]

A few days later, Captain King rode to Brownsville to see Jim Wells at the familiar office. A new power of attorney was drawn up. Francisco Ytúrria, the captain's banker in Brownsville, was notified: "Mr. Wells will continue as my lawyer. Give him the money he needs and charge to my account." Peering around the office, the captain asked, "What about these books? You'll need some books." Jim Wells looked up at the library of Stephen Powers. "I haven't the money to buy them," Wells said. The captain advanced him the money.

The young lawyer asked questions. Exactly how often should he report on his progress? Captain King looked at him, squarely into his eyes. "Young man," he said, "the only thing I want to hear from you is when I can move my fences."[73]

During the later years of Stephen Powers' life, his client King's interests had become so diverse that it was impractical for Powers or his partner to represent King in every legal matter. A rough, long trip by stage from Brownsville to the Santa Gertrudis or to Corpus Christi where King had almost constant business was sometimes too great an inconvenience to ask of lawyers busy with their practice at Brownsville; consequently, King accustomed himself to retaining additional legal counsel at Corpus Christi.

In 1881, less than a year before the death of Powers, Richard King and Mifflin Kenedy had a lawyer at Corpus Christi bring suit for them in court there, to end a nuisance of trespass by a certain road across their lands. The counsel of the opposition happened to be a new arrival in town, trying his first case in Nueces County.

His name was Robert Justus Kleberg.

He handled his case so skillfully that when the verdict was rendered by the court at the close of the pleadings, the astonished Captains King and Kenedy found themselves soundly trounced.

That evening, the tired young lawyer Kleberg went to bed early, his happiness with victory shaded with irritation at the conduct of the burly King who during the recesses of the court had pointedly avoided recognizing or speaking to Kleberg, in spite of the fact that they had met and in spite of the fact that King was well acquainted with older members of Kleberg's family at Cuero, Victoria, Galveston.

Before Kleberg dropped off to sleep, he heard a knock.

He got up, lit a lamp and went to the door. It swung open to reveal the impressive figure of Captain Richard King with his black hat and black beard, his black boots, his watch chain glinting yellow in the lamplight.

Standing uncomfortably self-conscious in his night shirt, the young lawyer said, "Come in, Captain King."

He came in and closed the door.

"Kleberg."

"Yes, Captain King."

"I'm looking for a good lawyer. How would a retainer of five thousand a year suit you?"

Robert Kleberg gulped. "Why—when would that start, sir?"

"Now."

Robert Kleberg gulped again.

"Right now," the captain said. "We will drive out to the Santa Gertrudis."

The captain drove the trotting team along the dim road on the black prairie under the late stars. "The joke was on me," the captain said, laughing in his beard and slapping the reins. He explained his coolness during the trial. He said he had been so sure of winning that he did not want to appear friendly: after the trial, people might think Kleberg had lost by collusion. So King had been gruff.[74]

The two men talked in the darkness, in the smell of the dust churning up from the invisible trotting hooves. A little before day, they came up the slope of the rise on the prairie, to the dim shape of the two-story ranch house in the trees.

The captain went in and awakened his daughter, to ask her to make coffee for a visitor who had just had a long ride from town. Nineteen-year-old Alice, home from Mrs. Cuthbert's in St. Louis, got up and went out to the brick kitchen. She made coffee and took it with a plate of sugar cakes to the table in the dining room, and left hurriedly so that the visitor might not see her. Before she went back to her own room in the dawn light, she peered through the crack of the dining room door. Miss Alice Gertrudis King thought the young man who sat so earnestly talking to her father was very handsome. She met him later in the morning and that meeting, in the years to come, would shape the history of Richard King's mammoth rancho.[75]

XII "As a Pioneer He Came and Labored"

AS THE YEARS

went by and the sons and daughters grew up, the King family in its various comings and goings seldom found itself gathered under one roof. In August, 1880, the young graduate of Centre College, Richard King II, working for his father on the ranch, wrote his mother in St. Louis: "Lee, Bland & Papa are out on the front porch talking. All that's missing to make us happy is Mamacita, & the girls. I think there will be great rejoicing in camp when all the females return. . . . while I think of it, please inform Miss Ella, that we expect a box of candy when she returns. If not she need not expect *any more horse back rides.* Well, Mama there is no news at present. And as Papa is making great preparations to commence letter writing, I will retire

and leave him a clear field. So Adios, with love to all and from all.''[1]
The next year, young Lee would be back at school in Kentucky,
Alice would be graduating as salutatorian of her class from Mrs.
Cuthbert's at St. Louis, Richard II would be journeying there whenever he found it possible, to call upon Alice's classmate and best
friend at school, the charming Miss Pearl Ashbrook — and Ella King
would be getting married.

By the time Alice met her father's handsome new young lawyer,
Mr. Kleberg, her two sisters were already married and making homes
of their own, living at St. Louis. Nettie King had married Major
E. B. Atwood, of the United States Army Quartermaster Department, on November 23, 1878. Though the marriage appears to have
been ''against the captain's will,'' he and all his family were present
at the ceremony at the Lindell Hotel in St. Louis, where a newspaper reporting the event noted that the hotel's ''Parlor seventeen
had been transformed into a regular garden of flowers'' and that
''The presents were the handsomest ever given to a St. Louis bride,
there being several large cases filled with solid silverware, and other
precious objects, the whole amounting to over $10,000.''[2] At a cere-
mony held in the ranch house on the Santa Gertrudis three years
later, in 1881, Ella King had been married to Louis M. Welton, a
merchant of St. Louis and San Antonio.[3]

As grandchildren began to arrive, Mrs. King was often at St.
Louis on extended visits. The affectionate Alice, after her gradua-
tion from school, became her father's companion at the ranch and
the hostess of the Santa Gertrudis when Mrs. King was away.

Every letter the captain wrote to his wife during her travels to be
with her children contained an admonition: ''See that none of Papa's
pets wants for anything money will buy.'' Sometimes he phrased it,
''Life is short and why be so mean as not enjoy yourselves now.''
Again he would spell out, ''it is my wish to see you and all of my

pets now or never will want for anything that money will buy as long as Papa has it."

In this private correspondence with his wife there are undertones hinting that the captain might not have been entirely happy with his two sons-in-law, but he went on making certain, usually by drafts on The Mechanics Bank of St. Louis, that none of "Papa's pets" wanted for anything.[4]

The captain frequently arranged his business trips so that he might meet his family or accompany it part way on journeys from the ranch. When he traveled, he was never "mean" about enjoying himself. He spent freely, handed out big tips, and demanded the best "that money will buy." Sometimes, when the cattle King of Texas had been using a bottle or two of Rose Bud to damp down the dust of the road, his deportment dismayed his wife and startled the spectators.

On one occasion the captain arrived from New Orleans in a mellow mood, to meet his family at a hotel in Galveston. He found them in the hotel dining room where Mrs. King was entertaining one of her friends, a Galveston lady, at dinner. When the captain sat down at table, he noticed that his wife's guest had been served a tough piece of meat. She was having difficulty cutting it. Captain King, most generous of hosts, drinking or not drinking, complained to the waiter, then to the headwaiter, who made no offer to remedy the situation. Thereupon, the captain got up, strode out, crossed the street to another restaurant and ordered a completely new meal for his guest and for his family — to be served at Captain King's table in the hotel dining room. When the line of outside waiters arrived carrying the platters from across the street, the hotel waiters would not remove the plates already on the table. At this point, it is probable that one pants leg was in and the other pants leg was out of the captain's boot tops. The storm arrived. Captain King pulled the tablecloth from the table, dumping the hotel food, dishes and all, to the floor. He very carefully re-spread the tablecloth and riveted the waiters with his pale eyes. "Now," he said. "Serve *that* one." They served it.[5]

The Kings traveled often to San Antonio, where they stayed always in the same pleasant rooms at the city's best hostelry, the famed old Menger Hotel. One time the captain got there a little before his family did and made his way for a brief refreshment at the Menger Bar. When he came upstairs, Mrs. King was settling the family in their rooms facing the ornate balcony which looked down upon the marble-floored hotel lobby. She had ordered water for the pitcher on the washstand in her room. The water wasn't brought. Tired of waiting, Captain King picked up the pitcher, walked out upon the balcony to the balustrade and dropped the big piece of crockery over the side. It fell with a crash to the lobby floor. Leaning over the balustrade, the captain called out to the room clerk: "If we can't get any water up here, we don't need a pitcher." There were pitchers full of water in the captain's rooms, quickly.[6]

When the captain made a trip to Brownsville, news of his arrival would usually spread all over town, bringing drunks, tramps and borrowers to gather hopefully at the saloon of Celestin Jagou where the captain could be counted upon to pay a call before leaving town. He was invariably good for a drink or two for everybody, and usually for a touch. He kept money loose in his side coat pocket and would, depending upon how he felt, dispense ones, fives, tens, maybe a twenty upon the hearing of a sufficient woe. One of the captain's pleasures in having money was being able to give money away. He indulged his pleasure—and kept close tab on what the indulgence cost him. At night he would carefully count the cash left in his side pocket and make a memorandum, which he kept, of every appreciable handout. He would leave town in the dark, without anyone knowing when or by what road. Next day, the barflies would be at Jagou's, but not the captain. After his death, many of these jug acquaintances came to his lawyer, following an advertisement for the presentation of claims against the captain's estate, to claim that their old friend owed them $10, $20 or whatever. When they were shown the captain's carefully kept memoranda of the amounts he had dispensed, with names and dates, most of the would-be claimants left the lawyer's office without a further squeak.[7]

The captain had an almost infallible ability to judge the caliber of a man; at times he might lend from his *inside* coat pocket a very considerable sum of money to a total stranger. Such a stranger was W.E. Halsell. One night in San Antonio long past midnight, the two men came together as they walked in the direction of the Menger. They were unknown to each other but each recognized the other as a cattleman and they fell to talking as they walked. Halsell was in trouble, he was pacing the streets, he was unable to rest. He had made a contract to buy a herd of steers, he had put up ten thousand dollars and had made arrangements with the bank in San Antonio to put up the rest. Then the bank had welshed out on him. He was stuck. King listened to the exact details of the story, decided what the man's chances were at making a profit if the deal went through and he halted at a light. He reached into his pocket, counted out the stack of big-denomination bills the stranger needed and handed them to him. "Go on with the deal. I'm Captain King and you can pay me back when you have finished the drive." Halsell introduced himself and took the money. There was no other arrangement. When the drive was done, King was promptly repaid.[8]

The captain was as efficient in the making of money as he was generous in the spending of it. The ranch was where he made it. He occupied himself with the daily small details of ranching as well as the larger problems of his business concern. He worked not only with his lawyers and with the lines of figures Reuben Holbein totted in the ledger at the commissary office, he might spend a week with a fence-building crew at the far end of the ranch, or he might be found at the forge in the blacksmith shop, pounding from an old piece of scrap he had saved a new kind of latch for a corral gate.[9] Ranchman King ran his enterprise much as he had once run a steamboat: the captain was wide awake and the crew stepped lively.

He knew how the grass, the water, the livestock in every pasture were doing, because he went there himself to see. His vaqueros watched for the familiar figure, the bearded and sunburned face under the crimped black hat, the boss riding on the spring seat by the driver of the light slat-bottom buckboard hitched to the matched team fast-stepping through the grass across the prairie. Standard equipment by the spring seat was a Winchester rifle and a demijohn of Rose Bud. Sometimes the captain's navigation of his huge range was in error. *"Keep driving, Willie, we'll get there all right,"* the captain would say to his driver Willie Rawlinson, looking for a landmark. The buckboard often pulled up at headquarters when the captain's big biscuit watch and the stars said it was nearly morning.[10]

Willie Rawlinson had been one of the waifs that the captain was always interested in. Richard King never forgot he had been a friendless boy himself: he never missed a chance to give such a boy a job and a helping hand to honorable manhood. Willie had been brought to the ranch when he was about eleven, an orphan whose parents had died in Kansas. He had grown up with the cowboys on the Santa Gertrudis and he had become a fine and dependable hand.[11]

Some of the captain's homeless protégés did not work out so well. One young tramp, whom King had encountered in the smoking car aboard a train, was given money, then a job at the Santa Gertrudis. The captain soon realized he had made a mistake. "I will have to get that young fellow away from here," he worried aloud, "or he will steal a horse as sure as I live." The captain took an easy way out: he sent the vagabond with a cattle drive to Kansas—and from there he went his way.[12]

The captain kept a sharp eye on suspicious strangers drifting through his range. When he had reason to mistrust one, his orders to his hands could be as sharp as the note he wrote to his foreman John Fitch: "Have nothing to do with a long, tall, lean, lank man representing himself as Maj.Cobb. Turn him loose a-foot.R.KING. I want no educated man in camp. R.K."[13] In Captain King's parlance, "educated" meant smart aleck.

Another of the captain's foremen, by the name of Jensen, told how the captain used to say, "I have to make 'em think I'm a man-eater. If I don't they'll kill me."[14] The captain had a considerable success in attaining the reputation he tried for. Driving through the sands north from Brownsville on a blazing hot midsummer day during drouth, the captain came up to a tired wayfarer walking north by the side of the parched road. King stopped the coach and told the stranger to get in. As they drove along, the captain remarked that his guest looked tired and hungry. The man answered that he was. King glanced at the gun the man carried and asked, "Why didn't you kill a deer or a calf or something?" "Oh no," the man answered, "I'm on Captain *King's* ranch." The captain said nothing but took the stranger north to the Santa Gertrudis, fed him and rested him at the transient quarters for several days. Before he started again on his way the captain told him the next time he was "on Captain King's ranch" and found himself needing food, to kill something to eat. King explained that while he meant to make things rough for bandits, rustlers and hide-peelers, he wanted no decent man to go hungry.[15]

Remembering the ranch in the early days, the aged vaquero Alvarado told stories with glimpses of *El Cojo* as he appeared in his

Kineños' eyes. "King owned a very gentle saddle horse that he always rode," Alvarado said. "One time he came to where there were various boys on horseback. He reached us full speed and said, as if joking: 'Boys, have you ever seen a man mount a horse better than I?' We said, 'No sir, your mount is very beautiful!' He grinned and showed all his teeth and left."

At times the captain's humor with his men was more slapstick. "Now I can tell you many pranks of King with some of his helpers," Alvarado smiled. "Sometimes he was a man very serious and correct in his ways, but many times he chatted with some of his helpers. One time he had a Negro called Gabriel. He sent him to the creek to dig a well, and as the well had much mud, the poor Negro had mud all over his body. He finished and came to advise King that now his well was ready. When King saw him coming so dirty, he called his wife in a high voice: 'Mamma, bring my shotgun, quick. Here comes a bear.' When the Negro saw King with a shotgun in his hand, he yelled in a frightened voice: 'Captain, I'm Gabriel.' King pointed at the Negro, he ran, and was yelling 'I'm Gabriel, I'm not a bear.' This was a joke. The shotgun that King held was broken in two pieces and was good for nothing."

Alvarado said that the captain could also be very dry. "One day King went in his buggy to make a round of the herds. He encountered a very drunk sheep herder. This herder watched his sheep all mixed up, lame and crippled ones. When King reached him, King said: '*Alal.* Hard working man.' He answered: 'Yes sir, I work very hard with these animals, and I want you to give me a saddle horse to herd them.' King said with sarcasm: 'It would be better to send you a buggy so you wouldn't fall out.' He said, 'Yes sir.' And for a long time he was waiting for the buggy that never came."[16]

The years made the "Old Cap" a curious inward blend of pilot-house commander and hacienda patriarch. He disciplined his people

but he took care of them; he protected them; he never failed to match their faithfulness with his own. He knew the moods of men with rough hands and strong backs. He could humor them. One morning early, the vaqueros around headquarters came to tell the *patrón* that they had a wish just to sit, to enjoy life, as a *patrón* enjoyed life sitting in his house, his fine house. Captain King looked at the brown faces. "*Alal*," he said, "pass in, please." He got chairs and sat them all down in the parlor. After an hour or so, one of the vaqueros got up. "Where are you going?" the *patrón* asked. "Outside, to smoke." "You can smoke right here," the *patrón* said and the vaqueros sat in the parlor until twelve o'clock at noon and then everybody was ready to go to work.[17]

This may have been at about the time Captain King wrote the letter uttering the immemorial plaint of every ranchman who has ever ranched upon the borderlands of Texas: "Dear Rube: Where I have grass, I have no water. And where I have water, I have no grass. The Mexicans won't work and things are getting in a hell of a fix fast."[18]

It may have been at about the time, May of 1881, that Bland Chamberlain at the Santa Gertrudis wrote his lawyer friend Jim Wells at Brownsville: "The old man is alone. There being no local option in the country, you can judge the consequences."[19]

Rains were few and thin that year of 1881. Drouth began to wither the grass and to shrink the watering places on the Santa Gertrudis. Though there was a growing boom in the ranching business all over the West, though the general market for cattle was good and getting better, the cattlemen of South Texas were facing increased difficulties in moving their beef herds along the roads north to market.

Barbed wire fences were cutting across the old routes to the railroad sidings. Open ranges were becoming enclosed pastures, guarded by owners violently opposed to the endless waves of South Texas herds cropping and trampling grass on the way north. The herd bosses found longer and longer detours necessary to skirt the fenced lands constantly multiplying on the roads to Kansas.

Damages to fences and to grass were not the only local objections to Longhorn herds as they moved to market. The cattle from South Texas brought fatal contagion to cattle farther north. No one knew exactly how the disease was communicated, but its arrival always coincided with the arrival of the southern herds and it was called "Texas Fever." Northern cattlemen took steps to protect their own stock. "Winchester Quarantines," bands of armed men standing on the roads to divert Texas cattle from an area, brought on fights and further detours for the herd bosses from Texas.[20]

The drouth of 1881-1882 contributed to other difficulties. The movement of a herd across country was vitally dependent upon watering places. When drouth made them scarce, when rangemen guarded water for the use of their own stock, transient drovers and their herds fared badly.

The roundabout railroads built into Texas in the first years of the 1880's could handle only a small fraction of the cattle available for market. Limited as these facilities were, the railroads also began putting regulations in force which prohibited the shipment of Texas cattle to the north except in the months during frost.[21] It was noticed that Texas Fever was in abeyance in the cold season—which was, from the standpoint of the Texas stockmen, the poorest time of the year to ship.

Involved with the troubles of a drouth and with the difficulties of marketing, the owner of the Santa Gertrudis saw his ranges stocked with a surplus of cattle and at the same time suffering from a shortage of grass. The general livestock market was excellent and, in spite of the harassments which he believed were only temporary, King went about solving his problems not by reducing his herds but by acquiring more land, especially in the Carricitos—and building more fence while hoping for more rain. In the summer of 1881, he was writing Mrs. King at St. Louis about one of the fencing projects: "We are getting along very well with the fence but our greatest trouble is to furnish water along it while the work is going on . . . It is expensive; that is where the money goes."[22]

The next summer, there was less water and less grass. Working cattle at the Bóveda pasture in the stifling heat of late July, the 33-year-old Bland Chamberlain came down with a fever and was brought to the Santa Gertrudis headquarters, where his sickness grew steadily worse. The captain was away from the ranch; Bland Chamberlain in growing delirium asked for the bearded brother-in-law who had been like a father so many years—as if the captain's presence might make all things well. King received word and hurried home, arriving at the ranch on the fifth of August. When he came into the sickroom, Bland Chamberlain was dying. The captain walked to the side of the bed and leaned down. "Bland, do you know who this is?" the familiar voice asked. "Yes—*El Cojo*—" Bland smiled. Then he died.[23]

That fall of 1882, with the skies still a pitiless blue, with grass of the overstocked pastures still dusty and brown, the square-built, brawny body of Richard King began to tire. It had served him powerfully and without fail, in every way he ever called upon it, for fifty-eight years. Now it no longer refreshed itself in sleep: it stayed tired too often. Something was wrong. The captain blamed it on age, but he grew gradually aware of a recurrent trouble in his vitals. His stomach hurt. It was hard to swallow the burn that sometimes crept up in his gullet. He fell away from the hearty eating he had always enjoyed. Pain replaced gusto. To kill the pain, and the growing awareness that something was wrong with the body he had always taken for granted, the captain used whiskey. He had always liked the jug, yet he had done his drinking in stride: it had never fogged him, never interfered with the energy he had poured into a strenuous life and an immense work. Late in the year 1882, he began to drink more heavily, to cast himself loose from the pain that came gnawing often at his middle.

The new year of 1883 arrived, but no rain arrived with it. Surveying his overstocked pastures, Captain King realized that he must sell some of his herds or see many of his cattle die for lack of grass.

The great boom which had brought ranches springing all over the West was at its height. Under its influence, values of rangelands were climbing; there was a great demand and there were fine prices paid for breed herds to stock the new ranges spreading north to Wyoming and Montana. The reputed profits to be made by ranching in the Wild West had become the subject of writers in eastern journals and the object of eastern speculators. Glowing articles were circulated with such titles as *The Beef Bonanza* or *How to Get Rich on the Plains,* and the possibilities roused such interest that investors were found as far afield as England and Scotland. Big British syndicates, among others, were buying ranchlands from Texas to Wyoming. Most of the absentee investors would rue the day they were persuaded to a fling with the Romance of the Range, but in the easy money market of the early 1880's, before the bubble burst, hopes were high and buyers active.[24]

Mifflin Kenedy had believed that buyers' offers were too attractive to go unheeded. Early in 1882 he had sold his Los Laureles, lock, stock and barrel, for $1,100,000 to a syndicate of Dundee, Scotland, known as the Texas Land & Cattle Co., Ltd.[25] A month later Kenedy had organized the Kenedy Pasture Co. and had begun extensive land buying around the La Parra grant, headquarters of his new ranching property. He had not gone there to live as a stockman, however, but had moved with his family to Corpus Christi; his Kenedy Pasture Co. had been organized, at least partly, with speculative aims for a future sale.[26] Businessman Kenedy never became as interested in the actual work of breeding and raising livestock as his friend King, nor did he ever evince deep attachment to a piece of land that was his own—a trait which became a vital part of King at the Santa Gertrudis.

Nevertheless, Kenedy's shrewd business sense and Kenedy's handsome profit from the sale of Los Laureles were strongly in King's mind early in 1883, with his pastures overstocked, with the drouth on the land unrelieved, with the vigor in his own body diminishing.

Then a blow fell. The captain lost his younger son.

The nineteen-year-old Lee had not elected to graduate from Centre, but had chosen instead to finish his schooling in a way he considered more useful, with a year at a business college in St. Louis. The latter part of February, a telegram came from the Southern Hotel where Lee was staying. The wire notified his family that he was ill; his mother and his brother Richard started for St. Louis immediately. Captain King and Alice left soon afterward. Lee's illness was pneumonia and when his family reached him his condition was grave. He died on the first of March, 1883, and was buried in a St. Louis cemetery far from home.[27]

Lee's death stunned the King family. Mrs. King was so stricken she became seriously ill and remained in St. Louis for months. Affairs at the ranch called the captain back immediately and Alice returned with her father. The eighteenth of March, he was sending a letter: "My Dear Dear Wife. I cannot write with any heart to you . . ."[28] Lee had promised much for the future of the Santa Gertrudis. Lee the staunch boy who went out with the rawhide riders at the cow camps, Lee who knew the livestock, the grass, the water, Lee who loved the range, Lee who—was gone. So was his father's heart.

For the first and only time in his life, Richard King felt a faltering faith in what he had tried to achieve during the thirty long years since he and his good companion Legs Lewis together had looked out from the rise on the prairie and heard the murmur of water on the lonely creek. The eighth of April, 1883, Richard King wrote his wife: "I am tired of this business, as I at all times have made a mess of everything that I have undertaken . . . and now I want to quit the Rancho business and will so do."[29] He entered into negotiations for the sale of the Santa Gertrudis, "to get out of business, and move to some quiet place, and then spend the balance of my time quiet."[30] King had entertained the idea of selling his Santa Gertrudis earlier in the year; when his son died, the captain actively pursued arrangements to sell to a British syndicate.

The season wore away without the gathering of the herds for the road north. There is no record that a ᭩ boss made a drive that year. King waited for agents and representatives of the syndicate to appear at the ranch and close the deal after an examination of the property. In letters to his wife, the captain referred to the prospective purchasers as the "Johney Bulls." Their agent was a man named Hancock, mentioned repeatedly in the captain's correspondence with Mrs. King. On April 12, he was writing: "I hope Hancock and party will come up in the payment of the money . . . if we do not sell out, something must be done, and soon. . . . Everything is going up every day. Stock of all kinds, lands going going up up daily. In fact there is a great boom in all matters. . . . What do you want to do with your cattle and sheep? Will they go in the sale or do you want to keep them? But in my opinion the cash would be better. . . . Now write me fully on all matters and let me know your wishes—"[31]

The deal was never closed. Exactly what happened, no one knows. According to the *New Orleans Times Democrat,* April 15, 1885, Captain King's asking price for the ranch and its stock was $6,500,000, a sum which may well have frightened even a syndicate. The agent Hancock and his buyers came to the Santa Gertrudis sometime between the middle of April and the latter part of June, 1883. The only clue to their visit and to the collapse of the sale comes from the recollections of the vaquero Victor Alvarado who told it this way:

These men wished to see the cattle first, then the rest of the stuff. King called his cattle bosses, who at that time were Ramón Alvarado and Jack [Jap] Clark. He told them "Tomorrow morning by nine o'clock, I want a roundup in the Preso de las Tranquitas," and this we did. When King thought that the hour was at hand, he went to the lookout of the house with his field glass and saw that everything was ready. He ordered a large stage coach to be hitched so that all the buyers could go. He went in his buggy as was his custom. They reached the roundup, but as there were so many in the herd, they had to go in with the vehicles to the middle of the herd. Even this way they couldn't see well. The buyers on the edge of the herd had to climb on top of the coach. In this way they could see better. They rode around the herd about an hour. The herd, I calculate, to be of about 12,000 animals. When the buyers wanted to go back to the ranch, King called the bosses, Ramón Alvarado and Jack Clark, and said in English to Ramón Alvarado: "Why did you gather such a little herd?" "Señor, you wanted the roundup very early, we didn't have time to gather any more." "Well, tomorrow morning, I want another roundup larger than this in the corner of the Bóvedo." When the buyers heard this, they asked King if he could gather more of a herd than what they saw there, and King said he could give them four or five roundups equal to the one they had. Then the buyers looked at one another and said to King that they didn't want to see any more than that one, it was enough to know they couldn't buy even the herd they saw, much less the land, and they left very sad.[32]

The transaction was dropped. All reference to it, and any further desire on the part of Richard King to quit ranching, faded away. By June 22, the captain was writing to Mrs. King: "We are all well but no rain so far and it makes us all feel bad. Stock is suffering for grass but we hope for the best as we have at all times had our portion of good luck. My Dear all we wish is that you will not worry yourself about things. We will come out all right. I hope for the best — we are all on the move and are doing [our] best to see that we do not lose too much. I fear it be heavy. Richard is out all the time and doing his best in all matters which is gratifying to me."[33]

Then in July rains came again, falling like a benison upon the thirsty land. The life-giving sweet rain, which has assuaged the hearts of herdsmen since the time of Abraham, worked a restoration of spirit, spelled an end somehow to a time of trouble. It entered almost with a cadence of poetry into the gaunt hand of Richard King writing, "My Dear Wife, We are all well and the grass in the yard is green once more thanks be to God for it."[34] A touch of Irish, a hint of the distant Emerald Isle, found its way to the rough nib of the pen.

Captain King went to work again, carrying the load, planning for tomorrow as he always had. Young Lee was gone, but the captain recounted his own "portion of good luck" and remembered gratefully the son he still had with him.

That summer, young Richard was engaged to be married to Miss Pearl Ashbrook. It was a betrothal approved by both families; Captain King responded to his son's plans for the future by presenting him with a ranch. By a Deed of Gift signed July 15, 1883, the captain and his wife Henrietta, for a consideration "of Love and Affection," gave their son the forty thousand good and well-watered acres comprising the Rancho Puerta de Agua Dulce.[35] Richard King II was the owner and manager of his own ranching property when Miss Ashbrook became Mrs. King in a ceremony at the home of the bride's grandmother in Wentzville, Missouri, on the twelfth of December, 1883. Reporting the nuptials, a St. Louis newspaper said, "The young couple left for the East, to be gone two or three weeks. About January 15, Mr. and Mrs. R. King Jr. will leave for Texas to take possession of an elegant new home, built by Mr. King on his ranch the 'Puerta de Agua Dulce.' "[36]

The husky, good-natured, affectionate young man who bore the captain's name acquired his own ideas about the agronomical uses of land when he settled in his own home. In Missouri he bought out an heir to the old Ashbrook farm, near St. Louis, where he and his wife chose to live during the summer. He saw new possibilities for the Agua Dulce and began the conversion of pastures to farmlands. Transporting Missouri techniques to Texas, he added cotton growing to the livestock ranching his father had so successfully practiced. No spoiled ne'er-do-well, Richard II was endowed with his father's industry but lacked his assets to outlast drouths and reverses. On occasion beef from the grasslands of the Santa Gertrudis had to take care of the farmer's debits.[37]

Richard's marriage and residence at the Agua Dulce left the captain and his wife with only one of their children still a part of life in the ranch house on the Santa Gertrudis. As the last child remaining in her parents' household, the always gentle and complaisant Alice Gertrudis King grew closer and dearer to her father and mother. It is evident that Alice was her mother's favorite. The captain wrote of his youngest daughter, "She is a little lady in all things and so good I could not do without my little Pet...."[38] More and more, during her mother's frequent absences from the ranch, Alice was her father's companion—and her mother's agent, to watch and to try to curtail the captain's increasingly hard drinking. On one occasion, Alice added to a letter written by her father this postscript: "Mama precious one, wanted to write you tonight but Papa wants me to read to him, so all I can do is to send a heart full of loving thoughts to the dear absent ones. Papa came home today. — *All right* and as well as when he left, bless his heart."[39] Taking over the duty of trying to ride herd on Papa, Alice was joyful when she could report he came home *"All right."*

The dutiful Alice's thoughts were not entirely circumscribed by the household she lived in. Mr. Robert Justus Kleberg, who was often at the ranch on her father's business, was yet oftener in her mind—and she in his. Alice would tell her children in later years that she had known it was "love at first sight" the morning at dawn when she peeked through the dining room door at her father's guest. Between the cultivated young lawyer and the cattleman's winsome youngest daughter a most exceedingly proper, unhurried and fond Victorian courtship was in progress. There were dinner conversations in the pleasant room where the bearded captain sat at the head of the long table with many guests, there were chats in Mrs. King's bric-a-brac parlor, decorous walks beneath the trees shading the green grass by the ranch house, and there were letters:

Santa Gertrudis, Tex.
Aug. 30, '83

Mr. Kleberg—
> Kind Friend.
Again 'tis a pleasing duty to acknowledge my indebtedness, I feel, I can
> No other answer make but thanks
> And thanks & ever oft good turns
> Are shuffled off with such uncurrent pay.

> Papa left this afternoon, for Brownsville, much to my regret. I can't tell you how much we enjoyed the brief visit of your friends. I was charmed with the Judge—as to your "other Mother," suffice it to say, she is all my "fancy painted" her.
> Assuring you the grapes will not go a-begging.
> With kind regards from Mother, & a multiplicity of thanks from
>> Your sincere friend,
>> A. G. King.[40]

Since the night in Corpus Christi when the captain had impulsively put the 27-year-old Lawyer Kleberg on retainer, he had more than fulfilled King's expectations. Beyond his legal ability he had demonstrated such understanding of a stockman's problems with land and livestock, and such acumen in meeting them for his client King, that Lawyer Kleberg had become an important factor in the conduct of the Santa Gertrudis ranching operation. Richard King was pleased with Robert Kleberg not only as a lawyer. He found no objection whatever to the courtly attention being paid to Alice. Neither did Alice's mother. Henrietta King was pleased with the never-failing sense of propriety her husband's Corpus Christi attorney displayed: she considered him an entirely suitable young man for the company of her daughter. There was nothing hasty in the siege he laid for her heart; there was nothing ill-advised in his conduct of that siege. He had long since won the love of Alice King and earned the high regard of both her father and mother before he popped the question, in October of 1884. By that time his legal practice was devoted almost as entirely to King ranch business as his heart was devoted to Alice.[41]

Beyond announcement of the betrothal no definite plans for the wedding were made: the affianced couple were content to wait until the captain and Mrs. King considered the time propitious. Meanwhile there were the pleasant congratulations, the felicitations from the Kleberg and the King families and from their friends. There was something else. The ailing Captain Richard King, sixty years old, entertained a comforting thought, a growing belief, that Robert Justus Kleberg might be the man, the one to be depended upon when the burden of the mammoth Rancho Santa Gertrudis fell as it must to other shoulders.

The year 1884 saw a declining cattle market, an intimation of the crash that would come the following year. In spite of less favorable prices, King was selling cattle, both beef and stockers, putting herds on the road north. He was adding to ranch income by attention to the marketing of wool from his sheep, and by selling horse stock.

At one time King wrote of his ranching: "Horses made this a success."[42] He found his horse business profitable because the animals he offered for sale were superior to the ordinary range mount. For thirty years he had consistently infused his stock with the blood of good studs, sorting his mare bands carefully, breeding for type and color. Working *remudas* on the ranch were often composed of matched horses of one color only, of bay, sorrel, black or gray.[43] Among the very best of the King ranch horses were the iron grays. The stud that gave them their quality had a story. One evening at dusk a stranger rode to the Santa Gertrudis commissary and asked to spend the night. He was mounted on a beautiful iron gray stallion; he was hospitably asked to stay. Captain King himself came out to look at the gray horse. He told the stranger that the stallion was one of the finest animals he had ever seen. The gray stood sixteen hands — bigger than the horses the captain bred. When King had finished walking around the horse admiringly, he told the stranger to make himself at home, to stay awhile. The stranger expressed his thanks and explained that he must leave early the next morning. The captain came out to bid him fair journey and courteously sent a vaquero to put the stranger upon the San Antonio road. When the time came for the vaquero to turn back, the stranger said, "Get down. I want to change with you. Take this horse back to Captain King and tell him that Jesse James sent him as a gift with his compliments." Whether the stranger was Jesse James or not, the horse was an admirable fact. The big, strong, fine-limbed offspring he sired and the descendants carrying the iron gray's stamp were known at the ranch as the "Jesse James horses."[44]

The blood of the Durham bulls with which the captain had tried to improve his beef herds produced no such upbreeding as could be observed in the horses on the ranch. The best cattle at the Santa Gertrudis were bigger and heavier than the common South Texas range animal, yet their size and weight had little to do with the attempted admixture of fine blood. The strongest, thriftiest cattle in Richard King's pastures were still big Texas Longhorns.[45]

By 1884, the ᴞ brand these Longhorns wore and the ranch they came from had a fame that reached across the length and breadth of the West. Early that fall, Walter Billingsley, one of the best herd bosses King ever had, found himself at Fort Sidney, Nebraska, on the way to Cheyenne with 5600 steers, one of the largest herds ever recorded on the roads north. Billingsley needed money to pay off five cowboys he had fired for drunkenness and failure to return to the herd outside Fort Sidney. "They demanded the money," Billingsley wrote later, "and I told them they didn't want it any worse than I wanted to give it to them. So I went up to a little two by four bank and told the banker I wanted to draw on Aften Gardner of Ogallala for six hundred dollars.

" 'You look all right and talk all right,' the banker said. 'Can't you give me some identification?'

" 'I am fifteen hundred miles from home,' I said, 'never here before and never expect to be here again.'

" 'Look around a little and see what you can do,' the banker said.

"So an idea struck me. I told the boys to hit the grit for camp and catch horses, had the cook hitch up the mules to the wagon. Now I said, 'Round up those horses and all of you follow me.' We hit the road for the bank. We got in front of the bank and I called the banker out. I says, 'Here is a hundred and fifty saddle horses branded Running W, chuck wagon, mules and most everything has that brand on it, and the brand is known from the Rio Grande to Canada, and if that is not enough, I have fifty-six hundred steers out there about three miles, all the same brand.'

"The old boy laughed and said, 'I'll bet I am the only banker in the whole world who ever was offered this kind of identification. Get down and make out your draft!' "[46]

The owner of the Running W brand was prominent at the first national cattlemen's convention held at St. Louis that year of 1884. Beset with difficulties in moving their cattle north, in spite of the facilities offered by the lengthening spread of railways, the stockmen of Texas had interested themselves in an ambitious plan for a National Cattle Trail, to be authorized by Congress as a fenced passage three to six miles wide, with quarantine grounds and watering places en route, all the long way from Texas to Dakota. When the possibilities of Congressional authorization and subsidy had faded, Captain Richard King on the floor of the convention proposed the outright purchase, by a corporation to be formed by cattlemen, of the land required for the trail strip. Countering objections to the vast cost of such a project, King pointed out the immense value the land would surely have as a corporation asset when the strip was no longer useful as a cattle trail. The stockmen failed to act upon the captain's grandiose proposal—the utility of such a trail was declining even as it was being discussed—yet King's conception of a company of cattlemen owning a swathe of real estate across the continent's heartland clearly indicates the daring scope of King's pioneering faith in the future value of land.[47]

At the end of the year 1884, the "Old Cap" was back at the Santa Gertrudis, sick and infinitely tired. His coats hung loose upon his shoulders. His shirt collars seemed too big. The black beard, the swag of black hair above the creased forehead were grizzled an iron gray like that of his Jesse James horses. Though the weather-roughened straight lips opened little to utter it, the pain gnawing now continually at him hovered in the pale blue eyes. An icy fire that had so long lived in them went clouded, soft with the inadmissible anguish of mortality. He drove himself yet, carrying his will and his suffering inside, firing the will and dulling the pain with brown burning gulps of whiskey from a jug.

His friend Kenedy, driving often between the La Parra ranch and Corpus Christi—where he was building a big new house in town for his family and his old age—stopped his coach at the Santa Gertrudis to see Richard King, to learn how he fared, to urge him to care more for himself, to go to specialists for medical attention. Kenedy had anxieties and sorrows of his own. His beloved Petra Vela was ill. His son James Kenedy, who managed the La Parra and upon whom his father had built many hopes, died of typhoid fever in December —with a murder indictment still standing against him for the shooting of a drunken troublemaker at the entrance to the harness room on the La Parra eight months before.[48]

In the foreboding Christmas time of 1884 there was one clear beam of happiness: on December 17, Richard King III was born at the ranch house on the Puerta de Agua Dulce. His advent, his name, brought a smile of pride in the grizzled beard of his grandfather.

The thirteenth of January in the new year of 1885, when Captain King returned ashen-faced from a business trip to Corpus Christi, he could drive his failing body no longer.[49] He was mortally sick and he knew it. Yet it was more than a month before his wife Henrietta and his daughter Alice were able to persuade him to make arrangements for leaving the Santa Gertrudis in order to place himself under the care of his physician in San Antonio, Doctor Ferdinand Herff.[50]

On the day of the captain's departure from the ranch, the twenty-fifth of February, he gave last instructions to Reuben Holbein, for the writing of a letter to Jim Wells at Brownsville on a matter relating to lands in the San Juan de Carricitos. "Tell him to keep on buying," the captain said. "And tell him, tell him not to let a foot of dear old Santa Gertrudis get away from us—"[51]

Outside the window, the Santa Gertrudis reached far across and beyond the horizon. It took a man on a good horse a whole week of steady riding to circuit the fence.[52] Out there on the miles beyond miles of grass there were more than forty thousand head of cattle branded ᏇᏇ. There were nearly seven thousand horses, there were twelve thousand sheep;[53] yet no livestock tally, no vault drawer full of warranty deeds, no set of facts or figures or fences to enclose counted possessions, could sensibly describe to a man what he had done with his own vivid life, with his strength, when it was expended. Looking out the window, the captain found no description which words could shape—except that it was time to go.

The big coach was drawn up by the steps leading down from the white porch at the front of the house. A warming sun caught silky lights on the lustrous coats of the waiting horses. They had been groomed. The harness had been soaped and polished for the lonesome road. All the satchels were stowed and closed in the maw of the clean leather boot. The driver sat looking down at the faces of the quiet people who stood by the gate, by the step on the tracked dirt in the shade of the opened coach door, along the thin shadow of the winter-bare branches of a willow tree. A faintest hint of new green hazed the long twigs of the sunny willow. It was a hard time to go. It was the season of the roundups for the road north across the far plains, when the great steers on the wild spring-steel legs came clattering their horns through the thickets, when scores of shouting centaurs rode in the dust to the bellowing music of the gathered herds.

The captain came out of the house and down the steps with his wife and his daughter Alice. There were the hands to grip, and the words—none of them shaping the thought yet—the Santa Gertrudis lurked somewhere in the grip of these hands. The captain climbed in the coach with his wife and his daughter. There was the strong pain. There was the strong goodbye. The coach moved. Then there was the brown-faced, bareheaded horseman on the sorrel standing still in the sunlight at the corner of the corral by the turning of the lane. There was the straight back of the horseman, the salute of the thorn-torn hat held high. *Adiós patrón!* Those were tears.

The coach carried the captain northwest by the winding road to Collins Station, away from the rise on the prairie, away from the morning sun.

Two days later the Kings arrived at the familiar Menger Hotel. Doctor Herff came to attend the captain in his room. The patient was suffering a cancer of the stomach in its terminal stage. When the captain was told that he could not live long, he received the news with the calm of his own prescience.

He was still using whiskey to dull the sweating, racking pain clamped at his middle. When Doctor Herff told Mrs. King that her husband's drinking was radically shortening the time left to him, she implored the doctor to ask the captain if he would give up the drinking she had always hated. "Tell him with a smile," Henrietta King said, "that I need him a while longer."

When the doctor told him, Captain King jerked himself up. "Give me my boots," he stormed. The doctor objected. "I'm going — you try to keep me in bed if you think you can —" The captain stuffed his nightshirt into the waistband of his trousers, walked into his wife's room, and slammed the door. "Etta. Did you say you needed me a while longer?" What else was said is shrouded in silence. Richard King finished his life without more whiskey.[54]

Members of the family, all but Nettie whose husband was ill, gathered at San Antonio. Richard II and his wife, Ella and her husband, came to the Menger Hotel. So did Robert Kleberg. There were many friends. The loyal Mifflin Kenedy, heavy with grief at the death of his wife on the seventeenth of March, left the sorrowful house he had just finished building for her and came immediately to

San Antonio, to sit day and night at the bedside of the man whose life, whose whole destiny, had been so interwoven with his own.[55]

On the second day of April, Richard King directed the making of his will, then signed the words his lawyer Kleberg had cast into legal form:

THE STATE OF TEXAS }
COUNTY OF BEXAR }

I, Richard King, of the County of Nueces, in the State of Texas, being of sound and disposing mind and memory do make and publish this my Last Will and Testament, intending thereby to dispose of all my worldly estate of which I shall be possessed at the time of my decease.

1. I direct that all my just debts, including funeral expenses and the expenses of administration be paid out of my estate.

2. I devise and bequeath all my estate, real, personal and mixed wheresoever situated, and of whatsoever kind, character or description, to my beloved wife, Henrietta M. King, to be by her used and disposed of precisely the same as I myself might do were I living, and to appoint the same by Will after her decease, according to her judgment and discretion.

3. I hereby appoint my said wife, Henrietta M. King, and my trusted friends, Mifflin Kenedy and Perry Doddridge, Executors of this my Last Will and Testament and direct that no other action shall be had in the County Court or in any Court having jurisdiction in matters of probate, in relation to the settlement of my estate, than the probating and recording of this my Will and the return of an Inventory, Appraisement and List of Claims of my estate, and I further direct that my Executors herein before named shall not be required to give bond.

In Witness Whereof, I, Richard King, the Testator, have hereunder set my hand this the second day of April, in the year of our Lord, one thousand eight hundred and eighty five.

R. KING

Signed, published and declared by the said Richard King as his Last Will and Testament in the presence of us, who in his presence and in the presence of each other, and at his request have hereunto set our hands as witnesses.

Jacob Waelder
Uriah Lott[56]

Twelve days later, on the evening of the fourteenth of April, as dusk fell on the Alamo Plaza outside his hotel window and the lamps were being lighted, Richard King came to the end of his life. With his family and friends around him he took quiet leave of a long quest and moved beyond it to enfolding silence.

What the quest had been was as difficult to shape in words as the farewell to the Santa Gertrudis the final morning, when the facts and figures and fences had not enclosed the meaning of a man's life, when the grip of hands reluctant to say goodbye had touched at the measure of a man's work when it was done.

Sixty-seven years later, the trail driver Walter Billingsley made an estimate.

"Mr. Billingsley, what kind of a man was Captain King?"

The reply came mixed with long thoughts mirrored in Billingsley's wise eyes remembering spacious times, horseback men, the strength of youth. "He was a rough man," Billingsley answered. "But he was a good man. I never knew a rougher man, nor a better man."[57]

The lonesome, hungry, tough-willed, hard-muscled runaway apprentice from Manhattan never lost the song his quick blood sang. It had led him listening to a frontier, to a place for striving, for battle. That was the song. The league beyond league of wilderness standing to the horizon like a mystery beckoning, upon the day the young steamboat pilot had stepped ashore alone in Texas, had blended the wind-whisper of its grass into the song and at length had become its burden. The steamboat captain, seasoned with striving, had left the river and come to grips with the land. In the dusk of the evening on the fourteenth of April thirty years later, the land was not wilderness. Its grass was no longer untenanted. The riverman who became ranchman had added to the hacienda economy of Latin herdsmen the dynamics of Anglo-Saxon business, and in this blend pioneered a basic industry for the western half of his continent. With his own sweat and treasure he had ruggedly devised a method for the harvest of a New World's grass.

To create handsome pastures from savage wilderness, to build a place for fruitful husbandry in a land torn by a bitter history of bloodshed, violence, hatred, contention, was not work for a gentle hand or an irresolute mind. The ranch on the Santa Gertrudis could not have been wrested from the Wild Horse Desert by a courtly display of pleasant intention. It was rough. It was no less honorable. It demanded a rough and honorable man.

Richard King had not shaped words for the meaning of his life, but they were clear. He had not come merely to possess a piece of the continent. It had come to possess him. His life, his strength expended, became a part of the land itself, its reward, its obligation, its promise.

On the fifteenth day of April in the year 1885, after a funeral service in the parlors of the Menger Hotel at four-thirty in the afternoon, a long cortège moved through the streets to the city cemetery of San Antonio. When the Reverend J.W. Neil, pastor of the First Presbyterian Church, had finished with prayer, the coffin enclosing the clay that had been Richard King was lowered into a grave and covered with earth.[58]

The press of the nation noted the passing of "the Texas millionaire cattleraiser." Among many eulogistic obituaries, a Texas newspaper pointed out that "his history is almost a history of this frontier." The final tribute, clean as the aim along the sights of a ranger's rifle, had already come from old Rip Ford. He wrote of his friend and companion the words to enclose it all, "As a pioneer he came and labored."[59]

APPENDICES

Early Spanish and Mexican Land Grants from the Rio Grande to the Nueces

THE MAP *accompanying this discussion was developed by the surveyor E. M. Card of McAllen, Texas, and Robert C. Wells, King Ranch Land and Tax Consultant, using early maps, deeds, abstracts, and other records of Nueces, Cameron, Hidalgo, and Starr counties and information and maps from the General Land Office of Texas. Mr. Card was an early-day surveyor who participated in surveying many portions of the area between the Nueces and the Rio Grande during the complications of ownership brought on by the coming of the railroad and the transition necessary to modern development.*

THE DEVELOPMENT OF MINES in the Monterrey area brought permanent Spanish settlements to northeastern Mexico as early as 1579. Beyond the Rio Grande minerals were so scarce and Indians were so fierce that Spaniards were little tempted to occupy the immense space claimed by the Crown in what is now Texas. French expeditions on the coast raised alarm enough to cause several official military *entradas* and the establishment of a few fortified mission-colonies, but such occupation of Texas as Spain achieved was generally half-hearted and unprosperous.

The able colonizer and administrator José de Escandón brought life and energy to the Spanish northeastern frontier. He arrived on the Rio Grande in 1749, with a royal commission to conquer and colonize the coastal areas reaching from Tampico in the south to the San Antonio River in the north. He named this territory *Nuevo Santander;* its boundaries approximately enclosed what later became the early Mexican Republic's State of Tamaulipas.

To conquer and colonize it, Escandón commanded a military force of 750 men, and with them he escorted overland from distant Querétaro a well-equipped company of 2500 colonists, with their livestock and their implements of husbandry. Their arrival in Nuevo Santander marked the beginning of a flourishing colonial administration during which Escandón managed to build a sturdy line of twenty-three new settlements upon the Spanish frontier. Among the most successful were Camargo, Reynosa and Mier.

Escandón brought a new concept to Spanish colonization technique. Instead of building missions as defensive strong points manned by garrisons of paid soldiers and managed by church fathers, Escandón founded civil towns and entrusted the main defense of the land to the citizen-colonists. To keep them from scattering to isolated holdings and becoming defenseless against Indian raids by living too far from the collective strength of the newborn towns, Escandón delayed any arrangement for the granting of farm or pasture lands to individuals.

The Rio Grande settlements functioned for eighteen years without any private ownership of land.

In 1767 a Royal Commission arrived to allot each family its own property. The basic allotments were for small but vital tracts of the most desirable land in the area: river-frontage in the proximity of the towns. A tract of this frontage was called a *porción;* it was a long and very thin rectangle, usually 1500 varas wide and 25,000 varas long with one face of its narrow width on the river's edge. A *porción* was awarded to the head of each established family of colonists to provide that family with its own minimum parcel of arable bottomland and an entry to unfailing water for livestock.

Beyond the crowded *porciones* stretched unmeasured grassland, capable of supporting countless herds and flocks. Ambitious and influential citizens on the river naturally sought title to promising tracts of that grassland for future development, and it was the business of the Royal Commission to issue such titles.

These proceedings were called "The Acts of the General Visit" and from them, beginning in 1767, stem not only the charters of the early Spanish Rio Grande towns and the private ownership of riverfront *porciones,* but also the original titles, later upheld by the governments of the United States and Texas, for the vast pasture lands granted to Spanish subjects from the Rio Grande north to the Nueces.

Escandón made one exception and allowed one private grant of land before "The Acts of the General Visit." Anxious to establish an outpost to link the Rio Grande towns with the fortified mission of La Bahía del Espíritu Santo at the northern extremity of Nuevo Santander on the San Antonio River, he sent Blas María de la Garza Falcón — Captain, Chief Justice and founder of Camargo — to establish a stronghold and way station in the wilderness near the Nueces.

Falcón moved north some time in the early 1760's, with his family, scores of retainers and a company of soldiers. Carefully he chose a position for his establishment that was defensible against the murderous Karankawas in the vicinity; Escandón awarded him private title to large lands surrounding his outpost. Some of them later became a part of the King Ranch and, still later, the Chapman Ranch on the flat blackland prairie southwest of Corpus Christi, and many small farms.

By the time of "The Acts of the General Visit" in 1767, Falcón's establishment had already become a flourishing rancho known as *Rancho Real de Santa Petronila* — for royal soldiers garrisoned it even though it was privately owned. The military force not only protected the stronghold, it probed and patrolled into a wide area, including Padre Island across the Laguna Madre, and it appears to have had a considerable success at keeping hostile Indians in check.

The rancho, located on Blas María Falcón's grant, El Chiltipín, roughly fifteen miles northeast of what is now Kingsville, was the first land grant in the King Ranch area. As the first settler in an uninhabited area, the captain from Camargo undoubtedly exercised the privilege of naming many of its geographical features. Blas María Falcón's first residence on the frontier, at the Villa de Señora Santa Ana de Camargo he founded, stood against a background of distant hills, Los Cerros de Santa Gertrudis, probably named after the patron saint of his only daughter, María Gertrudis. As the doughty first ranchero moved northward, so did his daughter's name. It next appeared on the creek that is the flowing life-stream through the heart of the King Ranch.

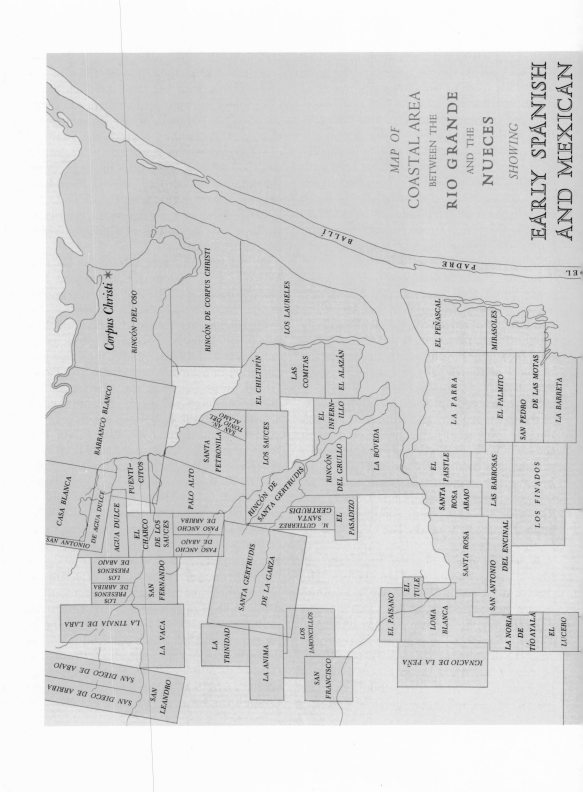

MAP OF
COASTAL AREA
BETWEEN THE
RIO GRANDE
AND THE
NUECES
SHOWING

EARLY SPÁNISH
ÁND MEXICÁN

EL.

PADRE

BALLÍ

Corpus Christi ★

RINCÓN DEL OSO

RINCÓN DE CORPUS CHRISTI

LOS LAURELES

EL CHILTIPÍN

LAS COMITAS

EL ALAZÁN

EL PEÑASCAL

MIRASOLES

BARRANCO BLANCO

SANTA PETRONILA

SAN AN-
TONIO DEL
ALAMO

LOS SAUCES

EL
INFERN-
ILLO

LA PARRA

EL PALMITO

SAN PEDRO
DE LAS MOTAS

LA BARRETA

CASA BLANCA

SAN ANTONIO

DE AGUA DULCE

PUENTI-
CITOS

AGUA DULCE

PALO ALTO

PASO ANCHO
DE ARRIBA

RINCÓN DE
SANTA GERTRUDIS

RINCÓN
DEL GRULLO

LA BÓVEDA

EL
PAISTLE

SANTA
ROSA
ABAJO

LAS BARROSAS

LOS FINADOS

EL
CHARCO
DE LOS
SAUCES

PASO ANCHO
DE ABAJO

M. GUTIERREZ
SANTA
GERTRUDIS

EL
PASADIZO

LOS PRESENOS
DE ABAJO

SAN
FERNANDO

SANTA GERTRUDIS
DE LA GARZA

SANTA ROSA

SAN ANTONIO
DEL ENCINAL

LOS PRESENOS
DE ARRIBA

LA TINAIA DE LARA

LA VACA

LA
TRINIDAD

LA ANIMA

LOS
JABONCILLOS

SAN
FRANCISCO

EL PAISANO

EL
TULE

LOMA
BLANCA

LA NORIA
DE
TÍO AYALA

EL
LUCERO

SAN DIEGO DE ABAJO

SAN DIEGO DE ARRIBA

SAN
LEANDRO

IGNACIO DE LA PEÑA

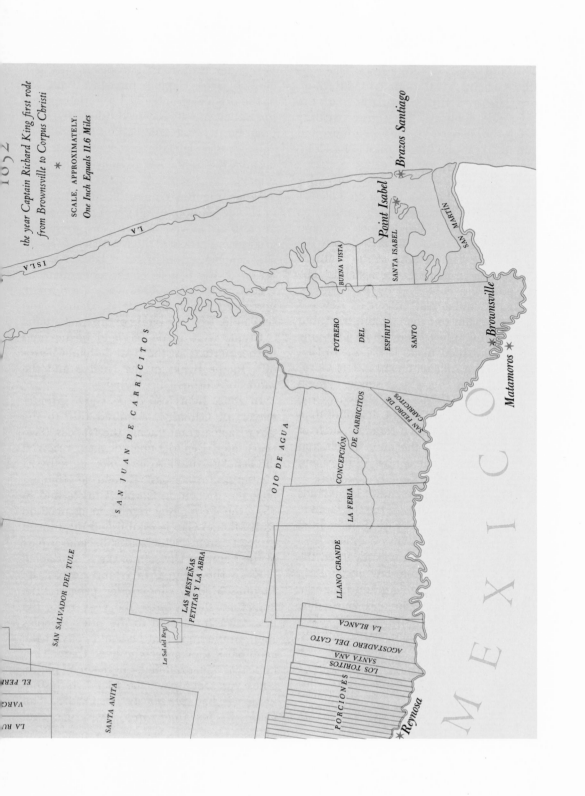

1852

*the year Captain Richard King first rode
from Brownsville to Corpus Christi*

★

SCALE: APPROXIMATELY:
One Inch Equals 11.6 Miles

ISLA

LA

★ Brazos Santiago

Point Isabel ★

BUENA VISTA

SANTA ISABEL

SAN MARTÍN

POTRERO

DEL

ESPÍRITU

SANTO

★ Brownsville ★

★ Matamoros

M E X I C O

SAN JUAN DE CARRICITOS

OJO DE AGUA

CONCEPCIÓN

DE CARRICITOS

SAN PEDRO DE
CARRICITOS

LA FERIA

LLANO GRANDE

SAN SALVADOR DEL TULE

LAS MESTEÑAS
PETITAS Y LA ABRA

La Sal del Rey

SANTA ANITA

EL PERI

VARC

LA RU

LA BLANCA

AGOSTADERO DEL GATO

SANTA ANA

LOS TORITOS

P O R C I O N E S

★ Reynosa

The land grants resulting from "The Acts of the General Visit" added to the vigor, prosperity and future prospects of the Rio Grande colonists. They grew wealthy through the increase of their livestock, and acquired larger and larger grants of grazing lands.

In 1772, Spanish-born José Salvador de la Garza, husband of Captain Falcón's daughter María Gertrudis, filed application for the fifty-nine square leagues* of land known as *El Potrero del Espíritu Santo*, the Pasture of the Holy Ghost, at the southern end of which Brownsville now stands. The application was contested by José Narciso Cavazos, an influential citizen of Reynosa who made claim to a part of the tract, but in 1781 a full title to the whole fifty-nine leagues was issued to de la Garza. In that same year, as a sufficient consolation, Cavazos was granted the largest single tract in the region, the vast acreage known as the *San Juan de Carricitos* grant. Its more than half a million acres later formed much of the Norias Division of the King Ranch, and included most of what is now Willacy and parts of Hidalgo and Kenedy counties.

Between 1777 and 1798, other large lands fronting on the north bank of the Rio Grande were granted to wealthy and influential citizens of the river towns. Captain Juan José Hinojosa of Reynosa was awarded the Llano Grande. His son-in-law José María Ballí received the adjoining grant, La Feria. Reynosa citizens Eugénio and Bartolomé

Fernández acquired Concepción de Carricitos. In 1794, Captain Juan José Ballí, son of the original grantee of La Feria, applied for and eventually received title to the huge grant north of the *porciones* of Reynosa, the San Salvador del Tule, a part of which later became the Santa Fé division of the King Ranch.

When the Rio Grande flooded Reynosa in 1801, the Captain and Chief Justice Francisco Ballí moved the citizens to higher ground and provided them with a new townsite which was on his own land. For this action to the benefit of the townsmen, he was given a big grant known as *La Barreta,* north of the San Juan de Carricitos — and sixty miles from the banks of the Rio Grande.

Grants were made for land farther and farther north, past the Real de Santa Petronila, to the banks of the Nueces and the shores of Corpus Christi Bay.

In 1804, Juan José de la Garza Montemayor, of Camargo, acquired title to the Casa Blanca grant, facing the Nueces. Two years later, Benito López de Jaen received the San Agustín de Agua Dulce, close by El Chiltipín. Farther east, Ramón de Hinojosa took the Rincón de Corpus Christi, and in 1807 the Pérez Rey family in association with Manuel García established the Rincón de los Laureles, which later became a part of the Laureles Division of the King Ranch.

Even the long, thin island across the Laguna Madre came under private title. Sometime shortly after the year 1800, the island was presented to the priest Nicolás Ballí, in the hope that he could convert the cannibal Karankawas who lived there. That hope was never fulfilled, but the good padre, whose presence gave the island its lasting name (it had previously been called *San Carlos de los Malaguitos*), was successful

* "In Spanish and Mexican law, the league, as a legal measure of length, consisted of 5,000 varas, and a vara was equivalent to 33-1/3 English inches, making the league equal to a little more than 2.63 miles, and the square league to 4,428 acres. This is its meaning as used in Texas land grants. United States v. Perot, 98 U.S. 428, 25 L. Ed. 251; Hunter v. Morse, 49 Tex. 219."—*Black's Law Dictionary,* Third Ed. (St. Paul, 1933), p. 1081.

in building up a rancho at the island's southern end, where he labored until his death by natural causes, not Karankawas, in 1829. A part of Padre Ballí's island grant later became the property of Richard King.

By decree of the Superior Council for Royal Lands, issued in 1802, the sale or adjudication of new lands for use as pastures was limited to a maximum of four square leagues for "people of ample faculties" and one or two square leagues for "poor people." In actual practice, the "poor people" qualified for nothing: the Council made no grants except to citizens of wealth or influence — and these partially evaded the four-league limitation by applying for larger grants using the name or names of additional male members of the family. Don José Lorenzo de la Garza, for example, received the twelve square leagues of the Santa Gertrudis grant in 1808 by applying for the land in his own name together with the names of two of his sons (see Appendix II).

The owners of all grants held their lands "by establishing ranchos—hamlets or settlements—occupied sometimes by the proprietor, more often by one or more of his sons, or other members of the family; always by his servants and vaqueros; and usually by *arrimados*, friends or distant relatives, who resided on a proprietor's lands with his permission, but without duties or obligation other than loyalty to the owner of the soil." *

The Mexican Republic continued the granting of lands under the precedent set by the previous Spanish regime. The State

* Harbert Davenport.

of Tamaulipas was especially active during the years between 1829 and 1836 in making new grants, officially encouraging residents on the Rio Grande to develop tracts in the north and to resettle such already existing ranchos as had been deserted due to Indian depredations during the revolt from Spain. The violence of the Texas Revolution brought an end to all granting and occupation of land in the vicinity which later became the King Ranch. By 1836 the outspread patchwork of granted and titled lands shown on the accompanying map was already formed. (Texas recognized no grants made by Mexico after December 19, 1836.) Such areas as remained ungranted at that time became public lands under the later administration and disposition of the General Land Office of Texas.

Following the Mexican War, the Bourland-Miller Commission was appointed to investigate the validity of titles to land grants. During the course of the investigation, many valuable records were lost in a steamboat accident. However, the commission finally produced a list of titles which were confirmed by the Texas Legislature on February 10, 1852: "An act to confirm certain land titles herein named and to require the Commissioners of the General Land Office to issue patents on same as approved, September 4, 1850."

Because of the lost papers and the fact that the commission's list did not include all lands, many grants were not validated by the "Act of Confirmation." This provided much material for subsequent litigation.

APPENDIX II

The Santa Gertrudis de la Garza Land Grant

UNDER THE LAWS governing land concessions during the Spanish colonial period in Texas, grants emanated from the Crown. They were made in the King's name by specially delegated officers according to elaborate protocol. The colonist or his agent addressed a formal petition to the provincial governor or his delegate. If the petition was approved a local officer was designated to examine, survey and appraise the tract and, finally, with due attention to proper procedure, to administer at the ceremony of giving official possession of the land to the applicant. A complete written record of events was made during the proceedings; this record served as a title to the land. A *testimonio* or certified copy of the file of documents was given to the owner.

The twelve leagues of the grant to become known as the Santa Gertrudis de la Garza, on which the King Ranch headquarters is now located, was originally granted — in three four-league tracts — to Don José Lorenzo de la Garza and his two sons, Don José Domingo and Don Julián. The entire procedure occupied a period of more than two years, from December, 1805, to January, 1808. The original *testimonios* of all three grantees have been preserved and are in the King Ranch vault. On the following pages is a translation of one of the documents, omitting such portions as are duplication or deal with legal technicalities rather than the actual acquisition of the land.

The facsimile on opposite page is the first page of the original document. The translation begins on page 384.

Quarenta y ocho reales.

SELLO PRIMERO, QVAREN-
TA Y OCHO REALES, AÑOS DE
MIL OCHOCIENTOS, Y MIL
OCHOCIENTOS Y VNO.

El Lic.do D.n Jose Manuel Ruiz de Aguir-
re, Abogado de los Reales Consejos, Teniente
Letrado Asesor ordinario, Encarg.do de esta
Intendencia, Juez Privativo de Tierras, y
Aguas en toda su comprension &.a

Por quanto D.n Jose Ygnacio de Almeira de esta Vecindad como Apoderado de Don Jose Lorenzo de
la Garza, D.n Jose Domingo y D.n Julian de la Garza, Vecinos de la Villa de Camargo en la Colonia
del Nuevo Santander con fecha diez y sette de
Enero del año proximo pasado de mil ochocientos seis presento en esta Intendencia un Escrito,
cuyo tenor con el de el Poder que le acompaño es
el siguiente = D.n Jose Ygnacio de Almeira à nom-
bre de D.n Jose Lorenzo de la Garza, D.n Jose Domingo,
y D.n Julian de la Garza, Vecinos de la Villa de Camargo, cuyo Poder presento en dos foxas utiles,
como mas haiga lugar en dro digo: Que mis
Partes son Criadores de ganado mayores, y menores, como tambien de conocidas facultades,
en cuya virtud, y en la de que en el Paraxe nombrado Santa Gertrudis se halla realengo, y ex-

Escrito.}

TITLE *to Four Leagues of* UNAPPROPRIATED CATTLE LAND *located in the place called* SANTA GERTRUDIS, *Colony of Nuevo Santander, in favor of Don José Domingo de la Garza, a resident of the Town of Camargo.*

THE LICENTIATE Don José Manuel Ruiz de Aguirre, Advocate of the Royal Councils, Legal Advisor, Ordinary Assessor, Commissioner of this District,* Exclusive Judge in charge of land and water in the entire jurisdiction, et cetera:

Whereas Don Ignacio de Alustiza, a resident of this town, having been granted full power of attorney [at Camargo, December 13, 1805] by Don José Lorenzo de la Garza, Don José Domingo, and Don Julián de la Garza, residents of the Town of Camargo in the Colony of Nuevo Santander, on the seventeenth of January of last year, 1806, filed with this Administration a document the import of which, together with the power of attorney, is as follows:

Brief:

I, Don Ignacio de Alustiza, by virtue of the power of attorney granted me by Don José Lorenzo de la Garza, Don José Domingo and Don Julián de la Garza, residents of the Town of Camargo, (I herewith submit my power of attorney on two sheets) declare in due form of law: That my clients are cattle- and sheep-raisers and known to be experienced as such, in view of which fact and of the fact that the place known as Santa Gertrudis is unappropriated, waste

* At this time New Spain was divided into twelve districts or *Intendencias,* each taking the name of its capital. Texas was attached to the *Intendencia* of San Luis Potosí.

and unpopulated, in the area which extends from the far side of the Rio Grande to the river called Nueces, I claim in the name of my clients twelve leagues suitable for cattle and request that each one be granted four leagues, considering as the center the aforesaid place, Santa Gertrudis, thence to the creek called San Fernando, offering to pay its value as set by just appraisal and the Royal tax of *medianata* as may be adjudged. Wherefore: I petition you so to order in accordance with my request as is just and provided by law.—José Ignacio de Alustiza.

Resolution of the Fiscal Officer:

To the Acting Treasurer of the District:

The Fiscal Officer states that Don José Ignacio Alustiza, acting for Don José Lorenzo de la Garza, Don José Domingo and Don Julián de la Garza, residents of the Town of Camargo, is claiming twelve leagues of pasture land in the place called Santa Gertrudis, with boundaries which he designates in his Deed, it being understood that the claim is for four leagues for each party.

This petition is not contrary to the agreement reached by the Superior Council of the Royal Exchequer at its meeting on the tenth of May, 1802; wherefore you will please to commission the Governor of Nuevo Santander, in whose jurisdiction the said town appears to be, personally, or through a deputy deemed reliable by him, and after the appointment of an appraiser, duly sworn in, and the summoning of adjacent landholders, to proceed to the inspection, appraisal and measurement of the claimed land: designating the lands which are allotted and correspond to each interested party, in order to prevent confusion and future litigation among them; and to draw up a map, and specify the quality, goodness, uses and applications of the lands, with the understanding that the leagues that have flowing water should be appraised at seventy pesos at least; thirty, those which can obtain it by means of draw wells, wells or other devices; and ten, those which lack this benefit, in accordance with the aforecited Higher Decree; and that then, having made thirty public proclamations in the nearest town, let him see to the judicial proceedings, and the summoning of whatever bidders may appear to this District, Potosí, January 25, 1806.

Gordoa

And this District, in compliance with the said officer's request, has ordered, by a decree of the same date, that the appropriate writ should be transmitted to the Governor of the Colony of Nuevo Santander, requesting that he himself, or a reliable deputy, should proceed to carry out the prescribed proceedings; and after the claimants have been advised of this, the aforesaid writ, dated the twenty-sixth of the same month of January was drafted, which, having been presented to the abovementioned Governor, Lieutenant Colonel Don Manuel de Yturbe é Yraeta, on the thirteenth of February of the same year, the latter accordingly gave orders that Don José de Goceascoechea, Captain of Militia of the said Town of Camargo, should put into effect that requested proceedings; to which purpose he notified the interested party, Don José Domingo de la Garza that, for the four leagues which concern him, he should see to the persons and other requirements necessary to the discharge of his commission; the said Garza, accordingly, whose leagues were to be measured, agreeing to the persons named by his father Don José Lorenzo, who are: Don Antonio Margil Cano, Surveyor; José Rafael Gonzalez, experienced Appraiser; Don Luis Olivares and Don Andrés Fernandez de la Fuente, accountants; after the acceptance and swearing in of these persons, the land was thereupon measured by the methods described as follows:

The Survey Begins:

Being in the place called Santa Gertrudis, and on the boundary line of San Julián belonging to Don José Lorenzo de la Garza (for the four leagues of pasture land that have been measured for him and adjudged [to him] by me), the thirty-first of the month of July, 1806:

I, the said Judge, commissioned for the purpose established by me, and in accord with Don José Lorenzo de la Garza as by the judicial decree of yesterday, ordered Don José Domingo de la Garza, the party concerned with the four leagues to be measured, the adjacent landholder Don José Lorenzo de la Garza, a Surveyor, an Appraiser, Accountants, and other assistants, that we should proceed to survey these four leagues.

First of all, the Surveyor took the cord destined for the purpose, of which he measured off fifty ordinary varas, and tying both ends of the said cord to two staffs of adequate strength, so that they might measure the distance only from one staff to the other, he set a boundary marker on the boundary of San Julián, and turning his line from south to north on the west side, he measured with the cord eighty-three lengths, sixteen varas, whereupon we found ourselves before the pond called La Trinidad, at which place I ordered a post to be set as a fixed boundary marker, with the name of San Rafael, and turning from here from west to east on the north side, two hundred twenty cord-lengths were measured off, whereupon we reached a knoll to which we gave the name of El Castillo.

At this place I ordered the survey to be interrupted, because it was the noon hour, and to be continued in the afternoon; I swear that the present document, which I have signed along with those assisting me, is a true and accurate record of my actions.

José de Goceascoechea

José Faustino Contreras, *Assistant*

José Antonio Prieto y Garza,
Assistant

The Survey Continues:

On the same day, I, the said Judge, continuing this survey, ordered the party concerned, and other associates, that we should continue it as established by my previous decree, and the Surveyor, accordingly, proceeded to measure off on the said cord fifty varas, and continuing a straight line in the same direction from west to east

along the north side, two hundred fifty cord-lengths were measured off, whereby the four hundred seventy of the opposite side were completed and we reached the Mogote del Lucero, where I had a post cut and set in this place as a fixed boundary marker with the same name of Lucero. Whereupon, the sun having set, I saw fit to interrupt the said survey and to continue it on the following day, recording it in the present document which I have signed with those assisting me as previously explained and to the accuracy of which I swear.

José de Goceascoechea

José Faustino Contreras, *Assistant*

José Antonio Prieto y Garza,
Assistant

Conclusion of the Survey:

At the said boundary marker of Lucero and on the first of August of this present year, I, the aforesaid Judge, in accordance with my orders in the previous decree, ordered the party concerned, Surveyor and individuals included in these documents, that we should proceed with its continuation, and, so doing, the said Surveyor prepared the cord for this purpose in the manner previously described, and stretched his line from the said boundary marker of Lucero in a north to south direction along the east side until he had completed eighty-three cord-lengths, sixteen varas, whereupon we reached the boundary marker of San George and had, consequently, measured off a distance equal to that of the opposite side; in accordance with which, and since the line from San Julián to San George had already been measured by Don José

Lorenzo, I saw fit to omit a second measurement of the said line and to declare as sufficient and complete the survey of these four leagues adjudged to Don José Domingo de la Garza, who was satisfied with it.

And since it was necessary to return to the boundary of San Rafael to begin the survey of the four leagues corresponding to Don José Julián de la Garza, I saw fit to order that this be done, and to provide for spending the noon hour there, and accordingly to summon the aforementioned Don José Domingo, as the adjacent landholder of his brother Don José Julián; and likewise to notify him that after the remaining survey had been concluded, the other proceedings would be taken care of; and having been advised of all this, he signed with me, along with [other] persons and the assistants with whom I act as Receiver, as has been explained; to the truth of the foregoing I swear,

José de Goceascoechea

Antonio Margil Cano

Andrés Fernandez de la Fuente

José Domingo de la Garza

José Luis Olivares, *Assistant*

José Faustino Contreras, *Assistant*

José Antonio Prieto y Garza

Appraisal:

Consequently, I, the aforementioned Judge, in view of the completion of the survey of the four leagues of pasture land described in these edicts, saw fit to notify José Rafael Gonzalez, as an experienced Appraiser, to set a just price upon and declare the value of each league with regard to the qualities of this pasture, its location, under his legal oath; and he, so doing, said that the only value or price that the said four leagues deserved was that of ten pesos apiece, which appraisal he made on the basis of his own experience and under the said oath; I had the foregoing set down in legal form, which the abovementioned did not sign, since he did not know how, and I, the said Judge, signed for him, along with those assisting me, as has been explained; to all of which I swear,

José de Goceascoechea

Andrés Fernandez de la Fuente

José Faustino Contreras, *Assistant*

José Antonio Prieto y Garza,
Assistant

Return of Documents:

In the said town [of Santa Ana de Camargo], and on the sixteenth day of the aforesaid month and year [August, 1806], the aforesaid Surveyor, Don Antonio Margil Cano, appeared before me, the said Judge, and upon appearing returned the present documents, and thereupon showed and delivered to me the Map prepared in accordance with the said documents, to which I order the said Map to be added, and that the remaining judicial proceedings be taken. And I, the aforesaid Judge, so determined and ordered by this document, which I signed with those who assist me and with whom I act as has been said, to which I swear,

José de Goceascoechea

José Faustino Contreras, *Assistant*

José Antonio Prieto y Garza,
Assistant

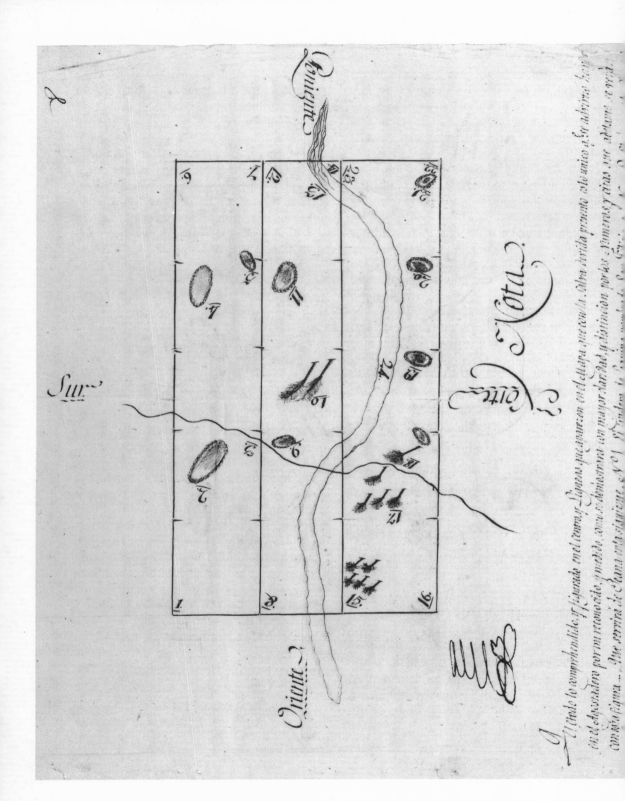

No 3. El camino N.3 mensionado N... ... el cuadro mas mortal... 61.... ... cuadro mas mortal... ... ... de Aguila mayoral—

San Lorenzo N.7. El lindero de Aguina nombrado S.M. Julian= N.8. El lindero de Aguina combibido S.M. Victoria, empor termini al mo Alta debo quatro sitios p.a menudear á Don José Lorenzo el la garza segun se cuenta. = N.o el Charro á las someras N.9. Alta. 1140. = N.11. El charro el Sans. = N.12. El mirado lindero de San Julian divisorio de la tierra p.a menudear á Don José Lorenzo y D.n José Domingo. = N.13. El charro de la Trinidad. = N.14. El lindero nombrado S.M. Rafael. = N.15. El lindero de Aguina nombrado el Lucero, divisorio entre Don José Domingo, y Don José Julian de la garza. = S.16. El lindero nombrado S.M. Juan Nepom cena = N.17. Los Tancililes. = N.18. El Desamer = N.19. La Laguna acantida. = N.20. El charro de los Amoladores. = N.21. El charro de Melmires. = N.22. El lindero en San Rafael divisorio, y ter mivare estos quatro sitios señalados á Don José Julian de la garza. = N.23. El lindero nombrado el Febro. = N.24. El Arroyo de Aguina divisorio. Y termina estos quatro sitios señalados á Don José Julian de la garza. = N.24. El Arroyo de Aguina Reservado que todo es Ciénaga, y Ciénaga reconocido, y medido, y prebenido de Don José Domingo, y Don José Domingo, las mismas que se han demarcado, registrado, reconocido, y medido, y prebenido en la autoridad de el S.r Señor Don José Domingo, y que se han aclarado (de esta vecindad) en conformidad el aqual, por una de lo prebenido en esta superior orden expedida por mayor, las mismas que se han aclarado (de esta vecindad) en conformidad el aqual, por una de lo prebenido en esta superior orden expedida por Don José Julian el la fabrica (de esta vecindad) en conformidad el aqual, por una de lo prebenido en esta superior orden expedida por el Señor el Señor Yntendente de San Luis Obispo, en 6 de Febrero M. pasado de año de Ochosientos cinco, mus abien valuar o decir p.a cada un sitio, en arencion aque la citada tierra, no prome se seguir, segun sus circunstancias) otra utilidad, que la de criadero de ganados mayores, excepto el habitar, escular, y ganados menores, aunque expone a la hostilidad de los Indios Barbaros, y por lo imble pedida en las Rigorias Secas, que por lo comun se experimentan, a causa esta ma ninguna conveniencia, a patuación de la Charque ria, y en dicha tierra reconocer, de consiguiente la cria da Ynnancia abaca los Ahados, y Pahar Irancia el Caballada Atencira, y el ma minimo de unido de minisque la reducida, y crecita. En conformidad el aqual, y reminiendame ata gracia que se me ace, y juzgan que falce, cargo he tenido a bien, valuar dicho Sitios a precios con dicho dinero de diezy ocho uno. A sí lo declaro, y firmé en esta dicho Villa el Señor lanza anno estampado, y en diez, y seis días el mes de Agosto y mil ochocientos cinco, usando de qua te qui pere de Pluma, ó tinta. = Antonio Marqui Cano.

KEY TO THE MAP

I HEREBY CERTIFY that everything comprised and drawn within the Map, and the lines appearing thereon, are, with permissible omissions, all that there was found to be in the Pasture-tract surveyed and measured by me, as will more clearly and distinctly appear from the numbers and references given with this figure, which will serve as a Key:

No. 1 The corner post called San Feliciano

No. 2 El Charco de la Escondida

No. 3 The impassible road

No. 4 El Charco de los Borregos

No. 5 El Charco de la Rosa

No. 6 The corner post called San Lorenzo

No. 7 The corner post called San Julián

No. 8 The corner post called San George, at which, as stated, the survey of the four leagues belonging to Don Lorenzo de la Garza ended

No. 9 El Charco de los Tomates

No. 10 El Castillo

No. 11 El Saus

No. 12 The aforementioned boundary of San Julián, dividing the land belonging to Don José Lorenzo from that of Don José Domingo

No. 13 El Charco de la Trinidad

No. 14 The boundary called San Rafael

No. 15 The corner post called El Luzero, dividing the land of Don José Domingo from that of Don Julián de la Garza

No. 16 The boundary called San Juan Nepomuceno

No. 17 Los Jaboncillos

No. 18 El Descanso

No. 19 La Laguna Escondida

No. 20 Los Huajolotes

No. 21 El Charco de San Andrés

No. 22 The boundary called El Lobo

No. 23 The San Rafael boundary, dividing off and ending the four leagues assigned to Don José Julián de la Garza

No. 24 El Arroyo de Santa Gertrudis

THE ENTIRE DIAMETER, center, lines and circumference of these lands comprises twelve leagues of pasture land, which have been claimed, examined, surveyed and measured at the request of Don José Lorenzo, Don José Domingo, and Don Julián de la Garza (all residents of this town), in accordance with which, and in view of the provisions of the superior decree by the Assessor Intendent of San Luis Potosí, on February 6 of the past year of 1805, I decided to appraise the leagues at ten pesos apiece, because the said land is such that it is fit only for the raising of stock (except horses, mules and sheep), although it is exposed to the hostile acts of the savage Indians, and to considerable loss of stock during severe drouths which are of common occurrence, because of the temporary nature and little duration of the waterholes found on the said land; as well as the great distance from the settlements, and the abundance of wild horses, which represent a constant danger to the tame breeding stock.

Accordingly, on the basis of my practical experience, and under legal oath, I have decided to set the abovesaid value of ten pesos apiece on the said leagues. So I declare, and hereto subscribe, in this said Town of Our Lady of Santa Ana de Camargo, on the sixteenth day of the month of August, 1806. Excepting all errors of writing or calculation.

—Antonio Margil Cano.

The Auction:

In the City of San Luis Potosí, on the twenty-third of the current month of April, 1807, there having gathered for Auctions the President, the Legal Advisor, the Ordinary Assessor in charge of this District, Licentiate Don José Ruiz de Aguirre, the Ministers of the Royal Exchequer of this Provincial Treasury, Treasurer Don Cristóbal Corvalán and Accountant Don José Caballero Basave, Honorary Auditing Commissioner of the Army, the Royal Fiscal Officer, Licentiate Don Francisco Gerónimo de Gordoa, and Don José Ignacio de Alustiza, as legal representative of Don José Lorenzo de la Garza, Don José Domingo and Don Julián de la Garza, for the purpose of holding the third one of the Auctions officially established, and in it, the sale of the twelve leagues of land which the former had claimed for the latter, and for which purpose they had gathered in the room destined thereto in this Royal House; at eleven o'clock today the proclamation of the land sale was begun by the official auctioneer, who announced in a loud voice:

"Anyone who wishes to bid on twelve leagues of unappropriated land situated in the place called Santa Gertrudis within the jurisdiction of the Town of Camargo, Colony of Nuevo Santander, and which have been claimed by Don José Lorenzo, Don José Domingo and Don Julián de la Garza, appraised at ten pesos apiece, let him appear, and his bid with the required bond of security will be received, and the sale will take place today after the noon call to prayer."

This announcement having been repeated several times without any bidder coming forward to place a higher bid on the said lands, and after an effort had been made to persuade Alustiza to do so, for reasons expressed by the Gentlemen of the Council —he stated that he could give only two pesos more for each league—the noon call to prayers having been made, without the appearance of any bidder other than the aforementioned Alustiza, the sale was ordered, which took place in the following terms:

"Since there is no one who will bid up the price, nor give more than the twelve pesos offered by Don José Ignacio Alustiza, acting with power of attorney of Don José Lorenzo, Don José Domingo and Don Julián de la Garza, for each league of the twelve which he has claimed, a total amount of one hundred forty-four pesos—much good, much good, much good may it do him— with the necessary condition that after the said lands have been delivered into the possession of the parties concerned, they must settle, farm and cultivate them within one year, under penalty of losing possession of them, and the said lands can then be sold to the highest bidder claiming them; and the higher authorities shall be advised of this sale for their approval by the Presiding Officer of this District."

These conditions were accepted by Alustiza who, in the name of the parties whom he represents, promised to abide by them. Thereupon this judicial act was concluded and was signed by all, including the Proxy Bidder; all of whom I certify,

Licentiate José Ruiz de Aguirre
Cristóbal Corvalán
José Caballero Basave
Licentiate Francisco
          Gerónimo de Gordoa
José Ignacio de Alustiza

Before me, Silvestre Suárez, Notary Public of the Royal Exchequer and War.

After this, the party concerned having paid into the Royal Treasury of this Capital the full value of the lands adjudicated, and the whole of the documents having been transmitted to the Supreme Authority of the Most Excellent Lord Viceroy of these Realms, so that in the Superior Council of the Royal Exchequer he may kindly decide what is his pleasure, His Excellency saw fit to approve in the said Council the aforementioned adjudication to the highest bidder, having received a petition to that effect from the Fiscal Officer of the Royal Exchequer, as will appear below:

Certification of payment to Royal Treasury:

The Ministers of the Royal Exchequer of the Provincial Treasury of this Province:

We certify that on this date Don José Ignacio de Alustiza, acting with power of attorney for Don José Lorenzo, Don José Domingo and Don Julián de la Garza, residents of the Town of Camargo in the Colony of Nuevo Santander, has paid to us one hundred fifty-four pesos one real, as follows: one hundred forty-four pesos which we have credited to the Land Division as the value of the twelve leagues claimed by the aforesaid individuals and which have been knocked down to them as by the preceding records of proceedings in an official Public Auction; two pesos seven reals for the said Land Division, being two per cent on said amount for the privilege of not appearing for the Confirmation; four pesos two reals for the Royal Tax of *medianata;* three pesos three-fourths real for five per cent on half of the value of the said lands; five pesos three-fourths real for the eighteen per cent transportation charge

to Spain; and the remaining three pesos for fees to the Auditor's Office of Royal Taxes, as entered on folio 146 reverse and 147 of Manual Book . . . . 154 pesos, 1 real.

To certify which, we grant these presents in the City of San Luis Potosí, April 27, 1807.

Cristóbal Corvalán
José de Caballero Basave

Approval of the Higher Council:

Higher Council of the Royal Exchequer: May 27, 1807:

After examination of the final adjudication of the unappropriated lands forming the subject matter of these proceedings, the same is hereby approved with the assent of the Fiscal Officer of the Royal Exchequer in his previous reply of the twenty-third instant, complying with the same in every respect. Agreed to and signed by:

[Viceroy Don José de] Iturrigaray
Castillo
Borbón
Monterde
Vildosola
Félix Sandoval

Conclusion:

I have, accordingly, ordered issued the present Title, by which, in the name of His Majesty (God save him!), and by virtue of the fact that all the respective and required payments have been made for the adjudicated lands, tax of *medianata,* and so forth, as have been indicated, and as will appear from the inserted Certification of the Officers of the Royal Exchequer, I do hereby in due and proper form of law declare Don José Domingo de la Garza, a resident of the Town of Camargo, the lawful owner in possession, proprietorship, ownership and full use of the four leagues of unappropriated land which has been adjudicated to him and described in the foregoing instrument, and of all that may concern and pertain to the said land in any manner whatsoever, divesting the Royal Exchequer from this day henceforth and forever of the interest, possession and ownership of the aforementioned four leagues; and I release, resign and transfer it all to the said Garza, his heirs and successors and whoever may represent his rights, with all clauses, requirements and formalities of importance, which latter will be deemed here implied as if they had been literally inserted; but with the express proviso and condition that said leagues may not be sold, resigned nor alienated to any Church or Monastary, under penalty of losing them; and that within the first three months after the presentation of this title before the Governor of Nuevo Santander, he [de la Garza] must receive and take possession of the aforesaid four leagues, so that, thus being in possession, he may plant along all the limits and boundaries willows and other trees in the proper season, as required by the Law 10 and 11, Book 4, Title 12 of the Code of this realm; and, finally, that he must occupy them within a time limit of one year in accordance with the stipulations of the act of adjudication, of which the necessary proofs shall be annexed hereto, the necessary evidence to remain in the Files of the Capital.

Given in San Luis Potosí, August 29, 1807.

Licentiate José Ruiz de Aguirre

By order of the Legal Advisor of this District,
Silvestre Suárez
Notary Public of the City Council and Royal Exchequer and War.

This title has been registered in the proper book in this District:

Title to four leagues of unappropriated pasture land, located in the Colony of Nuevo Santander in the Place called Santa Gertrudis, in the name of Don José Domingo de la Garza, Resident of the Town of Camargo.

San Carlos, 27 November, 1807.

Having examined the preceding Title, presented at this Government Office by the interested party, Don José Domingo de la Garza, resident of the Town of Camargo in this Province, in order to comply with the same in every particular punctually and duly, I hereby give sufficient and full commission as required by law to Captain Don José de Goceascocchea, Justice of the aforementioned Town of Camargo, to deliver at the earliest possible moment to the abovenamed Don José Domingo de la Garza the respective four leagues of land that have been granted to him, and likewise to give him formal and legal possession of them, after the fulfillment of all legal requisites and so forth as directed in the said Title.

Manuel de Yturbe é Yraeta
Manuel Nogaro, *Assistant*
Manuel Garza, *Assistant*

In the aforesaid town, and on the twenty-first day of the present month and year [January, 1808], the aforecited Don José Domingo de la Garza, having appeared before this court as a result of my notification, declared that he was ready to travel to the aforementioned pasture, as he had been ordered to by me; and in proceeding to the said journey, I had it set down in legal form and signed by the abovenamed, before me and those assisting me, with whom I act as Notary as already set forth; all of which I certify,

José de Goceascoechea

José Faustino Contreras, *Assistant*

Eusebio Treviño, *Assistant*

Being at the Charco de los Tomates on the twenty-fifth of the present month and said year [January, 1808]: I, the aforenamed Captain and Justice, an associate of Don José Domingo de la Garza, the interested party, together with assistants and other individuals accompanying me in order to place the said Don José Domingo de la Garza in Legal Possession of this pasture; I took him by the hand, and leading him about on that land, I said to him in a loud and clearly audible voice:

"Don José Domingo de la Garza, in the name of His Majesty (God save him) and by virtue of the powers granted me by sufficient commission, conferred upon me for this purpose by the Governor of this Province, in his abovecited Superior Decree, I hereby place you in legal possession of this pasture and of everything contained within its limits and confines as shown on the map inserted in these proceedings at folio 8, with all its entrances, exits, uses, customs and easements, and accordingly, from today henceforth I constitute, name and declare you Exclusive Lord and Legitimate owner in fee of the said pasture, through having examined it, bought and paid for it at public sale at the District of San Luis Potosí, as shown in the present Title which will be given to you for your protection. Wherefore, within the next six months, you will have strong and durable boundary markers of Lime and Stone set on all the aforecited limits and confines, with the understanding that in failing to do so you will lose the use, ownership, dominion and right which you have to the said pasture."

To this the interested party replied that he would do so, and, expressing his gratitude, he gave thanks to Your Majesty and said to the bystanders who were there:

"Gentlemen, you will bear witness that His Honor the Judge here present has placed me in Legal Possession of this pasture, without any third party gainsaying."

And, as a sign of possession, he tore up grass, spilled water, broke sticks and made other demonstrations of gratitude and pleasure. Thereupon I deemed the present proceedings complete and concluded. They were signed by the abovementioned before me and those assisting me, with whom I act as Notary as has been said; which I certify,

José de Goceascoechea

José Faustino Contreras, *Assistant*

Eusebio Treviño, *Assistant*

The present title is to be delivered to the interested party, Don José Domingo de la Garza, for his protection as provided by law, in sixteen folios; I place hereto my flourish.

Ynico Señor y Dueño lexmo. en propiedad el enunciado Agos=
tadero, por haverlo V. Registrado, Comprado y pagado en Ca=
xas Res. e Publica Almoñoneda é Yntendencia de S. Luis Poto=
si, segun se manifiesta en el prexente titulo que para su Res=
guardo se le entregará; Por tanto dispondrá V. que dentro del
texmino de los seys mexes siguientes, se pongan Mohoneras
fixmes y Conciztentes de Cal y Piedra en todos los Lindes y
Confines vitado, con apercevimto. de que en no verificarlo en
el texmino y tmpo. asignado, decaerá el Uso, señorio, Domi=
nio y Propiedad que á dho. Agostadero tiene; á que resolvió el
Ynterezado que así lo exeecutaria, y en muexza de Reconocimto.
dió las gracias á S. Ill. y dixo á los Circunstantes que allí ha=
via, Señores Amos. me sean testigos, como el prexente Señr. Juez
me ha puesto en Pocecion Juridica de este Agostadero sin
contadicion de tercero, y en señal de propiedad, Arranó
Sacate, Regó Agua, quebró Palos é hizo otras demonstracio=
nes de agradecimto. y complacencia; Con lo que di por bastante
y Concluida la prexente diligencia que fixma el suyo Refe=
xido por ante mí, y los testis asstes. con quienes acctuo por
Receptoria como dho. es: doy fé—

José de Goeazcoechea

asstª
José Faustino Contrerar

asstª
Eusebio Terviño

Se entrega el prexente titulo al Ynterezado D. José Dominga
de la Parza, para su Resguardo segun se manda, en diez y
seis foxas utiles: lo Rubrico.

R.

Typical Pages from the First Account Book Rancho Santa Gertrudis

THE ORIGINAL ACCOUNT BOOK in which Richard King started keeping financial records of ranching operations on the Santa Gertrudis in 1854 was discovered among other old papers in a storeroom in the ranch's Commissary Building in the mid-1920's. The account book was in a remarkable state of preservation. It contained a wealth of detailed entries of expenditures and receipts during the ranch's beginning days that have been invaluable in reconstructing early ranching methods. The pages reproduced here in facsimile show a portion of the record of disbursements by Captain King.

Ranch Santa Gertrudes
              In a/c with Richard King ——— Dr

1854.
Jany 1. To cash Expended in various sums at various times
            to date as follows
                pd R. Ryan for 3 yearling horse colts, 1 mare,
                    2 three year old horses & 2 saddle horses   50.—
            " Marco Radick for 76 mares   649.—
            " Expenses on same   20.—
            " David Vandenberger Expns on mares at Santa Rita   5.—
            advanced do to take of Stock at Rancho Viejo
                    1 Miss Rifle $15.—
                    1 Saddle & Bridle   20,—
                    1 blk pacing pony   30.—
                    Cash $10 & $10,—   20,—
                    1 pr pistol   10,—   95.—
            pd for 11 mares 7 colts &c & a Jack at Long Reach   140.—
            " Expns on same $15— to take same to Brownsville $10.— 25,—
            " for a horse for Jno Canter to drive same   15,
            " Alex So for a Bell mare   5.—
            amt Cash taken by me at to the Rancho   100.—
            " do borrd by me of H Clay Davis at do   100.—
            " do " " " " J Walworth at do   25.—
            pd E M Anderson for paint horse for Fogg   30.—
            " Jno Fogg to take Stock to Gregory & Richardson   50.—
            " J R Barnard amt borrd of him   30.—
            " Evaristo Mayor Domo   9.—
            " blk Hunter   6.—
            " for 2 Miss Rifles @ $12.—   24.—
            " " 1 govt Carbine   8.—
            " " 1 double barreled Gun   15,—
            " " 1 musket   6.—
            " " 4 Sett mule Harness   30.—
            " Franco 2 mos Services at Rancho Viejo   20.—
            " Juan Canter 5 mos do @ $15.   75.—
            " for ½ Cargo beans Sent fr Munguillas   5.—
            " Cart Hire   " do   20,—
                        amt carried forward $1,557.—

1854.   Amt Brot forward ──── $9.777.36

Aug.t 23	To Cash p.d Lewis order to Pedro Ramos	J.W.	9. 25
" " "	do " for grass &c	"	9. 50
" 31 "	do " Lewis order to Jamison's woman	"	8.—
" " "	do " das do " Andrw Majorga	"	8.—
Sept 8 "	do " Ylario to buy grass		.50
" 10 "	do " do on a/c of Services		3.—
" 17 "	do " Felipe to buy Corn		4.—
" 19 "	do " Ylario on a/c of Services		5.—
" " "	do " Munguillas (10 Mules & 16 mares)		300.—
" " "	do " for sundries by Howlett		.50
" " "	do " Mex at Capota		10.—
" " "	do " Ylario Chapa		3.—
Oct 28 "	do " Serra for ½ Cargo Corn		2.—
" 31 "	do " for grass		1.62
" " "	do " Howlett		17.94
" " "	do " G.K.Lewis dft for $1200, 200 Cows 2.d inst	1.200.—
Nov.r 2 "	do " for shoeing horses		2.—
" 4 "	do " " Pants & Shirts for Martin Brown		4.75
" " "	do " " Corn 8/- grass 12/ Corn 20/-		5.—
" 8 "	do " Wm Houston	J.W.	40.—
Dec.r 31 "	do " by Howlett for sundries on trip		16.43
" " "	do " Putiguat for Clothing for Martin Brown		7. 25
" " "	1 Saddle & Bridle left with Lewis		25.—
" " "	1 gun , d.b. " " do		25.—
" " "	1 pr. Blanket " " do		7.—
" " "	Cash p.d Fradin repairing guns pistols &c		25.—
" " "	do " Pagan for doctoring & feeding horse		5.—
" " "	do " Martin Brown for 2 mo.s Service		30.—
" " "	do " Fit out to go the trip to Rancho		25.—
" " "	do " Exp.s on the road there and back		20.—
" " "	do " Ch Parcell for 1 bay horse thro E.D.Smith $10.—		
	do " Provision by E.D.S. , G.K.L. took the horse, 2.69		12.69
" "	Fret and feed of Sundry Animals		30.—
" " "	do on sundry things to Munguillas & other points		30.—
" " "	Sundry saddles bridles blankets & arms bot for the Rancho at		
	Sundry times and not before Chg.d , Estimated at, ⎰	100.—
	Amt Carried Forward ──── $11.769.29		

1854.   Amt Brought Forward $ 11.769.79

Dec 31 To Sundry tools implements &c furnished the Rancho
        at Sundry times   250. —
"   " " Cash p by Galvan to Luis pr G.K.L's order 4 inst   15.13
"   " " do " " do   " Pedro Ramos pr do 14. "   8. —
"   " " do " for 6 sacks Corn sent in by Pedro Ramos   12. —
"   " " do " " 2 Brush bitts 2½ Tobacco by   3.75
"   " " do " Morgan Barclay Ferriage 19 inst   1.12
"   " " do " J.R Palmer for Shaving utensils G.K.L   4. —
"   " " do " do's   " Knife & mem book Howlett   3. —
"   " " do " Wm Houston on the road 8 Nov ulto   10. —
"   " " do " for 10 mares 2 Horses Colt &c 9   " "   68. —
"   " " do " G.K Lewis 16   " "   46. —
"   " " do " for 4 horses left at the Rancho, viz:
                    1 Roan "Pendleton" Horse $8. —
                    1 Clay Bank "Brown"   do   16. —
                    1 Sorrel "Howlett"   do   15. —
1855.   1 bay   "Soldier"   do   15. —   54. —
Jany 12 " Saddle bridle & blanket sent by Andres Majorca   20. —
"   " " To Cash advanced Andres Majorca , Self, $10. —
        do   "   do   p to Turner   20. —
        do   "   do   Self   50   30.50
"   " " do p yr, G.K Lewis order drawn on me or Rudolph   14. —
Feby 22 " do " Ygnacio Neira As pr his due bill   30. —
Mch 9 " do " yr order to L.I. Kennon , G.K.L.   56. —
"   12 " do " Corn, grass, Horse Shoeing, fit out,
                Provisions &c to go out to the Ranch   30. —
"   " " do " Dr E. Garey for 5 mares   60 —
                                                              12.479.29

                    Credit :

1854
Novr 28 By Two promissory notes drawn by W W White at San
        Antonio Texas and remitted me by G.K Lewis for my
        own benefit viz: $750 Each $ 1.500. —
"   " " 1 grey "Doddridge" horse traded off by me   30. —
1855
Feby 28 1 American Horse, &o,   100. —
         1 Buggy, Covered   125. —
         1 blk pacing Pony (valued by R King)   15. —   1.770. —
                                                              $ 10.709.29

Contract between United States Army Quartermaster and Richard King

1856

FROM THE AVAILABLE RECORDS, it becomes obvious that Captain King took the lead in promoting local business from the Army. The contract reproduced here in facsimile is typical of many which M. Kenedy & Co. fulfilled for the Quartermaster Department. It will be noted that James Walworth witnessed the contract.

Article of Agreement made this Fourteenth day of November in the Year One thousand Eight hundred and fifty Six, between first Lieut Lewis O. Morris first Artillery, A. A. Q. master United States Army, for and in behalf of the United States, On the One part, and Richard King of the City of Brownsville County of Cameron, State of Texas, on the Other part,

Witnesseth, That for and in Consideration of the Sum of Nine hundred and fifty Dollars, the Said King doth Covenant and agree to transport on a good Steam Boat or Boats from Brazos Santiago Texas, to Fort Brown Texas, Two Companies L. and M. first Artillery U. S. Army and twelve men, Band of 2d Cavalry with All their Baggage, Stores, and all other property of and belonging to Said Companies.

And the Said Lieut Lewis O. Morris A. A. Q. m. U. S. Army for and on behalf of the United State, doth Covenant and agree to pay to Said King, his heirs and Assigns the Said Sum of Nine hundred and fifty Dollars, on the Completion of the above Agreement, or as soon thereafter as there may be Sufficient funds in hand for that purpose.

In Witness whereof we have hereunto set our hands and Seal (using Scrawl for Seals) this Fourteenth day of November in the Year One thousand Eight hundred and fifty Six

In presence of
P. Wadsworth

Lewis O. Morris
First Lieut A A Q m

Richard King

Registration of
Early King Ranch Brands
and the
Running W

THE LACONIC OFFICIAL WORDING of the registration of these first brands and the brief tracings of their shapes paint a graphic picture of a ranch in its beginning. Captain King's *Ere Flecha*—or R Arrow—perhaps proved impractical because of its intricacy: the susceptibility to blurring and the many corners inviting deep spots in the burn to be attacked by insects and screw worms. As partners came into the enterprise, by marriage and by financial arrangement, their presence traced itself in the brand history of the ranch.

Henrietta M. King's Brand.

HK

THE STATE OF TEXAS
COUNTY OF NUECES

BE IT REMEMBERED *that Mistress Henrietta M. King, wife of Richard King, having deposited her brand in this office for record as described and laid down in the margin, the same was this day recorded in Book "B," of the registry of brands, Nueces County, on page 57.*

Witness my official signature, at my office in Corpus Christi, this 20th day of March, A.D. *1859.*

REUBEN HOLBEIN, *Clerk,* C. C. N. C.

Richard King's Brands.

R

Rancho Brand thus.

K

THE STATE OF TEXAS
COUNTY OF NUECES

BE IT REMEMBERED *that Richard King, having deposited his brands in this office for Record, as described and laid down in the Margin, the same were this day recorded in Book "B," of the registry of brands, Nueces County, on page 61.*

Witness my official signature, at my office in Corpus Christi, this 27th day of June A.D. *1859.*

REUBEN HOLBEIN, *Clerk,* C. C. N. C.

King & Walworth's Brands.

K

THE STATE OF TEXAS
COUNTY OF NUECES

BE IT REMEMBERED *that Richard King and James Walworth, having deposited their brands in this office for Record, as described and laid down in the Margin, the same was this day recorded in Book "B," of the registry of Brands, Nueces County, on page 61.*

Witness my official signature, at my office in Corpus Christi, this 27th day of June A.D. *1859.*

REUBEN HOLBEIN, *Clerk,* C. C. N. C.

Richard King's Horse & Cattle Brand

W

Ear Mark

Right Ear. Cut off Hole and Split in left —

All animals are also Branded K on left Cheek

THE STATE OF TEXAS
COUNTY OF NUECES

BE IT REMEMBERED *that on this The Ninth day of February A.D. 1869, Richard King having deposited his Brand and Ear Mark for Horses & Cattle as described and laid down in the Margin hereof, the same was and is hereby duly Recorded in Book "B" for the Registry of Brands in said Nueces County on page 181.*

Witness my Official Signature at Office in Corpus Christi, the day and date above written.

JOSEPH FITZSIMMONS, *Clk.* C. C. N. CO.

Contract between
Confederate States of America and
Richard King, Mifflin Kenedy
and Charles Stillman

1863

THIS CONTRACT — now faded brown script upon worn blue paper, fragile with age — opened up a Confederate lifeline of supplies in 1863. Profits from fulfilling the contract — received in gold rather than in Confederate currency of dwindling value — made possible later development of Rancho Santa Gertrudis by partners King and Kenedy. It played an important part in the future of the King Ranch.

M Kenedy

Chas Stillman

R King

The State of Texas
County of Cameron

    On this first day of the month of May
A. D. Eighteen hundred and Sixty three, personally
appeared before me, Henry Lyman Howlett, a Notary
Public in and for the Said County and State, duly
Commissioned and Sworn, —————————————

Charles Stillman,
————— Major Charles Russell, Miffline Kenedy
and Richard King, each to me well and personally
Known, who Severally Executed the foregoing Articles
of Agreement in my presence, And Severally acknowledged
to me they Executed the Same As their own proper act
and deed for the uses, purposes and considerations
therein Set forth.

    In Testimony Whereof I hereto Set my hand
And affix my Notarial Seal at my office
in the City of Brownsville in Said County
on the day and year above written.

HL Howlett
Not Pub.

Articles of Agreement made and entered into this twenty eighth day of the month of April A.D. One thousand eight hundred and sixty three, between Major Charles Russell Brigade Quarter master, an officer in the Confederate Army, on the one part, and Mifflin Kenedy and Charles Stillman of Brownsville in Cameron County Texas, and Richard King of Nueces County, Texas, of the other part—

This Agreement witnesseth: That the said Maj. Chas. Russell for and on behalf of the Confederate States of America, and the said Mifflin Kenedy, Charles Stillman and Richard King, their heirs Executors and administrators, have covenanted and agreed and by these presents, do mutually Covenant and agree to and with each other as follows: viz:

First. That the said Kenedy Stillman & King, their heirs, Executors and administrators, shall supply or cause to be supplied and delivered to the Quarter master of Fort Brown, Texas, at the Bank of the Rio Grande at Brownsville aforesaid, all such Quarter Master's stores and Camp and Garrison Equipage as may from time to time be required for all that portion of the Confederate States Army occupying the Valley of the Rio Grande, for the period of Six months Commencing on the first day of June A.D. Eighteen hundred and Sixty three and Ending on the thirtieth day of November A.D. Eighteen hundred and Sixty three; they, the said Contractors, to wit: Kenedy Stillman & King to be paid the original cost of Same by original Invoices and all Expenses of transportation and charges incident to landing and delivery of the Same at the River Bank at Brownsville aforesaid, together with fifteen per Centum on the Said Cost and charges—

Item That the said Major Russell will furnish or cause to be furnished to the said Kenedy Stillman & King, all needful notice of the amounts and quantities and description of each article of such Quarter Master's Stores & Camp & Garrison Equipage required monthly by the troops of the said Valley of the Rio Grande—

Second. That the said Major Charles Russell will pay or cause to be paid to the said Kenedy Stillman & King, their heirs and assigns, the amount of the original cost of said supplies and charges thereon to the landing at Brownsville aforesaid, together with the fifteen
per Centum

per centum on said original Cost and Charges as aforesaid in the manner following, to wit:

That whereas the parties to this Instrument have made a **Third** Contract of even date herewith, for furnishing the Confederate States Government with Subsistence for the like purpose and for the Same period as herein Contracted for; and Whereas under Said referred to contract, the said Maj. Chas. Russell has obligated himself on behalf of his Government, to deliver to the said Kennedy Stillman & King, five hundred bales of Cotton per month for the said period of Six months;

Now it is understood that the Surplus of said Cotton, after sales of same are rendered, after paying for the Subsistence Stores delivered under that said Contract, shall be applied to the liquidation of this Contract — And that all Conditions, terms to specified in that said contract, here referred to, shall be in full force and virtue with regard to this Contract.

The said Kennedy Stillman & King Shall have Authority **Fourth** to use, in the transportation of said Cotton, all the Conscripts not employed by Major S. Hart or engaged in hauling for the Nitro Mining Bureau or the Medical Department.

It is understood that the Commission to be charged by **Fifth** said Kennedy Stillman & King, Shall be two and a half per cent on all amounts advanced for freight and charges on said Cotton, and two and a half per cent on Sales of all of said Cotton.

It is well understood that no member of Congress has any Interest, direct or indirect, in this Contract.

In witness whereof We, the parties to this Instrument or Articles of Agreement, have hereunto Subscribed our names and affixed our Seals at Brownsville aforesaid on the day and year first hereinbefore written —

(Done in Triplicate)

Approved
Ben. Head ???
M. S. Gail
???

Charles Russell
Major C.S.P.A.
Brig. ??? Master

Agreement and Final Settlement of Affairs of R. King & Co.

RICHARD KING

AND

MIFFLIN KENEDY

RECITES:

The State of Texas
County of Nueces

AGREEMENT.

Dated: February 26th, 1870.

Filed: September 21st, 1870.

Recorded in Vol. B, Bonds & Mortgage Records of Nueces County, Texas.

Recorded in Vol. A, pages 45-47, Transcribed Deed of Trust Records of Kleberg County, Texas.

In The Matter of the Liquidation of the late firm of R. King & Co., at Rancho Santa Gertrudis, in said County and State.

It is mutually understood and agreed by and between us, the undersigned, Richard King, and Mifflin Kenedy, both of said County and State, composing said firm the horse stock and horned cattle, have been divided equally between us, and also the accounts and minor details of said liquidation have been adjusted between us to our entire satisfaction:

Now, this agreement Witnesseth, that for the purpose of making a final settlement, of the affairs of said firm, in liquidation, we hereby make and declare the following division of the lands belonging to the said firm of R. King & Co., and for the better equalization of the values thereof, and to obviate the necessity of dividing any one tract of land, we have agreed to include in this division and settlement some other parcels of real estate which are situated in Brownsville, Texas, and on the Rio Grande in Texas, belong jointly to the undersigned but not belonging to the assets of said firm of R. King & Co.

Therefore, in consideration of the foregoing recited premises, Mifflin Kenedy, for himself, his heirs, executors and administrators does hereby grant, set over, assign, release and quit claim unto Richard King, his heirs and assigns, all his (M. Kenedy's) right, title, interest and claim in and to the following described real estate, viz:

1st: The tract of land known as "El Rincon de Santa Gertrudis" originally granted to Juan Mendiola, containing three and a half leagues, more or less, and situated at the junction of the Santa Gertrudis and San Fernando Creeks,

2nd: The tract of land known as "Santa Gertrudis" originally granted in three portions, to Jose Domingo de la Garza, Jose Julian de la Garza, and Jose Lorenzo de la Garza, containing twelve leagues, more or less and confirmed by the State of Texas, being the tract whereof is situated the principal residence in Rancho "Santa Gertrudis" and the improvements connected therewith,

3rd: The tract of land known as "Puerta de Agua Dulce" originally granted to

Raphael Garcia, containing five and a half leagues, more or less, situated on the Agua Dulce Creek, and confirmed by the State of Texas,

4th: The tract of land known as "San Leandro" originally granted to Rafael Garcia Sisneros, the portion belonging to said firm of R. King & Co., being two leagues thereof, more or less, situated on the San Diego Creek, and confirmed by the State of Texas, being the same tract formerly belonging to John Levy,

5th: The tract of land known as "El Saus" originally granted to Antonio Hinojosa, the portion belonging to said firm of R. King & Co., being three and one fifth leagues thereof, more or less, situated on the San Fernando Creek,

6th: Two lots or parcels of land situated in the townsite of Corpus Christi, with the buildings and improvements thereon conveyed by Esther S. Mann to the said firm of R. King & Co. by deed bearing date on the twenty fifth day of November A.D. 1866, to which deed reference is hereby made for a more full description,

7th: All his (M. Kenedy's) interest in and to all lands whatsoever situated on the Rio Grande in the State of Texas, which lands are acquired by him from the estate of the late James Walworth, deceased, and also in and to all those several tracts of land, located or surveyed, or which may be located or surveyed by virtue of the following Headright Certificates, or any other Certificates or Scrip now located by either him or R. King, or R. King & Co., on or near the lands just hereinbefore described, towit: Headright Certificate for 640 acres issued to M. J. Thurman; Headright Certificate 480 acres issued to Miguel Tijerina; Land Scrip or Certificate No. 13, issued to August Reuss.

Now, in consideration of the foregoing conveyance, from Mifflin Kenedy to Richard King, confirming Seven Items as enumerated, Richard King, for himself, his heirs, executors, and administrators doth hereby grant, set over, assign, release and quit claim unto Mifflin Kenedy, his heirs and assigns all his (R. King's) right, title, interest, and claim in and to the following described real estate, viz:

1st: The iron building situated in Brownsville, Texas, on part of Lot 14, in Block........., at the corner of Levee and Thirteenth Streets, and occupied for some time past by the firm of King, Kenedy & Co.,

2nd: That certain brick warehouse, situated in Brownsville, Texas, on Lot No. One and part of Lot No. Two in Block ......, at the corner of Elizabeth and Eleventh Streets, formerly occupied by the U. S. Custom House,

3rd: That certain lot of ground in Brownsville, Texas, being Lot No. 5, in Block No......, situated in Elizabeth Street nearly opposite the property of Joseph San Roman,

4th: That certain lot of ground in Brownsville, Texas, being Lot No. 6, in Block...... on the corner of Elizabeth and Thirteenth Street, and directly in front of H. Millers Hotel, on Elizabeth Street, with all the improvements thereon,

5th: That certain part of Lot No. 1, in Block......, at the corner of Washington and Thirteenth Streets, in Brownsville, Texas, with a one story brick building thereon, being nearly opposite the brick store of the late firm of Braunschuger & Levy, on 13th Street, and adjoining on the South West part of said lot, a building belonging to Francisco Yturria,

6th: That certain one half of Lot No...... in Block...... situated in Brownsville, Texas, in Levee Street, nearly opposite the Ferry landing (Main ferry) and known as the property occupied by Broll, Paschal & King, Beef Contractors, in the year 1866,

7th: That certain tract of land known as "El Paistle" originally granted to Juan Antonio Balli Cavazos, containing five leagues, more or less, and situated on the south side of the "Olmos Creek" in Cameron County, Texas,

8th: That certain tract of land called the "Carricitos" situated in Cameron County, Texas, fronting on the Rio Grande between seven and eight leagues, above Brownsville, Texas,

9th: That certain tract of land situated in Cameron County, Texas, adjoining the City of Brownsville limits above on the Rio Grande, being a part of the Espiritu Santo grant, and a part of that conveyed by Dona Feliciano Goseascochea Tijerina to Basse & Herd, as aforesaid, was conveyed by Elisha Basse to Richard King,

To HAVE AND TO HOLD the above described premises from each of us to the other, as herein provided, forever.

In Testimony Whereof, we the undersigned, Richard King and Mifflin Kenedy, have subscribed our names and affixed our seals (Using scrolls for seals) at The Rancho "Santa Gertrudis" in Nueces County, Texas, on this the twenty sixth day of the month of February, A. D. Eighteen Hundred & Seventy.

N.B. When the words, "Brownsville, Texas" occur in the foregoing instrument, it is understood to be Brownsville, in the County of Cameron, State of Texas.

(*Done in Duplicate*)

R. KING

M. KENEDY

In presence of:

REUBEN HOLBEIN

H. L. HOWLETT

Claim by Richard King Setting Forth Losses by Cattle Thieves

Original Petition No. 22 Submitted to the United States Commissioners to Texas, 1872-1873.

The United States of America
Lower Rio Grande

Brownsville, Texas,
August 28th, 1872.

To the Honorable U. S. Commissioners to Texas.

The petition of Richard King, a citizen of the State of Texas, and of the United States, residing at Rancho Santa Gertrudis in Nueces County, Texas, respectfully represents:

That, he is the sole owner of the Agostadero "Santa Gertrudis," of about 78,000 acres of land; and of the Rancho "Rincon de Santa Gertrudis," of about 17,712 acres of land; the Rancho "Sans" [Saus] of about 17,712 acres of land; the Rancho "Puerta de Agua Dulce" of about 35,424 acres of land; and the "San Leandro" Rancho of about 8,856 acres of land, all in Nueces County, Texas; the Rancho "Santa Cruz" on Padre Island of about 13,284 acres of land in Cameron County, Texas, besides several tracts surveyed under Texas Land Surveys in various places in said Nueces County, of about 2,560 acres of land; making a total of one hundred and seventy-three thousand, five hundred and forty-eight (173,548) acres of land, more or less; and of the stock of cattle and horses thereon, which on the 11th day of November, 1869, numbered thirty-three thousand and six hundred and sixty-four (33,664) head of cattle, and twenty-two hundred (2,200) head of breeding and other horse stock; that the increase of said cattle for the three years from the date aforesaid, to the corresponding date of the year 1872, at the usual rate of increase, should

have been double the number of the said original stock or sixty-seven thousand three hundred and twenty-eight (67,328) head of cattle; and the increase of said horses at the usual rate of increase would have been one thousand three hundred and twenty (1,320) head, making at the date aforesaid, thirty-five hundred and twenty (3,520) head to which should be added six hundred and seventy (670) head of horse stock purchased—less five hundred and eighty-two (582) head of horse stock sold; making a total number of three thousand six hundred and eight (3,608) head of horse stock and the aforesaid total of sixty-seven thousand three hundred and twenty-eight (67,328) head of cattle which petitioner should now have upon his said lands.

That his total sales have been thirteen thousand five hundred and one (13,501) head of cattle; and that he has now upon his said lands but twenty thousand (20,000) head of cattle left of the sixty-seven thousand, three hundred and twenty-eight (67,328) head, twenty-six hundred and thirty (2,630) head of horse stock, making a total loss to him (after deducting sales, aforesaid) of thirty-three thousand, eight hundred and twenty-seven (33,827) head of cattle, and nine hundred and seventy-eight (978) head of horse stock.

Petitioner further says that the cattle and horses, aforesaid, have been forcibly and unlawfully taken from him, out of their usual range by armed bands of Mexican robbers, who reside in Mexico, and by Mexican soldiers of the Army of Mexico, under the recognized Government thereof; and with the knowledge, consent and assistance of said army and the frontier authorities of Mexico, or many of them; and that said officers and some of said authorities have assisted in said robberies under the orders of General Juan Nepomucino Cortinas, the Military Commander in Chief of the frontier of Mexico, from the year 1870, to about the month of June, 1872, that his said recognized military authority then ceased, but that he still continues his depredations as before, with many of his former command, within the knowledge of the Mexican authorities, Civil and Military, and that no efforts are made by them now, or have ever been made to stop them.

Petitioner further says that the said lost cattle and horse stock were of the best class and quality—male and female—and that the cattle were worth ten ($10.) dollars per head, in gold and that the horses were worth sixty ($60) dollars in gold per head, upon the lands from whence they were taken; that the increase of cattle in Texas, is thirty-three and one-third (33 1/3) per cent, and of horse stock, twenty (20) per cent, per annum; and that the damages to petitioner have been as before stated from the loss of said cattle, horses and their increase in accordance with the rate aforesaid, and that said rate of increase should be so computed as aforesaid, from this time forward.

Petitioner further says that, the gold value of the said thirty-three thousand and eight hundred and twenty-seven (33,827) head of cattle taken from him as aforesaid, is three hundred and thirty-eight thousand, two hundred and seventy dollars ($338,-270.00) and that the gold value of the said nine hundred and seventy-eight (978) head of horses, is fifty-eight thousand, six hundred and eighty ($58,680.00) dollars, making a total value of three hundred and ninety-six thousand, nine hundred and fifty ($396,-950.00) dollars, is the just sum of the said losses to the present time from the injuries aforesaid.

Petitioner further says that, the Republic of Mexico, is justly liable to make reparation to, and indemnify him, for his losses and damages, which were originated by her remissness and omission in the observance of her international duties, and the treaty stipulations with the United States, by allowing such armed bodies of men to issue from her soil to rob and plunder on our territory and to return with impunity and receive asylum within her borders with the spoils of their forays.

Wherefore, Petitioner prays for relief and reclamation on the Government of the said Republic of Mexico for the said amount of three hundred and ninety-six thousand, nine hundred and fifty ($396,950.00) dollars, and interest thereon from date until recovery; and that he may file testimony in support of his said case; that it may be made part of this petition, and that the testimony filed in other causes and the general testimony so far as applicable, may also be used in support hereof.

F. J. PARKER, *Atty for Claimant.*
Attest: RICHARD KING.
RICHARD H. SAVAGE,
Commissioner & ex. off.
Recorder.

[412]

Contract for Northern Cattle Drive
1875

THIS CONTRACT between Richard King and John Fitch and A. C. Allen, for the driving of 4737 head of cattle "to the Market in the State of Kansas, or in the State of Texas," dated March 12, 1875, is an excellent example of the manner of conducting business during this era of the cattle drives. It comes from the Fitch Papers, in the possession of Mrs. Lennie E. Stubblefield, Premont, Texas.

The State of Texas

County of Nueces

It is hereby Mutually understood and agreed, by and between Richard King and John Fitch and Albert, C, Allen all of said County, and State as follows to wit:—

Richard King is to furnish Four herds of Beef Cattle, Numbering in the aggregate to Four thousand Seven hundred and thirty Seven (4737) head more or less (quantity to be receipted for on delivery to said Fitch and Allen; the said Cattle to be driven by said John Fitch and Albert C. Allen to a Market in the State of Kansas, or in the State of Texas.— John Fitch and Albert, C. Allen agree to receive from said King the said herds of Cattle for the purpose above expressed and to use all due personal diligence and care in driving the same to said Market or Markets and to protect the same from Waste or loss; and agree to obtain the best price for the same — in Cash, the said Market or Markets will afford and to pay said Richard King the price and Sum of ($12.00) Twelve dollars in lawful Currency of the United States or its Equivalent in the lawful Coin thereof, for each and every head of said Cattle so delivered, and receipted for by the said Fitch and Allen,—as aforesaid; Which price and Sum the said Richard King hereby agrees to receive:— It being distinctly understood that all of said Cattle are to be Sold by said Fitch and Allen as Speedily as possible, and for Cash in hand, at the time of Sale or Sales of the Same, and under no circumstances Whatever to be Sold on a Credit, farmed out—or Wintered, to any person Whomsoever, in Texas, Kansas or Elsewhere ————————

———————— It is further understood and agreed that, after the payment of ($12) twelve dollars in Currency per head for the said Cattle or its Equivalent in Coin as aforesaid to said King, and the further re-imbursement to their parties respectively, of all Expenses incident to the Driving and Sales of the Same in such Market or Markets, then the Surplus or Profits, if any, to be divided between the parties to this Instrument, in the following manner to wit:————————

———— One half of said Surplus or profits to be paid to said Richard King, and the Re=maining half thereof to be equally divided between the said John Fitch and Albert C Allen, Share and Share alike—

———— It is also understood that the horses Mares and Mules, and other property, furnished by these parties for the purpose of driving said Cattle, Shall be included in the Expenses aforesaid; and if said horses mares and Mules, and other property be Sold, such to be accounted for, on the same terms as the Sales of said Cattle, after the Original Cost thereof Shall be ascertained and paid _____

_____ Witness our hands and Scrolls for Seals in good faith at Rancho Santa Gertrudes Nueces County, and State of Texas, aforesaid this 12th day of March A.D. Eighteen hundred and Seventyfive (1875) In triplicate. _____

Signed In presence of
John L. McLaughlin
James Downing

R. King
by Reuben Holbein
agents & attorney in fact.

John Fitch
(H)

A E Allen
(H)

The Estate of Richard King, Deceased

by ROBERT C. WELLS

AN ATTEMPT to arrive at the exact total of the acreage owned by Richard King at the time of his death confronts the researcher with numerous obstacles. Some of these difficulties are not new: They confronted the appraisers of the estate who wrestled with the problem in 1885.

The appraisers — John S. Greer, Thomas Beynon and Reuben Holbein — were obviously conscientious in approaching their task. They listed and appraised more than 250 pieces of property, producing a lengthy and minutely detailed document, "Estate of Richard King, Deceased: Inventory and Appraisement," which they signed, in company with Henrietta M. King, Executrix, before the County Judge of Nueces County, attesting "that said inventory and appraisement is a full and complete inventory and correct appraisement of all the property of the estate of the said Richard King deceased that has come to their knowledge." The document was recorded August 8, 1885, *Probate Minutes of Nueces County*, Book F, pages 18-27.

In view of the complex nature of Captain King's land holdings, his dealings and his partnerships, the appraisers did as precise a listing of his lands as could have been done under existing circumstances. After the passage of seventy years it is impossible to reconcile, confirm or refute some apparent discrepancies which appear in the inventory in the light of present-day knowledge. In other cases it becomes obvious how subsequent surveys and court decisions have modified the appraisers' listings.

Modern surveys have shown that Spanish and Mexican land grants are, by accurate measurement, often larger or smaller than the leagues called for in the original grant. In former years there was confusion as to the acre equivalent of a league. Some of the old grants were partially overlapping. As of 1885 some tracts had been purchased, but the sellers had not yet perfected title. The ownership of *derechos* was in many cases unsettled, so that what the appraisers listed as "an undivided interest" in a tract subsequently developed to be either more or less than listed.

Previous citations of land areas in the text of this book have been in accordance with contemporary knowledge and belief as of the date concerned. For example, in 1854 when Captain King acquired title to land on Padre Island he thought he was getting 13,284 acres; he later testified that Rancho "Santa Cruz" on Padre Island was composed of that much land; this is the first tract mentioned and the first figure which appears in the appraisers' inventory. However, many years later, in 1905, Mrs. King was awarded title to 6,000 acres by court decree.

Lands in the San Juan de Carricitos grant, the largest concession made by Spain in

Texas, made up the largest single bloc of acreage in the inventory. This grant is a typical example involving most of the difficulties involved in attempting to arrive at a total as of 1885. Various authorities have cited this grant as containing "a hundred and six and one half leagues," "more than 600,000 acres," and "a half million acres," as well as more precise statements. The appraisers listed it as containing "132 Leagues of Land," consisting of 518,617 acres, with Captain King owning an undivided interest. Four years later, a survey in connection with a partition suit proved the grant to total 575,545 acres. By findings of the court, as expressed in "Partition of the San Juan de Carricitos Grant approved as by Final Report and Supplement thereto of Commissioners of Partition," May 8, 1889, the Honorable John C. Russell, District Judge, the undivided interest turned out to be 312,279 acres.

Consequently, the best that can be proved today is that the appraisers miscalculated in many cases, through no lack of diligence or knowledge but on the basis of modern surveys and later partitions by court action. The appraisers listed the estate's lands at slightly in excess of 500,000 acres, thereby originating the oft-repeated family quotation that "Captain King left a half million acres of land."

At this late date, any attempt to adjust the appraisers' inventory will inevitably involve some approximation and omission. However—on the basis of maps, both old and new; abstracts; surveys; and many other sources—at the time of his death Captain King owned what would eventually become 614,140 acres, "more or less," as the legal phrase puts it:

Location of Lands	Acreage
San Juan de Carricitos grant . .	312,279
Santa Gertrudis and Laureles ranches:	
Spanish and Mexican land grants	193,347
Railroad sections and small tracts	42,554
Espíritu Santo grant	7,380
Hidalgo County	20,284
Duval County	8,856
Crockett County	29,440
	614,140

The acreage of lands in the San Juan de Carricitos grant was determined from court records. In the other categories above no attempt has been made to trace the areas of many small tracts and lots which were involved in the 1885 inventory but which are no longer a part of King Ranch properties. Consequently, the total of any or all of the latter six items may be incorrect. However, the error involved will not be great in comparison with the total amount of land.

After the difficulties of attempting to tabulate Captain King's lands, the appraisers must have taken some satisfaction in the brief but concise listing which they were able to make of his cattle. That portion of the "Inventory and Appraisement" has been reproduced in facsimile on the opposite page.

Personal property of every discription belonging to estate of Richard King deceased - the
same being community property held in
community with Henrietta M. King his surviving widow - the interest owned by the estate
of R King decd - being undivided one half -

Class of Stock. N°.	N° of head -	
Cattle of all Kinds. more or less -	40000. head	400,000 - 00
horses al Kinds - " " "	6600 "	60 000
Jacks & Jenets " " "	500	1500
Sheep & goats all Kinds " " "	12000	12000
Wagons of all Kinds	3 0 -	3200

& personal property including
ice machines + other miscellenous
property of every nature   2000000 -

Henrietta. M. King
Executrix

John S. Green
Thos Beyon
Reuben Holbein
Appraisers

NOTES
and
SOURCES

THIS SECTION serves two purposes: To give credit where credit is due, to the extent that is practical, and to elaborate upon information contained in the text.

In many cases of data gathered by interview, only one or two principal informants are credited for facts and anecdotes which have been pieced together from and corroborated by many sources. An attempt to name each of the many, many individuals who cooperated by furnishing confirming evidence to back up the multitudinous details of the research would be a cataloging task beyond the realm of practicality.

Documentation follows the standard practice of giving complete bibliographic information with the first citation of a source and abbreviating succeeding references.

As a convenience to the reader, the notes are keyed to the text in the upper outside corner of each page with a notation showing the chapter number and text pages containing the citations for the notes on that particular page.

CHAPTER I

¹ Such information as Richard King's family and friends possessed concerning his origin and early life is found, in various versions, in the following sources: John Henry Brown, *The Indian Wars and Pioneers of Texas* (Austin, n.d.), pp. 229-232, 369-370; James Cox (ed.), *Historical and Biographical Record of the Cattle Industry and the Cattlemen of Texas and Adjacent Territory* (St. Louis, 1895), pp. 589-591; Lewis E. Daniell, *Personnel of the Texas State Government, with Sketches of Representative Men of Texas* (San Antonio, 1892), pp. 436-449, 642-650; Ellis A. Davis and Edwin H. Grobe (eds.), *The New Encyclopedia of Texas* (Dallas, n.d.), I, pp. 862-867; *Prose and Poetry of the Live Stock Industry of the United States*, prepared by authority of the National Live Stock Association (Kansas City, 1905), pp. 80-86; Obituary of Richard King, *San Antonio Express*, April 15, 1885; Obituary of Mifflin Kenedy, *The (Corpus Christi) Daily Caller*, March 15, 1895.

² Positive identification of the *Desdemona* spoken of by Richard King has not been established. The only information of seeming significance concerning any vessel of that name came to Holland McCombs from William H. Tripp, Curator of the Old Dartmouth Historical Society and Whaling Museum, New Bedford, Mass.:

There was a whaleship named *Desdemona* which sailed from New Bedford. She was registered in New Bedford on October 16, 1843, and made whaling voyages until April 30, 1894. Our *Desdemona* was built at Middletown, Conn., in 1823; 236.69 tons burden, length 98.6, beam 26.6 ft., depth 14.7 ft., two decks, three masts, square stern, and the figurehead the bust of a woman. The registry of our *Desdemona* being 1843 would indicate that she was purchased in New York. From Starbuck's *History of the Whale Fishery* we learn the following: "The ship *Desdemona* was registered in New York. . . . She sailed for the South Atlantic Ocean in May, 1834, under Captain Smith. . . . She returned on April 28, 1835, with 1550 bbls. of whale oil. She sailed again under Captain Smith on June 18, 1835, and returned on May 4, 1837, having taken 50 bbls. sperm oil, 1850 bbls. whale oil."

Either of the sailing dates, May of 1834 or June of 1835, could conform to the meager information at hand concerning Richard King's departure from New York. An exhaustive search of the records of the Marine Curator at the Museum of the City of New York has revealed no other ship named *Desdemona* registered at that port at that time.

Yet there are grounds for doubting that a whaleship took Richard King to Mobile: (1) in recounting his experience, King said he hid behind cargo in the hold. Outbound whaleships crowded their holds with stinking oil barrels and specialized whaling equipment that King would surely have remembered and mentioned; (2) Mobile seems an unlikely port of call for a whaleship unless forced to put in for emergency repairs, a circumstance of which there is not the slightest hint in King's story; (3) whaleships and whalemen were special enough, as every reader of *Moby Dick* knows, and there is every likelihood that if the *Desdemona* had been a whaleship, King would have told of it. Moreover, the sturdy and venturesome King was the kind of small boy to be lured by a prospect of sea adventure and far voyaging. If the *Desdemona* had been a whaleship, it is very possible that the destiny of Richard King and the history of the livestock ranching industry in Texas might have been different.

³ The following affidavit was subscribed and sworn to by Richard King before F. J. Parker, United States Commissioner Eastern District of Texas, on April 11, 1870, and filed with the United States and Mexican Claims Commission, Washington, D.C., on August 30 of that year:

"Personally appeared before me the undersigned authority, Richard King, who being by me duly sworn, deposes and states; that he was born in the City of New York, County of New York in the State of New York, in the United States of America, on the Tenth day of July AD 1824: . . ." — *Records of Boundary and Claims Commissions and Arbitrations, Claims vs. Mexico — 1868, Claim No. 579*, RG 76, General Services Administration, National Archives and Records Service, Washington, D. C. (hereafter cited as "National Archives").

Prior to the recent discovery of the above deposition, all biographical sketches of Richard King printed by hearsay that he was born in

Orange County, New York, July 10, 1825. His own sworn statement is preferable.

4   Mrs. Mildred P. Seese, Goshen, New York, reported that she "came across reference to a King family living in an area [in Orange County] where there were, prior to 1850, a number of families of rather recent Irish origin. . . . I suspect that King family was of Presbyterian affiliation, since most of the families of the neighborhood were Presbyterian." It is probable that the King family moved to Orange County after Richard's birth. Unfortunately records of birth were not recorded by the City of New York prior to July 1, 1853.

5   Richard M. Kleberg, Sr., related that he understood that Richard King's parents died when little Richard was about five years old and that it was an aunt who placed him in apprenticeship. This would explain Richard King's making no effort to contact members of his family at a later date when he went north to school.

Furthermore, Dr. John Ashton, who spent many years during the early part of the century gathering material for a history of the King Ranch, mentioned an aunt but apparently knew nothing about the death of Richard King's father and mother.

The late Dr. Ashton was an author, linguist, authority on breeds of horses and cattle, and associate professor of agricultural journalism at Texas A. and M. College. Holland McCombs interviewed Dr. Ashton prior to his death on February 28, 1952.

6   Daniell, p. 436.

7   Brown, p. 369.

8   Same.

9   Same; Mrs. Robert J. Kleberg, Jr., to Holland McCombs.

10   Dr. Ashton to Holland McCombs.

11   Same. Dr. Ashton stated that he "heard this years ago from some of the family."

12   Brown, p. 369. Most of the small flotilla of shallow-draft steamboats used as military transports during the latter phase of the Seminole

campaign were under contract to the army, probably on a *per diem* basis, since payment of individual officers and crew members is not recorded on official service payrolls.

13   Same; John T. Sprague, *The Origin, Progress, and Conclusion of the Florida War* . . . (New York, 1848), pp. 299-303. Writers vary in their spelling of the chief's name: Hospetarke, Hospotoche, Hospetakke, Hospertacke, Hospetake. Sprague's version is accepted as the one most likely in contemporary usage, since he was Colonel Worth's aide during the campaign and wrote from firsthand knowledge.

14   Kenedy's obituary.

15   Same.

16   Faustino Villa to Richard M. Kleberg, Sr. Villa was a steamboater who worked for King and Kenedy. He said that Kenedy "could pick up a heavy anchor and throw it over the rail easily."

17   Brown, p. 230.

18   Capt. John Sanders to T. S. Jesup, Pittsburgh, July 2, 1846, *Correspondence with General Taylor*, Ex. Doc. 119, H.R., 29th Cong., 2d Sess., p. 422:

The success of these boats will depend entirely upon the manner in which they are handled and managed. I shall send out on each of the other boats two experienced and skilful men—one as master, the other as pilot. I have requested the owners to take with them down the river such crews as would be willing to reship at New Orleans in the government service.

19   Lt. Col. Thomas F. Hunt to T. S. Jesup, New Orleans, October 26, 1846: "The *Corvette*, arrived July 16, paid for July 27, $16,000, and despatched [for Brazos Santiago] August 6." —Same, pp. 385-387.

20   Kenedy's obituary.

21   Late in July, 1846, Bagdad was described by a contemporary observer as "a small collection of mud and reed huts, occupied by Mexican fishermen and herdsmen." About a year later this officer returned and discovered that Bagdad "had been somewhat improved and American-

ized."—An Officer of the First Regiment of Ohio Volunteers [Luther Giddings], *Sketches of the Campaign in Northern Mexico . . .* (New York, 1853), pp. 34-35.

By September 11, 1847, the *American Flag,* published in Matamoros, was citing Bagdad as a trap designed to extract money from visitors by fair means or foul.

CHAPTER II

1 For example, Andrew Jackson's letter to General Planche of New Orleans (Hermitage, June 14, 1844):

Texas is the key to our safety from British influence and British invasion. I say accept her hand while she holds it out to us, . . . Then let Polk, Dallas and Texas be the watchword and countersign. . . . Let Texas be the watchword, and victory will be certain.— *San Augustine Red-Lander,* August 3, 1844, as quoted by John Salmon Ford, *Memoirs,* II, pp. 356-357.

The Ford *Memoirs* are located in the Archives, Eugene C. Barker Texas History Center of The University of Texas Library, Austin, Texas (hereafter cited as "Archives, University of Texas"). Page citations of this and future references to the Ford *Memoirs* are to the typescript copy.

2 *Hostilities by Mexico,* Ex. Doc. 196, H.R., 29th Cong., 2d Sess. This document reproduces the diplomatic correspondence during the attempted negotiations by Slidell and the movements of General Taylor's "Army of Occupation" in Texas. On April 24, 1846, the Mexican General Mariano Arista arrived at Matamoros, across the Rio Grande from Taylor's camp. On the following day a reconnoitering party of United States Army dragoons, sixty-three strong, was attacked on the Texas side of the river. Taylor's dispatch reported "Hostilities may now be considered as commenced, . . ." See also Allan Nevins (ed.), *Polk, The Diary of a President 1845-1849 . . .* (New York, 1952), pp. 9-11, 25-26, 50-53, 65-67, 70, 71-72, 78-89.

3 Taylor's detailed reports of the two battles are contained in Pub. Doc. 388, Sen. 29th Cong., 1st Sess., pp. 2-30. In his initial terse battlefield dis-

patch, written at 10 p.m. on the night of Resaca de la Palma, Taylor remarked: "The enemy has recrossed the river, and I am sure will not again molest us on this bank."—Ex. Doc. 207, H. R., 29th Cong., 1st Sess., p. 3.

4 William L. Marcy, Secretary of War, to Brigadier General Taylor, August 30, 1845, *Hostilities by Mexico,* pp. 75-76.

5 Official reports on the battle of Monterrey will be found in Pub. Doc. 1, Sen., 29th Cong., 2d Sess. and Ex. Doc. 17, H.R., 30th Cong., 1st Sess. Eyewitness accounts will be found in Giddings, as cited; William S. Henry, *Campaign Sketches of the War with Mexico* (New York, 1847); John R. Kenly, *Memoirs of a Maryland Volunteer* (Philadelphia, 1873); Thomas B. Thorpe, *Our Army at Monterey* (Philadelphia, 1847).

In November, General John Wool with a force of about 3000 men crossed the Rio Grande north of Taylor's theater of action. Wool crossed Coahuila without a battle and penetrated to contact with Taylor near Saltillo. Another force, Missouri Volunteers under Colonel Alexander Doniphan, on his famed march from Independence, Missouri, invaded a more western segment of Mexico at El Paso del Norte, won Chihuahua against great odds at the battle of Sacramento and, in the late spring of 1847, came into Taylor's command on the Rio Grande.

6 General Taylor to Adjutant General, January 27, 1847, Ex. Doc. 56, H. R., 30th Cong., 1st Sess., pp. 290-292.

7 On January 3, Scott prepared orders and dispatched a courier, Lieutenant John A. Richey, to Taylor. At Villa Gran, Tamaulipas, near Linares, he was lassoed by Mexican partisans. They brutally killed Richey and sent his dispatch pouch to the Mexican Commander-in-Chief, General Antonio López de Santa Anna.—Ex. Doc. 56, H.R., 30th Cong., 1st Sess., pp. 288-289.

8 Official reports of the Battle of Buena Vista will be found in Ex. Doc. 1, Sen., 30th Cong., 1st Sess. Statistics on Taylor's losses are contained in Ex. Doc. 62, H. R., 30th Cong., 1st Sess.,

pp. 19, 79. For statistics on Santa Anna's forces see George L. Rives, *The United States and Mexico 1821-1848* (New York, 1913), II, p. 362.

9 As of 1909 when Steele published his critique. Matthew Forney Steele, *American Campaigns* (Washington, 1909), I, p. 95.

10 *Records of the Office of the Quartermaster General,* "Report of Persons and Articles Hired by Capt. E. A. Ogden, Asst. QM Depot Mouth of the Rio Grande, June 1847," R.G. 92, National Archives.

11 Scott to Secretary of War, January 12, 1847, Ex. Doc. 56, H. R., 30th Cong., 1st Sess., pp., 34-36.

12 The earliest effort at steamboat navigation of the Rio Grande, above Matamoros, was that by Henry Austin in 1829. He brought to the Rio Grande a stout, well-built steamboat called the *Ariel* and operated it between Matamoros and Camargo for several months. . . . there is a story that an ordinance of either Reynosa or Camargo forbade steamboats to tie up within the municipal limits, on the ground that gases from their smokestacks were deleterious to the inhabitants' health. Since the *Ariel* was of too deep draft for successful navigation of the Rio Grande, Austin gave up after a few months.— Harbert Davenport, "Notes on Early Steamboating on the Rio Grande," *The Southwestern Historical Quarterly,* XLIX (Oct., 1945), p. 286.

For a full account of Henry Austin's adventure on the Rio Grande, see Paul Horgan, *Great River, The Rio Grande in North American History* (New York, 1954), II, pp. 481-484, 493-494.

13 I had seen and heard tell of the crookedness of this grand river, but there is no way of showing how tortuous is its course except by the illustration given by an Alabama volunteer; he said "he had seen a crow fly from the top of a tree, follow up the course of the river for fifteen minutes, then light; and it *lit* on the same tree it had started from."— Kenly, pp. 48-49.

14 W. H. Chatfield, *The Twin Cities of the Border* (Brownsville, 1893), p. 43. For an account of the brief history of the Republic of the Rio Grande—whose founders hoped would encompass Texas, Nuevo León, Tamaulipas, Coahuila, Durango, New Mexico, and both Upper and Lower California—see Horgan, II, pp. 559-569.

15 William Neale, "History of the City of Brownsville, from 1848 to 1876," *Evening Ranchero,* July 5, 1876, as quoted by Chatfield, p. `14.

16 Though the installation's official name may have been Fort Texas, it was more commonly called Fort Taylor, in honor of the army's commander, even in official communications. General Taylor, however, held a low view of naming places after men before they were dead. He headed his dispatches "The Camp Opposite Matamoros" or "Camp on the Left Bank of the Rio Grande." On May 4, 1846, Major Jacob Brown, the commander, in his last report from the "little sand bag fort," called it Fort Texas.

17 A steamboat was also named in the hero's honor. The *Major Brown* held the record for the farthest steamboat passage up the Rio Grande. During the high water of 1846, the *Major Brown* steamed all the way to Laredo. The high water receded before she could return, and she was stranded for weeks.— *American Flag,* Matamoros, November 4, 1846.

But this did not deter military dreaming. On February 1, 1847, an officer making a topographical survey wrote:

I also understand that examinations have recently been made of the Rio Grande from Camargo to a point some thirty miles above Presidio, which encourage the hope that this noble river may become navigable, with slight improvements, at certain seasons of the year, nearly as high up as the Conchos, and render it not improbable that steamboats may at no distant day ascend even to Chihuahua, to Paso del Norte, and to the vicinity of Santa Fe. This, however, is venturing on the field of speculation.— George W. Hughes, *Memoir Descriptive of a Division of the United States Army, under the command of Brigadier General John E. Wool, from San Antonio de Bexar, in Texas, to Saltillo, in Mexico,* Ex. Doc. 32, Sen., 31st Cong., 1st Sess., p. 37.

18 Lloyd Lewis, *Captain Sam Grant* (Boston, 1950), p. 162.

19 Same, p. 163.

20 Same, p. 161.

21 John Francis Hamtramck Claiborne, *Life and Correspondence of John A. Quitman . . .* (New York, 1860), as quoted by Lewis, pp. 164-165.

22   Lewis, p. 157.

23   Same.

24   John Sedgwick, *Correspondence of John Sedgwick* . . . (New York, 1902-1903), as quoted by Lewis, pp. 157-158.

25   A proclamation by General Francisco Mejía, Matamoros, March 18, 1846, *Hostilities by Mexico*, pp. 109-110.

26   Lewis, p. 187.

27   Col. William Bowen Campbell, as quoted by Lewis, p. 159.

28   For an eyewitness account of the Texans at Monterrey see Giddings, pp. 143-144.

29   By October, 1846, Lieutenant Colonel Thomas F. Hunt, Deputy Quartermaster General, reported from New Orleans that thirteen vessels had been purchased for service on the Rio Grande or between the river's mouth and supply depots: *Hatchee Eagle*, $5,000; *Whiteville*, $5,500; *Troy*, $6,000; *J. E. Roberts*, $9,000; *Brownsville*, $9,000; *Mentoria*, $12,000; *Rough and Ready*, $12,000; *Major Brown*, $12,600; *Undine*, $13,000; *Colonel Cross*, $14,000; *Corvette*, $16,000; *Telegraph*, $10,491.67 (retained at New Orleans for trips to Brazos Santiago, La Vaca, and other points); *James Cage*, $18,000 (a steam-schooner propeller, to be used as a sea boat and lighter).—T. F. Hunt to T. S. Jesup, July 4, 1846; T. F. Hunt to Henry Stanton, October 26, 1846, Ex. Doc. 119, H. R., 29th Cong., 1st Sess., pp. 382-383, 385-387.

30   General Winfield Scott . . . at the mouth of the Rio Grande, desired to go to Camargo, and consult with General Worth. Captain Kenedy's vessel, the *Corvette*, was the best in the service and he was selected to take General Scott and staff up the river.— Brown, p. 369.

It has been stated by numerous biographers of Kenedy that the *Corvette* carried General Taylor to Camargo in July, 1846. This is an error. According to the August 6, 1846, issue of the *American Flag*, Taylor departed from Matamoros for Camargo on the *Whiteville*. This is confirmed by Thomas B. Thorpe in *Our Army at Monterey*. On the way up the river, Taylor apparently transferred from the *Whiteville* to the *Hatchee Eagle*, for, according to Major Barbour in his journal, Rhoda van Bibber Tanner Doubleday (ed.), *Journals of the Late Brevet Major Philip Norbourne Barbour* . . . (New York, 1936), and Captain W. S. Henry in his *Campaign Sketches of the War with Mexico*, Taylor arrived at Camargo aboard the *Hatchee Eagle*. No eyewitness reporters mention the *Corvette* in relation to Taylor's journey upriver.

The error probably originated in later years when Mifflin Kenedy and his crew told about transporting "the General" to Camargo. The activities of Taylor being better known on the Rio Grande, the reporters and biographers assumed incorrectly that "the General" was Zachary Taylor. It was in fact Winfield Scott.

31   LeRoy P. Graf, *The Economic History of the Lower Rio Grande Valley 1820-1875* (Doctoral Thesis, Harvard University, 1942), I, p. 199; Capt. John Sanders to T. S. Jesup, as cited.

32   *Steamboat Explosion*. By passengers arrived on the steamer *Hatchee Eagle* on Monday evening from Camargo, we are informed that the steamer *Enterprise* on her upward trip, having on board Captain Wood's Company of Texas Volunteers, with two companies, we believe, from Tennessee, burst her boilers a short distance above Reynosa. The boiler deck was raised from its supports and fell below, precipitating many who were on that part of the boat into the river, several of whom were drowned. One or two were killed by pieces of timber which were blown off, and some were cast into the fire-bed where they were burnt severely. . . . The wounded, amongst whom was the Captain, were brought down to Reynosa and placed in the hospital. Carelessness on the part of the Engineer in charge at the time, who we understand has been arrested, is assigned as a reason for the catastrophe.— *American Flag*, August 26, 1846.

33   Same, October 14, 1846.

34   Same, September 26, 1846.

35   Same, October 1, 1846.

36   Lieutenant Colonel Hunt reported on four boats which had been chartered: *Big Hatchee* at $135 1/3 per day "and we to find her fuel;" *Warren*, *Exchange* and *W. N. Mercer* at $125

per day plus fuel. Each was to receive $1,000 expenses to the Rio Grande. "The charter [of the *Big Hatchee]* is conditioned that she will answer our purposes; and the test is to be, that she will take 100 tons of freight up the river to Matamoros, provided there be 3½ feet water in the river."— Hunt to Jesup, July 4, 1846, as cited.

There were apparently several other vessels chartered during the war on a similar *per diem* basis.

37 Graf, I, pp. 200-201.

Captain John Sanders reported from Pittsburgh, on June 21, 1846, on a Captain William Stewart who was taking two boats to the Rio Grande, one under thirty days' charter and the other "on his own venture, with the understanding that he was to be patronized when the government had more freight than its own boats could carry." — Ex. Doc. 119, 29th Cong., 2d Sess., pp. 420-421.

While the army still had but one steamboat in the river, a Mississippi River captain put the *Frontier* steamboat in commercial service with deck passage between Matamoros and Point Isabel at $3.00, and passage in the cabin, $10.— Robert Selph Henry, *The Story of the Mexican War* (New York, 1950), p. 89.

Other steamers engaged in private trade on the Rio Grande during the war were the *Lama, Tom Kirkman, Laurel, Del Norte, Gazelle* and *Monroe,* as evidenced by various advertisements and articles in the *American Flag.* Concerning the *Monroe,* the following news item was published in the August 17, 1846, issue of the *American Flag:*

Steamer Monroe. This fine steamer, commanded by Captain Hugh Monroe, an experienced steamboat officer, and brother, we believe, to the gallant Major Monroe, in command at Point Isabel, arrived here on Thursday. The *Monroe* has been built expressly for the Rio Grande, is of very light draft, carries a heavy freight, and has a powerful engine, which enables her to stem the rapid current of the stream with greater speed than almost any other boat on the river. She is to run, we understand, independent of Government charter, and will be devoted to the interests both of the Government and private individuals. Captain Monroe will be found an accommodating and gentlemanly commander, and his boat a speedy and safe means of transportation.

This Captain Hugh Monroe is evidently none other than Richard King's employer and benefactor at Mobile Bay. There is no record of a meeting of Monroe and King on the Rio Grande, but there is no reason to doubt that meeting took place, renewing their friendship after the passage of a decade.

Hugh Monroe sold his boat *Monroe* in 1847 and evidently left the border country. His boat stayed. On November 3, 1847, the *American Flag* reported as follows:

Steamer Wrecked. The steamer *Monroe,* Capt. McGowan, bound from the mouth of the Rio Grande to Lavaca Bay, Texas, in attempting to get out to sea a few days since, struck on the bar at the mouth of the river and was afterward driven ashore, becoming a complete wreck. The *Monroe* has been running for the past year on the Rio Grande, and was recently purchased here with a view to run her on the Trinity river, in Texas. The captain was the chief owner, and suffers a serious loss by the wreck of the boat.

38 *American Flag,* October 30, 1847.

39 Holman Hamilton, *Zachary Taylor, Soldier of the Republic* (New York, 1941), pp. 248-249.

CHAPTER III

1 *The* (Corpus Christi) *World,* May 23, 1878; Mrs. Henrietta M. King to her granddaughter, Mrs. Thomas R. Armstrong; Captain William Kelly, an early steamboater on the Rio Grande and employee of King and Kenedy, remembered while reminiscing to Harbert Davenport that stories of Richard King's having served as bartender and bouncer of his "inn" at Boca del Rio were common knowledge in the Brownsville area in the early days. Kelly came to Texas during the Civil War and was employed by King and Kenedy in 1866.— Chatfield, p. 21.

2 "Consolidated Correspondence File, Brazos Santiago, Texas," *Records of the Office of the Quartermaster General,* R. G. 92, National Archives.

Some boats were sold "at private sale" prior to the auction. In his letter of March 1, 1849, from Brazos Santiago, Assistant Quartermaster Brevet Major W. W. Chapman reported to

Quartermaster General T. S. Jesup that the public sale was postponed to March 15 and that the *Colonel Hunt* had been disposed of privately for $5,000. "All consider this a very advantageous sale." And in comparison with prices which other steamboats brought at auction, it was very advantageous indeed.

3 Same.

4 Same.

5 *American Flag*, November 29, 1848. The steamer was reported "a total wreck" on a trip from Brazos Santiago to the mouth of the Rio Grande. "The cargo was luckily all saved—principally iron and other articles belonging to the government."

Obviously Major Chapman was unaware of this catastrophe at the time he prepared the "Notice of Quartermaster's Sale" (page 43) for publication.

6 In 1820 a wave of liberalism swept the Mediterranean states. The Spanish government issued a decree directing that "The Mouth of the Rio Bravo and four other ports on the Mexican Gulf" should be opened for commerce. But Mexican officialdom was absorbed in the turmoil of a burgeoning revolution. The decree was never carried out.

7 Victor M. Rose, *Some Historical Facts in Regard to the Settlement of Victoria, Texas; Its Progress and Present Status* (Laredo, [1883]), pp. 10-14, 151. Zachary T. Fulmore, *The History and Geography of Texas, as Told in County Names* (Rev. ed., Austin, 1926), p. 32.

8 Rose, pp. 151-153.

In Mr. Rose's book Ramón Lafon appears as "Lafou." According to Harbert Davenport, authority on history of the Lower Rio Grande area, "The name is unquestionably 'Lafon.' He married Angela de García, daughter of the original grantee of the Santa Isabel Grant. They had one son, Ramón, Jr., who lived to be known to many of the people of Brownsville and who was a large landowner in the country prior to his death."

9 Emperor Iturbide had made Congregación del Refugio a port of entry by a decree dated January 28, 1823. The government of the newly independent Mexico was in close financial straits. It opened seaports to the commerce of all nations and imposed a duty of twenty-five per cent on all imports; the *alcabala* (excise tax) added another eighteen per cent. This made entry by an unlicensed port such as Brazos Santiago particularly attractive: the purchase of official honors was more reasonable than the payment of official taxes.

10 The land on which the city of Matamoros stands was included in a subdivision of six and three-fourths leagues called *San Juan de los Esteros,* purchased for $750 by Lorenzo de la Garza from Pedro López Prieto, March 18, 1794.— Harbert Davenport.

11 Francisco Ytúrria had a humble beginning. He was born in Matamoros. His father, Manuel Ytúrria, who had been an officer in the Spanish army, died young; his mother, Paula Navarro y Ortosu, was the daughter of refugees from the town of Palafox, destroyed by Indians about 1818. Francisco received his business training as an employee of Charles Stillman. He attained great wealth beginning with an association with Stillman, King and Kenedy, particularly during "Los Algodones."—Same.

12 Ford, V, pp. 882-883.

John S. Ford's *Memoirs* provide some of the straightest, some of the most intelligent and some of the most interesting source material on the history of the King Ranch region. He wrote, as a participating eyewitness, of a vital span of Texas history.

Ford was born in South Carolina on May 26, 1815. He had little real schooling but, by virtue of his love of reading, he qualified as a country schoolteacher at the age of sixteen. He was completing medical studies at the age of twenty-one in Tennessee when he decided to go to Texas. He arrived at San Augustine June 20, 1836. His first military service in Texas was enlistment under Captain William Kimbro for a Cherokee campaign. In autumn of 1844 Ford was elected to the House of Representatives of the last Congress of the Republic of Texas. In the spring of 1845, in partnership with a printer, he established *The Texas Democrat* in Austin. On May 14, 1847, he enlisted for service in Mexico as adjutant of Colonel John C. Hays' First Texas Mounted Volunteers. He was discharged June 30, 1848, and returned to his newspaper. From that time until his death, November 3, 1897, John S. Ford continued to alternate between military service, public service and newspaper work.

Equipped with newspaper experience and having been in the vanguard of virtually every significant frontier political and military activity in Texas for a full half a century, John S. Ford was ideally fitted to write of the events in which he had participated. In 1885 he began compiling his *Memoirs*. They present a graphic view of the sweep of history through which he lived.

13 Graf, I, p. 52.

14 Same, pp. 273-274.

15 Same, pp. 212-213.

16 Testimony of Robert S. Leman. Jacob Mussina *v.* William Alling et al, *Louisiana Annotated Reports*, XI, p. 568.

The Brownsville Town Company was officially contracted on December 9, 1848, between Charles Stillman, Samuel A. Belden and Jacob Mussina for a joint venture "within what is termed the *ejidos* of the City of Matamoros situated on the left bank of the Rio Grande embracing the town tract of Brownsville and the land upon which United States Government improvements [Fort Brown] now exist."

17 Davenport, "Notes on Early Steamboating," p. 288.

18 Graf, I, pp. 77-78.

19 Archives of Matamoros, Mexico. For data on Stillman and his family see Henry R. Stiles, *History of Ancient Wethersfield, Connecticut* (New York, 1904).

20 Ford, V, p. 884.

21 Graf, I, pp. 160-161.

22 *Records* "At a special session of the Commissioner's Court of Cameron County, Texas, Dec. 7, 1849" show the *Whiteville* tied up at Brownsville. The *Frankland* and the *Aid* were also tied up. See *American Flag*, April 19, 1848.

23 This deduction is based on facts contained in Graf's study of the steamboat trade.

24 Graf, I, pp. 4-5.

25 Captain William Kelly to Harbert Davenport. See also Kenedy's Obituary.

26 Graf, I, p. 235.

27 Captain William Kelly to Harbert Davenport.

28 Kenedy's Obituary.

29 Same.

30 This date is an inference based on recorded dates of preceding and succeeding events.

31 This account of the Stillman-Kenedy interview is based on the reminiscences of Captain Kelly to Harbert Davenport.

32 Graf, I, p. 358.

33 This account of the Kenedy-King conversation is based on the following sources: Captain Kelly to Harbert Davenport; John D. Finnegan, retired business manager of the King Ranch, who recounted the conversation as related to him by R. J. Kleberg, Sr., who had heard it from Mifflin Kenedy himself; Davenport, "Notes on Early Steamboating," pp. 288-289; King's Obituary; Kenedy's Obituary.

34 In a deposition by Mifflin Kenedy, September 23, 1872, he stated that the firm of M. Kenedy & Co. had started business as "common carriers on March 1, 1850."

35 Davenport, "Notes on Early Steamboating," p. 289.

36 Same.

From a study of the *Comanche's* requirements, it becomes obvious that the boat's draft had to be "less than twenty-four inches loaded."

37 Graf, I, p. 360.

38 Same, p. 359.

39 Penciled note in the handwriting of Mrs. Henrietta M. King, King Ranch vault.

40 This account of the first encounter between Richard King and Henrietta Maria Morse Chamberlain is based on the following sources: Penciled notes of Mrs. Henrietta M. King; notes by Mrs. R. J. Kleberg, a daughter; notes "As told to Sarah Kleberg [a granddaughter] by H. M. M. C. King"— all preserved in the King Ranch vault; Dr. John Ashton to Holland McCombs.

41 Florence Bell, *A History of the First Presbyterian Church of Brownsville, Texas*, n.p., n.d.; *Diamond Jubilee October 4-11, 1925, Celebrating the Organization of the First Presbyterian Church Brownsville, Texas, 1850-1925,* n.p., n.d.; J. L. Allhands, *Gringo Builders* (Privately Printed, 1931), p. 19. Teresa Griffin Vielé, *Following the Drum, A Glimpse of Frontier Life* (New York, 1858), p. 109.

Mrs. Vielé, the wife of an army officer, accompanied her husband to the border, arriving in 1851. She spent a year at Ringgold Barracks. She remarked of Brownsville: "In 1852 when we were there, there was no church, and but one preacher . . . a wandering Presbyterian . . ."

42 Dr. John Ashton to Holland McCombs.

43 Same.

44 *A Chamberlain Geneological Record*, n.p., n.d.

45 H. Chamberlain, Windsor, Conn., "New Year's Eve, 1823," to Miss Maria Morse, Lewis, Essex County, New York, preserved in the King Ranch vault.

Hiram Chamberlain continued to give a detailed account of his rather stormy teaching experiences in Windsor, "a *natural garden,* but almost a *moral wilderness.*" Miss Morse was also a teacher. Chamberlain complained "You have not told me, *where, how long,* and for *how much,* you teach in Lewis."

46 *Chamberlain Geneological Record;* unidentified Essex County, Vermont, newspaper clipping.

47 *Chamberlain Geneological Record.*

48 Same.

49 Preserved in King Ranch vault.

50 H. Chamberlain to Miss Henrietta Chamberlain, March 26, 1847, King Ranch vault.

51 Samples of the verse and the flower painting are in a scrapbook in the King Ranch vault.

52 The story of Hiram Chamberlain's riding a mule to Texas is a family story that has passed from generation to generation.— Robert J. Kleberg, Jr.

53 Although the First Congress of the Republic of Texas had by resolution declared the Rio Grande the boundary of Texas, the republic was unable to make good this declared extension of territory by force of arms. When Texas was annexed to the Union, it first undertook the appearance of civil government south of the Nueces River by the creation of Nueces County April 18, 1846. Its county seat, Corpus Christi, at the extreme northern edge of the county, was impossibly located for administration of law over the huge area embraced by the county—from Corpus Christi to Laredo to Brownsville. Until the actual promulgation of the Treaty of Guadalupe Hidalgo, any civil government visible to the naked eye in the lower Rio Grande country was furnished by the State of Tamaulipas.

With the coming of peace and settlements of growing importance on the Texas side of the river, Cameron County, containing an area facing the lowest reaches of the Rio Grande, was carved from Nueces County on February 12, 1848. Administration of the county government was first organized at the tiny village of Santa Rita, six miles upriver from Brownsville, but when the first officials were elected in August, Brownsville was designated as the county seat.

From that time we began to feel that we were actually American citizens. Although Texas had been in the Union for three years, and we had been citizens of Nueces County in the Lone Star State, the fact was that we might almost as well have been living in the very heart of Mexico.— Adolphus Glaevecke, as quoted by Chatfield, p. 23.

The first action of the county administration at Brownsville was the construction of a strong jail. Not until January 24, 1850, was the town of Brownsville officially incorporated.

Cameron County took its name from the brave Captain Ewen Cameron, a Scot who served in the army of the Republic of Texas. He met death before a Mexican firing squad during the Mier Expedition. The original Cameron County ran from the Rio Grande to Los Olmos Creek—that is, all of present day Cameron, Willacy and Kenedy counties. Willacy County was created in 1911 from Cameron and Hidalgo counties; in 1921 Cameron, Willacy and Hidalgo counties provided land for Kenedy County.

From 1848 until 1911 the entire area from the Rio Grande to Los Olmos Creek, comprising the Kenedy Ranch and large sections of the King Ranch, was "governed" from Brownsville; it was still border country.

54 Jovial Henry Miller had a talent for hospitality. He rebuilt and expanded Miller's Hotel in 1858. It prospered for years. Though no longer under the same name, it is still a hotel today.

55 Stillman journeyed to Connecticut and married Miss Elizabeth Goodrich at Wethersfield on August 17, 1849. He returned to Brownsville with his bride and built a new house, the first solid brick residence in town. It was said by Stillman's niece, Miss Hattie Case, that Stillman brought his bride to Brownsville by schooner because he was "afraid of steamboats."

56 This account of Richard King's celebration of his twenty-sixth birthday comes from a story told by the Combe family. It is familiar to old-timers in Brownsville. Richard King's words are here placed in direct quotation for the first time in this book.

Dr. Charles Berthoud Combe was en route to Mexico City, but he liked the atmosphere or the people of Brownsville so well that he stayed. This was the beginning of a long friendship with Captain King. Doctor Combe died in Brownsville in 1907, in his seventy-eighth year, after a long and honored medical career on the border.

The dashing young Kentuckian's rough companion on that night in July, 1850, was a character who came to be well known in Brownsville as "Hell Bent" Miller, so-called not only because his actions earned the name but to distinguish him from "Heaven Bent" Miller, a very pious

fellow. During an epidemic in later years both of them were stricken and—contrary to expectations—Heaven Bent died and Hell Bent survived. Neither was related to Henry Miller, the owner of the hotel.

CHAPTER IV

1 As evidenced by an advertisement in the *American Flag*, August 21, 1850.

2 The disposition of the boats is a logical conclusion from facts available about M. Kenedy & Co.'s operation.

3 The August 21 issue of the *American Flag* listed "M. Kenedy, Master" for the *Grampus*. Contrary to most published accounts, King did not skipper the *Grampus* and Kenedy did not skipper the *Comanche* for several months after the arrival of these boats.

4 Davenport, "Notes on Early Steamboating," p. 289; Ford, V, pp. 891-892.

5 The discovery of gold in California was a boon to general business activities in Brownsville and particularly to the newly organized company. Referring to the year 1850, William Neale said:

Stage lines and steamboats plied between our city and the mouth of the river, Brazos St. Jago [Santiago] and Point Isabel, and they did a thriving business at that time, for on the first excitement regarding the California gold diggings, and for some time after, great numbers of travellers passed through our city on their way to the Pacific coast by land, and expended considerable amounts of money here in purchasing outfits from our traders and stock raisers.—Chatfield, p. 14.

6 The monopoly eventually drew public complaint and a cry was raised for overland competition by way of "the Corpus route."—*Nueces Valley*, March 13, 1858, as quoted by Graf, I, p. 362.

7 Graf, I, pp. 358-359.

8 Same, p. 360. For the deposition see Nathaniel Wilson, Special Counsel for Claimants, *The Steamboat "Swan." Before the Mixed Commission on American and Mexican Claims. M. Kenedy & Co. vs. Mexico. No. 340. Brief for*

Claim on Merits (Judd & Detweiler, Printers, n.d.) This legal action was a claim for indemnity for Mexican seizure of the steamboat *Swan* in 1858.

9 Allhands, p. 19; Frank Cushing Pierce, *A Brief History of the Lower Rio Grande Valley* (Menasha, Wis., 1917), p. 123; Harbert Davenport to Holland McCombs.

10 Graf, I, p. 360.

11 Same, p. 361.

12 Harbert Davenport to Holland McCombs. Mr. Davenport came to Brownsville to practice law in 1912 with a great and growing curiosity about local history. He interviewed available old-timers, accumulating a wealth of experiences and gossip of earlier days.

13 In her later years Mrs. Henrietta M. King made notes on her early experiences, or in some cases dictated them to a daughter or granddaughter. This note is preserved in the King Ranch vault. It survived the fire which destroyed the ranch house in 1912.

14 Victor Rodríguez Alvarado, "Memoirs." Alvarado, an early-day employee on the King Ranch, recounted his experiences in an interview on August 15, 1937. A translation is on file in the King Ranch vault.

15 Henry Bamford Parks, *A History of Mexico* (Boston, 1938), p. 222.

16 Same.

17 Vielé, pp. 191-193.
From Ringgold Barracks Mrs. Vielé had a ringside seat on the unfolding of the abortive *Plan de la Loba*. It becomes obvious from her narration of events that she was rooting for Carvajal and the filibusters.
Various spellings of Carvajal's name will be found: Carbajal, Caravajal, Carabajal. The spelling used in this work is taken from his signature.

18 Harbert Davenport, "General Jose Maria Jesus Carabajal," *The Southwestern Historical Quarterly*, LV (April, 1952), pp. 475-483.

19 Vielé, p. 192.

20 Ford, V, p. 880; Ernest C. Shearer, "The Carvajal Disturbances," *The Southwestern Historical Quarterly*, LV (October, 1951), pp. 215-216.

21 Ford, IV, pp. 636-637.

22 Same, pp. 637-638.

23 Same, p. 638.

24 There are many accounts and records regarding the Carvajal Revolution. For official documents and investigations see: *Texas Frontier Troubles*, Report No. 343, H.R., 44th Cong., 1st Sess.; *Message on Hostilities on the Rio Grande*, Ex. Doc. 21, Sen., 36th Cong., 1st Sess.; *Difficulties on the Southwestern Frontier. Message of the President of the United States*, Ex. Doc. 52, 36th Cong., 1st Sess.; *Troubles on the Texas Frontier*, Ex. Doc. 81, 36th Cong., 1st Sess.; *Reports of the Committee of Investigation Sent in 1873 by the Mexican Government to the Frontier of Texas* (New York, 1875); *Report of the Permanent Committee Appointed at a Meeting of the Citizens of Brownsville, Tex., April 17, 1875* (Brownsville, 1875). Ford's *Memoirs*, IV, pp. 624-641, provides an excellent picture from the viewpoint of a participant. Vielé (as cited) and Emmanuel Domenech, *Missionary Adventures in Texas and Mexico: A Personal Narrative of Six Years' Sojourn in Those Regions* (London, 1858) are from the viewpoint of spectators. See also Davenport, "General Jose Maria Jesus Carabajal;" Pierce (as cited); Shearer (as cited); Coleman McCampbell, *Saga of a Frontier Seaport* (Dallas, 1934).

25 M. L. Crimmins (ed.), "W. G. Freeman's Report on the Eighth Military Department," *The Southwestern Historical Quarterly*, LII (July, 1948), pp. 101, 104.
A comparison of the rates for transportation of supplies from Brazos Santiago to Fort Brown and from Brazos Santiago to Ringgold Barracks shows that the *Comanche* end of the enterprise was not working for peanuts:
[Ringgold Barracks] is supplied by water transportation, under contract, and the following rates are paid from Brazos Santiago:—corn & oats, 38 cents per bushel; hay, $5 per bale; lumber, $28 per 1,000 feet; shingles,

$3.75 per thousand; for all pound freight, $1. per 100 lbs; for all measurement freight, 30 cents per cubic foot; soldiers, $8 per man; horses and mules, $12 per head. For Subsistence stores the rates paid are:—flour, beans, bread, rice, coffee, sugar, salt, apples, onions, or any other *dry barrel*, taking the flour barrel as the standard, $1.60 per barrel; for pork, molasses, vinegar, or any *wet barrel*, $2.20 per barrel. The cost of transportation between any intermediate points is in proportion.—Same, LII (October, 1948), pp. 231-232.

26 Buckingham Smith, United States *chargé d'affaires*, Mexico City, to Major W. W. Chapman, Commanding Officer, Fort Brown, Texas. Smith ordered Chapman to prevent "directly or indirectly the support of insurgents by men and arms."—William R. Manning (ed.), *Diplomatic Correspondence of the United States, Inter-American Affairs, 1831-1860* (Washington, 1932-1939), IX, p. 414.

27 Graf, I, pp. 356-357.

28 Brownsville *Daily Cosmopolitan*, March 17, 1886.

29 Father Verdet officiated at the service in St. Mary's Church. Marriage records are on file in the office of the County Clerk, Cameron County, Texas.

30 C. G. Norton, *Austin Times*, June 4, 1937.
This feature article dates a letter from Kinney, written in Brownsville, as "1842." This is an obvious typographical error. In 1842 there was no Brownsville: no steamboats and no "General A." to whom to sell a boat.

31 George C. Furber, *The Twelve Months Volunteer . . .* (Cincinnati, 1848), p. 163; Walter Paye Lane, *The Adventures and Recollections of General Walter P. Lane . . .* (Marshall, Tex., 1928), pp. 72-73.

32 Josiah Turner, "Deposition No. 95," *Memorial of the United States, No. 230, Before the General Claims Commission of the United States and Mexico, Under Convention Concluded September 8, 1923, United States of America on Behalf of Robert J. Kleberg, Sr. . . . Richard King v. United Mexican States* (Washington, n. d.) (hereafter cited as *"Memorial No. 230"*), p. 146.

CHAPTER V

1 Lewis, p. 135.

2 Captain King's party took the route which was known for many years after Taylor's march from Corpus Christi to Matamoros as "General Taylor's Road."—Capt. John James Dix, "Indian Troubles," as quoted by Ford, II, p. 327.

The road proceeded southwestward from Corpus Christi for about thirty miles and then turned south to the Rio Grande. It was a thirsty trace through a wild country, but it gave graphic testimony of its grazing potential. The future General "Grant would ride out onto high ground to see the wild mustangs covering the plain clear to the horizon in three directions, too many . . . to be corraled in the whole state of Rhode Island."—Lewis, p. 135.

3 According to Kinney's report to President Lamar, "he was first deceived in the purchase of the property, having bought of a person who had no title to it." At the arrival of Villareal's force, all but eight of Kinney's forty men, hired as soldiers "in constant pay," deserted him. But Kinney intimated to the Mexicans that he had buried bombs and other secret destructive devices. "This led to an interview, in which sharp words first ensued; and a peaceful trade for the land followed."—Charles Adams Gulick, Jr., and Winnie Allen (eds.), *The Papers of Mirabeau Buonaparte Lamar* (Austin, 1924) (hereafter cited as *"Lamar Papers"*), No. 2422, IV, pp. 213-214.
Kinney agreed to pay $4,000—$3,000 in United States currency and $1,000 in merchandise. The down payment was only 845 reales.—Coleman McCampbell, *Texas Seaport, The Story of the Growth of Corpus Christi and the Coastal Bend Area* (New York, 1952), p. 26.

4 Same, p. 27; Lewis, p. 124; Shearer, pp. 205-207; Edward S. Wallace, *General William Jenkins Worth, Monterey's Forgotten Hero* (Dallas, 1953), p. 66.

5 *Lamar Papers*, No. 2422, IV, pp. 213-214.

6 McCampbell, *Texas Seaport*, pp. 27-29.

7 *The Corpus Christi Caller-Times,* November 26, 1933; *San Antonio Express,* Feburary 17, 1952; McCampbell, *Texas Seaport,* pp. 30-31.

8 Hortense Warner Ward, "It Was Texas' First State Fair," *The Houston Chronicle Magazine,* April 27, 1952, p. 22.

9 Shearer, pp. 223-224.

10 Ford, IV, p. 638.

11 Same, p. 641.

12 Ward, p. 22.

13 Mifflin Kenedy related this conversation to Robert J. Kleberg, who repeated it to his son, Richard M. Kleberg, Sr.

14 Walter Prescott Webb, *The Texas Rangers, A Century of Frontier Defense* (New York, 1935), p. 143; *Muster Roll of Texas Mounted Volunteers,* Archives, Texas State Library, Austin.

15 *Nueces County Records,* Book E, p. 57, shows that on June 5, 1852, G. K. Lewis bought Colonel H. L. Kinney's part-interest in what had been the *Corpus Christi Star* printing establishment. This same page of the record book reveals that Lewis bought many bayfront lots, paying as much as $100 and $150 per lot. Lewis was also engaged in a mercantile venture with John Willett of Corpus Christi. Willett became one of the administrators of the Lewis estate, according to the "Petition of John Willett for Appointment as Administrator," filed with the Nueces County Court April 16, 1855.

16 *Records of Real Estate of Nueces County,* Book E, pp. 347-350.

17 The fact that the legal documents attendant to the purchase by King from the heirs of the original grantee and to the sale of the half-interest to Lewis were filed at the same time indicates that the two transactions were part of a plan upon which the partners had agreed.

18 *Records of Real Estate of Nueces County,* Book E, pp. 347-350.

19 According to "Field Notes of a Survey on 3½ Sitios of Land called 'Rincón de Santa Gertrudis',", recorded September 10, 1855, and on file in the General Land Office of Texas, Austin, the tract was surveyed on November 18, 19 and 20, 1853, and again on July 6 and 7, 1855, by Felix A. Blucher, Special Deputy District Surveyor for Nueces District. Chain carriers for the survey are recorded as Frank Abbe, Wm. Denning, Nicolás Alvarado, Domingo Escamilla and R. King.

20 Dawson Duncan, "Huge Land Area Is Lost in Pioneer Surveys," *Houston Chronicle,* May 18, 1930; Florence Johnson Scott, *Historical Heritage of the Lower Río Grande, A Historical Record of Spanish Exploration, Subujugation and Colonization of the Lower Río Grande Valley and the Activities of José Escandón, Count of Sierra Gorda, together with the Development of Towns and Ranches Under Spanish, Mexican and Texas Sovereignties, 1747-1848* (San Antonio, 1937), p. 87.

21 A legal instrument testifying to the death of José Lorenzo de la Garza, executed in the Congregación de Refugio, June 12, 1814, signed by de la Garza's sons.—King Ranch vault.

22 John Henry Brown, *History of Texas from 1685 to 1892* (St. Louis, 1893), II, pp. 138-139.

The activities of the Cow Boys quickly got out of hand as the supply of cattle dwindled. They made inroads upon those engaged in the smuggling trade which was beginning to flourish between Mexico and the Republic of Texas. There was retaliation and counter-retaliation. On September 13, 1839, a Lieutenant John Browne made an official report to the Adjutant General of the Texas army:

When I arrived in Victoria I found it filled with a set of men who have given themselves the title of a *band of Brothers....* They are all in the cow stealing business, and are scattered all over this frontier. They pretend ... they steal only from the enemy; but I am convinced, to the contrary, that they steal from Texans as well as Mexicans. ... he then said that he was one of the *band of Brothers* and wished me to know that they could defend themselves against any force the government could send to oppose them. ... I am convinced that there are no less than three or four hundred men engaged in this business. ... one of them told me that they had their expresses better regulated than any regular army that has ever been in the country.— *Lamar Papers,* No. 1447, III, pp. 106-107.

Two days later H. S. Foote wrote to President Lamar, registering his protest as an aggrieved citizen of the area:

I am . . . constrained upon unquestionable evidence to State . . . that there is a strange combination of marauders along the whole western frontier; composed in part of Mexicans, in part of Comanches, and in part of men claiming to be Texian citizens, who are allied in order to plunder and devastate indiscriminately the private property of as good citizens as any in Texas; men who have served you in war and served you in peace, and who are heart and soul devoted to the interests of the Republic. . . . The most valuable tract which the republic possesses is almost entirely extirpated. Distress has fallen upon men, women and children, and the whole population is speaking seriously of abandoning the country, and abandoning it forever.—*Lamar Papers*, No. 1449, III, pp. 108-109.

Late in 1839 the pillage upon private citizenry was somewhat alleviated by Carvajal, who recruited Cow Boys to fight in the Federalist War under General Antonio Canales. This filibustering was excellent training for, if not a step toward, the Mexican War to follow.

[23] The spelling of the name varies in early legal documents examined: Prahedes, Prugedes, Pragides, Pragidis. These variations were presumably attempts at Anglicization of a christian name rather uncommon to the Spanish language.

[24] *Deed Records*, Nueces County, Book E, pp. 498-499 and *Transcribed Deed Records*, Kleberg County, Vol. A, p. 89; *Deed Records*, Nueces County, Book E, pp. 499-500 and *Transcribed Deed Records*, Kleberg County, Vol. A, pp. 89-90.

[25] Ford, V, p. 881.

CHAPTER VI

[1] Alvar Nuñez Cabeza de Vaca, *The Journey of Alvar Nuñez Cabeza de Vaca*, tr. Fanny Bandelier (New York, 1905), p. 97.

[2] Charles W. Hackett, *Historical Documents Relating to New Mexico, Nueva Viscaya, and Approaches Thereto* (Washington, 1923), I, p. 41.

[3] J. Frank Dobie, *The Longhorns* (Boston, 1941), p. 4.

[4] Captain George W. Hughes, who kept notes during General Wool's march from San Antonio to Saltillo, recorded the Mexican vaquero in his native land:

Fancy to yourself a rather light-colored Indian, dressed in a pair of leather unmentionables, without suspenders, buttoning from the knee downwards, which are usually left open in warm weather for comfort, and to exhibit the white drawers underneath; a common cotton shirt, often wanting; a red sash tied tightly around the waist; a pair of sandals on his feet, and enormous iron spurs on heel; with a heavy conical felt hat (that would almost resist a sabre cut) on head, and a long iron-pointed aspen goad in hand, and you have a perfect picture of the ranchero, or rather vachero [*sic*]. Mounted on a spirited pony, with a lasso at his saddle-bow, he is no mean adversary for a single man to encounter. He rides well and fearlessly, and throws the lasso with unerring aim. It is a beautiful sight to see him with his red blanket (worn as a poncho in cold weather) streaming in the wind, his head bent eagerly forward, and lasso whirling in circles high in air, riding down some refractory animal that he seldom fails to catch, at the first throw, by the neck or hind foot, bringing him violently to the ground. The animal thus caught feels that the contest is ended, and quietly submits to his captor. It is amusing to see the young urchins following the example of their elders, and practising on little pigs and tender kids, who by no means appear to enjoy the fun . . . Every Mexican, whatever his condition may be, is expert with the lasso, and the throwing of it may be regarded as a national amusement. One of our men became intoxicated at the hacienda of Lorenzo, near Parras, and was in the act of raising his carbine to shoot Don Manuel, its amiable and accomplished proprietor, who, quick as thought, threw the noose over him and pinioned him by the arms, when our stalwart Arkansas cavalier became as meek and quiet as a lamb.—Hughes, p. 41.

[5] On March 4, 1832, R. H. Chisholm wrote a request to Ezekiel Williams that he record his brand (HC) at Gonzales. This was the beginning of our present system of brand recording. —Richard M. Kleberg, Sr., "Cowmen Have Problems to Solve," *The Cattleman*, XIII (October, 1926), p. 21. For a facsimile reproduction of this historic Texas cattle brand see Dee Brown and Martin F. Schmitt, *Trail Driving Days* (New York, 1952), p. 48.

[6] Walter Prescott Webb, "The Cattle Kingdom," *The Great Plains* (Boston, 1931), pp. 205-269.

[7] *Corpus Christi Caller-Times*, November 26, 1933.

[8] The dam forming the big tank, now ruined and dry, at the old Spanish rancho called *Randado,* in the brush of Jim Hogg County, is said to have been made in the late 1700's—and by a curious method. Peons loaded dirt on dried cowhides. Vaqueros fastened one end of their *reatas* to the cowhides and the other to the pommels of their saddles and rode, dragging the loads of dirt to the embankment which formed the dam.

[9] Graf, II, p. 464.

[10] Ford, V, p. 880; Pierce, p. 33.

[11] Ford, V, p. 888.

[12] Alvarado, "Memoirs."

[13] Same. Alvarado was probably the only man to call Captain King "mister."

[14] Victoriano Ochoa Gonzalez, of Camargo, an authority on local history.

[15] Dr. John Ashton to Holland McCombs.

Employment on the King Ranch is no shortlived thing; it goes on through generations, and it is not unusual to find fathers and sons and grandsons working side by side on the same division of the ranch . . .

Capt. King solved most of the employment problems when he signed on his original crews. Today, a large majority of the ranch employes are grandsons and great-grandsons, grandnephews and cousins of all degrees of the King-employed cowpunchers. And, while some of the family names that were prominent on the ranch 75 years ago have disappeared, they are still represented by blood relationship in other families. —*King Ranch, 100 Years of Ranching* (Corpus Christi, 1953), pp. 64, 98.

[16] Harbert Davenport stated that when he came to Brownsville in 1912 there was "affection between the Canales family and the King family, and Richard King had once said that 'he could not have kept on and held on if Andrés Canales had not been adjoining'." — Davenport to McCombs, November 5, 1952.

[17] Thomas R. Armstrong (grandson of Major Durst) to McCombs, March 15, 1953.

[18] Ford, V, p. 885.

The San Salvador del Tule ranch was destroyed by Cortina in 1859. In his later years Kenedy told Richard M. Kleberg, Sr., that it was King who spurred him to turn to ranching as a serious business.

[19] Graf, II, pp. 466-470.

Graf's economic study of the area cites the two types of ranch operation prevalent during this period: The owner-operator, like Captain King, or the partnership arrangement in which one partner was always present, as contrasted with absentee-ownership with the ranch operated by a manager, as in the case of Stillman.—pp. 463ff.

[20] Abstract of Rincón de Santa Gertrudis; *Probate Minutes*, Nueces County, Book B, p. 229; Testimony of James Bryden, King Ranch vault; James Bryden, "Deposition No. 495," *Memorial No. 230*, p. 185.

[21] In writing an account of her mother's early life, presumably from dictation, Mrs. Alice G. K. Kleberg, the youngest daughter, carefully stressed the passage of time in noting her grandfather's acceptance: "In time Rev. Hiram Chamberlain grew to admire this young captain's sterling qualities and strong personality . . ."

[22] James L. Allhands, *Uriah Lott* (San Antonio, 1949), p. 87; *Kansas City Star*, July 4, 1926: "When Henrietta grew to young womanhood she began teaching in Brownsville."

The Rio Grande Female Institute was founded by the Reverend Hiram Chamberlain. It was undoubtedly in this institution that Henrietta taught.

[23] Mifflin Kenedy and his bride had built a house on Elizabeth Street in 1853.

[24] *Marriage Records*, Cameron County, Vol. A, p. 387.

[25] Mrs. King described her wedding dress in great detail to her granddaughter, Henrietta Rosa Kleberg (now Mrs. Thomas R. Armstrong), who took down the description and made a

watercolor sketch of the dress. The drawing and the note are preserved in the King Ranch vault.

26 Notes in Mrs. Henrietta M. King's writing, trembled with age.—King Ranch vault.

27 Alpheus Morse to Mrs. Henrietta M. King. —King Ranch vault.

28 Present *Kineños* keep her memory green with the title *La Patrona*.

29 George Buchanan Fife, New York *Evening World,* as quoted in "Mrs. King — Indeed a Queen," *Literary Digest,* LXXXV (April 25, 1925), p. 40.

30 I, Guadalupe Ballí, . . . for and in consideration of the services already rendered and to be hereafter rendered towards the prosecution and final settlement of all my interests in the United States of Mexico and in the State of Texas, by Gideon K. Lewis . . . have granted, bargained, sold and conveyed and by these presents do grant, sell, bargain and convey unto the said Gideon K. Lewis, one half of all my interests in all property both real and personal in the aforesaid United States of Mexico and in the State of Texas.—*Deed Records,* Cameron County, Vol. F, p. 28.

31 *Deed Records,* Kenedy County, Vol. G, pp. 15-17.

The Padre Island tract has been the subject of much litigation. In 1905, by the Laredo Decree, Mrs. H. M. King was awarded title to 6,000 acres.

There is so much conflicting evidence . . . I recall that in the suit which we had with the State of Texas over the title to the Island we could not even agree with the State on where the island is located.—Leroy G. Denman, Jr., of San Antonio, King Ranch attorney.

32 "Inventory and Appraisement, Estate of Gideon K. Lewis, Deceased, April 27, 1855," *Minutes Probate Court,* Nueces County, Vol. B, pp. 55-57.

CHAPTER VII

1 *Minutes of the Probate Court,* Nueces County, trace the lengthy and complicated settlement of the Lewis estate by an array of legal documents, beginning with the "Order Appointing Temporary Administrator and Appraisers, Estate of Gideon K. Lewis, Deceased, April 16, 1855,"

Book B, pp. 47-48, and stretching through numerous orders appointing administrators and appraisers, petitions and grants of petitions for orders of sale of properties, and reports and accounts of sale. Most of these documents are contained in Book B. The culmination was the "Order Dismissing Estate of Gideon K. Lewis, Deceased, November 5, 1874," No. 227, Book E.

2 Testimony of James Bryden; Abstract of title to Rincón de Santa Gertrudis—King Ranch vault. "Administrator's Deed, Estate of Gideon K. Lewis, by H. P. Bee, Administrator . . . to Richard King and W. W. Chapman," *Records of Deeds,* Nueces County, Vol. 13, pp. 117-119; "Simple Mortgage to Secure Promissory Note, for $1,575.00. Richard King and W. W. Chapman to Estate of Gideon K. Lewis, deceased," dated August 1, 1856, recorded July 21, 1858, *Deed Records,* Nueces County, Book G, pp. 169-170.

3 The warranty deed from Uribe to Walworth was filed on January 28, 1857, after the formal recording of the cancellation.

4 Ownership of the de la Garza Santa Gertrudis grant was entirely vested in James Walworth from December, 1856, until June 10, 1859, when, for $2,500, he sold a one-half undivided interest to Mrs. Henrietta M. King. Tax receipts are on file in the King Ranch vault showing that Walworth paid the taxes on the property during the years he owned it. The taxes on the whole twelve leagues for the year 1857 were just $59.49.

5 Harbert Davenport to Holland McCombs.

6 Biographical data on Stephen Powers was furnished by Harbert Davenport, who became associated with the firm in 1912.

7 From the time of its establishment in 1849 the law firm changed members and names many times: Powers and [Nestor] Maxan; Powers and [James B.] Wells; Wells and [Robert B.] Rentfro; Wells, Rentfro and [Benjamin O.] Hicks; Wells, [Robert W.] Stayton and [Robert J.] Kleberg; James B. Wells; Wells and [Joseph K.] Wells.

[8] Thomas Rusk and P. H. Bell to T. S. Jesup, February 15, 1856, "Capt. Mifflin Kennedy [*sic*]," *Records of the Office of the Quartermaster General, Consolidated Correspondence File*, R.G. 92, National Archives.

[9] "Certification of debts due by QM at Ft. Brown, Nov. 17, 1856," same. Both items involved the movement of troops.

[10] Carl Coke Rister, *Robert E. Lee in Texas* (Norman, Okla., 1946), pp. 70, 75.

[11] Lee had been sent to San Antonio to join General Wool's force. "He was to assist Captain William D. Fraser in collecting tools for road- and bridge-building and pontoons" to improve Wool's route to the Rio Grande. The work included the construction of a pontoon bridge across the Rio Grande about thirty miles south of what is now Eagle Pass.—Same, pp. 7-10.

[12] Same, pp. 75-76.

[13] Bell, *History of the First Presbyterian Church;* Mrs. May H. Dickens, Kingsville.

Mrs. Dickens is a historian and lecturer. She taught in the Brownsville schools from 1909 until 1923 and was a Professor of History at the Texas College of Arts and Industries from 1925 until 1947.

[14] Armistead L. Long, *Memoirs of Robert E. Lee, His Military and Personal History* . . . (Philadelphia, 1886), p. 79.

[15] The road network of the day made the Santa Gertrudis a natural stopping place (see Rister, p. 41). Lee recorded one such stop in his Memorandum Book.

[16] Notes in the handwriting of Alice Gertrudis King Kleberg, obviously dictated by Mrs. Henrietta M. King.—King Ranch vault.

[17] More and more the greatness of Texas impressed Lee. Its rolling hills and valleys, its sparkling rivers and fine forests, its vast farms and ranches, its diversified climate, and its friendly, hospitable people affected him strongly, while the spirit of optimism which he observed in the state was unlike anything he had seen or felt elsewhere . . . His letters home at this time reveal the spiritual change that was taking place within him, . . . Brother officers who witnessed his metamorphosis stood in awe . . . Yet each knew . . . that he could go to him with any problem, however personal, and find a sympathetic listener and friend, whose advice would be sound, for when Lee spoke, all took heed of his counsel.—Rister, p. 69.

[18] Family reminiscences record this phrase as having been repeated by Mrs. King so often that it became a byword.

[19] Many published accounts — magazine and newspaper articles about the King Ranch—have recorded that Robert E. Lee selected the ranch site in the wilderness. This is not true. Lee was stationed in Baltimore when King and Lewis chose the site for the ranch and its headquarters. The misconception about Lee choosing the site for the King Ranch probably grew from the fact that Lee did give his young friend King advice about the rancho and that, in all probability, Lee did recommend the building site for the permanent ranch home of the Kings at Santa Gertrudis.

[20] Dr. Zachary T. Scott, Austin, who made an extensive study of King Ranch history, to Holland McCombs.

[21] From family reminiscences as quoted by Robert J. Kleberg, Sr.

[22] As related by Mrs. King to members of her family.

[23] Same.

[24] On March 10, 1857, Major Chapman reported to the Quartermaster General that forty-three wagons were leaving for San Antonio that day with the "remainder of the stores at this depot," except what was to be sold at auction. All purchasers of warehouses and other buildings were given until the last day of the month to remove their property from the premises.—*Records of the Office of the Quartermaster General*, National Archives.

[25] The anaqua trees were called *los arboles del rodeo* because that was where the roundup was always held. "These trees were where grandma used to bring grandfather his lunch."—As told to Russell Cook of the Texas College of Arts and Industries in 1927 by Mrs. Robert J. Kleberg, Sr.

Only two of these trees remain today, in Kingsville on West Santa Gertrudis between Second and Third streets in front of the Flato Elementary School. The Tranquitas dam was located at the site of the present Kleberg County Courthouse.

26 Notes in the handwriting of Mrs. Henrietta M. King, King Ranch vault.

27 James Bryden, "Deposition No. 495," *Memorial No. 230,* p. 186.

28 Graf, II, pp. 482-483.

29 Daniel Evander McArthur, *Cattle Industry of Texas, 1685-1918* (Thesis, University of Texas, 1918), p. 211.

30 J. Frank Dobie, *A Vaquero of the Brush Country* (Dallas, 1929), pp. 26-27. Mrs. Alice G. K. Kleberg stated it was in 1859.

31 Dobie, *Vaquero of the Brush Country,* p. 27:
He [King] "attempted to preserve meat for shipment by infusing brine into veins of cattle immediately after they were slaughtered." The experiment proved unsuccessful, however, and thereafter he had his Mexicans pour the tallow into barrels, hang the hides on fences, and cast the meat to some six or seven thousand hogs.

32 *Austin Times,* June 25, 1937; James B. Wells and Fred E. Starck to Harbert Davenport; *Probate Minutes,* Nueces County, Vol. C, p. 369.

33 William P. Aubrey was the first postmaster of Corpus Christi.

34 Perry Doddridge went to Brownsville in 1853, worked for the King-Kenedy enterprise, and finally moved to Corpus Christi where he set up a mercantile business, then a commission business, established the first bank, served as mayor, and was for many years one of the community's most progressive citizens. He was named one of the executors of Richard King's will.

35 Forbes Britton came to Texas with Taylor's army. In 1849 he established a wagon freight line. He built an impressive house overlooking Corpus Christi Bay and served in the Texas Senate from 1857 until his death in 1861. He was a trusted friend of Houston. In 1860 Houston sent him to Washington to seek more protection for the Rio Grande frontier.

36 William B. Mann was an early citizen and merchant in the Corpus Christi-Brownsville area. He was one of Britton's partners in the freighting business. He built a block-sized southern colonial house. It became known as "Mann's Red House." Later a house to be known as "The King House" was built on the same site.

37 German-born and -educated Felix A. Blucher came to Kinney's Ranch in the 1840's. He served as interpreter for Taylor's army, assisted as a surveyor in founding New Braunfels. He later moved to Corpus Christi after returning to Germany for a bride. In Corpus Christi he continued the surveying and civil engineering business and also practiced as an attorney.

38 Benjamin F. Neal was a Virginian by birth and a lawyer by education. In 1852 he was elected Corpus Christi's first mayor and served again in 1855. He was a district judge and edited *The Nueces Valley,* one of the earliest newspapers.

39 Henry A. Maltby, who had furnished the tent for Kinney's Fair, came to Corpus Christi in 1850. He was Corpus Christi's mayor in 1856. He became editor and proprietor of *The Ranchero* in 1859. He later moved to Brownsville and became a prominent citizen of that community.

40 Reuben Holbein went to the Santa Gertrudis in 1863.

41 Various legal documents indicate that Richard King maintained his legal residence in Brownsville, Cameron County, until he moved to the Santa Gertrudis, Nueces County, in December, 1860.

42 Ford, V, pp. 884-885.

43 Graf, I, pp. 357-362. Corpus Christians admitted "the steamboats could always underbid land transportation up the valley."

44 A report to the United States Secretary of State stated this free zone "is granted so as to establish a depot for smuggling on our immediate borders, and is given to no other section of that country . . . and in its operations inducing smugglers, adventurers, and thieves to flock to

the right bank of the Rio Bravo, . . . To such an extent did this decree encourage smuggling and lawlessness, that eminent Mexican authority, at one time, estimated the floating population in the City of Matamoros at over forty thousand. . . Mexico has made the Zona Libre . . . for the reception of goods, duty free, to be smuggled over our borders."—Ex. Doc. 39, H.R., 42nd Cong., 3rd Sess.

⁴⁵ *Report of the Permanent Committee*, pp. 4-5; Ford, IV, p. 783.

⁴⁶ Webb, *Texas Rangers*, p. 178.

⁴⁷ Juan Nepomuceno Cortina (sometimes called "Cortinas," although his father dropped the "s" from the name) was the great-great-grandson of Blas María Falcón, the founder of the Rancho Real de Santa Petronila, first ranchero in the wilderness between the Rio Grande and the Nueces. Cortina was the great-grandson of the María Gertrudis Falcón, after whom Santa Gertrudis Creek was named, who married Don José Salvador de la Garza, owner of the 59-square league Potrero del Espíritu Santo grant. Cortina was connected by ties of kinship with a large number of the wealthiest and most eminent early families in the Lower Rio Grande region.

⁴⁸ Ford, IV, pp. 784-785.

⁴⁹ Adolphus Glaevecke, as quoted by Webb, *Texas Rangers*, p. 176.

⁵⁰ Ford, IV, pp. 787-788.

⁵¹ The intricate story of the litigation concerning the Brownsville Town Company may be read in a maze of court records and decisions. From January, 1850, until return of a mandate of the Supreme Court of the United States in 1880, titles to property within the City of Brownsville were unsettled.

⁵² Antonio Tijerina, "Deposition No. 31," *Memorial No. 230*, pp. 112-113.

⁵³ John S. Ford related an anecdote which sheds light upon Cortina's knowledge of human psychology by which he maintained political control:

He understands his countrymen of the lower classes almost thoroughly . . . Cortina was approached by one

of his men; who asked him for money to buy a suit of clothes. He finished his business with Nesmith, handed the soldier twenty-five cents, saying "Here, my man, take this money, and go buy a suit of clothes." Nesmith remarked "General, why do you fool that poor fellow; you know two bits will not purchase a suit of clothes?" "Yes, sir, I do, and so does he. I know he only wanted money to get drunk on, and he has it."—Ford, IV, p. 785.

As the Honorable William Neale put it, "he was a useful 'striker' at elections."—Chatfield, p. 15.

⁵⁴ Webb, *Texas Rangers*, pp. 177-178; Pierce, p. 35.

⁵⁵ *Difficulties on the Southwestern Frontier*, pp. 79-82.

⁵⁶ Accounts of the Brownsville raid of September 28, 1859, will be found in various versions in numerous sources: Adolphus Glaevecke (a participating eyewitness, who had he been "quicker on the trigger" would have shot Cortina), Chatfield, p. 23; Major S. P. Heintzelman (later in command of troops operating against Cortina), Chatfield, p. 2; William Neale (a besieged citizen whose son was a victim), Chatfield, p. 15; Webb (the historian), *Texas Rangers*, pp. 178-179; aggrieved citizens speak in *Difficulties on the Southwestern Frontier*, pp. 20ff.

⁵⁷ Webb, *Texas Rangers*, p. 179.

⁵⁸ *Difficulties on the Southwestern Frontier*, pp. 70-72.

⁵⁹ Rister, p. 110.

⁶⁰ Ford, IV, pp. 789-793; Webb, *Texas Rangers*, pp. 180-183.

⁶¹ Ford expressed the opinion that Britton's alarm was "an act" designed to elicit immediate action from the governor. If it was Britton was a good actor. The first order conferred on Ford the rank of lieutenant colonel. A subsequent order modified the rank to major.—Ford, IV, pp. 789-791.

⁶² Webb, *Texas Rangers*, p. 185.

⁶³ On arriving in Brownsville, Ford's force was greeted by a company of home guards, under Captain Mifflin Kenedy, formed across the street in battle order. The rangers had been sighted from a church steeple and mistaken for the enemy.—Ford, IV, pp. 792-793.

[64] Webb, *Texas Rangers*, p. 186; for Heintzelman's report see *Difficulties on the Southwestern Frontier*, pp. 97-98.

[65] Ford, IV, pp. 805-806.

[66] Webb, *Texas Rangers*, p. 192.

[67] "Memorandum Book No. 3," *Lee Papers*, Library of Congress, Washington, D. C.

[68] Ford, IV, p. 820.

[69] For an excellent account of the whole Cortina War, including the inglorious feats of arms of the Brownsville Tigers, a civil guard organization, see Webb, *Texas Rangers*, pp. 175-192. Ford, IV, pp. 783-835, gives a spirited account from the viewpoint of an active participant.

[70] Richard King went to Kentucky to buy horses several times before the Civil War. Family stories indicate that he accompanied his family to Kentucky when Hiram Chamberlain, Jr., entered Centre College. Centre College records list a Hiram Chamberlain as "a non-graduate, year '59."

[71] In writing Ford's original orders to purchase supplies and raise troops for the Cortina campaign the important word "horses" was omitted. —Ford, IV, pp. 790-791.

[72] The claim found its way to a State Department file where it reposes to this day, unpaid.

[73] Webb, *Texas Rangers*, p. 193.

[74] Graf, I, p. 403.

[75] Same, pp. 400-401.

[76] Letter, "F. F. Fenn," June, 1860, Brownsville, "Gilbert D. Kingsbury Papers," Archives, University of Texas (hereafter cited as "Kingsbury Papers").

"F. F. Fenn" was the assumed name of Gilbert D. Kingsbury, who came to Brownsville in 1855. At the time he wrote this letter to his brother, "Fenn" was postmaster and deputy county clerk. His sympathies were with the Union. At the beginning of the Civil War he was removed from office and charged with treason. He escaped to the sanctuary of Matamoros. After the Civil War he resumed his proper name and moved to Central Texas.

[77] Richard King, "Deposition No. 125," *Memorial No. 230*, pp. 169-170.

[78] Kenedy sold an undivided interest of twelve leagues in the Las Mesteñas grant to the Salomé Ballí Young-McAllen estate, presumably to raise money for the new partnership.—"James K. Wells Papers," Archives, University of Texas (hereafter cited as "Wells Papers").

[79] Abstract of title to the Santa Gertrudis de la Garza grant, King Ranch vault.

[80] The expression the "Puerta de Agua Dulce" became common by local usage to designate an area west of Corpus Christi, the vicinity of the Agua Dulce Spanish grants and Agua Dulce Creek. No record of a land grant by this specific name has been found. It is probable that this terminology came about to designate the area where the old road leading out of Corpus Christi entered the Agua Dulce country and was, therefore, "La Puerta de Agua Dulce" or "the door to the Agua Dulce."—Robert C. Wells, Land and Tax Consultant, King Ranch.

[81] One of the documents attendant to the later dissolution of the firm stated the situation clearly:

This indenture . . . by and between Richard King of the first part, and Mifflin Kenedy of the second part . . . Witnesseth:—That whereas the said parties with James Walworth, now deceased, on the fifth day of December A. D. 1860, entered a partnership under the style of R. King & Co. for the purpose of Stockraising, and put into said partnership the cattle, horses, mules, sheep, goats and other stock belonging to them, as well as the tracts of land, known as Santa Gertrudis, Rincón de Santa Gertrudis or Mendiola Grant, and Agua Dulce situated in the County of Nueces, and State of Texas . . . —*Records of Real Estate*, Cameron County, Book B, pp. 120-123.

[82] Mrs. Minerva King Patch (granddaughter of Captain King) to Holland McCombs, March 7, 1952.

[83] Note in the handwriting of Hiram Chamberlain, King Ranch vault.

CHAPTER VIII

[1] Secessionists besieged Governor Houston to call a special session of the legislature. He refused and leaders of the movement organized a "People's Convention," composed of delegates from each representative district. This convention, completely extraofficial in beginning, convened January 28, 1861, and was then authorized by an extraordinary session of the legislature to act for the people provided the question of secession be submitted to popular vote. The election was called for February 23. The convention reconvened on March 2 to canvass the vote and the secession ordinance passed with a more than 3 to 1 majority. On March 5, 1861, the convention voted to unite Texas with the Confederate States of America.

[2] *The War of the Rebellion: Official Records of the Union and Confederate Armies* (hereafter cited as "*Official Army Records*"), Ser. I, Vol. I, pp. 503ff.

[3] Mrs. Caroline Baldwin Darrow, "Recollections of the Twiggs Surrender," *Battles and Leaders of the Civil War*, ed. by Robert U. Johnson and Clarence C. Buell (New York, 1887), I, pp. 35-36.

[4] *Official Army Records*, Ser. I, Vol. I, pp. 536ff.

[5] Ford, V, pp. 914-917, 998-1001.

Oran M. Roberts, leader of the secessionists, said of Ford's early activities on the Rio Grande:
I do believe that, but for his prudence and masterly management of the troops, and his address with the United States officers, the war would have opened there, before we had finally seceded, and very probably to our disadvantage . . . As soon as he got possession of the public property, on the Rio Grande, he set about establishing pacific relations with the Mexican authorities on the other side of the river. He did it with admirable skill.—Same, p. 996.

[6] "Accounts of M. Kenedy & Co. with H. E. Woodhouse, of Matamoros, November 1861— May 1863," *Account Books of H. E. Woodhouse.*—Courtesy of Harbert Davenport.

[7] Lieutenant Colonel Backus, commander of the Third Infantry at Ringgold Barracks, to Major F. J. Porter, Assistant Adjutant General, Fort Brown, February 6, 1861:
Company A, Third Infantry, leaves by land tomorrow and should be at Brownsville on the 11th. The baggage goes by steamer, and being an invalid I shall go by the same means . . . Our property is already on board the steamer *Mustang*, . . . —*Official Army Records*, Ser. II, Vol. I, p. 19.

[8] . . . up to the time of final annexation of Texas to the Southern Confederacy, the Lone Star flag, the former emblem of our independence as a Republic, was generally used all over the State in evidence of the almost universal desire to resume our State sovereignty.—*The Texas Almanac for 1862*, p. 16.

[9] Ford, V, pp. 931, 1003.
Having recd information of the commencement of hostilities between the Confederate States and the government of Mr. Lincoln and having learned that an expedition is sailing for the coast of Texas—supposed to be destined for Brazos Santiago—I request of you to allow the use of your steamers in transporting public property and stores from Brazos to this point . . . Your compliance will be a favor to the State of Texas and promotive to public good.—Headqrs. Rio Grande Mil Dist., Fort Brown, to Capt. M. Kenedy, Firm M. Kenedy & Co., Brownsville, April 18, 1861.—Courtesy Mrs. Harbert Davenport.

[10] When the Civil War came, King and Kenedy were recognized as Confederates. They had made common cause with the people with whom they had relations of business, friendship, and affection. Their steamboats were at the use of the Confederate forces. They performed many useful purposes for the South.—Ford, V, p. 893.

[11] Same, pp. 921-926.

[12] Same, p. 982.
Walworth apparently remained in Austin to serve on the Committee of Public Safety. In the records which have been examined, there has been no further mention of him until his death in Austin at the war's end.

[13] Graf, II, p. 556.

[14] Same, p. 474.

[15] McArthur, p. 204.

[16] Same, p. 74; *Prose and Poetry of the Live Stock Industry*, p. 395.

[17] Charles Stillman, Brownsville, to Capt. R. King, Santa Gertrudis, August 10, 1862.—King Ranch vault.

18 *Woodhouse Accounts.*

19 Graf, II, p. 453.

20 From Stillman's letters it is obvious that King had been in communication with Stillman prior to March, 1862, in regard to the purchase of Stillman's Laureles ranch, and Stillman was "open to any further proposition you may deem proper to make me for the property."—Stillman to King, March 18, 1862, King Ranch vault.

This land was acquired by the King Ranch after 1900. The purchase is discussed in Volume II of this work.

21 "Indenture between Richard King and Mifflin Kenedy, November 5, 1867," *Deed Records,* Cameron County, Supplemental Vol. B, pp. 120-123.

The Mann brands included the M which could have been the origin of the King Ranch's present brand, the Running W (see pages 257-258).

22 Pierce, pp. 36-38.

23 For a discussion of the unrest in Mexico and the diplomatic and military affairs leading up to the regime of Maximilian see Parks, pp. 242-258.

24 Pryor Lea, State Military Board Receiving Agent for the Brownsville area, urged that the route to the Rio Grande be divided into three parts: from Alleyton, end of the railroad line, to Goliad; from Goliad to King's Ranch on Santa Gertrudis Creek; from King's Ranch to the river.—Graf, II, p. 496.

25 In general this [see above] division of the route was adhered to not only by state cotton but also by Confederate and private cotton. King's Ranch became a great depot for cotton moving southward. From time to time the [State Military] board supplied King with funds with which to pay freight and incidental expenses on state cotton.—Same.

26 Stillman to King, February 25, 1862, King Ranch vault.

27 Same, March 11, 1862.

28 Graf, II, pp. 532, 685.

King & Kenedy [M. Kenedy & Co.] felt cramped in their transporting operations. They could not visit Brazos Santiago without being captured by the blockader. They consulted Ford in regard to placing their boats under the Mexican flag. He advised them to do so. The boats of that firm were then allowed to navigate the waters of the Gulf of Mexico and the Rio Grande. They were laden with freight intended for the government and the citizens of the Confederate States, and no one interfered.—Ford, V, p. 1005.

29 Rear Admiral David G. Farragut dispatched Commander Henry French and the *Albatross* to the mouth of the Rio Grande with a mission "of a most delicate character . . . to prevent the introduction of munitions of war . . . and the exit of cotton from Texas." Commander French examined many ships of many nations and expressed his frustration in a report to his superior:

This may be all honest but I do not believe it . . . My belief is that every ounce of this cotton comes from Brownsville, and only goes through the form of a transfer to Mexican merchants.—*The War of the Rebellion: Union and Confederate Navies* (hereafter cited as "*Official Navy Records*"), Ser. I, Vol. XIX, pp. 168, 180-181.

The American Consul at Matamoros wrote to Commander French on September 16, 1862:
As to the cotton, there is not one pound in fifty that ever belonged to a Mexican; neither is there one bale in ten that ever remained a week on Mexican soil.—Same, p. 295.

30 Stillman to King, March 18, 1862, King Ranch vault.

31 In reporting on his activities Ford wrote:
I would have been compelled to abandon the country to the enemy . . . I have been able to remain here only by means of the supplies for which the cotton was sold.—Ford, VI, p. 1094.

32 Jerome E. Brooks, *The Mighty Leaf* (Boston, 1952), p. 181.

33 For a detailed study of the Confederate cotton policy see Frank Lawrence Owsley, *King Cotton Diplomacy, Foreign Relations of the Confederate States of America* (Chicago, 1931).

34 John Warren Hunter, "The Fall of Browns-ville on the Rio Grande, November 1863," manuscript, Archives, University of Texas, p. 5.

Hunter was sixteen or seventeen years old when he secured a job as a teamster on the cotton road. He went from Hopkins County to "King's Ranch," then to Brownsville. He was on his way to Mexico to avoid conscription. He crossed over into Matamoros and remained there until the end of the war.

35 Federal Writers' Project, *San Antonio, An Authoritative Guide to the City and its Environs* (hereafter cited as "*San Antonio Guide*") (San Antonio, 1938), p. 30.

36 As quoted by F. H. Morse, U. S. Consul in London, to William H. Seward, U. S. Secretary of State, November 28, 1862, *Official Army Records*, Ser. III, Vol. II, pp. 948-949.

In many maps and records contemporary with the Civil War, including military corres-pondence, "Matamoros" will be found spelled with an "-as" ending. To avoid the possibility of confusion, in such cases occurring in quoted passages the ending has been changed to "-os" to conform with current spelling.

37 Carl Sandburg, *Abraham Lincoln, the War Years* (New York, 1939), II, p. 186.

38 Matamoros was the chief mart . . . Thousands of bales belonging to firms and individuals found their way to the same point . . . In passing by way of Banquete, and above there were cotton roads in every direction . . . The chaparral would be almost white in places from the lint detached from passing bales.—Ford, VI, pp. 1092-1093.

39 In the fall of 1862 various departments of the Confederacy started purchasing and collecting cotton in competition with each other. For the complicated story of Confederate finances see Owsley, pp. 384-417.

40 Hunter, pp. 4-6; *San Antonio Guide*, p. 30.

41 This was in Confederate money, "which at that time [1861] was current at par."—Hunter, p. 5.

42 James Arthur Lyon Fremantle, *The Fre-mantle Diary*, ed. by Walter Lord (Boston, 1954), p. 7.

Lieutenant Colonel James Fremantle, of the Coldstream Guards, was on military leave from the British army when he landed in Browns-ville April 2, 1863. He traveled across Texas, Louisiana, Mississippi, Georgia, Tennessee, Vir-ginia, and on to New York. He saw the Con-federacy at its high tide and kept an invaluable journal, a revealing firsthand picture of the South at war.

43 The following sources were used in compiling the table of cotton prices at the mouth of the Rio Grande: Stillman to King, August 10, 1862, King Ranch vault; General Magruder to Assist-ant Adjutant General, Trans-Mississippi De-partment, December 15, 1862, *Official Army Records*, Ser. I, Vol. XV, pp. 900-901; Fre-mantle, p. 7; Graf, II, p. 523; Hunter, p. 6.

44 The following sources were used in compiling the record of ships anchored at the mouth of the Rio Grande: Commander French to Ad-miral Farragut, September 8, 1862, *Official Navy Records*, Ser. I, Vol. XIX, pp. 180-181; Fremantle, p. 6; Graf, II, pp. 533-534; Pierce, p. 55.

Frank C. Pierce, who was on the scene at the time, reported:

From 200 to 300 vessels ranging in size from a 20-ton schooner to a 2000-ton steamship were constantly an-chored three or four miles from its [Bagdad's] beach, while hundreds of laborers engaged as lightermen in bringing merchandise across the bar from the Gulf to the harbor in the river, enlivened the town.

45 Hunter, pp. 7-8.

46 On September 18, 1862, Commander French wrote Admiral Farragut:

. . . the only way to prevent it [the cotton trade under the subterfuge of Mexican ownership] will be to occupy Fort Brown with a small force. If there was sufficient water on the bar I would not hesitate to go up there. There are only about 20 soldiers in the Fort, no guns, and no other troops near them.—*Official Navy Records*, Ser. I, Vol. XIX, p. 295.

It was just as well for Commander French that he did not put his proposal to test. His idea was that "the Mexican steamer which brings cotton out of the river could . . . be easily chartered or bought" for use as a Union gunboat. Doubtless he would have found an incredibly high price on the M. Kenedy & Co.-controlled river steamer.

47 In Corpus Christi the war took on more the aspect of comic opera than mortal conflict. On August 7, 1862, the Federal blockaders demanded the surrender of the town; the demand was refused. The blockaders began to bombard. A cannon ball passed through a saloon, much to the annoyance of one of the occupants.

Felix A. Blucher, Captain King's surveyor for the Santa Gertrudis grant, was now a Confederate major. He gathered a few companions and headed for the beach and an old cannon. Major Blucher eyed the ship. "I believe I'll take a pop at it," he said. The shot barely missed. "I believe I'll take another one," Blucher decided. After that one the Yankee ship departed.—"Robert Adams Memoirs," La Retama Public Library, Corpus Christi.

For other accounts and anecdotes see Mc-Campbell, *Saga of a Frontier Seaport*, pp. 24-25; Mrs. Mary A. Sutherland, *The Story of Corpus Christi* (Corpus Christi, 1916), pp. 111-115.

48 For reports on the capture of Galveston by the Union fleet see *Official Army Records*, Ser. I, Vol. XV, pp. 147-153.

49 J. Thomas Scharf, *History of the Confederate States Navy . . .* (New York, 1887), pp. 504-517. For official reports and military correspondence on the recapture of Galveston by Confederate forces see *Official Army Records*, Ser. I, Vol. XV, pp. 199-227.

50 Ford was temporarily relieved by Colonel P. N. Luckett and then by General H. P. Bee.

51 I regard him [Ford] as unquestionably the very best military man that we had in Texas at the time of the war, and so I believe he was generally regarded by those who were well acquainted with him. He should

have been in the field, and "Old Rip," as his frontier boys called him, would have made his mark. For unlike most of our frontier officers he had studied war as a science, has a fine military library, and had for years devoted himself to it.—Oran S. Roberts, as quoted by Ford, V, p. 995.

52 General Magruder to James A. Seddon, January 6, 1863, *Official Army Records*, Ser. I, Vol. XV, pp. 932-933.

53 Sutherland, pp. 132-133.

54 Hunter, pp. 5-6; "Robert Adams Memoirs."

55 From available correspondence between Stillman and Captain King as well as remarks by contemporaries, it is obvious that King operated the Santa Gertrudis end of the cotton transportation. In the early stages of organizing the depot and managing the ranch, he was so out of contact with the outside world that Stillman took pains to bring him up to date on news of the world and the market situation.

56 Fremantle, pp. 33-34.

57 General Magruder to General Cooper, March 31, 1863, *Official Army Records*, Ser. I, Vol. XV, pp. 1030-1032.

58 Magruder to Cooper, June 8, 1863, same, Ser. I, Vol. XXVI, Pt. II, p. 63.

59 Major Russell to Lieutenant Colonel McNeil, May 4, 1863, same, Ser. I, Vol. XV, pp. 1073-1074.

60 There are many sources and tables available on the depreciation of Confederate currency, but perhaps the most contemporary and graphic example is Colonel Fremantle's journal notation of receiving on April 13, 1863, "four times the value of my gold in Confederate notes." At Charleston, two months later, he was offered six to one; at Richmond, two weeks after Charleston, he was offered eight to one.—Fremantle, p. 22.

61 As part of his labor in fulfilling the Confederate contract Captain King took on the title and duties of a Quartermaster's Agent and shortly had occasion to worry about compliance with official orders. On May 27, 1863, he wrote Quartermaster Simeon Hart:

Sir: It is my duty to report to you that a very large number of wagons, loaded with cotton for Brownsville, belonging to private persons, and driven by conscript teamsters, have passed my ranch since the date of General Magruder's Orders, No. 65, on the subject of such transportation. Daily and hourly such wagons and teams, which, by the department orders, properly pertain to the Government service, are passing my place without regard to the commanding general's order on the subject.

There is no force at my ranch, nor elsewhere on the route, so far as I know, by which the regulations on this matter can be enforced. Of course, it is out of my power to stop them and turn them over for the service of the Government, but it does seem essential that some prompt and efficient action should be taken by the proper military authorities to carry out General Magruder's orders.

Very respectfully, &c.,

R. KING,
Quartermaster's Agent.

On June 9 an order was issued that two regiments, Colonel Wood's and Colonel Buchel's "will remain at or in the vicinity of King's Ranch." These units were later removed to support the Texas coast after the fall of Vicksburg.—*Official Army Records,* Ser. I, Vol. XXVI, Pt. II, pp. 18-19, 42.

[62] Major Russell to Lieutenant Colonel McNeil, May 4, 1863, same, Ser. I, Vol. XV, pp. 1073-1074.

[63] General Bee to Captain Edmund P. Turner, June 23, 1863, same, Ser. I, Vol. XXVI, Pt. II, pp. 78-79.

[64] The complexity of the cotton business and the trials and tribulations of military supply on the Rio Grande are reflected in the reply to a letter from General Bee about paying for the cargoes of three British ships that were off Bagdad:

You [Bee] say that you deduct 3,000 bales of cotton from the amount at the Rio Grande and arriving there, as the probable amount that will belong to the State, to associations for the benefit of soldiers' families, to planters expecting to buy supplies, &c., and that the whole amount is about 11,000 bales. This will leave about 8,000 bales at your disposal. These quantities are modified . . . the tax law . . . This will give us 880 bales, for under this law there is no exemption either

for State, foreign, or any other cotton. Of this 240 is derived from the 3,000 bales belonging to the planters and State, and we have 7,380 at our service.

Now, if one-half of this belongs to foreigners, the other half, 3,690, will be the available quantity on hand with which to send back the three vessels, each with a load of cotton . . . but you say that cotton is only worth about 20 cents per pound in market at Brownsville, and that the teamsters were promised 16 cents per pound in gold by their employers, and that you offered them 8 cents per pound, but that they refused this, and have remained unpaid. The major-general commanding understands that cotton is now worth 25 cents per pound in Brownsville.—Captain Turner to General Bee, July 29, 1863, same, pp. 122-125.

[65] General Magruder to General Cooper, June 8, 1863, same, pp. 57-65.

[66] Pierce, p. 42.

[67] Same, pp. 41-42.
Colonel Fremantle came across Montgomery's body shortly after landing at Bagdad:

He had been slightly buried, but his head and arms were above the ground, his arms tied together, the rope still round his neck, but part of it still dangling from quite a small mesquite tree. Dogs or wolves had probably scraped the earth from the body, and there was no flesh on the bones . . .

I understand this Montgomery was a man of very bad character, and that, confiding in the neutrality of the Mexican soil, he was in the habit of calling the Confederates all sorts of insulting epithets from the Bagdad bank of the river; and a party of his *renegados* had also crossed over and killed some unarmed cotton teamsters, which had roused the fury of the Confederates.—Fremantle, pp. 8-9.

[68] General Bee to Captain Turner, October 28, 1863, *Official Army Records,* Ser. I, Vol. XXIV, Pt. I, pp. 448-449.

[69] Fred E. Starck to Harbert Davenport.

[70] Adrian Vidal was captured and court-martialed in Mexico in 1865 by the Imperialists, "presumably for treason, and was executed pursuant to the findings of the court-martial." — Harbert Davenport to Holland McCombs, November 20, 1952.

[71] General Bee to Captain Turner, October 28, 1863, *Official Army Records,* Ser. I, Vol. XXVI, Pt. I, pp. 448-449.

⁷² "Some of them very large," according to General Bee's official report of November 5, 1863, same, p. 433.

⁷³ "Strength and composition of the Rio Grande Expedition, October 31, 1863," same, p. 398.

⁷⁴ For official reports and correspondence, both Union and Confederate, on the affair see "October 27–December 2, 1863. The Rio Grande Expedition, and operations on the coast of Texas," same, pp. 395-447.

⁷⁵ General Bee to Assistant Adjutant General, November 8, 1863, same, p. 434.

John Warren Hunter's account gives an idea of the magnitude ot the rumors and misinformation:

On the morning of November 3, 1863, a runner brought the startling news that a Federal fleet had appeared off Brazos Santiago 15 miles distant from Brownsville and that 50,000 men were being landed, infantry, cavalry and artillery and that a cavalry force of at least 4000 troops was approaching the defenseless city.—Hunter, p. 9.

⁷⁶ General Bee to Assistant Adjutant General, November 8, 1863, *Official Army Records,* Ser. I, Vol. XXVI, Pt. I, pp. 448-449.

⁷⁷ J. A. Quintero to Hon. Judge P. Benjamin, November 26, 1863, same, Ser. I, Vol. XXXIV, Pt. II, pp. 888-890.

⁷⁸ General Bee to Assistant Adjutant General, November 8, 1863, same, Ser. I, Vol. XXVI, Pt. I, pp. 448-449.

⁷⁹ Hunter, p. 12.

⁸⁰ In his official report to the Assistant Adjutant General, General Bee said "peril was around me on all sides."

⁸¹ General Banks to General Halleck, November 6, 1863, *Official Army Records,* Ser. I, Vol. XXVI, Pt. I, pp. 399-401.

⁸² See the accounts of William Neale and John Warren Hunter for contemporary descriptions of events.

Neale, quoting from his journal for November 3, 1863, charged that General Bee was "pretty high from the effects of champagne"

consumed at Henry Miller's convivial establishment when he ordered the firing of Fort Brown. —Chatfield, p. 15.

Hunter commented: "The rear-guard—if such it may be called—left the city, followed by the fierce imprecations of a maddened, betrayed people whose only safety now lay in sudden and precipitate flight to Matamoros."—Hunter, pp. 12-13.

⁸³ Hunter, pp. 12-15.

⁸⁴ Same, p. 16.

⁸⁵ Graf, II, p. 593.

⁸⁶ Chatfield, p. 13.

⁸⁷ Official correspondence and translations of various proclamations issued by Cobos, Ruiz and Cortina will be found in *Official Army Records,* Ser. I, Vol. XXVI, Pt. II, pp. 399-409.

The rapidity with which the situation progressed can be indicated by extracts from the letters written by the commanding general of the Union forces and the United States Consul in Matamoros:

NOVEMBER 6, 10 P.M.—"On the evening of the 5th, after the arrival of our troops, Cobos crossed the river . . . and took possession of Matamoros." *General Banks.*

NOVEMBER 7—"We anticipate a riot (or what is called, in Mexican phraseology, a revolution) to-night, and I am fearful . . ."—*L. Pierce, Jr., United States Consul.*

NOVEMBER 7, 8 P.M.—"Another revolution occurred to-day in Matamoros. General Cortinas . . . seized the reins."—*General Banks.*

NOVEMBER 9—"Three revolutions have occurred in Matamoros, . . . The first was adverse to the interests of Mexico and the United States. Everything is now as favorable as could be desired."—*General Banks.*

The invading Union forces had only to stand by and wait—anxiously—for the political situation in Matamoros to turn to their advantage.

⁸⁸ General Banks to General Halleck, November 9, 1863, same, p. 405.

³⁹ General Banks to General Halleck, November 18, 1863, same, pp. 409-410.

⁹⁰ Rev. Hiram Chamberlain San Patricio, to Lieutenant Colonel E. F. Gray, Third Texas

Infantry, January 1, 1864, "Report of a Raid on The King Ranch During Civil War," *The Kingsville Record,* July 3, 1929, as quoted from the *Houston Tri-Weekly Telegram,* February 1, 1864.

91 Colonel Duff to Aide-de-Camp and Acting Assistant Adjutant General, November 11, 1863, *Official Army Records,* Ser. I, Vol. XXVI, Pt. I, pp. 439-443.

92 Hunter, pp. 18-19.

93 General Bee to Captain Turner, November 12, 1863, *Official Army Records,* Ser. I, Vol. XXVI, Pt. II, pp. 408-409.

94 Major Benavides to General Bee, November 12, 1863, same, p. 409.

95 General Magruder to General Smith, December 24, 1863, same, p. 530.

96 General Dana to General Banks, November 21, 1863, same, Pt. I, pp. 414-415.

97 Same.

98 General Dana to General Stone, December 24, 1863, same, pp. 876-878.

General Dana was suggesting to his chief of staff that the base of Union operations be changed from Brownsville to Corpus Christi, hoping to get at a thorn which had developed in the Santa Gertrudis area:

From my spies, I am pretty well satisfied that there is now in the vicinity of King's ranch a body of 150 well-armed and well-mounted Texans. [Captain James Richardson's force of irregular cavalry organized by Captain King] Their horses are in fine condition, and they are on the other side of the sand desert, which is 30 miles wide and devoid of water. They are very much on the alert, and scout actively, besides having spies between them and us, with orders to signalize our approach by smokes or otherwise.

99 "Report of Col. Charles Black, . . . of expedition to Rio Grande City," same, pp. 423-424.

100 General Dana to General Stone, December 2, 1863, same, p. 830.

101 Dana attempted to foist the Benavides problem off on the Mexican government. On De-

cember 1 he wrote the United States Consul at Matamoros:

Benavides escaped across the river . . . Now, is he a Mexican or a Texan? . . . If he is a Texan, I shall demand him, as a renegade, for punishment. If he is a Mexican, it must be looked to that he answers properly to the Mexican authorities . . . I have full confidence that our friends of the Mexican nation will not object to helping us.—Same, p. 830.

He was working on the "King's ranch" problem with spies and non-military personnel. On December 11 he reported to the Chief of Staff that he had sent two spies to the ranch and "accepted the services of a refugee, by the name of McManus," for the purpose of "getting up a panic about the danger of the roads."—Same, p. 843.

McManus was apparently an "irregular," devoid of military status and low on funds. Dana had to furnish him with such a common item of border dress as a pistol.

102 General Dana to M. M. Kimmey, December 18, 1863, same, p. 865.

103 General Dana to General Banks, November 21, 1863, same, pp. 414-415.

104 General Dana to General Stone, December 24, 1863, same, p. 877.

105 General Dana to General Banks, December 24, 1863, same, p. 876.

106 Sources for the Union raid on the King Ranch are Alvarado's "Memoirs;" Rev. Hiram Chamberlain to Lieutenant Colonel Gray, as cited; Mrs. Lennie E. Stubblefield to Holland McCombs; Sutherland, p. 43.

107 Richard King to Major General Giles S. Smith, September 15, 1865, *Wells Papers.*

108 Only scraps of evidence are available to reveal Captain King's activities during these strident days. From the statement of Mrs. John Fitch to Mrs. Lennie E. Stubblefield, King fled from the Santa Gertrudis to Mexico. He returned as soon as possible to plague the marauding Union forces who were using his beeves as a supply source.

[109] Numerous letters, both Confederate and Union, will be found in the *Official Army Records* testifying to the trials and tribulations of the cotton trade.

[110] Graf, II, p. 685.

[111] General Dana to General Stone, January 7, 1864, *Official Army Records*, Ser. I, Vol. XXXIV, Pt. II, pp. 38-40.

[112] Colonel Ford to Captain Turner, December 25, 1863, same, Vol. XXVI, Pt. II, p. 535.

[113] In a communication dated December 19, Ford was authorized to organize "as many companies for special service for three months in the west" as he might be able to raise.—Same, n.b., p. 543.

[114] Captain Turner to Colonel Ford, December 22, 1863, same, pp. 525-526.

[115] Upon receipt of official authorization and instructions from General Magruder's headquarters, Ford was already in San Antonio engaged in a recruiting campaign for the "Cavalry of the West," presumably as Texas volunteers. After orders from Confederate headquarters urging secrecy the organization was designated as "Expeditionary Forces."—Ford, VI, p. 1047.

[116] Colonel Ford to Captain Turner, December 27, 1863, *Official Army Records*, Ser. I, Vol. XXVI, Pt. II, pp. 543-544.

[117] Ford, VI, p. 1050.

[118] Pierce, pp. 47-48.

[119] General Dana to General Stone, January 7, 1864, *Official Army Records*, Ser. I, Vol. XXXIV, Pt. II, p. 38.

[120] Ford, VI, pp. 1037-1038.

[121] By the end of the war it was estimated that 200,000 cattle, many of them bearing brands of owners as remote as the northern banks of the Colorado, had come into this country.—Graf, II, p. 473.

Before the days of fenced ranges, a severe winter inevitably caused drifting cattle and "die-ups," dreaded by cattlemen and welcomed by skinners who had no cattle. The winter of 1884-1885 resulted in what was probably the greatest drift in history; the two blizzard years of 1886 and 1887 were undoubtedly the most disastrous for cattlemen. For an account of drifts, see Dobie, *The Longhorns*, pp. 195-202.

[122] Colonel Ford to Captain Turner, December 29, 1863, *Official Army Records*, Ser. I, Vol. XXVI, Pt. II, pp. 560-561; Ford, VI, pp. 1041, 1048-1049.

[123] Colonel Ford to General Magruder, February 17, 1864, as quoted by Ford, VI, p. 1050.

[124] Same, V, p. 894.

[125] Same, VI, 1056-1058.

[126] Same, V, pp. 1012-1013.

[127] The original contract was for six months beginning June 1. Because of the shortage of supplies it became necessary for General Bee to call "at once for three months' supplies, even before their contract commenced," leaving only half to be completed before Bee's retreat from Brownsville.

[128] Ford, VI, pp. 1070-1071.

[129] Same, V, p. 1012.

[130] On July 7, 1864, Ford wrote the chief of staff that "Stillman declines filling the contract entered into with Captain King." Back in December Stillman's ranch had furnished the Union forces with horses; the letter does not clarify whether by purchase or impressment. Stillman arranged through George W. Brackenridge to visit General Dana, commander of the Union forces. — *Official Army Records*, Ser. I, Vol. XXVI, Pt. I, pp. 842-844.

[131] King could pull off those contracts because the people along the route trusted him and he could get teams and stopover places.—Harbert Davenport.

[132] Ford, V, p. 1011.

[133] Same, p. 1012.

[134] In a letter dated February 11, 1864, General F. J. Herron, commander at Brownsville, reported to his corps commander:

A majority of the merchants in Matamoros have large amounts due them . . . and will furnish both money and arms . . . One merchant, Belden, has already sent a large number of pistols to Col. Benavides at Laredo, and the clique to which he belongs confidently asserts that Ford will have this place within forty days. —*Official Army Records,* Ser. I, Vol. XXXIV, Pt. II, pp. 295-298.

This action by the merchants was perhaps in answer to Ford's complaint late in December that "no arrangement has been made to furnish funds for the expedition."—Same, Ser. I, Vol. XXVI, Pt. II, p. 561. However, on August 17, 1864, he reported "this command had not been paid either in Confederate notes or in coin."— Ford, VI, p. 1111.

135 Ford, V, p. 1011.

136 Same, pp. 1013-1014.

137 Same, VI, p. 1106.

138 Same, V, pp. 1015-1017.

139 Same, p. 1017.

140 Same, p. 1018.

141 Special Order No. 115, Hdqrs. Expdy. Forces, Fort Brown, August 11, 1864.—Courtesy Mrs. Harbert Davenport.

> Capt. Watson . . . will proceed with his company and station it as courier to King's Rancho, in following manner.
>
> Brownsville 6 men, Anaquito 6 men, Tajitos 8 men, Santa Rosa 8 men, King's Ranch 6 men. He will make his own Hdqrs at some conv. point for superintending the line.
>
> II. He will keep his horses well picketed and constantly in hand. Two men will travel together from station to station, due diligence will be used in arresting & sending to headquarters any person or persons travelling on or near this route without proper papers. The driving of stock without the proper authority is also prohibited and all stock thus taken will be reported to headquarters at once.
>
> The express will be carried thro with all possible dispatch and couriers receiving dispatch will see that the time of departure be noted on outside of packages.
>
> J. S. Ford

142 L. G. Aldrich to Colonel Ford, March 21, 1864, *Official Army Records,* Ser. I, Vol. XXIV, Pt. II, p. 1068.

143 Pierce, p. 49.

144 Ford, V, p. 1028.

145 Same, pp. 893-894.

146 Same, VI, p. 1108.

147 Brownsville was recovered and the line of the Rio Grande reoccupied, owing purely to the ability and personal influence of Colonels Santos Benavides and John S. Ford. No sooner was this accomplished, however, than the Confederate command in the Trans-Mississippi Department began to interfere. General Drayton was sent from San Antonio to supersede Ford. Drayton was relieved by Brigadier General James E. Slaughter.—Harbert Davenport to Holland McCombs.

148 Pierce, pp. 50-51; Ford, VI, pp. 1127-1143, 1146-1160.

149 Same, p. 1143.

150 Same, p. 1044.

151 Same, p. 1143.

152 Same, VI, pp. 1144-1145; VII, p. 1195.

153 Reams of Confederate correspondence testify to the confusion of policy.

154 For Ford's account of his meeting with General Wallace see his *Memoirs,* VII, pp. 1174-1189.

155 Harbert Davenport to Charles Edmands, December 27, 1945.

156 Ford, VII, p. 1190.

157 Same, V, p. 1024; VI, p. 1129. Ford wrote: "The writer never heard anything more inspiriting."

158 Same, V, p. 1031; VII, pp. 1191ff.

CHAPTER IX

1 See, for example, John N. Edwards, *Shelby and His Men* (Cincinnati, 1867), pp. 532-551.

2 For Sheridan's official orders see General Grant to General Sheridan, May 17, 1865, *Official Army Records,* Ser. I, Vol. XLVIII, Pt. II, p. 476.

3 The day before Grant issued orders to Sheridan he had received a letter from General Lew Wallace reporting that General E. Kirby Smith had refused to surrender and urged his soldiers to hold out and that there was "a secret arrangement existing between the Mexican Imperialists and the Texan Confederates."—Same, p. 457.

4   General Sheridan to General Grant, June 28, 1865, same, p. 1015; Pierce, p. 54.

5   Ford, VII, p. 1213.

6   Same, pp. 1197-1199.

7   Same, V, pp. 896-897.

8   Richard King to Major General Giles S. Smith, September 15, 1865, *Wells Papers.*

9   *San Antonio Express,* April 15, 1885. This was a portion of a dispatch written for the *Express* by John S. Ford a few days before the death of Captain King. It was included as a part of Captain King's obituary notice.

10 Following the death of James Walworth, Jane M. Walworth, widow, signed a release to Mifflin Kenedy and Richard King of all of Walworth's interests in the partnership for $50,000. The conveyance shows that Walworth was a member of the firms King and Walworth, M. Kenedy & Co., and R. King & Co.—"Release," dated May 10, 1865, filed September 17, 1866, *Deed Records of Nueces County,* Vol. H, p. 396; *Transcribed Deed Records of Kleberg County,* Vol. A, p. 245.

There is no mention in the document of Charles Stillman, indicating that he was not involved.

11 Graf, II, p. 685; a letter from the French Legation to the Secretary of State, October 19, 1865, places the *Señorita* as having been in use for the Imperialist cause since July.—*Official Army Records,* Ser. I, Vol. XLVIII, Pt. II, p. 1241.

12 The army was short on transportation, particularly shallow-draft vessels. Presumably the quartermaster did not have operational personnel for those which had been seized and was just as glad to have them in the hands of their former owners where they could be chartered for use.

13 General Granger to General Sheridan, June 19, 1865, *Official Army Records,* Ser. I, Vol. XLVIII, Pt. II, pp. 927-928.

14 Pierce, p. 56.
According to the Brownsville *Daily Ranchero,* November 8, 1865, the *Antonio* and the *Eugenia* were rigged out by the Imperialists as "gunboats." The *Antonio* was commanded by "Anderson," the *Eugenia* by "Col. Rubio."

15 A legal paper filed by Captain King in regard to insurance of a cargo on the *Camargo* which was involved in an accident on August 14, 1865, places this steamboat as having been in use on that date. The paper was among old records kept in the patio of Francisco Ytúrria's office, Brownsville.

16 Joseph Kleiber told of the Verlanders having chartered "their two new steamboats," the *Enterprise* and *El Primero,* to the quartermaster in a letter written September 30, 1865.—Kleiber to Forstall, *Joseph K. Kleiber Letters, 1860-1877,* (hereafter cited as "*Kleiber Letters*") Archives, University of Texas.

According to the bills of sale, which are among the *Wells Papers,* these two boats had been "built at the mouth of the Rio Grande in about the month of August A.D. 1865." King and Kenedy purchased them in February, 1866.

17 M. Kenedy & Co. were not only chartering steamers to the United States Quartermaster, they were selling and chartering vessels for use of the Imperialists under Mejía. Also, some of their vessels were in the use of the *Juarista* forces. The banker, Francisco Ytúrria, partner and front for M. Kenedy & Co., was an ardent Imperialist, knighted by Maximilian. He was obviously the contact man with Mejía for M. Kenedy & Co.

In later years Captain William Kelly prepared a list of their boats and noted that they owned "twelve boats for the lower river," ocean-going lighters, and "four boats for the upper river." Presumably this ownership was as of 1866 when Kelly worked for King and Kenedy.

18 ". . . there is now very little private freight, not enough for one boat; and the rates are 25¢ per bbl either way. This low rate of freight is a fair sample of how every other business now is."—Kleiber to Forstall, September 30, 1865. In another letter, Kleiber to Garey, October 3,

1865, Kleiber wrote "we do not sell $100 a week. . . . My expenses are enormous."—*Kleiber Letters.*

19 Shortly after coming to the border in 1912, Harbert Davenport met an escapee from the Battle of El Convoy, a former member of the virtually annihilated Austrian regiment which was involved on the Imperialist side. According to the Austrian's story, *Juarista* Colonel Servando Canales had been assigned to harass the convoy on its way to Monterrey. He had contacted the commander of the Imperialist cavalry, convinced him that since the Emperor could not raise funds to pay his troops the Empire was obviously nearing its end. The cavalry had only to change flags and they could pay themselves out of the rich cargo they were guarding. The argument was convincing; the opportunity was at hand.

At dawn on June 16, the wagon train found the *Juaristas* deployed across the road to Mier. The Imperialists advanced—the Austrian regiment on the right wing, Mexican infantry in the center and the larger force of Mexican cavalry on the left. The cavalrymen wheeled and opened a devastating cross fire on their erstwhile comrades-in-arms. By noon they were collecting their back pay in boots, shoes, woolens, silks and satins while they refreshed themselves with wines and brandies, consumed preserved meats and other delicacies, and topped it off with the finest cigars—courtesy of the merchants of Matamoros.

20 Stillman did not abandon his interests on the border or leave them untended. For example, Antonio Yznaga represented him in the cattle business after his departure. In 1871 Robert Carson, of Brownsville, took over his numerous business interests, including the plotting of 1200 acres into city lots and acting as agent for the tract of land on which La Sal del Rey is located. —Chatfield, p. 20.

The Stillman heirs continued to maintain business ventures in Brownsville under local management until 1921, when Homer Fitch made a bloc purchase of their interests. Joseph K. Wells was Fitch's attorney.—Robert C. Wells.

21 Biographical material on Charles Stillman came from a manuscript by Harbert Davenport.

22 Graf, II, p. 687.

23 General Sheridan, "Report . . . of Operations on Rio Grande after May 29, 1865," dated November 14, 1866, *Official Army Records,* Ser. I, Vol. XLVIII, Pt. I, pp. 297-303.

24 "Indebted Railroads," *Records of the Office of the Quartermaster General,* Pkg. No. 13, R.G. 92, National Archives.

25 The purchase was consumated May 10, 1865. —*Supplemental Records of Real Estate,* Cameron County, Book A, pp. 180-181.

26 "Indebted Railroads," as cited. The railroad was repossessed by the Quartermaster Department on March 2, 1867.

27 The railroad was sold on August 31, 1868, to the Indianola Railroad for $10,000, presumably for salvage.—Same.

28 Graf, II, p. 689.

This was not the first charter to be granted for a railroad in this area. On February 7, 1853, a charter was granted to a "group of Brownsville people among whom were Charles Stillman, J. A. Thompson, William P. Converse and Samuel A. Belden" for the Brownsville and Rio Grande Railway Company, to run "from a suitable point on the Laguna Madre to such a point on the Rio Grande up and down the river by way of 'Sal de Ray' as the Company may deem proper." The railroad was never built.— S. G. Reed, *A History of the Texas Railroads and of Transportation Conditions under Spain and Mexico and The Republic and The State* (Houston, 1941), pp. 466-467.

29 It may be that this [the railroad for which King and Kenedy had a charter] did not appeal to them as they were buying land in that section then for about $10.00 a league.—Same, p. 467.

This was the Potrero del Espíritu Santo grant (see map Appendix I).

30 Graf, II, p. 689. See, for example, "Mexican Border Railroad," a letter signed by John N. Singer, April 6, 1867, published in the *Houston Telegraph.*—"Brazos-Santiago R.R.," *Records of the Office of the Quartermaster General,* National Archives.

31 Reed, p. 467; "The Rio Grande Railroad," Chatfield, pp. 11-12; Allhands, *Gringo Builders,* pp. 110-112.

32 Had the suit been won the railroad would have been compelled to haul freight to the center of the city in oxcarts or by burro. E. J. Davis, later Reconstruction governor, won the case for the railroad.

33 Documents and letters in the *Wells Papers* indicate that Mifflin Kenedy filed suit in 1875. Accumulating complications, the affair dragged on for some time, egged on by a very stubborn Kenedy. The Woodhouse firm was responsible for the railroad's bills. In 1872 King and Kenedy had advanced $1,245 to the Woodhouse company to pay for a shipment of rails. The railroad was in receivership and refused to pay. To add to the complication, Stephen Powers, the King-Kenedy lawyer, was acting attorney for the railroad.

This difficulty in collection undoubtedly contributed to Kenedy's cantankerous frame of mind when the right-of-way question came up. In January, 1879, King and Kenedy sued the railroad for trespassing or building track on their land. By September, 1879, they had secured judgment against the railroad company and payments were scheduled to effect complete payment by October 16. A deed to the right-of-way was signed by King and Kenedy and mailed to Stephen Powers on September 21, 1879.

34 Graf, II, p. 685.

35 Eyewitness accounts of the hurricane can be found in Chatfield, pp. 10, 15. Joseph Kleiber reported on the financial devastation to A. M. Kleiber on November 5, 1867.—*Kleiber Letters.*

36 After September, 1868, Robert Dalzell is mentioned frequently in the press in connection with steamboats, rather than Kenedy and King. The change apparently dates from September 9, 1868, when the Brownsville *Daily Ranchero* carried the notice that "Capt. R. Dalzell and wife have returned from their trip to the north."

37 In "Articles of Agreement" entered into with Lieutenant Colonel James A. Ekin, Deputy Quartermaster General, on January 17, 1871, King and Kenedy agreed to transport between Brazos Santiago and Fort Brown at fifty cents per hundred pounds and between Ringgold Barracks and Fort Brown for eighty-five cents per hundred pounds. The contract was to run for the first half of the year 1871 and King and Kenedy posted a $30,000 performance bond.—"Kenedy and King Contract, Jan. 17, 1871," *Records of the Office of the Quartermaster General,* National Archives.

38 The folder for the year 1874 in the *Wells Papers* contains correspondence relative to the stockholders' meeting but no indication of the exact terms of the agreement.

39 Mr. Kelly succeeded to the business of King, Kenedy & Co., in 1874, since which time he has run the steamboating business on a constantly descending scale. From a fleet of twelve steamboats on the lower river and four on the upper, run constantly to their utmost, the "Bessie," making two trips a month (when there is water enough to float her), from Brownsville to Rio Grande City. . . . Mr. Kelly is prepared to abandon his last steamboat.—Chatfield, p. 21.

Chatfield's paper, published in January, 1893, carried a brave quarter-page advertisement for the *Bessie,* but one and a half pages were devoted to railroad advertising.

40 Acreage owned by R. King & Co. as of 1866 has been computed from the property inventory contained in the indenture, dated November 5, 1867, between King and Kenedy which was the initial formal step toward the dissolution of their partnership.—Filed December 16, 1867, *Deed Records of Nueces County,* Vol. H, p. 573; *Transcribed Deed Records of Kleberg County,* Vol. A, p. 254.

The property listed in the inventory consisted of the following tracts and grants of land: El Rincón de Santa Gertrudis, 3½ leagues; Santa Gertrudis de la Garza ("being the tract whereon is situated the principal residence and the improvements connected therewith"), 12 leagues; Puerta de Agua Dulce, 5½ leagues; San Leandro, 2 leagues; El Saus, 3⅛ leagues; El Paistle, 5 leagues; "a tract of land adjoining the said Rincón de Agua Dulce on the north," 7500 acres; and several additional small tracts, some of undesignated area, totaling more than a thousand acres.

It is interesting to note that as the steps toward the liquidation of the partnership proceeded to its final stage the inventory of property became more specific in its detail. See Appendix VII for the "Agreement and Final Settlement of Affairs of R. King & Co."

Also note the acreage totals contained in Richard King's petition before the United States Commissioners to Texas, dated August 28, 1872 (Appendix VIII). By that time *agostadero* Santa Gertrudis, containing the headquarters, had grown by the acquisition of adjacent areas as King persisted in his policy of buying land.

41 This indenture was also recorded in Cameron County on November 13, 1867, *Records of Real Estate*, Cameron County, Book B, pp. 120-123.

42 "Partnership agreement between King and Kenedy, Nov. 5, 1867," King Ranch vault.

43 "Articles of Agreement and Settlement between R. King and M. Kenedy," May 31, 1868, King Ranch vault.

44 The warranty deed, dated June 3, 1868, was acknowledged on that same day by Ol Ferish, Clerk, Galveston. It was recorded July 27, 1868, Book I, pp. 66ff.—Abstract of title.

45 Graf, II, p. 476.

46 At the early part of the Civil War quite a number of stockraisers carried large herds of cattle south of the Nueces River. They squatted on the lands of others. . . . The cessation of hostilities did not change the situation materially. The squatters remained, also their stock upon the bosoms of the prairies. Those holding titles to these broad acres complained that they were deprived of the use of property they had owned for many years. For these, and other reasons, landholders in that part of Texas conceived the idea of enclosing their lands by fences. Capt. Kenedy was a pioneer in the matter of building pasture fences. . . . This [the Laureles Ranch] soon became a place of note, others followed suit. The actuating motive was self-protection.—Ford, V, pp. 895-896.

Kenedy advertised his intent in the November 12, 1868, issue of the *Corpus Christi Advertiser:*

> By the first of Dec. next, my line of fence, extending from the Oso to the Laureles Creek, will be completed, and my lands below and southeast of said fence will be completely enclosed.
> Owners of such stocks . . . now at large on my lands, will therefore oblige me by causing the same to be driven off and removed beyond and outside of my said enclosure.

47 The fence cost from $500 to $1000 per mile. —*Prose and Poetry of the Live Stock Industry,* p. 83. The fence was constructed of 1 x 6 x 20 planks, freighted from Corpus Christi by wagon. Vincente Patino was King's *caporal* for the fencing project. "He put three boards on the fence, and when the pasture was ready, . . . The division began."—Alvarado.

48 Mifflin Kenedy, "Deposition No. 90," *Memorial No. 230,* p. 138.

49 Mifflin Kenedy to Richard M. Kleberg, Sr., as quoted to Holland McCombs.

50 In a record book which belonged to Mrs. Robert J. Kleberg is the notation under the heading "Information given by John G. Kenedy":

> . . . in 1867 when the company liquidated and the stock was divided Capt. King branded his share with the W known as the running W and called by the Mexicans La Vivorita—the snake brand.—King Ranch vault.

51 *Corpus Christi Advertiser,* May 9, 1868.

52 Contemporary newspapers of the area show the Running W at the head of King's stock

brand notices. For example, the Running W headed a list of thirty-four brands in the *Brownsville Sentinel,* May 11, 1877 (see p. 270).

53 Prof. W. G. Sutherland, "Sage of Bluntzer Describes Earlier Days When South Texas was Covered with Cactus, Mesquite and Bandits," *Corpus Christi Caller-Times,* April 6, 1930; Graf, II, p. 484.

54 Reuben Holbein, R. King & Co.'s bookkeeper, testified that "to the best of my recollection" one thousand head of cattle were sold by the company during the period August 20, 1866, to November 11, 1869.—"Deposition No. 91," *Memorial 230,* p. 141.

Existing ranch journals for the period show more sales than this, though not a roaring trade in relation to the number of cattle in the pastures. The journals also show a fairly brisk business with the Army Quartermaster.

In addition to managing the interests of R. King & Co., King was also participating in numerous financial and trade ventures—or "adventures" as they were listed in the account books—in partnership with others. For example, such headings appear as "Brownsville Adventure," "King & Pashal," "King and Glaevecke," "Adventure with EDR" [E. D. Rowe, a transaction involving the marketing of mules in New Orleans] and other surprisingly diversified listings.

As Victor Rodríguez Alvarado later expressed it in his "Memoirs":

Capt. King had such an eye for business, he didn't care what they brought him to sell, he wanted always to buy it, if it was cheap.

55 For detailed historical and economic discussions—as well as many rich anecdotes—of that phase of American history which became known as "The Cattle Kingdom" see such volumes as Andy Adams, *The Log of a Cowboy* (Boston, 1927); J. Frank Dobie, *The Longhorns;* Walter Prescott Webb, *The Great Plains;* Paul I. Wellman, *The Trampling Herd* (New York, 1939).

CHAPTER X

1 . . . early in 1867 the evil [cattle stealing] broke out again . . . under a guise . . . difficult to class . . . as such owing to the imprudence of some cattle owners residing on or near the Nueces River who gave other parties verbal authority to drive and dispose for their account . . . all stock in their brands found strayed from their range. Some of these parties had as many as 500 brands which they claimed . . . authority to dispose of. These men would hire Mexican horsemen . . . to gather cattle . . . the Mexicans saw . . . that they could get more by selling . . . than by turning them over to their employers. Accordingly they would gather not only of the brands they were confided with, but also of all American brands they came across. Twenty or thirty miles before reaching town they would divide the drove in two, the one with the authorized brands they would drive into town and deliver to their employers; the other drove was crossed into Mexico and sold for their own benefit. Others were more bold and started on their own hook gathering all cattle in American brands, drove them across the river and sold them to the butchers at Matamoros. At first they got good prices . . . but this fact induced so many to take a hand . . . that beeves . . . often sold [for] less than the butchers got for the hides alone.— Antonio Yznaga, "Cattle Stealing on the Rio Grande Frontier," a manuscript in the possession of Harbert Davenport.

2 Webb, *Texas Rangers,* p. 219.

3 Carpetbagger Governor E. J. Davis organized the State Police as a law enforcement agency. Walter Prescott Webb succinctly thumbnailed the sorry history of this organization: "The career of the state police affords a story of official murder and legalized oppression."— Same, p. 221.

4 Ford, V, p. 901.

5 The futility of dealing with Mexican authorities is illustrated by the official testimony of Alexander Werbiski on August 28, 1872:

Question. Did you make effort to reclaim any of those [stolen] cattle?

Answer. I did and they would not give them to me. I conversed with the persons holding the cattle, and they told me I might see the alcalde, and I knew it was no use to reply. Dionisio Cardenas, the First Alcalde of Matamoros now, and then a leading butcher, said there was no law in Mexico compelling the holders to deliver the cattle. I made legal effort and was unsuccessful. The judge told me that he did not dare to give judgment against the robbers. This was in 1869.—"Deposition No. 106," *Memorial No. 230,* p. 156.

6 William D. Thomas, "Deposition No. 16," same, pp. 80-89.

7 Dobie, *Vaquero of the Brush Country,* pp. 55, 72.

8 *Texas Frontier Troubles,* p. v; *Report of the Permanent Committee,* pp. 6-7.

9 *Memorial No. 230,* p. 4.

10 Charles Goldfinch, *Juan N. Cortina 1824-1892: A Re-appraisal,* Thesis (University of Chicago, 1949), pp. 52-58; *Reports of the Committee of . . . the Mexican Government,* pp. 153-154.

11 Report of the Grand Jury, impaneled at the March term, A.D. 1872, of the United States District Court, held in Brownsville, within the Eastern District of Texas.

12 *Report of the Permanent Committee,* p. 7; Webb, *Texas Rangers,* p. 239.

13 "Historical Resume of Mexican Raids in Texas and Texas Border Troubles From 1859 to 1878," *Memorial No. 230,* pp. 55-56; "Mexican Border Troubles," *Texas Frontier Historical,* a report to Secretary of State Hamilton Fish by United States Commissioners to Texas Thomas P. Robb, J. J. Mead, and Richard H. Savage, Ex. Doc. 39, H.R., 42nd Cong., 3rd Sess., p. 99.

14 "Historical Resume of Mexican Raids . . . ," p. 60.

15 *Corpus Christi Gazette* of early 1873, as quoted by *Corpus Christi Caller-Times,* November 26, 1933.

16 *Corpus Christi Gazette,* June 7, 1873.
The conflict between ranchers and hide-peelers became known as the "Skinning War." Testimonies of internal revenue agents and inspectors of hides and animals reveal something of the volume of the trade and the futility of legal efforts to cope with the situation. For example, see "Deposition No. 117," "Deposition No. 124," and "Deposition No. 127," *Memorial No. 230.*

17 Antonio Yznaga, from a manuscript in the possession of Harbert Davenport. The manuscript is in letter form, addressed "Editor Texas New Yorker" and signed "A Sufferer."
Yznaga apparently served as a correspondent for the *New Yorker,* published by G. H. Sweet & Company. "His vigorously written contributions to that paper undoubtedly influenced the sending to Texas of the American Commission in 1872."—Harbert Davenport.

18 John S. Greer, "Deposition No. 494," *Memorial No. 230,* p. 184.

19 Same.

20 For example, during 1869 "Expenses of B. [land] Chamberlain for his trip to Mexico to recover lost Manada," . . . "Expenses for August Tambreño on trip to Mexico with Bland recovering animals."—Journal No. 3, King Ranch vault.

21 Richard King, deposition, April 11, 1870.— "Stillman vs. Mexico," *Records of Boundary and Claims Commissions and Arbitrations, Mexican Claims, 1868, No. 961,* R.G. 76, National Archives.

22 Graf, II, p. 622.

23 These advertisements appeared in the *Corpus Christi Advertiser, Nueces Valley, Goliad Guard, Brownsville Ranchero, Brownsville Sentinel.*

24 The Mexicans seeing that our authorities refused to prosecute them, and that their acts of hostility were not only winked at but encouraged by the Mexican authorities, became reckless and were driving off the cattle in such large numbers that in August 1869 Genl Reynolds had to issue special orders authorizing Post Commanders to appoint hide and cattle inspectors requesting them to endeavor to break up the traffic. —Yznaga, "Cattle Stealing on the Rio Grande Frontier."

25 William D. Thomas, "Deposition No. 16," *Memorial No. 230,* pp. 88-89.

[26] Ford, VII, pp. 1226-1228:

This expedition was an assurance that the military would endeavor to protect the property of the citizens. It had a good effect. Though it did little, if anything, towards checking the frequent forays made by Mexicans upon our citizens.

[27] Webb, *Texas Rangers*, pp. 219-229.

[28] Richard M. Kleberg, Sr., to Holland McCombs.

However, the shotgun was not Captain King's only weapon. Many border tales testify to his proficiency with a pistol. He was described as "a capital marksman."—Daniell, p. 441.

[29] Journal No. 3, King Ranch vault.

[30] Dr. John Ashton to Holland McCombs.

[31] Same.

[32] An extract of the commissioners' report to the Secretary of State was published in "Mexican Border Troubles," as cited.

[33] The commissioners had the opportunity to gather firsthand evidence. On September 6, 1872, they were aboard the steamer *San Juan* heading upriver. At a bend a half-mile above Las Cuevas they came upon a herd of cattle being crossed over to the Mexican side under protection of mounted men but without benefit of customs officer. There were no troops aboard the steamer; no attempt could be made to recapture the stolen herd. But the recorder of the commission made an "official memorandum."— Same, pp. 106-107.

[34] Richard King, "Deposition No. 89," *Memorial No. 230*, p. 136.

[35] John S. Greer, "Deposition No. 183," same, p. 184.

[36] Allhands, *Gringo Builders*, p. 20.

[37] Apolinario Hernandez, "Deposition No. 38," *Memorial No. 230*, pp. 120-122.

[38] *Reports of the Committee of . . . the Mexican Government*," pp. 61-62.

[39] *Report of the Permanent Committee*, as cited.

[40] *Texas Frontier Troubles*, as cited.

[41] "Historical Resume of Mexican Raids . . . ," pp. 56-58.

[42] *Texas Frontier Troubles*, p. vi.

As Uriah Lott put it in his testimony before the Congressional committee in Washington, January 29, 1876:

It is not now so much a question of loss of property that has excited our people, but the increasing feeling of insecurity for life that has become so widespread, resulting from the almost daily occurrence of some brutal murder committed by bands of armed men from Mexico.—Same, p. 19.

[43] Ford, V, p. 900.

[44] John S. Greer, "Deposition No. 494," *Memorial No. 230*, pp. 183-185.

[45] John S. McCampbell was testifying before a Congressional committee in Washington on January 26, 1876. The chairman of the committee was quizzing him about conditions in South Texas:

Q. Does Captain King live at his ranch with his family?

A. Yes; he lives at his ranch. He has an armed force there to defend himself. He has hired men all the time armed, and has good fortifications. He thinks he can defend himself.—*Texas Frontier Troubles*, p. 6.

[46] Captain H. C. Corbin, testimony, same, p. 59.

[47] Same, p. 73.

[48] Richard M. Kleberg, Sr., heard a story from *Kineño* Eleno Alvarado which is the only record available of a direct attack upon the Santa Gertrudis headquarters. Alvarado was fifteen years old at the time of the fray.

According to Eleno, the bandits were down by the Tranquitas lake trying to roundup some cattle to drive off. A group of *Kineños*, probably under James Richardson or Thomas Beynon, found them and hit them, head-on. The fight turned into a melee of hard-riding and shooting. Eleno saw the battle going on, got hold of an old octagon-shaped rim-fire .22 rifle that belonged to young Richard King, and joined in. It was pretty close. Afterwards Eleno told about it with a grin:

"*Me fuí agatas hasta atras de un nopal y estaba uno [bandido] en una mula tirandonos tiros y yo le di un tiro a la mula en una nalga y se fue reparando—y lo tumbó—y el bandido calló en un nopal. Entonces yo corrí.*"

49 "The Corpus Christi Raid," *Texas Frontier Troubles*, pp. 52-53.

50 *Report of the Permanent Committee*, pp. 21-22.

51 Webb, *Texas Rangers*, p. 238.

52 Same.

53 Joseph E. Dwyer to General E. O. C. Ord, July 5, 1875, *Texas Frontier Troubles*, pp. 41-42.

54 For a full account of this fight, including McNelly's official report to General Steele, see Webb, *Texas Rangers*, pp. 239-252. See also McNelly's testimony before the Congressional committee, *Texas Frontier Troubles*, pp. 13-17; J. L. Haynes, p. 87.

55 For an eyewitness account of this remarkable group of frontier fighters see N. A. Jennings, *A Texas Ranger* (Dallas, 1930).

56 McNelly, *Texas Frontier Troubles*, pp. 8-9.

57 Webb, *Texas Rangers*, p. 258.

58 Jennings, pp. 134-142.
The burning of Sandobal's ranch must have taken place after May 3, 1875. On that date he testified as to his troubles before F. J. Parker, United States circuit court clerk:

I have been a peaceable citizen of the United States since 1853; at least, I have voted and held office for that season. I have many enemies in Mexico. They say I am Americanized and consequently criminal—a traitor to Mexico. They have persecuted me, threatened my life, and attempted to assassinate me. For seven months I have not slept in my house. I have slept in the chaparral, and have been a solitary sentinel over my own person. On the 21st day of April of the present year three armed Mexicans, from beyond the Rio Grande, went to my house and asked for me. They told my wife if she did not tell where I was they would kill her.—*Texas Frontier Troubles*, p. 84.

59 Webb, *Texas Rangers*, pp. 255-257.

60 This Edinburg was not on the site of the present city of that name. The Edinburg of the 1870's was located almost due north of Reynosa on the Texas side of the Rio Grande at the northern apex of a looping U the river made. Eventually the Rio Grande claimed the old town of Edinburg.

61 This account of the affair at Las Cuevas is based upon Webb, "McNelly and the War of Las Cuevas," *Texas Rangers*, pp. 255-280. Quotations and extracts are from that source. For the official reports of Major A. J. Alexander, Major D. R. Clendenin, and Captain James F. Randlett see *Texas Frontier Troubles*, pp. 90-96. See also Jennings, pp. 143-182.

62 Ford, VII, pp. 1237-1238.

63 Cortina's life was undoubtedly spared because of John S. Ford. After Cortina had been tried and condemned to death, Ford went to General Canales and said to him:

"It is known to everyone that yourself and Gen. Cortina are deadly personal enemies, if you approve of the proceedings of the Court Martial by which he was tried, and he is shot, it will be said that personal ill feeling actuated your approval. It will, in my opinion, be a stain on your memory for all time to come. Send the prisoner and the proceedings to President Díaz. Let him act as it may suit him."—Same, pp. 1239-1240.

64 Misc. Doc. 64, H.R., 45th Cong., 2nd Sess., p. 175.

65 Webb, *Texas Rangers*, p. 288.

66 *Texas Frontier Troubles*, p. 175; Jennings, p. 178.

67 Dobie, "Foreword" to Jennings, pp. x-xi.

68 Webb, *Texas Rangers*, pp. 288-294. See also Dora Neill Raymond, *Captain Lee Hall of Texas* (Norman, Okla., 1940).

69 From the *Fitch Papers*, documents belonging to the heirs of Captain John Fitch, courtesy Mrs. Lennie E. Stubblefield, Premont. Captain Fitch was a foreman and herd boss employed by Captain King in the 1870's and 1880's.

In the course of his subsequent duties as a Texas Ranger, Pablino Coy encountered two horse thieves. During the resulting mixing of gun smoke, he killed them both. Riding back toward Santa Gertrudis on the train, Pablino sat across the aisle from two gentlemen who had heard of the shooting but were unaware of his identity. They were scandalized by the act and had few compliments for the man who did the shooting. As they warmed to the subject, they engaged Pablino in the conversation.

"I understand they were very bad men," Pablino remarked blandly.

70 Prof. W. G. Sutherland, as cited.

71 Durham, Talley and Wright worked for the King Ranch for the rest of their long and faithful lives. John B. Armstrong, whose exploits are recounted by Jennings, Raymond, Webb and others who wrote of the Texas Rangers, established ties of friendship with the King Ranch which have become stronger and stronger with the passing of the years. Richard King's granddaughter, Henrietta Kleberg, married John B. Armstrong's son, Major Thomas R. Armstrong, and their home is on the Armstrong Ranch adjoining the Norias Division of the King Ranch.

John Armstrong's first meeting with Captain King was during a Cortina raid. Armstrong and Lee Hall had returned some stolen cattle to the King Ranch. Captain King said, "Go down and pick out any horse you want." Later John Armstrong told about it: "I picked out the best horse I could find. And that horse pitched all the way to the Rio Grande."—Major Armstrong to Holland McCombs.

72 *Memorial No. 230.*

73 I am willing to take a good many chances, but I certainly would not live on a stock-ranch west of the Nueces River, at any point from the mouth of the Devil's River to the mouth of the Rio Grande. I think the risk is too great—so great that scarcely any compensation would pay for it. My position, in command of a company of troops, I do not consider half so hazardous as that of those men living on ranches.—L. H. McNelly, *Texas Frontier Troubles,* p. 10.

CHAPTER XI

1 Webb, *Great Plains,* pp. 220-222.

2 For a great study of the durable animal that shaped the economy of the early West, see Dobie, *The Longhorns.*

3 John Ashton, "Texas Cattle Trade in 1870," *The Cattleman,* XXXVIII (July, 1951), pp. 21, 74-75.

4 Webb, *Great Plains,* p. 223.

5 Though the records are incomplete, available ranch journals and account books for the period and testimony before the Congressional committee, *Memorial No. 230,* allow a fairly accurate estimate of the proportion of cattle marketed during this period. This estimate is further attested to by the volume of cattle marketed later.

6 See Appendix VIII.

7 Years later, in 1915, a group of old-time trail men met in San Antonio for the purpose of organizing an association. The Old Trail Drivers' Association was born, largely through the efforts of George W. Saunders. He began accumulating letters and papers from members of the association relating to their experiences on the various cattle trails. Eventually *The Trail Drivers of Texas* (Nashville, 1924-1925) was published, compiled and edited by J. Marvin Hunter. The work contains more than a thousand pages of miscellaneous "Interesting Sketches of Early Cowboys and Their Experiences on the Range and on the Trail during the Days that Tried Men's Souls—True Narratives Related by Real Cow-Punchers and Men who Fathered the Cattle Industry in Texas."

8 *Fitch Papers;* entries in early King Ranch account books.

9 Alvarado's "Memoirs" give the barest account of this early drive:

. . . he rounded up all the steers he could from three years and up. He went by land to St. Louis, took some thousand steers, and the following cowboys: Ramon Adelardo, Egenio Pisano, William Brai, the latter was boss of other cowboys. He arrived in St. Louis and sold at good price by weight, he also sold all his horses and camp equipment, and he shipped his cowboys by boat to Corpus.

10 In 1867 and 1868 some of our most venturesome stockmen took a few small herds of cattle to New Orleans, Baxter Springs, Abilene, Kansas, and other markets. The Northern drives proved fairly successful, though they experienced many hardships and dangers going through an uncivilized and partly unexplored country. The news of their success spread like wildfire, and the same men and others tackled the trail in 1869. . . . The 1869 drives proved successful, which caused many other stockmen to join the trail drivers in 1870.—George W. Saunders, "Origin and Close of the Old-Time Northern Trail," *Trail Drivers of Texas,* pp. 20-21.

11 By this time going up the trail was all a rage; 1870 was a banner year at all markets. The drivers came home and began preparing for the 1871 drives.—Same, p. 21.

See also Webb, *Great Plains,* pp. 223, 231.

12 Richard King was at Abilene on August 4, 1871. He signed for a registered letter in reference to the purchase of shares in the International Railroad Co.—a proposed line which would later become the Missouri Pacific. Shortly after the 1871 cattle season King invested large sums in the railroad, risking his cattle profits to get a railroad to South Texas.—*Wells Papers.*

13 Webb, *Great Plains,* p. 231.

14 E. T. Merriman, *Corpus Christi Caller,* October 29, 1922.

15 *Corpus Christi Gazette,* February 1, 1873.— Courtesy Mrs. Lennie E. Stubblefield.

16 Webb, *Great Plains,* pp. 231-232.

17 Available ranch records are incomplete for this period. That Captain King sold his herds prior to the crash is an inference based upon the fact that there is no evidence of serious loss at that time and the further fact that immediately following he spent a considerable sum in ranch expansion—more than he would likely have spent in the face of financial reverses.

18 Initial steps in the purchase of the San Juan de Carricitos grant began earlier and the process lasted for many years. King was deeded his first interest on September 13, 1873, by

María Clemencia García, who had inherited it from José María Cavazos. She was paid $4,000.

The process of acquiring the various outstanding interests in this grant stretched over more than fifteen years. The *Wells Papers* tell of King's buying *derechos,* or interests in the grant, in 1879. He and the heirs of Narciso Cavazos — sixty-seven of them — jointly owned 106½ leagues of land, granted in 1792.

In 1879 there was a suit to establish ownership of certain tracts; on May 29, 1889, the Final Decree of Partition was rendered. Richard King's attorney indicated the complexity of the affair years later when he was preparing an opinion to accompany an abstract of a portion of the area: ". . . to have attempted to have embraced in this abstract such chain of title to said Captain Richard King, and Mrs. Henrietta M. King, and the Court files, in said Partition suit, would necessarily make this abstract fully two thousand pages in length."—James B. Wells to Robert J. Kleberg, Sr., April 14, 1906.

19 Stirling W. Bass, *The History of Kleberg County,* Thesis (University of Texas, 1931), p. 485; *San Antonio Express,* June 17, 1934.

20 Merriman, as cited. The *Corpus Christi Gazette* of 1873, as quoted by Bass, p. 478, reported that sheep raising "now forms the largest part of the stock raising in this area." Richard King and five other ranchers were listed as chief breeders of the area. They were importing bucks from Pennsylvania, Ohio and New York.

21 Graf, II, p. 477.

22 The statistics cited by the *Gazette* reporter indicate a ratio of less than five acres per head of livestock. Such a ratio would be considered overgrazing in most parts of the country with today's cattle under today's range conditions, but it was not an uncommon ratio in the 1870's.

Richard King's letters to members of his family who were away from the ranch support this. During periods of drouth the opening paragraph of almost every letter expressed great concern over the grass that was invariably "growing short."

But then as now, the land of the Santa Gertrudis would recover quickly after a rain. Captain King's letters would open on an optimistic note: "We have had fine rains and plenty of them here. The stock is all right . . . the grass is growing fast." Or "everything looking well at home. Plenty of water and grass from Brownsville to San Antonio."

²³ Webb, *Great Plains*, pp. 205-269.

²⁴ *Wells Papers.*

²⁵ John Maltsberger, of Cotulla, ran away from home to join the trail drives when he was fifteen. Later he told about them:

> The long herds of the King Ranch . . [were] . . a pretty sight. The herds of cattle and horses were of a color. The horses were uniform and beautiful. They had long manes and tails, long hair and fetlocks. . . .There would be bay horses with red cattle, black horses and black cattle, brown horses with brown cattle.—As quoted by J. T. Maltsberger, Jr., to Holland McCombs.

²⁶ The documents used in reconstructing this trail drive are in the *Fitch Papers*. It is believed that this accounting of a trail drive may be the only extant complete bookkeeping on a herd moving to northern markets during the trail drive days.

²⁷ There are no accurate statistics available today on the cost of producing cattle in the 1870's. It is known that after the Civil War when the market was low herds sold for $1 and $2 per head (*Prose and Poetry of the Live Stock Industry*, p. 395). Hides and tallow from large fat cows netted owners $2 to $4 (Bass, p. 75), and it was said "it cost about as much to raise a cow in Texas as it did a chicken."—McArthur, p. 76.

The figure of $2 a head follows the custom of the times, so to speak, in that it does not take into account the many intangibles and dependent costs which in these times, under a modern cost accounting system, would be charged against breeding and raising cattle: Cost of land, depreciation of equipment, taxes, legal expenses, wages, interest and innumerable other items. Seldom did the rancher of the 1870's, and later, count the cost of getting money into his hands. Cash in hand was operating capital; if that operating capital produced more money it was again cash in hand.

²⁸ It is estimated by the most conservative old-time trail drivers that an average of 350,000 cattle were driven up the trails from Texas each year for 28 years, making 9,800,000 cattle at $10 a head received by the ranchmen at home, making $98,000,000; 1,000,000 horse stock at $10 per head received by the ranchmen at home, making $10,000,000, or a total of $108,000,000. —Saunders, p. 24.

²⁹ Letters preserved in the King Ranch vault.

³⁰ Mrs. Minerva King Patch to Holland McCombs, March 7, 1952.

³¹ An oft-repeated family story.

³² From the inscription on the tomb of the Rev. Hiram Chamberlain, City Cemetery, Brownsville.

³³ Mrs. Patch to Holland McCombs.

³⁴ A family story. The autographed photograph of General Lee which the Kings received on the occasion of this visit is preserved in the King Ranch vault—a rare print of the photograph taken by Rees & Co., Richmond, Virginia, in 1867.

³⁵ Mrs. Patch to Holland McCombs.

³⁶ Mrs. Alice Gertrudis King Kleberg to Mrs. Jeff Miller and Stirling Bass, as told to Holland McCombs.

³⁷ Mathew John Kivlin to Holland McCombs, summer of 1952.

³⁸ Reuben Holbein II to Mrs. Lennie E. Stubblefield, as told to Holland McCombs.

³⁹ In most of the several family portraits existing, probably taken by itinerant photographers, Captain King is in noticeable contrast with the neatly combed and freshly dressed appearance of the rest of the family. In some cases the captain obviously stepped in from his work about the ranch just long enough to have his picture taken.

40 Richard M. Kleberg, Sr., John D. Finnegan, Robert C. Wells.

The anchor chain version of the injury is favored because it seems likely that had Richard King been wounded on one of his trips between Brownsville and Santa Gertrudis during the days of the cattle depredations King himself or one of his employees would have testified concerning the affair during the investigations by the Robb Commission.

41 Mrs. Patch to Holland McCombs.

42 Ed Durham to Holland McCombs.

43 Mifflin Kenedy to Richard M. Kleberg, Sr.

44 Branch Isbell to J. Frank Dobie, as quoted to Holland McCombs.

45 Mifflin Kenedy to Richard M. Kleberg, Sr.

46 General Joseph D. Patch (son of the young lieutenant, Alexander M. Patch) to Holland McCombs.

47 Daniell, pp. 442-443.

48 April 4th [1879]. On my way to Brownsville, preached at night in Trinity Church Galveston. . . . Reached Brownsville Saturday, April 22, overland from the Santa Gertrudes Ranch. I am much indebted to Captain Richard King and Mrs. King for their genuine hospitality, and for making the journey down as rapidly and as pleasantly as possible. The vehicle known as a "jerkey" is felicitous in name, but it is seen under the most flattering auspices when prepared for its journey by the kind friends at Santa Gertrudes. The one hundred and twenty-four miles was accomplished in 28 hours.—From Bishop Robert W. B. Elliott's diary for the year 1879, courtesy Bishop Everett H. Jones, Episcopal Diocesan Center, San Antonio.

49 Judge [James B.] Wells told me that shortly after he became established in Brownsville, Captain King employed him, . . . to buy legitimate claims to undivided interests in the King Ranch lands. This employment required young Wells to examine King's titles, ascertain whether any given claim had a legitimate basis, draw the necessary deeds, and have them executed and draw on Captain King for the standard price. . . . As a result of this arrangement, Judge Wells devoted a greater portion of seven years to clearing title to the King lands. . . . Between them [Powers and Wells, King's attorneys] they kept Richard King

out of the courts and free from the trammels of litigation for more than thirty years.—Harbert Davenport to Robert C. Wells, August 23, 1951, and April 19, 1952.

50 In beginning to purchase a tract of land at this early date, the first step was to locate the individual with the best legal claim to that tract, if possible a direct descendant of the original grantee who was occupying the land. From him the purchaser would get an undivided interest in a piece of terrain with inexact boundaries, because of the crudeness of early surveys, and of inexact area, because it might be subject to claim by other direct descendants with equally strong undivided interests.

The purchaser would then have to deal with all other individuals holding rights or interests in the tract of land—*derechos* these rights were called. The holders of *derechos* would be multiple branches of the family tree of the original grantee or purchasers of their rights. They would confront the purchaser, bearing marriage records, birth records and similar proofs of connection with the original grantee. By the 1870's or 1880's a grant which was made by the Spanish Crown in the first decade of the nineteenth century might have accumulated hundreds of legitimate holders of *derechos,* to say nothing of spurious claimants and those who thought they had rights.

51 *Wells Papers.*

52 Harbert Davenport to Robert C. Wells, August 23, 1951.

53 "Special Warranty Deed, July 25, 1853, Richard King to Heirs of Juan Mendiola," recorded November 14, 1853, *Records of Real Estate,* Nueces County, Book E, pp. 347-350.

54 "Special Warranty Deed, November 11, 1853, Richard King to Gideon K. Lewis," *Records of Real Estate,* Nueces County, Book E, pp. 347-350.

55 See *Probate Minutes,* Nueces County, Book B, p. 119, for reports of sale of the Lewis estate; "Simple Mortgage to Secure Promissory Note, for $1,575.00," August 1, 1856, Richard King

and W. W. Chapman to Estate of Gideon K. Lewis, deceased, *Deed Records,* Nueces County, Book G, pp. 169-170.

[56] See Chapter IX, note 10.

[57] Confirmation of Title for the Rincón de Santa Gertrudis was recorded "Richard King, assignee of the heirs of Juan Mendiola v. The State of Texas, No. 580," *Minutes of the District Court,* Book C, pp. 184-186. See also *Transcribed Minutes of District Court,* Kleberg County, Vol. A, pp. 7-9.

[58] "Final Judgment by Consent of District Court of Nueces County, Texas, rendered April 6, 1883," *District Court Minutes,* Nueces County, Book E, p. 522.

[59] The land would come into litigation one more time. In the early 1900's the General Land Office of Texas brought suit against many owners of former Spanish and Mexican land grants to determine exact acreage and boundaries, since there was overlapping and conflict with Texas grants. James B. Wells defended the Juan Mendiola grant title and secured confirmation on November 30, 1904, according to the abstract records.

[60] Entries in early King Ranch account books and documents in the *Wells Papers* show these side ventures doing a brisk business immediately after the Civil War.

[61] In 1877 Eli T. Merriman and William Maltby established the *Corpus Christi Free Press,* forerunner of the *Caller-Times.* Both King and Kenedy were partners in the enterprise, according to Mrs. Marion Clemmer, a daughter of Merriman.

[62] W. R. Woolrich, "Mechanical Refrigeration —Its American Birthright," *Refrigerating Engineering* (April, 1947).

The Brownsville *Weekly Ranchero,* June 1, 1878, advertised that the Brownsville Ice Factory would deliver crystal ice to places of business and private residences for 1½ cents per pound.

[63] King made a contract with the government to deliver correspondence and passengers in forty-eight hours from San Antonio to Brownsville, and he bought four or five stage coaches for the passengers. This wasn't very successful financially because of the scarcity of passengers.—Alvarado.

Richard King III relates an anecdote which reveals that the difficulty may not have been entirely a scarcity of passengers. Captain King put his son Richard in charge of the stage line. Soon everybody was riding on a pass and the business was rapidly going into the red. Captain King instituted a policy of nobody riding free. A few days after the ultimatum the stage arrived at the Santa Gertrudis stop loaded with some of Captain King's old friends. Young Richard informed them of the new rule; they complained bitterly. Captain King arrived on the scene. He grinned. "Guess we'll have to waive the new order this time," he said.

One of the old stage coaches used on the line is now on exhibit in the Witte Museum, San Antonio.

[64] Allhands, *Gringo Builders,* pp. 62-64.

[65] Merriman, *Corpus Christi Caller,* October 29, 1922.

[66] *Wells Papers.*

[67] Uriah Lott was promised $20,000 by King as soon as a herd of cattle then en route to Kansas City was sold. Immediately Lott left Corpus Christi by boat. In a few days he arrived in Kansas City and presented himself to Reuben Holbein to collect the subscription. It was this money that purchased the railroad's first locomotive.—Allhands, *Uriah Lott,* pp. 14-15.

[68] Allhands, *Gringo Builders,* pp. 73-75. See also *Uriah Lott,* pp. 13-20.

[69] Merrily the train whizzed along at twenty miles an hour and all went well until the official mixers went into the coach. . . . Soon there was a great milling around that barrel and a few of them snickered knowingly . . . some one had sneaked three gallons of Rose Bud and twelve quarts of champagne into the brew. —Same, pp. 21-22.

The brew inspired a lengthy and graphic description of the trip which was published in the *Laredo Times* (date unknown), complete with a poem entitled "The King-Kenedy Excursion to Laredo."

70 *Brownsville Democrat*, March 3, 1878.

71 Harbert Davenport, "Life of James B. Wells," manuscript, Archives, University of Texas.

72 *Wells Papers.*

73 Robert C. Wells to Holland McCombs.

74 Daniell, pp. 443-444.

75 The story of Alice Gertrudis King's meeting with Robert J. Kleberg, Sr., has been passed down by the two participants to their children and their grandchildren.

CHAPTER XII

1 The letter, dated August 29, 1880, is in the King Ranch vault. In spite of the "great preparations," Captain King's letter to Mrs. King was dated September 2.

2 *St. Louis Globe-Democrat*, November 24, 1878.

3 Family records.

4 From the file of letters preserved in the King Ranch vault.

5 Family anecdote, as told to Holland McCombs.

6 Mrs. Henrietta M. King to Mrs. Jeff N. Miller, as quoted to Holland McCombs, August, 1954.

7 Daniell, pp. 444-445; family stories.

8 Robert J. Kleberg, Jr., to Holland McCombs.

9 Mrs. Henrietta M. King to Richard M. Kleberg, Sr., as told to Holland McCombs.

10 Mrs. Lennie E. Stubblefield to Holland McCombs.

11 Same.

12 Daniell, p. 443.

13 *Fitch Papers.*

14 Mrs. Bessie Kirkland to Colonel William Sterling, as quoted to Tom Lea and Holland McCombs, November 10, 1953.

15 John D. Finnegan to Holland McCombs.

16 Anecdotes from Alvarado's "Memoirs."

17 Richard King III to Holland McCombs.

18 Same.

19 *Wells Papers.*

20 As early as 1884, the United States government began its effort to stop the spread of Texas fever. The Secretary of Agriculture drew a quarantine line from the northern border of Arkansas across Kansas and then southwest to the Rio Grande. The purpose was to prevent cattle from passing from north to south across this line between July and November, or during the frostless season.—Bass, pp. 65-70.

21 Quarantine pens were established at terminal points, cars which had carried southern cattle were disinfected, and inspection for tick infestation was established at railroad loading points. —T. C. Richardson, "Cattle Tick," *The Handbook of Texas* (Austin, 1952), I, pp. 315-316.

22 Letter in King Ranch vault.

23 Unidentifiable newspaper clipping in the King Ranch vault.

24 Wellman, "High Profits and Noble Profiteers," *The Trampling Herd*, pp. 295-303.

25 Abstract of Records, Los Laureles grant, King Ranch vault. The British syndicate was represented by F. L. Underwood and William A. Clark.

26 The first stockholders meeting of the Kenedy Pasture Co. was held on March 10, 1882. The firm was organized with shares totaling one million dollars. The *Wells Papers* include the Articles of Incorporation.

27 Robert E. Lee King's body was moved to San Antonio and later to the family plot in the cemetery in Kingsville.

28 Letter written from Santa Gertrudis, March 18, 1883, King Ranch vault.

29 Same.

30 Same.

31 Same.

32 Alvarado.

33 Letter, June 22, 1883, King Ranch vault.

34 July 8, 1883, same.

35 The wedding gift consisted of "5 sitios and 37 caballerias . . . and all interest in the Casa Blanca." The deed was acknowledged on July 30, 1883, and recorded September 25, 1883, *Deed Records*, Nueces County, Vol. P.

36 Unidentified newspaper clipping, King Ranch vault.

37 Richard King III, of Corpus Christi, to Holland McCombs.

38 Richard King to Mrs. Richard King, March 18, 1883, King Ranch vault.

39 Letter, March 24, 1883, same.

40 Same.

41 On October 12, 1884, Robert J. Kleberg addressed a letter to Alice's mother in which he followed the courtly Victorian custom of asking her daughter's hand in marriage.—King Ranch vault.

42 Richard King to Mrs. King, April 18, 1883, same.

When the price of cattle dropped on the market, as in the early seventies and after the boom years of 1881-1883, Captain King gave more attention to raising and selling horses. —Bass, p. 80.

43 J. T. Maltsberger, Jr., to Holland McCombs, as cited. See Chap. XI, Note 25.

44 The story of the "Jesse James horses" has been told and retold. The closest rendition to the event was that of John G. Kenedy, son of Mifflin Kenedy.

Students of the Jesse James story might debate the point of whether Jesse James was a guest at the King Ranch. If it is true—and there are strong points in its favor—it probably happened in May, 1875.

On May 12 of that year, a stage was robbed between Austin and San Antonio. Though there was an attempted refutation of a confession implicating the James-Younger gang, the method of operation tallied with their tactics, even to entertaining the unfortunate passengers with wisecracks during the holdup. Jesse James could have stopped by the King Ranch on his way either to or from the affair.

It is a known fact that he was a superb horseman and a connoisseur of horses. In addition, he had a sense of humor which makes the story probable: He liked to announce his identity in unexpected places, to astound people after the fact by letting them know who their recent associate had been. The presentation of the iron gray horse to Captain King carries the stamp of a typical Jesse James joke.

45 Early ranch account books show that Captain King consistently bought good bulls whenever he found them south of the Rio Grande. He culled his range stock, turning those which did not measure up into hide and tallow.

Captain King's hide and tallow factory was located at a point about seven miles west of modern Kingsville, on the north side of State Highway 141. The pasture was called, appropriately enough, Matanza Pasture. Two of Captain King's old rendering vats remained in the pasture until just after World War I. At that time one vat was moved to the scene of a small oil development southeast of Kingsville to serve as a storage tank.

Later it was again moved to Plomo Pens and used to store the molasses being used for cattle feed. Then the vat was moved to the Silo Barro Mill for use as a water tank. It proved too small and was superseded by an earthen tank. However, the old vat remains there today, rusted and weathered. It is a cylindrical container eighteen feet long and six feet in diameter.

The second vat was cut up during a World War II scrap metal drive.

46 From a letter by A. W. Billingsley dated January 27, 1939.

47 Wellman, *Trampling Herd*, pp. 225-226.

48   The depths of Mifflin Kenedy's worries are graphically indicated by letters written during this time.—*Wells Papers.*

49   Dr. John Ashton to Holland McCombs.

50   Bass, pp. 369-370.

51   Dr. John Ashton.

52   According to Jack Kivlin, when Wesley Stevens went to work at the King Ranch—on La Ebonita, about one-third the area of the present Santa Gertrudis Division—the captain said: "Go around the ranch, around the fence." It took Stevens a full week — Sunday to Monday — to carry out the captain's order to encircle La Ebonita.

53   From an inventory of Captain King's estate: See Appendix X.

54   Robert J. Kleberg, Sr., and Mrs. Alice G. K. Kleberg to Richard M. Kleberg, Sr.

55   Daniell, p. 448. Kenedy telegraphed for specialists from New Orleans. It was in vain.—*New Orleans Times Democrat,* April 18, 1885.

56   Richard King's will was filed April 23, 1885, recorded *Probate Minutes,* Nueces County, Vol. F, pp. 16-17.

57   A. W. Billingsley to Holland McCombs.

58   Obituary of Richard King; *New Orleans Times Democrat,* April 15, 1885; Unidentified newspaper clipping, King Ranch vault; *Corpus Christi Caller,* July 20, 1884.

THIS BOOK

was designed, printed and bound in Texas by the photo-offset process; plates and presswork by Guynes Printing Company.

The type for the text is 16 point *Centaur* Roman with *Arrighi* Italic, composed on the Monotype and reworked by hand; chapter titles and initials handset in larger sizes of the same types. Appendices and Notes are in *Caledonia,* composed on the Linotype, headings handset in *Legenda.* Bold titles are in *Hadriano.* Typography by Carl Hertzog of El Paso. The chapter title pages were designed by the author.

Colortones on the maps and the portraits are from separate drawings also made by the author, and printed with special inks.

Binding by the Universal of San Antonio.

EL PASO
TEXAS